Treatment and Management of Maladaptive Schemas

The complexity of thought-process: artistic interpretation by Christopher Kreuter

Eric A. Kreuter • Kenneth M. Moltner

Treatment and Management of Maladaptive Schemas

Foreword by
Laurence Allen Steckman, Esq., M.Phil.
and
Lodze Steckman, M.D., FACS

Afterword by
Cathleen M. Kreuter, MS-MFT

Springer

Eric A. Kreuter
Yorktown Heights
New York
USA

Kenneth M. Moltner
New York
New York
USA

ISBN 978-3-319-06816-9 ISBN 978-3-319-06817-6 (eBook)
DOI 10.1007/978-3-319-06817-6
Springer Cham Heidelberg New York Dordrecht London

Library of Congress Control Number: 2014940858

Printed on acid-free paper

Springer is part of Springer Science+Business Media (www.springer.com)

Foreword

Laurence Allen Steckman, Esq., M.Phil. and Lodze Steckman, M.D., FACS

Maladaptive Schemas and the Transfiguration of Core Beliefs—
When and How Paradigms of Consciousness Shift—an Introduction to
Dr. Kreuter's and Counselor Moltner's Analysis and Recommendations
Regarding Counseling and the Treatment of Certain Psychic Disorders

Introduction

Dr. Kreuter and counselor Kenneth Moltner integrate philosophical and psychological insights regarding the treatment and/or mentoring of persons whose past experiences prevent them from attaining life goals and achieving optimal psychic health. Their goal is to examine "the phenomenology of adapting or not adapting well to stimuli," and to suggest strategies which may be helpful to persons seeking to achieve more integrated and fulfilling lives. We introduce vocabulary and key concepts of schema-focused therapies, which the authors discuss as successful change modalities for many persons suffering so-called maladaptive schema. We comment, as well, on certain philosophical insights the authors provide as guidance to mental health professionals and others engaged in therapeutic/transformational efforts.

A. Vocabulary and Key Concepts

Schemas are psychic structures that some mental health practitioners and research professionals believe play an important role in the maintenance and expression of many personality disorders (Young et al. 2003). Manifesting themselves as patterns of memories, emotions, and perceptions, schema structures are hypothesized to form during early stages of human maturation, largely due, in many cases, to early, serious trauma and/or parental failure to provide a child's basic needs (Young et al. 2003). They are hypothesized to strongly influence later-life behaviors, playing a substantial causal role in the etiology, maintenance, and recurrence of maladaptive personality traits (Young et al. 2003).

The term "schema" has been variously defined in cognitive science literature, *inter alia*, as a "structure, theme, or pattern of cognitive content" or a "blueprint imposed on experience" to help individuals explain it, to mediate perception, and to guide responses (Cockram 2009, p. 32). Schema are thought to partly determine how people interpret, evaluate, and categorize their experiences and, for this reason, hypothesized to be constitutive of who we are and who we experience ourselves to be. Among those who posit their existence, schema are regarded as difficult to modify, even when one is fully aware of them and motivated to change, and even where professional help is available to facilitate such change (Young 2003; Cockram 2009).

"Maladaptive schemas" are schema thought to contribute to later life cognitive or behavioral dysfunctions. They may give rise to unreasonable or exaggerated fears of abuse, a sense of deprivation, or a mistrust of people or groups; they may result in feelings of isolation, shame, inadequacy, or a sense that one is doomed to fail, with disaster looming just over the horizon, when little objective basis for such feelings may exist (Young et al. 2003). Such schema may impair a person's ability to achieve goals or life satisfactions, resulting in feelings of hopelessness; in a vicious circle, they may create the situations persons so afflicted, fear most.

"Paradigms" are global systems of hypotheses, beliefs, rules, and principles, frequently discussed in scientific and social science literature, as making up the fabric of human knowledge domain. In certain respects, they are similar to schema. Thomas Kuhn, author of "The Structure of Scientific Revolutions" (*Structure*), is generally credited with popularizing the concept of "paradigm," as now understood. In *Structure*, Kuhn argued science history shows scientific knowledge evolves unevenly through revolutionary shifts in paradigms which have the effect of altering, in fundamental ways, how science proceeds.

The phrase "paradigm shift," for Kuhn, denotes the movement from the complex of prevailing views constituting a subject knowledge domain, to a new, better adapted complex. Frequently cited examples of paradigm shifts include replacement of Ptolemy's earth-centered universe with Copernicus' sun-centered universe and Einstein's replacement of Newton's clockwork universe with relativity; each providing superior predictive and explanatory capacities relative to the replaced paradigm. Understanding how paradigms deform and shift, the authors suggest, provide considerable insight into ways therapeutic tools may be designed and used to help clients alter or eliminate maladaptive schema underlying many psychic disorders.

B. Paradigms and Paradigm Shifts in Science—The Inability to See What Is Actually Before One's Eyes

Structure was Kuhn's most famous attempt to describe what paradigms are and the way in which scientific knowledge evolves within the global networks of definitions, causal hypotheses, and experimental protocols of what he called "normal science." *Structure* became a classic in philosophy of sciences and the humanities, generally, in large part because it challenged a then widely held view that scientific knowledge increases in a linear manner, with experimental results simply adding one upon another, growing society's store of correct facts. It was commonly believed scientists apply neutral theories in experiments which reveal nature's truths, verifying or refuting theories, in a straightforward manner, adding to science knowledge through unbiased verification of science theories (the "Traditional View").

Kuhn, in contrast, argued scientific knowledge evolves, in large measure, through nonlinear science "revolutions" in which radically new idea complexes replace whole systems of previously confirmed definitions, theories, and experimental, interpretive, and assessment protocols. Scientists, he observed, spend most of their careers engaged in "puzzle-solving" within frameworks that not only provide the instruments, theories, and procedures to address current science problems, but which, as well, define how experimental results will be interpreted and their significance understood. He referred to this as "normal science."

Because existing paradigms are the result of many successful experiments, practitioners of normal science puzzle-solving tend to be highly confident in paradigm-endorsed theories and procedures. From that well-reasoned optimism, however, flows a specious overconfidence that paradigm instrumentalities will be adequate to solve all presenting problems in the science domains in which they operate as they largely determine scientist expectancies, influencing postexperiment understandings of data and data significance, in a paradigm-preserving manner.

Nevertheless, scientific instruments and procedures become more precise over time allowing scientists to probe ever more deeply into the universe. With new and more precise data disclosed, researchers may be confronted with "anomalies," i.e., experimental outcomes difficult or impossible to explain within existing paradigm hypotheses. If such anomalies are serious and unresolved for long periods of time, paradigm definitions, hypotheses, and experimental rules sometimes begin to loosen. As experimental design and interpretation expand in an effort to try to satisfactorily explain observations, competing schools of explanation may begin to arise, challenging assumptions and concepts upon which the paradigm is based.

The search to adequately explain anomalies, over time, may intensify as paradigm boundaries are pushed, potentially to a breaking point. Further experiment, within paradigm protocols, may, of course, show that what were initially thought to be anomalies are, in fact, outcomes consistent with a current paradigm, properly interpreted or understood. In other, where consistency is not shown, ad hoc hypotheses may be added to the paradigm, supplementing existing theories, in an effort to explain anomalies otherwise unexplainable within existing theories, no matter how interpreted.

But, sometimes, a point comes where anomalies accumulate to such a degree, that they present a clear and very present danger to the whole complex of definitions, theories, and hypotheses of then-current normal science. If efforts to recharacterize or explain growing anomalous outcomes continue to fail, a phase of "revolutionary science" may begin to emerge and a "crisis" within the current paradigm may become apparent. At that point, alternatives to once obvious-seeming assumptions may begin to be taken seriously. The premises of an entire field, once thought largely unchallengeable, may begin to be reexamined. Rival theories to established frameworks which would not have been seriously considered before a crisis emerged may slowly (or even suddenly) be perceived as new and serious contender paradigms.

The scientific community will naturally oppose any major, conceptual change in a then-prevailing paradigm. Science cherishes successful paradigms because their procedures and instrumentalities have a history of success. What has worked in the past is often a fair guide to future efforts, whereas new, untested hypotheses are often unsuccessful. Normal science practitioners will tend to view any threat to their existing systems of understanding negatively and, thus, tend to view favorably any new explanation that might save the current paradigm.

Scientists only reluctantly give up paradigm-established hypotheses, even where their instrumental value and practical efficacy are challenged by actual observations. The reasons are fundamentally psychological and sociological. The intensity of effort to preserve the paradigm status quo results, in large part, from the damage acceptance of a new paradigm does to the comfort levels of those who conduct normal science. Science professionals, especially those at the top of their fields, will have spent considerable time and resources to become experts in their fields. Their identities may be intertwined in their status as experts within the existing paradigm and they may be ill-disposed to give up that status.

Over time and in the face of potentially very substantial resistance, however, an existing paradigm will, in rare cases, collapse. A new one will emerge and solidify—in Kuhn's language, a "paradigm shift" will have occurred. Once the new paradigm is established, work within it will again take on the attributes of what will then be regarded as "normal science" puzzle-solving, guided by the new paradigm's definitions, hypotheses, protocols, and interpretive procedures.

Kuhn (2002) likened the recognition and acceptance of the new paradigm by science practitioners as analogous to what occurs during a "gestalt switch" or "religious" illumination:

> Paradigms are not corrigible by normal science at all … normal science ultimately leads only to the recognition of anomalies and to crises. And these are terminated, not by deliberations and interpretation, but by a relatively sudden and unstructured event like the gestalt switch. Scientists then often speak of the 'scales falling from the eyes' or of the 'lightning flash' that "inundates" a previously obscure puzzle. On other occasions the relevant illumination comes in sleep. No ordinary sense of the term 'interpretation' fits these flashes of intuition through which a new paradigm is borne (p. 122).

The language Kuhn used to describe the phenomenology of acceptance of paradigm shifts is similar to that frequently used to describe religious/mystical experiences. The language of "scales falling from the eyes" is frequently associated with New Testament theology and blinding revelations of the divine. The development of science is, per Kuhn, not the rational, linear, cumulative and aggregative process the Traditional View reflects but an uneven process, influenced by psychological and sociological factors, which largely prevent science practitioners from seeing what is before their eyes.

Paradigm shifts thus resemble psychic shifts in the modification and/or replacement of maladaptive schema. In revolutionary science, explanatory and predictive theories may only forcibly replace with theories better adapted to their environments under the crushing weight of anomalous observations which cannot be explained by the addition of ad hoc hypotheses. In similar fashion, maladaptive schema will only be replaced with better adapted ones, with great effort, and only when psychic defenses directed to preserving existing schema are forcibly overcome, resulting in an experience similar to a gestalt switch, as described below.

Kuhn's analytics of science history were, of course, fundamentally *descriptive* of the evolution of science theories. He was not addressing whether scientists could or should be attempting to alter paradigm-consistent beliefs. Rather, he was explaining the dynamics of normal and revolutionary science and how and why paradigm shifts occur in the way they do.

The design and implementation of therapeutic strategies are obviously not fundamentally descriptive. The manner in which the status quo in science domains is preserved in the face of contradicting observations, however, is very similar to the manner in which psychic defenses preserve the maladaptive schema status quo of the human psyche, even where they are not well adapted to the actual environment in which the client functions and contradict and impair the ability of the person having them to realize his or her life goals.

The *prescriptive* efforts of psychology to identify strategies to help clients replace maladaptive schema with healthier ones can learn much from the ways in which science practitioners act to preserve paradigm theories that guide their conduct even when they have ceased to be effective guides to current or future experimentation, observation and interpretation. Restated, the resistance patterns scientists show in conscious and unconscious efforts to preserve paradigms present a strong and informative analogy to client efforts, conscious and unconscious, to avoid the schema-shifts therapists attempt to facilitate, for their benefit.

C. Maladaptive Schemas and Therapeutic Methodologies

Therapists have successfully employed various strategies to help loosen the grip of the maladaptive schemas, including some the authors discuss. These strategies reflect the fact that human information processing is strongly biased in favor or maintaining schema content; studies show people better remember schema-consistent information, tend to make errors in a schema-consistent pattern and interpret new information so as to support preexisting schemas that are: "self-maintained by the magnification of information that is consistent with the schema and through minimization or negation of information that is inconsistent, with it" (Cockram 2009, pp. 32–33).

(i) Maladaptive Schemas and Paradigms of Consciousness

Schemas, as noted above, are thought to be psychological structures which allow individuals to screen, evaluate and categorize environmental stimuli to which they are exposed. They arise as a natural part of the organism's cognitive maturation, helping individuals organize their world. "Meaning making structures," they provide "enduring thematic representations of cognitive statements, networks and associations" (Dowd et al. 2010, p. 90). Schema are said to be "triggered" or "activated" by life events or stressors, consciously or unconsciously apprehended to be similar to the traumatic childhood experiences that some psychologists posit caused them in the first instance (p. 90). They are sometimes viewed as underlying beliefs that manifest in biased, distorted patterns of thinking or emotional responses and/or a range of other psychic dysfunctions (DeRubeis and Beck 1988, p. 275).

Early maladaptive schemas are sometimes understood to arise where a child fails to have his or her core needs met, e.g., lack of affection, empathy and guidance, or where the child is traumatized or victimized (Young et al. 2003). Closely related to affective states with the capacity to powerfully influence behavioral patterns, schemas contribute to what we observe, attend to and remember; thus, they are thought to be intertwined with our concepts of ourselves and, for this reason, tend to be highly resistant to even sustained modification efforts:

> Once formed, schemas are maintained in the face of contradictory evidence through the processes of distorting, not noticing, and discounting contradictory information or by seeing this information as an exception to the schematic, and therefore 'normative' rule ... The ease with which schemas are maintained even in the face of contradictory evidence poses a dilemma for cognitive therapists. Much of cognitive therapy relies on modifying beliefs through the review or production of evidence that contradicts negative or maladaptive conclusions drawn by a client (Padesky 1994, p. 268).

Schema-focused therapy (SFT) differs from traditional cognitive behavioral therapy (CBT) in several ways:

> [T]he demands and assumptions of CBT are at odds with the needs of patients with PDs [personality disorders]. Specifically, CBT's structured, instructive, problem-focused approach may be ill-suited to patients who present with vague or diffuse problems, cognitive rigidity, poor emotional awareness or an interpersonal style that undermines collaborative relationships [notes omitted]. Schema-focused therapy (SFT) retains a cognitive theoretical framework, and suggests that PDs result from early maladaptive schemas that interfere with the individual's ability to meet his or her core needs. The individual develops patterns of avoidance and compensation to avoid triggering the schema, but these patterns become over-generalized and rigid. To modify early maladaptive schemas, SFT employs a broad range of techniques, including behavioral, psychodynamic, experiential and interpersonal strategies. As a result, the treatment is more flexible, elaborative and emotion-focused than traditional cognitive approaches ... SFT treatments also tend to be longer, ranging from one to four years in duration ... (notes omitted) (Matusiewicz et al. 2010, un-paginated pdf text, at notes 45–48).

The goals of SFT include replacing maladaptive schema with healthy beliefs better suited to achieving client psychic health and life goals. Such therapy focuses on early childhood experiences attempting to achieve high levels of affect in therapy.

SFT generally assumes insight, in and of itself, will rarely lead to profound cognitive or behavioral change, absent concomitant substantial emotive change and it places great emphasis on addressing affect. The therapeutic relationship is itself viewed as a key component of treatment; SFT attempts to target the unconscious mechanisms that theorists posit are determining our understanding of the world. Commentators have observed that our ability to regulate our behavior is largely a function of our ability to identify and try to overcome the automatic impulses and emotions that influence all aspects of our waking life (Bargh 2014, p. 33). People are prone to misunderstanding regarding the true causes of their feelings and "studies suggest that an unconsciously perceived stimulus may suffice to cause someone to actually pursue a goal without any awareness of how it originated—no conscious deliberation or free will required" (p. 37).

Therapies often involve efforts to develop coping skills. These may include skills designed to give the client instruments to cope with problem situations giving rise to stress, problem-solving therapies, providing clients with strategies to deal with a wide range of personal difficulties, and restructuring therapies, which assume emotional problems are a consequence of maladaptive thoughts, with treatment directed toward reframing distorted thinking patterns and promoting effective, adaptive thoughts (Knapp and Beck 2008, p. 55).

(ii) Therapeutic Methodologies

Therapy may proceed in many different ways. The following outlines in broad terms steps frequently involved in efforts to address client maladaptive schema.

Preliminarily, the therapist attempts to create a therapeutic environment in which security, control, acceptance, and appreciation are maximized (Prasko et al. 2012). Emotional support must be provided and care taken to assure the client seeking help understands therapeutic activities will be within his or her control. The hope is that as inner attitudes of control develop, they help set the stage for therapeutic interventions to "neutralize lifelong feelings of defeat, helplessness, and a lack of control" (p. 115). Assessment of the client's condition must be made to determine whether and to what extent maladaptive beliefs/schemas are present and adversely influencing client behaviors, a task for which various strategies have been devised.

Clinicians may, for example, use detailed questionnaires as a prelude for more detailed inquiry to suggest what beliefs/schemas may be at work (Young et al. 2003). Clinicians may ask indirect questions regarding people "in general," rather than directly confronting the client, asking, for example, what the behavior in issue might suggest of "a person" acting in some particular way. The idea is to have the client understand his or her own situation while, at the same time, minimizing, in the assessment phase, to the extent possible, a perception of threat to the client's personal identity, which is, at least in part, a function of the schema itself.

In the assessment phase, the therapist seeks to "identify core cognitive structures, dysfunctional information-processing strategies, or maladaptive behavioral patterns that are central to the presenting symptoms"—the idea is to put together a preliminary picture of the client's cognitive and behavioral life so interventions can be selected or created to effectively address presenting symptoms (Dowd et al. 2010, p. 92). In SFT, the therapeutic relationship is viewed as fundamental to the change process (Pitchford 2009). Therapists may engage in empathic confrontation (validating the development and continued perpetuation of schemas while simultaneously confronting the necessity of change) and limited re-parenting (providing what the individual needed, but did not get from their parents, within therapeutic relationship boundaries, to help the client understand the present in terms of the past, and ultimately effect a gradual weakening of dysfunctional parts of personality structure) (Beckley 2013). These views are well explicated in the literature (Young et al. 2003). The clinician's task is to determine what schema might be involved so, in continuing therapy, to be able to help the client reformulate his or her thinking.

In the assessment phase, clients are frequently encouraged to view their initial reactions as "hypotheses" rather than as facts or certainly true propositions. By framing beliefs as hypotheses, distance is created, allowing the client to slowly disassociate from maladaptive beliefs. The clinician and client jointly attempt to identify "consistencies or themes that run through the individual instances of upset," to help determine what mechanisms may possibly be in issue (DeRubeis and Beck 1988, pp. 274–275). "By searching and assembling common cognitive denominators across diverse life situations and the patient's evaluation of them, a cognitive pattern can be identified" (Knapp and Beck 2008, p. 59). Once the client accepts the *possibility* that schemas may be involved in maladaptive behaviors or responses, the likelihood that client/therapist will find ways to favorably address presenting problems increases. The therapist then attempts to determine which schemas appear to be involved in presenting dysfunctions, to enable the process of changing the client's beliefs or systems of beliefs to ones better suited to client goals and interests.

The therapist may start by questioning the content of client reactions to stimuli and providing better alternatives to his or her reactions or behaviors. Over time, this may have the effect of loosening the maladaptive schema as the client learns, by repeated processing of alternatives, to do so on his or her own, outside the therapeutic context (DeRubeis and Beck 1988, pp. 274–276). Over time, the client may come to realize that his or her initial understanding of events and the inferences made based on such understandings were faulty, thus allowing the possibility of different interpretations of events:

> Throughout the treatment, the collaborative and psycho educational approach to treatment is used, with specific learning experiences designed to teach clients to: 1) monitor and identify automatic thoughts; 2) recognize the relationships among cognition, affect, and behavior; 3) test the validity of automatic thoughts and core beliefs; 4) correct biased conceptualizations by replacing distorted thoughts with more realistic cognitions; and 5) identify and alter beliefs, assumptions, or schemas that underlie faulty thinking patterns … In contrast to psychoanalytical therapies, CT [cognitive therapy] sessions have a structure in which the cognitive therapist plays an active role in helping the patient identify and focus on important areas, proposing and rehearsing specific cognitive and behavioral techniques, and collaboratively planning between-sessions assignments … The cognitive therapist has to be a good strategist to devise specific therapeutic procedures that have higher chances of producing specific changes for that particular patient…. CT encourages their patients to

adopt the empirical problem-solving approach of scientists, and the therapist serves as a role model for their patients by instilling self-efficacy, enthusiasm and hopefulness about the challenging work of changing maladaptive cognitions (Knapp and Beck 2008, p. 58).

(iii) Coping Mechanisms

Throughout the therapeutic process, clients frequently exhibit coping strategies that have allowed them to coexist with maladaptive schema and they tend to fall into broad categories.

"Schema surrender" occurs where the client "surrenders" to the schema by acting ways that continue to trigger the schema, e.g., staying in an abusive relationship, thus allowing abuse to continue, but, nevertheless, feeling a sense of the appropriateness of the relationship because the client may deserve such abuse for some conduct. "Schema avoidance" occurs where the client attempts to avoid the conditions that will activate the schema, e.g., by avoiding the formation of relationships to avoid being taken advantage of or to avoid being left alone if those are present schema. "Schema over-compensation" occurs where the client over-compensates, for example, by externalizing the schema by blaming others because the client fears he/she will be blamed. Some or all of the above coping strategies may be at play, singly, serially, or simultaneously, and techniques need to be employed to help the client address them.

Such coping strategies may have been in place for a very long time and the client may not only be comfortable with them, but view them, consciously or unconsciously, as a central component of their personal identity. The therapist may encourage the client to accept the possibility that such coping strategies are at work and, critically, that if the underlying problem is addressed, she/he will come to feel the coping strategies will become unnecessary as maladaptive schema are favorably addressed.

Once the client understands the adverse effects of the coping strategies being employed, the therapist will be in a position to try to identify therapeutic means to impact both them and the schema structures underlying the client's presenting problems:

> [T]he way individuals perceive and process reality will influence the way they feel and behave. Thus, the therapeutic goal … been to reframe and correct these distorted thoughts, and collaboratively endeavor pragmatic solutions to engender behavioral change and ameliorate emotional disorders … Once a particular basic belief is formed it may influence the subsequent formation of new related beliefs, and if they persist, they are incorporated into the enduring cognitive structure or schema. Core beliefs embedded in these cognitive structures shape an individual's thinking style and foster the cognitive errors encountered in psychopathology. Schemas are acquired early in an individual's development, and act as "filters" through which current information and experience is processed. These beliefs are molded by personal experiences and derived from identification with significant others and from the perception of other people's attitudes toward them. The child's environment either facilitates the emergence of particular types of schemas or tends to inhibit them. The schemas of well-adjusted individuals allow for realistic appraisals, while those of maladjusted individuals lead to distortions of reality, fostering, in turn, psychological disorder

> … Schemas have a variety of properties, such as permeability, flexibility, breadth, density, and also a degree of emotional charge, which may determine the difficulties or facilities encountered in the treatment process … The activation of these schemas interferes with the capacity for objective appraisal of events, and reasoning becomes impaired. Systematic cognitive distortions (e.g., catastrophizing, emotional reasoning, and selective abstraction) occur as dysfunctional schemas are activated. As tentative coping strategies to avoid getting in contact with their core and underlying beliefs, patients may engage in compensatory strategies. Although these cognitive and behavioral maneuvers alleviate their emotional suffering momentarily, in the long run compensatory strategies may reinforce and worsen dysfunctional beliefs (notes omitted) (Knapp and Beck 2008, pp. 57–58).

(iv) Limited Re-parenting and the Use of Imagery in Rescripting Experiences

SFT, in many cases, attempts to impact maladaptive schema structures through so-called limited re-parenting. This is accomplished by trying to address client needs not met in childhood by the client's actual parents, through the therapist's own efforts to provide what was missing, in the first instance. The client may, for example, be asked to imagine that a traumatic event is presently occurring so that she/he may re-live through the situation in imagery.

Within the imagery and guided by the therapist, the client may exploit coping strategies unavailable at the time the time the traumatic events occurred, enabling the client, in imagery, to change the outcome of experienced event(s). The idea is to neutralize existing schema arising from the child's unmet needs or trauma and/or replace them with better adapted psychic structures created in the therapeutic context and fostered, throughout the therapeutic relationship as a means of changing responses outside the therapeutic context. As the client begins to recurrently experience his or her needs being met, albeit in imagery guided by the therapist, she/he begins to learn to more effectively self-regulate schema-relative emotions. Such regulation is fostered by the establishing of a so-called secure attachment between therapist and client, over the duration of therapy. Techniques range from (empathetic) confrontation, on the one hand, to providing the warmth and nurturing initially missing in the parent–child interaction.

The client may, initially, become dependent on the therapist in such interactions, but dependency, in SFT, is encouraged, contrary to many other treatment modalities. The therapist also places substantial reliance on client self-reports regarding the idiosyncratic meaning of his or her own experiences and views the therapeutic process as largely collaborative (DeRubeis and Beck 1988, p. 277). Mutual trust develops and has the effect of bringing client and therapist closer together. By providing consistent warmth, nurturing, and support needed to develop an adult "mode" of behavior, intervention encourages the client to develop his or her own ability to engage in a healthy regulation of affect, not only inside the therapy session, but outside it, facilitating maximization of real world autonomy.

Guided imagery is particularly useful in attempting to directly influence client affect. (Young 2003; Hagenaars and Holmes 2012). The reasons have to do with brain structure and, in particular, the manner in which maladaptive schemas are thought to be encoded in human brains (Young et al. 2003). In early childhood, the brain's right hemisphere is dominant and strongly linked to the brain's limbic system which is the seat of human emotion, processing, and organizing information mainly through imagery, not logical or conceptual processes (Young et al. 2003). Holmes et al. (2007) wrote:

> [M]uch of the cognitive-affective disturbance associated with intrusive trauma-related memories is embedded in the traumatic images themselves, directly challenging and modifying the traumatic imagery becomes a powerful, if not preferred, means of processing the traumatic material … in the context of traumatic stimuli … emotional memory is perceptual in that it is imagery-based in nature … experimental findings lead us to two proposals with clinical implications: (1) Imagery has a more powerful impact on negative emotion than verbal processing of the same material, and therefore imagery should be examined during clinical assessment across disorders, and (2) Imagery also has a more powerful impact on positive emotion than does verbal processing, and therefore cognitive behavior techniques used to promote positive change should also employ imagery … an increase in perceptual processing subsequently led to an increase in conceptual processing, which in turn has been shown to have a beneficial effect …(pp. 298–299).

SFT therapists frequently attempt to access childhood memories in the form of images given that restructuring of ideas and interpretations has been found to be far more effective if imagery is involved than if purely rational interventions are used (Arntz 2012; Boysen and Zarbock 2012). Clinicians will ask clients to explain how retrieved images relate to feelings and needs as of the time images were formed and efforts are made to try connect client feelings/needs when schema were established to feelings/needs activated by current experiences. Once the client's then thoughts and emotions are disclosed, experiential modalities may be systematically alternated so that painful experiences once hidden by denial and dissociation may emerge and so be integrated as a conscious part of the psyche (Prasko et al. 2012, p. 115).

The therapist may, for example "enter into" the imagery process and function, for a limited time, as a source of new "parenting" (Young 2003, pp. 129–133). Within the imagery, clients may be encouraged to, for example, express anger, assert rights, or grieve and, in so doing, respond to past circumstances, guided by the therapist. The expression of emotion toward aggressors or of anger at persons who could and should have helped protect the client, as a child, but did not do so, is viewed as a healthy means of starting to assert control absent in current behaviors. The client may be encouraged to enter into "conversations" with persons who should have been there to provide support or protection and to state the consequences of the person's failure to provide such security, with the therapist responding either as one of the persons imagined or, alternatively, an outside facilitator.

Recurrent healthy responses developed in therapy begin to form patterns more consistent with those of a healthy adult not only inside therapeutic imagery, but in the client's interaction outside it. Over time, a healthy adult pattern or "mode" of behavior becomes dominant in the client's psyche, replacing maladaptive patterns of responses to stimuli which previously would have activated maladaptive schema. Other tools may be used to facilitate change. Flashcards, for example, are written statements authored by the therapist and/or coauthored by the therapist and client reflecting types of statements a parent made or might have made to the client when the maladaptive schema formed (Young 2003, pp. 104–107). Diaries may be prepared by the client in-between sessions, helping the client organize his or her thoughts (DeRubeis and Beck 1988, pp. 286–287). The process of translating thoughts, reactions, and emotions to a writing, whether in flash cards or diaries, may facilitate client internalization of positive reactions to re-parenting efforts.

It is particularly important that alternative schema comport closely with reality to assure, to the extent possible, embodiment of better adapted schema structures will not be compromised before the client's new way of reacting to stimuli, has solidified. Within the imagery context but most importantly outside it, the client will have been enabled to experience feelings that would have ensued had different conduct been undertaken by people who could have positively intervened to lessen or eliminate the trauma causing event(s), in the first instance. Substantial empirical evidence supports the causal efficacy of schema-focused therapy (Boysen and Zarbock 2012; Cockram 2009; Knapp and Beck 2008; Young 2003).

D. Kreuter and Moltner's Philosophical and Strategic Insights

Kreuter and Moltner urge therapists and mentors to work with their clients to develop a deep sense of meaning and optimism in their lives. The authors focus largely on ten subjects about which philosophers and psychologies have had much to say. We address some of them, in outline form, noting their significance to the authors' project on transformation and development of the integrated life.

First, Risk—Kreuter and Moltner explain that therapeutic efforts involve client willingness to accept risk which is omnipresent in all phases of transformative programs. Clients who enter therapy risk learning things about themselves that, at least initially, might make them even more uncomfortable than the maladaptive schema afflicting them. Clients may be encouraged to engage in new behaviors, but there are no guarantees such behaviors will always have positive consequences. Clients need to understand, however, that failing to undertake risk will effectively guarantee nonachievement of goals, at least in many cases. Quoting Camus, the authors explain that all choice involves acceptance of the consequences of one's action. There are no guarantees client choices will be good ones. Risk, however, is ineluctably involved in understanding one's self and an inescapable concomitant of efforts to locate meaning. Transformation, they urge, is an act of bravery, and risk cannot be avoided, as made clear by diverse philosophers, e.g., Nietzsche, Kierkegaard, James and Dewey (Steckman 2013).

Second, Creativity—Kreuter and Moltner, citing Nietzsche, explain that optimal satisfaction with one's life requires that the person interact authentically with the world. To do so, she/he must create values consistent with his own being rather than just accepting the values society or other people provide. Few people attempt to define values for themselves, in the sense about which Nietzsche wrote, but those seeking authenticity should welcome the opportunity to create and re-create the persons they wish be. They should welcome, as well, the opportunity to realize their own values in action and to find new ways of interacting with others. The conscious creation of oneself is, the authors argue, a profound activity and the human capacity to do so underscores for the client his or her own potential to overcome limiting psychic impediments. Life should be lived, the authors argue, with a deep sense that one has been born for a reason.

Third, Achievement—Achievement fosters a sense of integration. Defined, in part, by what we do and what we accomplish, achievement, especially of goals believed to be valuable for others, improves the quality of one's own life (Steckman 2013). Goal-seeking should be rationally undertaken to optimize success chances and mentors and coaches may encourage and help clients to prepare reasonable, straightforward action plans. Such plans should emphasize immediate action, focused on what can be done, right now, to proactively move forward. Therapy or counseling should endeavor to replace magical thinking, a legacy of childhood, and false notions of causation, with more accurate understandings of events. Commenting pragmatically, the authors note that interim success regarding small goals may help clients sustain efforts to undertake increasingly challenging and potentially rewarding projects, fostering a sense of increased integration.

Fourth, Commitment—For Kreuter and Moltner, the person likely to achieve his goals is unlikely to approach them in a casual manner. It has always been difficult to achieve great things and, today, as a practical matter, it is particularly difficult given the numerous complexes of economic, environmental and social problems facing the world. Commitment, the authors write, requires that one understand what she/he really values and this requires being in touch with the deepest parts of who we are. The process of making and keeping commitments is recommended not merely because of its instrumental value in fostering achievement of goals, but because commitment to goals larger than one's self is one way individuals may effectively transcend the limitations of their own subjectivity.

Fifth, Integrity—The individual with integrity may be engaged in the focused, intelligent pursuit of goals, be willing to sacrifice to achieve them and willing to take ownership of and be held accountable if goals are not accomplished. Mentors and coaches may encourage conduct with integrity by helping clients more fully understand and clarify what is really important to them. First and foremost, they need to learn, frequently with help to be honest with themselves and this may involve exploring, in therapy, the benefits of a life of integrity in one's personal life, as well as the pursuit of business, social, or societal goals. The client who, with integrity, pursues his ends is not only more likely to achieve them, but more likely to experience a heightened quality of life in doing so, regardless of actual outcomes.

Sixth, Faith—Faith, not necessarily religious faith, fosters an optimally fulfilling life. They cite Kierkegaard, who maintained that the "knight of faith" embodies Christianity's solution to the "fear and trembling" and "sickness unto death" that arise from the subject's experience of a potentially godless universe wherein no values—or being itself—have an absolute foundation (Steckman 2013). They cite theologian, Paul Tillich, who was heavily influenced by Kierkegaard and defined "god" as that which is man's object of "ultimate concern." Kreuter and Moltner argue that faith, whether understood as the ultimate foundation of being or the object man's ultimate concern, has instrumental value, potentially inspiring acts of altruism or even heroism. Faith may, in addition, facilitate achievement of goals that might not have even been attempted, a point argued for famously by pragmatist William James, in his influential essay "The Will to Believe."

Seventh, Courage—For Kreuter and Moltner, undertaking to improve one's life requires courage, specifically leaving behind the comfort of old ways in which problems have been addressed. Courage, they explain "allows the will to benefit from a new sense of internal energy, enough to push through previously established limitations." A key goal for therapists, mentors and coaches is the elimination of the masks that obscure the client's deep beliefs, and disclosure of same takes courage.

For Tillich, the human condition involves multiple anxieties arising from our human finitudes, i.e., biological finitude (the fact we know sooner or later we die), moral finitude (the fact we cannot know with certainty what we ought to do, if anything, and the inability to act consistently with our beliefs, even when we are confident we know what we ought to do), and existential finitude (the fact we know neither our values nor existence may have any absolute foundation). Although such finitudes may give rises to a sense of aimlessness, isolation, and despair, man may, nevertheless, be saved, per Tillich, through the courageous act of affirming one's existence and one's faith in god. Per Kierkegaard, even if such affirmation is directly contrary to evidence one and reason itself, acting courageously is worthwhile.

Courage, Kierkegaard argued, is needed for the Christian to make a "leap of faith," even if the leap is compelled by the dread the Christian experiences as a result of the omnipresent possibility that there may turn out to be no god to catch him (Steckman 2013). Nietzsche's "superman" acts courageously in affirming self-created values by an act of will, in the absence of any absolute foundation, including a Christian-style personal deity (Steckman 2013). For the authors, courage is necessary to uncover and/or create personal meaning, to discover one's authentic self and, ultimately, realize one's own highest values and purposes.

Eighth, Being and Becoming. Kreuter and Moltner cite Rollo May, who urged that human beings are engaged in a simultaneous process of being and becoming; rather than collections of static substances, once freed from the barriers of unawareness, fearfulness, and sometimes paralyzing anxieties, human beings have the capacity to understand our potential and, armed with that knowledge, to live transformed, positive lives (Pitchford 2009; Kreuter 2013a). For the authors, the being/becoming relationship provides access to a matrix of possibilities.

Ninth, Truth—The truths about which Kreuter and Moltner are primarily concerned are not focused on the correspondence of human beliefs to the facts the world presents (the correspondence theory of truth) or discussions about the coherence of propositions we may believe (the coherence theory), although both are, in their way, important to transformational efforts. The truths about which they write concern the fundamental question of what makes one's existence meaningful (existential/subjective truths) and what truths work best for each individual, given who she/he really is or can be (pragmatic truths). Kierkegaard famously wrote that "truth is subjectivity." By this, he meant each human encounters truth not in objective relations with the world but through the intensification of his inner/subjective life, through commitment to the possibility that the object of faith may be real.

Restated, one's own truth(s) is not found in the propositions to which a person assents or the relations between belief and the world, a view commonly associated with Twentieth Century analytic philosophy, but in the intensity of affect achieved through faith and commitment in and to those things believed valuable, along with the pursuit of them, with all ones' hearts. The purpose-driven life is, for Kreuter/Moltner, an achievement, in itself, and a source of transcendent meaning.

Tenth, Living in the Present Moment—Kreuter and Moltner urge that we need to live in the present moment if we are to live optimally rewarding lives, an exhortation easier to articulate than actually live. Where past traumatic events play an outsized, adverse causal role in obstructing efforts to achieve one's dreams, the present become little more than an extension of the past, with attenuated possibilities of transformation, rather than a healthy matrix in which unlimited human potentials may be realized. For the authors, living in the present moment means finding ways of assure one's past traumas do not indelibly define who we are or who we have the capacity to become.

Therapeutic tools exist which may help each person determine, by acts of his or her own will, who they are and who they will be in each of their future, present moments.

Conclusion

Kreuter and Moltner explain that therapists, mentors and coaches must deeply empathize with their clients if they are to successfully encourage attitude revision and the beneficial restructuring of client reference frames. Clients may develop more accurate causal understanding of their behaviors by rational strategies, but optimal efficacy of change modalities, where schema are present, require the employment of transformational strategies directed toward affect, including strategies such as imagery rescripting. Proper assessment of situations, realistic expectancies about what can be reasonably achieved, over realistic time frames, and the client's commitment to goals she/he believes are worthy of pursuit, are part and parcel of living a human with integrity.

The authors observe that the development of "authenticity" requires each of us to "enter into the abyss of ourselves" and to "navigate the waters" of not only who we are but who we hope to. In the presence of maladaptive schema, such "entry" and "navigation" is difficult.

Empirical studies, however, indicate forward movement is possible, especially where such movement is facilitated by empathetic, concerned, well-trained mental health professionals, including not just therapists, but mentors and coaches. In marital relationships, Kreuter and Moltner counsel that each partner should strive to be a "custodian of each other's dreams." In the therapeutic relationship, the counselor may not be such a "custodian," but she/he will be optimally effective in achieving therapeutic goals if the client's dreams, over time, grow in a manner consistent with increasing capacities to engage in healthy, adult behaviors, regardless of the toxicity of past experiences.

Preface

> To thine own self be true, and it must follow,
> as the night the day, thou canst not then be false to any man.
> William Shakespeare

The phenomenology of human behavior involves many forms of adaptation in response to stimuli encountered within the spectrum of everyday life. Such responses include identifiable patterns of negativity brought on by the perception of the individual or as the result of trauma from extraordinary events. These responses provide the basis for the thesis of this study. Recognizable patterns of behavior can be observed as organized reactions to recurring and similar forms of stimuli. Sometimes these patterns take on a negative tone, resulting consequences to the individual, which the authors refer to as maladaptive schemas.

The purpose of this book is to analyze these maladaptive schemas, identify their possible causes, and suggest some potential approaches to effective treatment. Perspectives from both the philosophical literature, as well as psychological constructs are covered in order to provide a wide base from which to review the topic. Case examples are included to illustrate the etiology of negative schema and to portray positive adaptations through individual effort as well as when appropriately supplemented by professional intervention. In writing about biological terms of patterns, Szasz (1974) offers:

> I do not deny, of course, that man is an animal with genetically determined biological equipment which sets the upper and lower limits within which he must function. I accept the limits, or the general range, and focus on the development of specific patterns of operating within them (p. 209).

Szasz' perspective resonates with the practical consideration that we, as humans, are either somewhat helped or handicapped by our genetic makeup and relative fortune in terms of environmental factors such as pollution, food supply, socioeconomic status, and intellectual and emotional capacity. As such, we must operate within these boundaries, though intrepid souls do all they can to break their own barriers and expand previously defined limits. In a way, each individual's life is a partially completed canvas where the paint is still wet and the brushes stand ready to alter the impressions. Behaviors are initiated through a combination of natural instinct and, as children, by mimicking the behavior of others, typically adults. The outcome or products of our behaviors derive cognizable results and/or consequences whether small or significant. When these outcomes are positive the behavior deemed responsible for the result/consequence is reinforced, ready for repetition when similar stimuli are presented. Negative results will typically cause an erosion of the prior pattern of behavior or, at least, inhibit formation of a new pattern. In cases where no better way of responding can be found, the eventual behavioral pattern is likely to be maladaptive.

The relative level of success (or lack thereof) that the individual perceives in life contributes heavily towards formation of schemas. Success can be defined as the favorable outcome of an attempt or endeavor, whether based on short- or long-term. Modern society tends to create pressures to succeed frequently measured by notions, such as accumulation of material wealth (money, property), attainment of power (business, political, social-standing), and abilities (professional, management, athletics, acting, or writing). Endeavors to succeed may be a relatively short span of an active life, such as an elected U. S. President or a professional football player, or span a major portion of one's lifetime, such as a person's career.

The human condition is defined by a range of possibilities with regard to success: total failure, partial success, complete success, and no desire at all for the achievement of success. Risks should be weighed juxtaposed to the potential feelings of regret for risks not taken. Those with high aspirations should exercise appropriate caution and evaluate the true purpose of each stated goal. When aspirations elevate in a distorted manner, they can develop into harmful fixations. Some excuse themselves for not branching out to try new things or feel inhibited from doing so because of some maltreatment endured during childhood. Murray (1955) named one type of fixation the *Icarus complex*, after the mythological personage who flew too near the sun in his attempt to surpass his father, and, as a result had the wax holding his artificial wings melt, leaving him unable to fly. "People with the Icarus complex are considered to have a special affinity for fire and water, strong narcissism, cravings for immortality, and great aspirations that crumble in the face of failure" (Maddi and Costa 1972, p. 78). As individuals, we are free to choose many of our options, especially those involving our will, desires, strivings, and preferences.

Some feel that the collective history of life experiences, impressions, etc. is inbred into our DNA, and continues to influence our behaviors throughout life. The age-old debate over nature vs. nurture indicates the disparate ways people feel about why they are the way they are. Extended further, some people are of the opinion that people cannot change themselves. The authors disagree and are of the belief that a willful person can, in fact, make considerable changes to the patterns of their behaviors. Despite even significant limitations, growth, improvements, and shifts in attitude remain possible.

Each of us has potential, as well as, at least in certain societies, ample room to make choices in our lives, which we can define as a form of personal freedom. "Choices are influenced by many factors, such as family, fears, and goals" (Kreuter 2014). We also each have gifts—those elements of native ability that enable us to do one or more exciting things in life. Those who are born disabled or become ill, or who are compromised due to accident, may lack certain abilities, but their gifts are not shuttered. Living within limits may be one of the aspects of being human, but not everyone adheres to such limits. Many persons in human history have triumphed despite their limitations by bravely overcoming obstacles. As an example, the famous American Helen Keller (1880–1968) was the first deaf and blind person to earn a Bachelor of Arts degree. Through the dedicated efforts of her teacher, Anne Sullivan, Ms. Keller was able to learn to communicate. Thus, through Ms. Sullivan's pioneering work, the isolation of lack of language was shattered, enabling Ms. Keller, by many accounts, to live a very fulfilling life. Naylor (1998) wrote:

> And so what I've learned in the last twenty years is that *I* am the sole judge and jury about what my limits will be. And as I look toward the horizon of the next twenty years, it is *no... no* limit. With that kind of knowledge, I've grown as old as I can possibly be; the aging has stopped here, and now I just grow better (p. 42).

We can also refer to freedom of choice as one's volition since it matters most what we do with our knowledge, skills, and abilities. Such freedom, which is to be particularly cherished when we realize that some do not have it, can help to define what we strive to accomplish in life. Some may consider that an element of luck interplays with success. Perhaps that is so. A person born into a wealthy family would presumably be initially exposed to opportunities that are much grander than a person born into an impoverished family. "[A] study, entitled: A Status Enhancement Account of Over Confidence," concluded: "The individuals among us who are elevated to positions of status wield undue influence, have access to more resources, get better information, and enjoy a variety of benefits" (Furness 2012, p. 1). This is not to imply that the wealthy person will succeed or that the poor person cannot. It does mean that sustained effort and some good fortune and/or mentoring would be helpful for a person who is at a distinct disadvantage. Even those with disadvantages can become noticed and earn the opportunity to demonstrate capability to the fullest extent possible. An example is a long-distance runner who was born in a very poor city, but whose efforts result in his or her running prowess being discovered and then nurtured. Bringing the person into an environment where opportunities can be presented, may lead to the person's potential of being realized. How many brilliant-minded or athletically gifted persons become lost in the crowd because of limitations of exposure?

As the purpose of this book is not to debate geopolitical issues, we can only focus on potential within the psychological, emotional, behavioral, and spiritual construct of a person as opposed to an entire society or culture. We also examine the phenomenology of adapting or not adapting well to stimuli regardless of the backdrop of societal influence or the relative levels of privilege and fortune. The authors do encourage other researchers to explore whether there are connections between privilege and lack thereof, which may encourage the formation of maladaptive schemas. Attitudes and paradigms become important considerations when analyzing the lack of progress towards transformative goals in the examined life.

The study of maladaptive schemas must include the older concept of paradigms. What is meant by the term "paradigm"? One important aspect of the definition of paradigm is how we are bound or confined by some form of pervasive or subtle limitation on our ability. It is also important to consider that a lack of flexibility in our thought process may result in the failure to achieve a goal, which can be interpreted as the failure to succeed. Or the lack of ability may result from a manner of perceiving or thinking, which can be changed. A deficit, with coaching, can be turned into a skill, especially with sustained effort and motivation. The lack of ability may be attributable to a physical factor (or factors) that affect the mental process, which is outside the scope of this book. Treatment protocols are certainly available for many conditions and maladies. Further, hope is always present that new or improved treatment regimens may become available in the future.

Logically, paradigms form the basis for paradigmatic thinking. Such cerebral effort is either deliberate or reactionary, perhaps guided by nothing more than pure habitual behavior. The proverbial "knee-jerk reaction" is one example of a response borne more out of habit than measured and thoughtful consideration. An example of habitual behavior is a person becoming unduly hostile towards a spouse during marriage counseling or some other confrontational event. Such a person may simply respond to new stimuli as if having the same reaction they always have without filtering the appropriateness of the response.[1] Limitations on the person's ability or willingness to self-judge his or her own reactions to stimuli can limit the possibility for interpersonal growth.

It is the reactivity to common or repetitive stimuli that result in a person exhibiting behavior that is routed in a boundary, recognized or unrecognized. Only the person receiving the stimuli can perceive it as the same type of stimuli. Whereas Kuhn conceptualized paradigmatic thinking from a societal perspective, for the purpose of this book, we are analyzing paradigms or schemas from the individual perspective. We adapt the basic concept, put forth by Kuhn, that paradigms are a belief system to the present subject matter. We engage in paradigmatic thinking because we think that it works (consciously or subconsciously) or has meaning to us. Normally, if we do not believe that it will work, we would not engage in it: an example coping or a way of dealing with reality.

Our organized patterns of thought and behavior, or schemas, can either work perfectly, work somewhat, or be maladaptive to our internal goals and best interests. Such organization is necessary in order to perceive and process new information received in the world, even to the extent such perception is incompatible to that which would ordinarily be considered appropriate. When strife is encountered (a roadblock), a person with insufficient coping skills may succumb to stress and become psychologically unable to deal with a given situation, leading to some level of dysfunction. Such dysfunction may manifest as behavioral problems or physical illness triggered by unstoppable reactions to stress. Prolonged stress can lead to major life-shortening medical emergencies. Career longevity, for example, can be cut short as a result of unchecked stress.

---

[1] "Filtering" is part of Executive Function." Incorporating retrospective thinking is helpful to a person who seeks to find superior ways of responding to stimuli.

Interrelated dysfunction compounds these developed negative schemas. For example, consider a person who has difficulty coping with the pressures and challenges of chronic unemployment and depression, but who also binges (eating, sexual behavior, drug-use, etc.) and sleeps through the morning on most days. Such a person may or may not be on medication and, if the person is being treated pharmacologically, may be taking multiple forms of medication (both legal and illegal). Unwinding the person's issues can be a complex undertaking. As a workable combination approach, the person likely is under the care of a psychiatrist, may be in treatment with a psychotherapist, and may also have one or more allies (peer/friends) who take on the role of coach. The central point of help from the humanistic perspective, respecting the theories of Carl Rogers and others, is client-centered. Where the coach's role becomes most prominent is in daily or, at least, frequent, communication with the person about the currency of events (stimuli) where immediate response is possible or demanded.

It is vital to point out to the client where the clients' thought-process may be deceptive to him or herself. Hegel (1977) wrote:

> The commonest way in which we deceive either ourselves or others about understanding is by assuming something as familiar, and accepting is on that account; with all its pros and cons, such knowing never is anywhere, and it knows not why (p. 18).

What forms our reactions? What affects them? We engage in paradigmatic behavior for one of two reasons: we cannot or do not care to control it or we expect it to lead to a certain result (consciously or subconsciously). Life, in reality, is a series of behaviors influenced by attitudes, stimuli and decisions, including nondecisions. Paradigmatic behavior is predicated on our reaction to stimuli. For example, it (stimuli-induced behavior) has meaning to us. If we did not believe it would work, we would not engage in it, often a form of coping mechanism or way to deal with reality.

We are taught to learn or develop paradigms from infancy, which is one reason they are so hard to change. We are surrounded by stimuli and with the ever-expanding onslaught of social networking. In some ways, we have become bombarded by this phenomenon. In fact, we are reacting to stimuli virtually every second of every moment when we are awake. Depending on the relevance of the stimuli to us, our reactions vary as to both intensity and conscious thought that we give to it. There are innumerable examples and we will provide some. Our reaction can be conscious or subconscious, to varying degrees, to the point of being rote. It can be planned or thought-out to varying degrees.

We react, overreact or we underrespond to or even completely ignore relevant stimuli. The person with an explosive personality may be likely to overreact at the slightest provocation and the depressed individual may not even care about what is occurring environmentally or may be incapable of finding effective ways of responding. Stimulus causes reactions. Stimulus is frustrating when our actions do not result in the reactions from other people that we seek or hope for—that we expect should be the consequence of our actions. As we discussed in *Fostering Resilience for Loss and Irrelevance* (Kreuter 2013a), we have certain expectations when, for example, we cross the street (or before we begin that walk) or when we begin our day. We have certain expectations that our reactions to stimuli will have a certain or desired effect. Individuals like to feel important and that their actions matter to others or, at the very least, get noticed.

There are many types of paradigms that are situation-dependent. Some categories include:

- How to spend time
- What is pleasurable
- What is painful
- How to respond to an abusive coworker
- How to react to a tragic event
- Dealing with death or illness
- Ways of handling stress
- Attitudes about money and finances
- How to hit a baseball
- Making decisions while grocery shopping; and
- How to handle a recurring problem

As an example of situational-dependent thinking: when a child pushes too far, when he/she refuses to listen and does things detrimental to him or herself because she/he perceives that she/he can "get away with it." Particularly with children, the expression "give an inch take a mile" has much meaning. Add to that the exasperation (perceived or real) when a spouse seemingly undermines the other spouse when she/he attempts to impose disciplinary constraints or to impose some semblance of discipline absent acknowledgment from the other spouse that such constraints are necessary.

Thus, the problem of maladaptive schema must be considered when dealing with a person in a treatment or coaching environment. Rogers (1988/1951) felt that treatment should be client-centered. According to Rogers (1995/1961), " … it is built upon close, intimate, and specific observations of man's behavior in a relationship, observations which it is believed transcend to some degree the limitations or influences of a given culture" (p. 5). Rogers firmly believed that his clients were not fixated on negativity. Rogers added:

> It has been my experience that persons have a basically positive direction. In my deepest contacts with individuals in therapy, even those whose troubles are most disturbing, whose behavior has been most anti-social, whose feelings seem most abnormal, I find this to be true (p. 26).

According to Rogers (1988/1951, 1956), for constructive personality change to occur, it is necessary that these conditions exist and continue over a period of time:

1. Two persons are in psychological contact;
2. The first, whom we shall term the client, is in a state of incongruence, being vulnerable or anxious;
3. The second person, whom we shall term the therapist, is congruent or integrated in the relationship;
4. The therapist experiences unconditional positive regard for the client;

5. The therapist experiences an empathic understanding of the client's internal frame of reference and endeavors to communicate this experience to the client; and,
6. The communication to the client of the therapist's empathic understanding and unconditional positive regard is to a minimal degree achieved (pp. 95–96).

No other conditions are necessary. If these six conditions exist, and continue over a period of time, this is sufficient. The process of constructive personality change will follow. It is in the sharing that the client is best able to accept notions of change required in the client's repertoire or behaviors, attitudes, and perceptions—all leading to the ways the client responds to stimuli. However, the client's struggle and ultimate ability to change must be recognized for it is the client who ultimately changes or at least should be credited with the responsibility to at least try to adapt. In many ways, it is far better for the person to accept ownership of any change in behavior.

The effective coach can help catalyze the ability of the person to adopt more effective paradigms and forge small breakthroughs, which can compound into dynamic and positive change, possibly leading to even grander breakthroughs. In a way, the coach is a more immediate and easily accessible person to take the role of sounding-board. Communication is much more casual and balanced than it could be under the (ethically appropriate) constraints of formal psychotherapy. Such informal communication can include email, texting, frequent telephone calls, letters, and in-person meetings. Events that cannot wait for the next scheduled session with therapist or psychiatrist can be discussed with the caring coach, usually an uncompensated individual. Just as a mentor, who is best recruited by the person needing mentoring, the relationship of coach and protégé is best done through direct request by the protégé, though it can occur through initial offering by the would-be coach. It is the sincerity and validity of the relationship that is of primary importance.

Coaching becomes essential to help the person overcome internally driven resistance (setbacks). Such resistance includes minor complaints, as well as overtures to give up. Reminding the person what goals they had set and asking them to speak about the importance of these goals will help steer the person back to a centering place in their life, specific to resumption of their progress towards his or her goals. It is important to respect these setbacks and find ways for redoubling the psychic energy to keep moving forward and break through obstacles.

Coaching and mentoring can be effective interventions to catalyzing meaningful change in the mindset of the individual. It is the process of instilling motivation to keep making an effort despite the short-term lack of progress that can lead to amazing breakthroughs in the person's life.

Therapeutic intervention, whether in the form of traditional psychotherapy or therapy using a multitude of modalities, such as poetry therapy, expressive art therapy, dance therapy, and others, can instigate positive change in a person's momentum. As an example, Wyatt and Rogers (2009) developed an instructor's manual on person-centered expressive arts therapy based on the work of Carl Rogers:

> Natalie Rogers' approach to person-centered expressive arts therapy developed out of the client-centered therapy work of her father, the late Carl Rogers, combined with the influences of her mother, who was an artist herself. The person-centered approach is more than just a theory of psychotherapy—it is a belief system and way of life. This philosophy holds that every one

> of us carries tremendous inner resources, and we each have the capacity to become more fully ourselves. The main task of the person-centered therapist is to create the facilitative environment with the proper conditions for the client's full self to come into bloom (p. 11).

Another example is bibliotherapy in which connections are more between literature and one's own development for intellectual, emotional, and behavioral growth (Jones 2006). "Bibliotherapy is an adjunct to psychological treatment that incorporates appropriate books or other written materials, usually intended to be read outside of psychotherapy sessions, into the treatment regimen" (Encyclopedia of Mental Disorders 2014, p. 1). Self-guided bibliotherapy offers individuals an important cost-saving and time-saving alternative to irrational thinking and negative emotions, without contacting any counselors or therapists (Frieswijk et al. 2006). Self-guided bibliotherapy was found to be "…a helpful tool to look at the family violence in a tolerant and understanding way" (Wang et al. 2013, p. 261). As well, it may be useful for others with other types of problems. "Bibliotherapy is not likely to be useful with clients suffering from thought disorders, psychoses, limited intellectual ability, dyslexia, or active resistance to treatment" (Encyclopedia of Mental Disorders 2014, p. 1).

Let us consider change itself. Can we really change our behavior—even when we really want to? If so, what leads to "real" change in the way we act? How hard it is to change depends on what we are changing and how deeply committed we are to change. Further, there may be external influences that either attempt to force us to change or encourage us to change. The following are just a few such influences:

- Imprisonment
- Sudden unemployment
- Death in family—loss of support system
- Disabling accident; and
- Intervention

Mistakes, worrying (which by definition is about the future), being subjected to the judgment of another person or the control they may have over us, and how we may be able to change any specific paradigm are important psychological constructs. To change our paradigms we have to understand why and how they are formed in the first place. Change is a word easily stated—but real change requires real understanding. Understanding often requires a catalyst who, or which, can challenge our previously ingrained notions. The timing of when we gain that understanding is critical to the process of change, if it is to be made. In the end, only we can determine when we have gained a sufficient understanding to realize whether we can effect real change, but we must be confident that we have, in fact, gained sufficiently new understanding and that such understanding is "correct," at least for the particular objective.

How do our paradigms impact on how we define success? Success is a very individualized concept. Depending upon how it is measured, success may not be that difficult to obtain. It can be as broad as a career change or as meaningful as a single experience viewing the want ads. Even movement toward a goal can be a success or, at least, a very positive first step. Many people stuck in a rut have a difficult time committing to start the process of change. In running it is not finishing that defines success, but a positive beginning. One cannot finish what one has not started. What meaning the individual ascribes to the success is critical because that can define whether she/he continues the straight and narrow road or veers off the path. The precipitating reason for a change or suppression with respect to one's goals (*e.g.*, boredom, believing it is not attainable, expectations not met) is also relevant. It is only when the goal or goals are set that we can know if we have met it and thus have succeeded. There may be a change in goals and thus a change in the change of paradigms necessary to meet the goal or goals. Sometimes success is measured by the attempt to reach a goal. An example is a runner who tries to win a race, but fails to do so. However, the completion of the race, albeit at a pace slower than that of the winner, can be felt as a successful endeavor. People have different levels of ability and not everyone has the same training regimen nor the same quest or even conceptualization of victory. Thus, pure physical ability and preparedness are ingredients that can make major differences in who can and will win. For some, the thought of actually winning might never enter the mind as a possibility. Just being an entrant and being there for the finish may be adequate and desirable.[2] The reality is that not everyone can win first place, but many can complete the course. If the only reason to enter is to win, then most who think rationally would never even try.

Thus, the paradigm of not engaging in a particular activity because of the self-admitted prophecy of defeat can derail any effort to be a participant solely because of the reality that winning is very unlikely. Some youth may avoid team sports in competitive leagues if the coach emphasizes "winning" more than sportsmanship, athleticism, and simply having fun. This may have more to do with why people compete. Some compete for prizes or trophies or bragging rights; others for the pure challenge and for the value of the established goal to motivate the person to stick to a training program.[3] There are those who deem "winning" to be equated to finishing. Kreuter has now completed 71 marathons and 24 half marathons. He has not won any of these races and winning has never been set as a goal. At age 54, trying to run 26.2 miles faster than runners under age 25 would be somewhat foolish, if not delusionary. Instead, a much more realistic and attainable goal would be to be fit enough to handle the physical demands of the distance and the specific challenges of the course, which invariably include steep hills, inclement weather and inhospitable temperatures. His attitude is "Bring it on" because there is no point (for

[2] An example is the recent 2014 Winter Olympics where the Jamaican bobsled team competed, but had no real chance to win a medal, according to expert sports commentators.

[3] Kreuter trained by running every day for one year before considering the challenge of a marathon. It was the original goal of improving his health that, once accomplished, turned into a lasting desire to compete in sanctioned distance-running events. The regimen of frequent competition in sanctioned events proved to be beneficial on physical, mental, and emotional levels.

him) in taking the easy road. The positive boost of energy and spirit is evident following each race despite the inevitable recovery period. Even the small amounts of pain and discomfort (blisters, lost toe nails, fatigue, dehydration, sore muscles) pale compared to the positive elements, thereby making the effort one of a producer of net positive results. In this way, the repetition of the experience of running becomes an adaptive schema, one that incorporates well with the lifestyle and persona of the runner. Nonrunners may speak of prolonged distance running as an addiction or a penchant for an endorphin rush, but such criticisms miss the point entirely. Some more sedentary people dislike those around them who are more active. Instead of cheering them on, they comment in the negative.

The personal challenge is the one most coveted internally. When we strive to reach new plateau's in our lives it is the result (positive or negative) that often drowns out the sheer excitement of the process. While it is always good to win at something or reach the highest level possible in a particular endeavor, coming in second (third, etc.) does not equate to failure. Just because one or more people are superior does not in any way diminish the effort or mute the achievement. Sincere competitors prefer strong adversaries because it provides a better challenge. It is better to lose to a superior team rather than easily defeat very inferior teams. The very essence of competition is that there are others who share the same dream. Thus, lining up on a track next to nine other qualified runners makes the race a "race." If in the end someone else breaks the tape at the finish line we should not be unduly disappointed except, perhaps if we know deep down that we did not put in the fullest effort we were then capable of. Thus, finishing well based on your current capabilities may be very beneficial for boosting self-confidence.

To overcome the negative schema of low esteem, depression, etc., a person can adopt a regimen of simple, sustainable, and increasingly challenging movement. This plan can consist of any number of goals, such as reaching a commitment to an eventual goal of a specific level of fitness or the attainment of a finisher medal in a marathon. Once a baseline of capability is established, the next goal would be to increase the effort. Staying with running as the example, the person wishing to climb out of their dilemma (the lethargy) can start on the first day by walking for 20 minutes at a normal pace. The prescription for achievement equates to nothing more than compounding the effort of day 1 by adding more effort in day 2. This can mean walking for 25 minutes at the same pace. For day 3, the distance can increase slightly to 30 or even 35 minutes and the pace could be quickened. Following suit, the days that follow can produce results of more time and more effort (read: progress). Of course the person needs to be committed to the program, allocate the time necessary, and be motivated. Excuses such as the weather must be set aside and overcome. This helps build confidence and toughness. By starting out easy (relative toward the ultimate goal) the mind–body–spirit connections all contribute to improved performance. Using this technique with the guide of a coach or therapist, the person can soon become capable of longer distances and faster paces.

There is no real measure of our limits except those we place on ourselves and those determined through trial. Kreuter noticed a famous T.S. Eliot quote on a shirt that said: "Only those who risk going too far can learn how far they can go." This saying proves quite apropos to the person beginning a sustainable regimen with increasing self-induced pressure. Staying with the program produces amazing results. Kreuter has described this technique to several persons he has coached and they have all benefited by the simplicity yet the effectiveness of the process. The human body is built to deliver performance based on demand as long as the training allows the body to be ready for the potential demand. In the movie *Rocky II* (United Artists 1982), Rocky Balboa's trainer, the character "Mickey," explains that to fight for 45 minutes (15 3-minutes rounds), a fighter needs to train for 45,000 minutes. So, then, applying this concept to the person needing to climb out of morass, the element of physical movement works wonders to use the process to also move the mind forward. It is the progression of the capability of the self as a physical entity that has positive reverberation on the mental, psychological, and spiritual aspects of the person.

Another such example is the material presented in Appendix E: Jewish Oncology, which is a comedic, though serious, essay written by Kreuter as a method of altering the negative mood of the cancer sufferer.[4] Using such writing, the current mood of a person, a form of transient paradigm, can be changed if even for a brief moment. Some people who are diagnosed with a serious disease say to themselves and others: "Why me?" But, they also could say: "Why not me?" Adapting to disease may take time and the process of acceptance following denial can lead to coping and actually embracing the illness and the treatment plan if there is one.

Laughter is a gift, an elixir of the heart and mind. It has long been known that humor can be involved in the healing process. Films have been made about the topic and books have been written covering the power of laughter, which has the medical benefit of reducing blood pressure. By looking at the onslaught of disease through the lens of a combatant, reducing the intense pressure of the disease from a psychological perspective can help stimulate the will to live and add to quality of life during the ordeal of treatment.

Today we seek immediate cure. Some illnesses are not able to be cured quickly and others are not curable at all. For example, cancer survivors typically have to wait five years and be cancer-free during that period for the "cure" word to even be mentioned by the medical community, if even then. Thus, remission becomes the in-between period of time wherein nobody can predict the ultimate prognosis, though there is, of course, plenty of available statistical data. Nonetheless, patience is required to cope with and deal with the required wait for more definitive medical news. Even with the news of "cure" worry may invade the person's conscious, resulting in the ongoing importance of keeping a positive attitude.

By starting out small, big things can happen. Breakthroughs occur when a person feels ready to advance to the next level in any effort to alter his or her present course. An example is a smoker whose habit contains both a physical and psychological component, where the person is determined to decrease the number of cigarettes smoked in a day by one per week to which there is both a physical and

[4] This essay was inspired by Kreuter's wife, who was undergoing surgery, chemotherapy, and radiation for breast cancer.

psychological component. Eventually, the decreased intake of nicotine will be tolerated and the tapering may lead to complete cessation of the unhealthy habit. It is the further hurdle of finding new ways to adapt to the future onslaught of emotional strife and stress that becomes necessary to manage.

Negative paradigms can be overcome. By breaking down the challenge into steps, one can achieve short-term and then eventually long-term goals. Discipline is necessary for perseverance and moving beyond immediate, and ultimately hollow, gratification.

Societal influences play a role on both how we view success and in the methods used to obtain it. Some individuals require a less complicated life (i.e., fewer activities); therefore, they set fewer goals, which means less to achieve success in order to feel fulfilled and happy. Others simplify their lives by focusing and removing what they perceive to be the clutter.

Camus (1913–1960) wrote about our sense of choice and acceptance of consequences. In an abstract of the philosophical writings of Camus, the complexities of choice are discussed (Lander.edu 2013):

> This specific sense of "choice" implies that I must accept the consequences of my choices, even when those consequences are undeserved since the consequences of actions cannot be reliably foreseen. Yet, when I am self-directed and my soul is clear, the existentialist recognizes my anguish of taking personal responsibility for fortuitous consequences. As an existentialist, when I am self-directed and my soul is clear, I recognize my anguish of taking personal responsibility for the fortuitous consequences (p. 1).

It is important for the client to accept personal responsibility for his or her life and the decisions that are made within the lifetime. "...to make a decision presupposes the willingness and capacity to assume responsibility for it. This would include the risk of making a wrong decision and the willingness to bear the consequences without blaming others for them" (Horney 1957, p. 26). Maslow (1961) wrote:

A problem we psychologists have been ducking is the problem of responsibility and, necessarily tied in with it, the concepts of courage and of will in the personality. Perhaps this is close to what the psychoanalysts are now calling 'ego strength' (p. 56). Sartre (1985/1957) discussed absolute responsibility as "...simply the logical requirement of the consequences of our freedom" (p. 53).

This book is the natural evolution of Kreuter's (2013a) book titled: *Fostering Resilience for Loss and Irrelevance* (Springer-Verlag, New York). In that book, Kreuter (and Moltner and other contributors) convey their viewpoints that the constructs of resilience and relevancy are related and, when tied together, form the added basis on which to base therapeutic intervention. In the present thesis, the authors join forces to extend the notion of what the problem is and how can the problem be resolved by examining the construct of the paradigmatic shift as a necessity along the continuum of self-improvement by dealing effectively with the problems of negative schema.

Synopsis of preface

- Patterns of behavior are organized reactions to recurring stimuli.
- Negative patterns can form maladaptive schemas, impacting the person's life.

- Success in life is a determinant of the formation of schemas.
- Each person has gifts, enabling potential to achieve in life.
- Attitudes and paradigms impact on the level of happiness in life.
- When treating a person, the problem of maladaptive schema should be considered.
- Constructive personality change requires certain conditions to occur.
- Interrelated dysfunction compounds the development of negative schemas.
- Coaching and psychotherapy are two approaches to helping a person overcome the impact of maladaptive schemas.
- Coping mechanisms help a person deal with reality.
- Movement is one way to overcome the negative schema of low esteem and depression.
- Societal influences play a role on how we perceive success.
- Paradigmatic behavior is predicated on our reaction to stimuli.

Commentary—The Legacy of Eugene I. Taylor

Dr. Kreuter's new book (together with Mr. Moltner) epitomizes the scholar-practitioner *ethos* of the University, which I lead, and from which Dr. Kreuter graduated. Like his prior excellent treatise, *Fostering Resilience for Loss and Irrelevance*, this new book not only honors the past in its broad and insightful analysis of the literature, but also breaks new ground in theory and *praxis*.

It is not a surprise to those of us at Saybrook that Dr. Kreuter skillfully weaves together the concepts from the luminaries of humanistic and existential psychology—including May, Rogers, Allport, Murray, Jung, and many others—with "down-to-earth" advice in this new book. In his time as a Saybrook student and in his career as what can only be called a "renaissance man," Dr. Kreuter has demonstrated a stunning capability to range widely through intellectual landscapes (and that is intentionally plural) and to be able to map the world in ways that illuminate territories (again, plural). He bridges C. P. Snow's two cultures in a manner not seen in many humans!

Treatment and Management of Maladaptive Schemas is about helping people change their thought patterns from negativity to more positive ways of responding to stimuli. It covers Thomas Kuhn's work on paradigm shift applied to the human being and person-centered psychology dealing with psychodynamic and humanistic models of counseling people, using various modalities and exercises. While much of the book is a scholarly exercise, the included case studies provide guidelines and lessons, with the appropriate *caveats*, to both "do the right thing and do things right."

In this exceptional effort, Dr. Kreuter demonstrates he has learned well the Saybrook mantra to take it "from the library to the street," meaning he is both book- and street-smart. He also shows his keen perceptivity in addressing the central organizing question at our University: "What does it mean to be human in the twenty-first century?"

A word about the Saybrook professor to whom the book is dedicated, Dr. Eugene Taylor: Until his death in 2013, Dr. Taylor was a central figure in the scholarly and student-inspiring universe that comprises the University. Dr. Kreuter has talked many times about the mentor-mentee relationship he had as a student who worked with Dr. Taylor in curriculum and as the chairperson of his doctoral committee.

An early student of humanistic psychology, Taylor was present at some of the earliest transpersonal psychology conferences in the 1970s. Combined with his long-standing interest in Eastern religions, this exposure helped develop his scholarly interest in the study of consciousness itself, which he placed at the center of the psychological experience. Psychology, he emphasized, is a "person centered science," in which the subjective experiences of everyone involved are at the center of best practice. He held that the current "neuro-revolution" in science will further affirm this: that the effort to study the neurons of the brain for the stirrings of consciousness will lead to the realization that there is no "empirical" way to study consciousness without involving radical subjectivity. To take that subjectivity into account as central to understanding rather than futilely trying to dismiss it was, he said, the essence of good science.

"There is no science anywhere that does not involve someone's personal consciousness somewhere," he wrote. His work at Saybrook, where he at various times chaired the programs in Consciousness Studies and Humanistic & Transpersonal Psychology, inspired many to follow in his footsteps and put existential psychology at the center of their own work and practice.

It is not unreasonable to say the Dr. Kreuter would not be the scholar and practitioner he has become without the influence of Dr. Taylor. Dr. Kreuter's own words explain it best; he wrote in a personal communication:

> [Dr. Taylor's] legacy as an authority on the history of humanistic and existential psychology and … his work and teaching through the wonderful Saybrookian system allowed people like me to broaden my notion of a purely debit and credit world to understanding the complexity of the human psyche while appreciating the simplicity of the person-centered approach towards treatment of mental illness.

So much more could be said about Dr. Taylor and his contribution to Saybrook, to psychology and to the world. But, to conclude, here is what Louis Hoffman, the President of the Society for Humanistic Psychology (APA Division 32) and a colleague of Taylor's on Saybrook's executive faculty, upon word of his death:

> Eugene gave much of his life to humanistic psychology, and served in many ways as our historian. His passion for humanistic psychology was evident to anyone who knew him. His scholarship and, more importantly, the man, will be dearly missed by his students, colleagues, and the whole humanistic community.

This book, then, is dedicated not only to Eugene Taylor, and to the University he served and loved, Saybrook, but to the human spirit and to the goal and task of every human achieving their full humanity.

Mark Schulman, Ph.D.
President,
Saybrook University

Eugene I. Taylor, Ph.D.
1947–2013

Commentary
A Reflection on Dr. Kreuter and Mr. Moltner's Thought-Leadership Book: "Treatment and Management of Maladaptive Schemas"
A. James Forbes, Jr.

Broad Perspective

I have been given the privilege of reading Dr. Kreuter and Mr. Moltner's book while in its development stage, for which I will be eternally grateful. I was given to making analogies in a number of business and life scenarios for inclusion as this Commentary. As a business executive who does not pretend to have anywhere near the depth of knowledge and experience in this area as Dr. Kreuter and Mr. Moltner, however, one with a long career in many business sectors, I quickly began to make mental notes on how these maladaptive schemas can and do profoundly impact the business world. Indeed, experience informs me that the behaviours and challenges described therein are amongst the most significant issues many organizations face.

Arguably, business is a collection of people from all walks of life who come together for the ostensible purpose of accomplishing a mission and vision. A business is also a "people laboratory" comprised of a collection of individuals with a certain percentage impeded by personal maladaptive schemas. For success, identification of these instances and remedial actions are often necessary.

We are no longer an evolutionary world but one in which there are revolutionary changes on a daily basis; thus raising the bar towards competing more effectively. Unchecked, these collective maladaptive schemas can be compounded and reinforced into an unhealthy environment, often to the gross detriment of the organization. And, depending upon the nature of the business, such schema adversely impacts the rest of us who benefit from the goods/services which support the common good. Certainly, then, our attention must be drawn to their identification and resolution.

An applicable example of the above I am given to think of is a bio-science organization for which I was engaged to assist in the commercialization of a new medicine which targeted children in developing countries who were afflicted with a disease causing about 5000 deaths per month. The science was right; the public interest would be served; the economics were strong, however the product was commercialized too late and the business was lost to a competitor. It was so unnecessary and lives were lost when they did not have to be. In this case, it was all due to a fundamental unjustified mistrust by the CEO of the experts working for him. Later it was discovered that he had a long history of this in other professional settings.

In the macro-sense, the Fortune 500 list of companies will serve as an example. More than 50% of those on the list 25 years ago are no longer on the list. In many cases, it might be argued, it was because of unresolved internal management/people driven issues. That's a separate case study. Mine is not to study those which demised for one reason or another, but business books are riddled with examples of leadership with maladaptive schemas drawn into the workplace and into positions of authority.

Recognizing When These Maladaptive Schemas Are at Play

The foregoing comments are not meant to be a broad condemnation of organizations and the fine, effective people in them. In fact, from my personal experience, it is a relatively small population of organizations wherein this is a critical factor. Having said that, we must be realistic—most organizations bring a certain amount of maladaptive schemas into the workplace.

The author's observations on the human scale can be noted in both the partially or fully dysfunctional workplace. I do not refer to low level office politics or debate; or an organization given to poor processes and controls, but more one where the mission/vision is not being accomplished because of materially insufficient well adapted leadership.

In the following, I have extracted and placed in quotes certain of the author's comments which struck me as very appropriate for interpretations in the business world. They are reflective of commonly faced challenges of which we need to be aware and then set a direction for course correction. Certain of them:

- "……Mistrust of people or groups….."—This exhibits itself in the leadership approach known as the "I know better than thou" form of leadership. There is little or no "group think". The consequences of such leadership can be devastating. It manifests itself with decisions made without consultation and unexplained deviations from previous plans. *A recent example was the matter of the well publicized near demise of the JC Penney retail chain because the CEO made dramatic changes in pricing policies and store design without consultation from outside focus groups and senior inside leadership. He openly admitted he listened to his own voice over that of others.*

- "...Global systems of hypotheses, beliefs, rules and principles...."—This is most commonly exhibited when organizations fail to realize that we are in a world wherein most commercialization is no longer an evolutionary process but a revolutionary one—*Apple gets the message; Kodak did not.* There is a high need to be open to re-think; modification of original plans and becoming a leader in change, especially in these times.
- "....Identities may be inter-twined in their status as experts within the existing paradigm and they may be ill-disposed to give up that status...." Interpretation: Narcissism and good business must be mutually excludable—to the benefit of the organization and the people it serves. *An example is a recent client which is well known in its field. The CEO was originally recruited because of his expertise in a particular programmatic area. When business conditions gave strong indications that the particular program approach was no longer viable, the CEO insisted that his experience and expertise and contacts in this area would pull the organization through. It did not and the organization nearly went bankrupt. This CEO could not look past his status as an expert.*

What Is an Organization to Do in Such Cases?

From a professional business perspective, I am only able to offer directional remedies as each situation can be quite different. The following are based on my collective experience which includes senior level executive positions and board level responsibilities—they are only highlights and not meant to be exhaustive–for sure; many have authored books on this topic as well as it being the topic of advanced studies:

- The Board must be the leader in establishing "tone-at-the-top" which will then permeate all the key activities and decision making from the board on down. A strong tone at the top environment governs key decisions on:
  - Tsuhe hiring of the CEO
  - Understanding and participating in the key policy making activities
  - Working closely with the CEO in driving a culture of openness and empowerment.
- Once the CEO is in place, after thorough referencing—and perhaps psychological testing, the board must check-in and not check-out. Hiring and governance over the CEO while in place is paramount and one of the board's highest priorities.
- Internal quality checkpoints must be in-place and supported at the board level on all key initiatives included in the strategic planning process.
- A firmly established whistleblower policy which reports outcomes on a collective basis and at times on an individual basis, to the board of directors or a committee thereof.

Conclusion

Dr. Kreuter and Mr. Moltner present a universal set of guidelines/thoughts for thinking about and charting a course in any number of settings. The author of this reflection saw it through the lens of a business person. It has opened my eyes to be more aware of the, not only complex personnel forces at play, but also the opportunities that lay ahead to create higher performing organizations. I commend Dr. Kreuter and Mr. Moltner for their efforts in sharing their most pertinent knowledge.

Acknowledgements

Eric Kreuter

The late Dr. Eugene I. Taylor, former faculty member of Saybrook University and Chair of Dr. Kreuter's dissertation committee in 2006 was instrumental in furthering the knowledge of many students through his courses, lectures and numerous published books. He was a true academic mentor and one of the most brilliant people I have known. His passing leaves behind a legacy of lifelong research and everlasting respect for the ideals of learning and the nobility of contributing to the fields of psychology and comparative religion. His profound impact is immutable.

I wish to express my appreciation to my co-author and friend, Ken Moltner for his insights and great additions of writing, editing, and conceptual development and to Mr. Laurence A. Steckman and Dr. Lodze Steckman for their eloquent and philosophically rich Foreword and to my beloved daughter Cathleen M. Kreuter, a psychotherapist, for her insightful Afterword and to the contributors of case material to our book and to all those who provided helpful guidance, constructive criticism or who just listened to a description of the purpose of the book.

Special thanks to my dear wife, Meryle, for her tireless editing and, as a skilled psychotherapist, for her suggestions and critique of ideas along the continuum of the process of writing this book and to my articulate 16-year-old son, Aaron for his contribution of an essay. Thank you as well to those who unselfishly contributed case study material for his book.

Deep appreciation is expressed as well to the unswervingly excellent team at Springer-Verlag, most notably: Sharon Panulla, Sylvana Ruggirello and Kanchan Kumari of Crest Premedia Solution Private Limited in India.

Kenneth Moltner

The most wondrous aspect of life is the people who bring into our lives joy and meaning. I am fortunate to say that there are many of those people in my life. And I now understand why so many acknowledgements are to an author's spouse and children as this one is to mine. Another of these people is Eric Kreuter, for whose friendship, support, and invitation to work with him on this book I am truly grateful. An acknowledgment also to the people in this book, who by selflessly sharing their inner challenges and selves will, I hope, contribute to a greater good.

Contents

About the Authors

Eric A. Kreuter is a partner with Marks Paneth LLP, a NYC-based regional accounting and business consulting firm. He specializes in litigation support and forensic investigations. Dr. Kreuter testifies as an expert witness in court. He has an undergraduate degree in Business Administration from Manhattan College, a Master of Arts degree in Industrial Psychology from Long Island University and a Doctorate in Clinical Psychology from Saybrook University, where he also serves as a Trustee of the Board. Dr. Kreuter served as a Research Fellow with the Cambridge Institute for Psychology and Religion and is Editor of the International Journal for Psychology Research, published by Nova Science Publishers. He is a Certified Public Accountant and also holds certifications in the fields of management accounting, forensic investigations and human resource management. Dr. Kreuter has numerous publications in the fields of psychology, business, poetry, and human resource management. He is a former Associate Professor of human resource management at Mercy College in Dobbs Ferry, New York. Dr. Kreuter is Treasurer of The National Association for Poetry, Inc and Board member of Hermandad, Inc.

Kenneth M. Moltner is counsel to a New York City law firm, practicing commercial litigation and matrimonial law. He has presented Continuing Legal Education lectures to attorneys at the New York City Bar Association and the New York County Lawyer's Association including on New York State litigation practice. He is an adjunct professor who teaches a continuing education course in Litigation at Hunter College and has taught at New York University's SCPS. Mr. Moltner is a graduate of New York University, Phi Beta Kappa with Honors in Politics, and obtained his J.D. from New York University School of

Law. His community experience includes service as a former Chair of a Manhattan Community Board, member of the board of a not-for-profit organization, and a Special Master for a New York State Supreme Court Justice, among other positions. He is also a recipient of a New York City Council Proclamation for Community Service.

Additional Contributors

Cathleen M. Kreuter MSMFT is a graduate from Mercy College in Dobbs Ferry, NY. She has a Master of Science degree in Marriage and Family Therapy and graduated with distinction. As a volunteer with Cross-Cultural Solutions, she helps educate potential volunteers about volunteering internationally. She is currently interested in pursuing a Doctorate in the field of psychology, and is currently working towards licensure while working at Suncoast Mental Health Center, Inc. Cathleen incorporates creative expression and emotional insight into psychotherapeutic services through art, poetry, movement, and play, specific to the given population. She currently treats children and adults with mental incapacities, including anxiety and depression, bipolar disorder and schizophrenia.

Laurence Allen Steckman Esq is a partner at the law firm of Eaton & Van Winkle LLP in New York City. He has been litigating securities and business disputes for 25 years. Mr. Steckman started his career at the law firm of Shea & Gould, handling rule 10b-5 securities fraud, civil RICO and complex commercial litigation cases. In July, 2006, Super Lawyers Magazine, in its premiere New York edition, identified Mr. Steckman as one of New York's "Super Lawyers" in the areas of securities and business litigation. He again received that honor in securities litigation in 2013. Mr. Steckman has handled billions of dollars in client matters and has been counsel in leading securities, derivatives and RICO litigations and commercial and securities arbitration disputes for domestic and foreign litigants. Mr. Steckman holds *summa cum laude* undergraduate degrees in classical music performance and philosophy and pursued doctoral studies at Columbia University where he received his Masters degree in philosophy before deciding to pursue a career in law. He graduated law school with honors, publishing scholarly articles authored during law school in all three of his law school law review journals. Mr. Steckman is the author or lead co-author of more than 40 published works on the law and has been repeatedly cited as an authority by courts and commentators in his practice areas. He has published and been cited as authority, as well, on public policy matters ranging from international terrorism to application of the Sixth Amendment right to counsel. Mr. Steckman is currently involved in several entrepreneurial projects in several countries focused primarily in the energy and infrastructure sectors. He has published, as well, on the psychology of resilience and the philosophy of Friedrich Nietzsche, Soren Kierkegaard, John Dewey and William James. Mr. Steckman has recorded several CDs of classic and original works for guitar and written several movie scripts.

Lodze Steckman MD, FACS has practiced medicine for more than twenty-five years. She is a Board Certified general surgeon, with a specialization in cardiothoracic surgery, and is an internationally recognized expert on disaster management. Born in Haiti, Dr. Steckman started medical school at age 16. Before she was 30, she had become Chief of Surgery at two hospitals. She served as the Chair for the Health Care Reform Committee for the University Hospital of Haiti from 1990 to 1991 and, in 1995, was appointed an Executive Committee Member of the National Commission for Disasters in Haiti. From 1995 to 1997, she served as Disaster Coordinator for the Haitian Red Cross and was in charge of disaster prevention, preparedness, response and mitigation, which included a water and sanitation program for the entire country. Dr. Steckman served as a consultant to the United Nations, focusing on international disaster-relief and, in Haiti, simultaneously, as Coordinator for Disaster Management for Haiti's Ministry of the Interior. Dr. Steckman came to the United States in 2000, completed a general surgery residency at Harlem Hospital where she twice received the woman of the year award. After becoming Board Certified in general surgery, she completed a fellowship in cardiothoracic surgery and then another fellowship, in Paris, on minimally invasive valve replacement. Dr. Steckman subsequently became a Research Fellow at Columbia University, where she focused on injury prevention for the elderly. In 2010, she returned to Haiti with a team of American doctors and surgeons to provide emergency care and medical treatment to people injured during the 2010 earthquake. Dr. Steckman is a Fellow of the American College of Surgeons, a Member of the American Society of Thoracic Surgery and sits on the Committee on Media Relations of the American Society of Thoracic Surgery. She is a Member of the Association of Haitian Physicians Abroad, a member of the American Academy of Aesthetic Medicine and has published on health-related subjects ranging from injury-related fracture hospitalizations and injury reduction in children and the elderly, to studies and reports on topics as diverse as breast cancer and typhoid perforation. Dr. Steckman has published health care assessments on Haiti's medical system and "*A Guide for Community Education on*

Water and Sanitation Management in Haiti." Fluent in French, Creole, English and Spanish, Dr. Steckman has trained in medicine, surgery and disaster management in Haiti, France, the United States and Israel. She is currently practicing surgery and emergency medicine full time in New York and simultaneously pursuing a double Masters Degrees in Business Administration and Public Health. At the same time, she is coordinating research and the collection of statistical data for a new injury-prevention program she designed for the elderly. Dr. Steckman is particularly interested in the interrelationship between medicine and psychology.

Mark Schulman PhD currently serves as president of Saybrook University, a premier graduate institution for humanistic studies in psychology, mind–body medicine, organizational systems, leadership, and human science. Throughout his career as an educator, consultant, writer, and administrator, Dr. Schulman has been dedicated to innovative and academically rigorous education. An academic leader with over three decades of experience in education consulting, higher education administration and in communications, Dr. Schulman previously served as president of Goddard College (Vermont), president and professor of humanities at Antioch University Southern California, Los Angeles and Santa Barbara. Dr. Schulman has published, consulted, and presented extensively on progressive and emancipatory education, distance learning, technology, communications, media, and culture. Dr. Schulman received his PhD in Communications from the Union Institute (Cincinnati), his MS in Education, Instructional Systems Technology at Indiana University, and his BA in Literature at Antioch College (Yellow Springs, Ohio).

A. James Forbes Jr. (Jim) is a financial and operations professional who has served both the for-profit and not-for-profit sectors. Jim is actively engaged in public policy discussions; providing leadership on global healthcare and aging issues through his professional experience which has included not-for-profits such as AARP where he is Secretary/Treasurer of the national Board of Directors and his working with organizations which have included *The National Institutes of Health, The United Nations, and the US Agency for International Development.* Prior to engaging in the not-for-profit sector, Jim successfully completed a career which included well known names such as *Price Waterhouse, Dun&Bradstreet, Mercedes-Benz* and others where he led significant financial and operational change through his senior executive roles. Subsequent to his for-profit roles, he entered the not-for-profit arena and was promoted to Executive Vice Chairman of *AmeriCares*, which provides international emergency relief and sustainable programs on a global basis. Since *AmeriCares*, Jim has been serving not-for-profit organizations through his own company, *Forbes Consulting*, as an Interim Executive Services professional. He has served prominent organizations in health care, research, associations, human rights, resource planning, biomedical science and others. In addition to his present AARP board role, he was formerly Founding Chairman of the *Board of the Biomedical Engineering Alliance and Consortium Foundation* in Hartford CT. He has spoken in the media (*CNN, NPR, NBC, and ABC*) and addressed the *National Institutes of Health* in Washington, DC on issues related to the international delivery of medical services and products. At the United Nations he addressed a plenary session on *Global Issues Facing the Aging Population.* Additionally, he contributed to a series of books on *Critical Issues in Global Health* (Editor: Clarence Pearson, global healthcare leader) and has also authored papers and spoken on contemporary topics in the not-for-profit sector. Jim is a *National Association of Corporate Directors* (*NACD*) Board Fellow in both Board Governance and Board Leadership. He was recently invited to join *Covington's Who's Who* of business leaders.

Dr. Charles King received his Masters degrees in psychology and social work from Montclair State College and Rutgers University. He completed his Ph.D. in School Community Psychology at Hofstra University and post-doctoral studies in Clinical Psychology at Hofstra and the Institute for Rational Living. Dr. King is a Diplomate in School Psychology of the American Board of Professional Psychology (ABPP) and a recipient of the Distinguished Service Award from the Council of Presidents of Psychology Specialty Academies of ABPP. Dr. King's hospital experience includes working with inpatients and outpatients for several years with Long Island Jewish/Hillside Medical Center, Essex County Hospital, Glen Cove Hospital, and Brunswick Hospital and has acted as a medical expert. Dr. King has been a member of the adjunct faculty of Hofstra University, St. John's University, and Queens College and his field supervision includes Adelphi University (School of Social Work), Iona College, and Touro College. He is President-Elect of the Nassau County Psychological Association and on its Executive Board. He has, in addition, served as the President of the School Division of the New York State Psychological Association, Chairman and Secretary of the Council of Presidents of the Psychology Specialty Academies of the American Board of Professional Psychology, President of the American Academy of School Psychology, and is a member of the Executive Committee of the Clinical Division of the New York State Psychological Association. Dr. King is a member of the American Psychological Association, American Association of Sex Educators, Counselors and Therapists, National Association of Social Workers and the Academy of Certified Social Workers. Since 1980, Dr. King has maintained a private psychology practice in New York.

John Enger PhD is a former 22-year law enforcement veteran holding the rank of Lieutenant Commander with the University of Minnesota Police Department. He held the following positions at the U of M: *Patrol Officer; Tactical Unit Supervisor; Criminal Investigator; Training Unit Commander; 911 Communications Commander; Executive Assistant to the Chief of Police; and Patrol Commander*. He was a regular guest lecturer for the U of M General College—School of Human Services, lecturing in the areas of police intervention into domestic violence and hostage negotiations. He is credited with starting the first successful Police Chaplains program in a "Big 10" University. Under his leadership he recruited and trained ten Chaplains, all of which took on a very active role within the police department and university community. While a police officer, John received numerous departmental commendations, including four Citations for Bravery in the line of duty, receiving the department's "Medal of Merit" for his involvement in each cited incident. He left his former agency being one of the highest decorated officers on record during his 22-year career. John is an ordained minister and is a Certified Master Chaplain with the International Conference of Police Chaplains and several other organizations. John has worked extensively with children and youth as a Youth Pastor and was Founder and Director of a successful Christian counseling ministry by the name of the "Rose of Sharon Christian Counseling Center" while living in the Minneapolis, MN area, where he did youth, family and marital counseling. He is certified in the following areas with the Faith Based Counselor Training Institute: Restorative Therapist; Crisis Chaplain; Anger Management Specialist and Youth Violence Intervention Specialist. In 1997 John retired from his career in law enforcement and moved to Sarasota, Florida to head the National Christian Counselors Association and the Sarasota Academy of Christian Counseling as its Executive Director. He was later recruited by the Sarasota Police Department as their Judicial Liaison Program Manager and Chief Police Chaplain and was nominated "Civilian Employee of the Year." He is an author and had his first book published in 1998 titled *The Prevailing Prayer of a Peace Officer*. The publication of his second book *Fingerprints* in 2013 was completed and is a moving book honoring not only his granddaughter's short life, but gives hope to those searching for answers to the meaning of life. John holds undergraduate degrees in Paralegal Studies and Business (Specialized Associates and B.S.) a graduate degree in Law Enforcement and Management (M.A.) as well as advanced seminary degrees in Ministry (D. Min), Clinical Pastoral Counseling (Ph.D.) and Theology (Th.D.). He has written numerous courses and worked as adjunct professor for several Bible Schools and Theological Seminaries. John is currently a Licensed Private Investigator in the state of Florida. He is still very active in counseling, ministry and running an international martial arts organization where he also teaches martial arts to a select group of private students.

The authors wish to thank Dr. Arthur Lothstein, who is the Director of the Institute for Peace and Social Justice at Long Island University, C.W. Post College, for reading and commenting on the Foreword to this work. Dr. Lothstein has taught philosophy for more than 40 years and lectures on the interface between philosophy and psychology. Thank you to Dr. Mark Schulman, President of Saybrook University, for your commentary on the work of Dr. Eugene I. Taylor and to Brendan D. Leonard, M.B.A. for agreeing to write a review of the book. Following Mr. Leonard's review of the manuscript he asked if he could forward Appendix F: Jewish Oncology, to a person he knows suffering with cancer. This is the exact purpose of the book—to help people who have troubles to reach a deeper level of self-understanding and to help them shift into a happier, more productive mindset. Even if only one person can be helped by having this material the process will have been worthwhile.

Chapter 1
Introduction

If you have inner peace, nobody can force you to be a slave to the outer reality.

—Sri Chinmoy

Overview

Throughout human history, people have searched for the greater meaning of life's many constructs, wondered about their origin and hungered for a greater understanding of their place in the cosmos. Today, there is an active search for life on other planets because earthlings have an earnest desire to explore and to know if we are the only populated planet (now or ever).[1] As civilizations began to flourish and revolutions of technology and philosophy became constant, the deep internal quest of man turned from finding new ways to make fire and hide from warring neighboring villagers to the contemplation of life, its purpose, and why people behave the way that they do. "…social attitudes and perceptions shape mental processes and behaviour. How people think about things plays a critical role in their approach to problems and their overall well-being" (Bishop 2013, p. 1). In essence, curiosity led us to seek out new lands to conquer, brought us to the depths of the ocean and to the moon and destinations beyond the immediate solar system. Knowing more about our history helps us to navigate into the future. So, too, increasing our understanding of our own thoughts, fears, dreams, and desires can lead to self-improvement whether catalyzed internally or with the help of another person.

Finding peace within oneself has also been a quest of the restless heart of man. Reaching outward for many encompasses a need to crash through boundaries to redefine limitations and then invent new ways to break through those. Just as United States Air Force Brigadier General (Ret.) Chuck Yeager became the first pilot to travel faster than sound in 1947, many have followed him and succeeded in exceeding his feats. "The very fact that man strives in his life for the realization of some

[1] Exploration of earth's deep oceans is for the same quest for knowledge and discovery.

E. A. Kreuter, K. M. Moltner, *Treatment and Management of Maladaptive Schemas*,
DOI 10.1007/978-3-319-06817-6_1, © Springer International Publishing Switzerland 2014

aspirations is a manifest criteria for unity. Man centers his effort on becoming what he wants to become" (Ghougassian 1972, p. 59). Consider the following "why" and "what" questions:

- Why do we not succeed at everything we try to do and in the time frame allotted?
- What causes us to stumble along the way or results in a derailing of our progress when things were proceeding so well?
- Why does our initial momentum slow down or stop at the slightest test of our fortitude or resilience?
- Why do other people around us seem to be thriving and we seem to be moving backwards?
- Why do we feel an ever-deepening sense of blah?
- What is this feeling of dread we have when faced with another day?
- Why do we not feel good just being alive?
- What is this feeling of depression even when good things happen in our lives?

If you or your clients have asked these burning existential "why" questions, please read the rest of this book. In Kreuter's previous book (*Fostering resilience for loss and irrelevance,* Springer-Verlag, New York, 2013a), he outlined a connection between two constructs: resilience and irrelevance. The important connection between them was explained as a way of helping the therapist (or a person attempting self-help) to open up new pathways of challenge into the thinking and attitudes of suffering individuals. This book takes that topic further by exploring head-on the problem of the fixed or static paradigm. But first, what is a fixed paradigm or, more precisely, paradigmatic thinking?

We are not suggesting that people should be, let alone are, "happy" or can always find the way to be within their comfort zone all of the time. Although that would be nice, the journey through life necessarily involves a mixture or a tidal wave of emotions, including sadness and unfortunately despairs. In one respect, that is the beauty of life. This book, however, is not an overview. Rather, the focus of this book is how people have, or in certain cases have not, overcome maladaptive thinking in varying but concerning particularized challenges, all of which had import to them. The authors do so by applying the concept of a paradigm shift to help them overcome negative schema in the context of guiding therapeutic principles, but that should not be confused with a conclusion that people are, or necessarily should be, satisfied with their lives all of the time.

Paradigmatic thinking is when a thought, idea, model, belief, or notion presents to a person as a rigid unrelentingly accurate perspective of truth applied to a problem in the world. Applying this to the study of archaeology, Hershel Shanks (2014), who has spent over 30 years asking questions about the location of biblical Mount Sinai, quoting, in part, the poet George Eliot writes, "It may well be that I have done more than weave an ingenious web of probabilities—the surest screen a wise man can place between himself and the truth" (1878–1885, p. 436). Parr (1996) added: "Perhaps final truth in archaeology is unattainable, but it is certain that progress towards it can come only through asking questions, for without questions there can be no answers" (p. 217).

An example will help to explain the phenomenon. Fred (a fictitious person) is a 50-year-old unemployed construction worker. He has had trouble regaining employment since his marriage failed and he was forced to declare bankruptcy under the mounting pressure of both secured and unsecured debt. Fred never thought he could actually fail or that he would ever face his present dilemma. His habits of reckless spending and weekend binge drinking led to the complete annihilation of much of the support structures within his existence. Fred's overriding attitude was that the world was at fault for "putting" him where he now found himself. Fred never took any personal responsibility for making bad choices and for doing little or nothing to climb out of the deep morass he was presently in and might always face. Essentially, Fred was stuck in neutral and his steadfastly anchored notion of responsibility was central to his innate ability to extract himself from his plight, except that he was incapable of seeing it, let alone dealing with it. Therapy was not in the cards for Fred because he always saw such engagement as either a waste of time and money or something only weak people did.

Fred continued to work out in his tiny one-room bunker inside an overcrowded state-subsidized apartment located in a tough part of town. And Fred was indeed tough. His attitude was tough. He did manage to see his daughter, Amy, now age 10, but visits were short and he just did not know what to do with her. His ex-wife yelled at Fred repeatedly for his failure to provide whatever level of meager support she was able to convince the court to mandate. Fred did not really care all that much since it was not his fault he was in such a predicament. "Screw them," he would say to himself between dead lifts.

Fred's hold on his paradigm blocks him from enlightenment, keeping him from any forward momentum in his narrow existence. He had few friends and came from a small family. His two brothers made regular attempts to help Fred, but he would not budge. People like Fred can be helped to face their inner obstacles and to choose new pathways in their lives. But they cannot usually transform on their own. Something or someone is needed to catalyze them from inaction to action. Success is not something we stumble on like a loose piece of slate on the sidewalk. It is something we must work at, develop, nurture, and then go willingly through the process of impasse, struggle, and self-doubt. We are fortunate to find success at all and even more fortunate to hold on to it once identified. Action takes work. Success is not something for the lazy person or the person who is overconfident and stubborn. Relative level of intellect is not the deciding factor on whether a person can be helped, but the relative nature of the person's integrity is the predominant factor. What is meant by this?

Personal integrity, for this purpose, is the ingrained sense of honesty with the self. All future transformation begins with this type of integrity. Does the person care about his or her life in a way that makes them open to discussion about how they add to their problems or is this just not possible? "Whether pushed by pain or pulled by possibilities, we are entering a new era in which our own choices create a new reality. We know that it is never too late or too soon to discover new paths for our lives" (Leider and Webber 2013, p. 146).

The Pattern of Negativity

Humans are creatures of habit. As such, we forge ahead in life as best we can by considering the state of our circumstances, making subtle and not so subtle changes to daily behavior dependent on mundane aspects such as weather or we may react to sudden events such as a car accident, sudden death of a loved one, or winning the lottery.

However, we each possess an unalienable right to select an attitude for each moment of conscious existence. Oftentimes, though, we do not actively consider attitude selection in our lives. Instead, we commonly just react. Some of our reactions form into notorious patterns. Some of these patterns can be viewed as negative when we consider the consequences or impact of such reactions, herein called "behaviors." Thus, our schema can become maladaptive without us even noticing such a phenomenon since it is often quite difficult to really see yourself as you operate in the world. Further, absent an intermediary, it is highly possible that any negativity is not viewed in that manner by the person since others might be the better jury.

We have all felt "in a rut" or heard someone else speak of their life in such a way. But what does that actually translate into? Perhaps being in a rut means not making any discernible progress in life as measured by our relative success in career, relationships, or other aspects. It could mean a person who is just "spinning his or her wheels" to use a modern cliché.

It is the negative energy associated with the negative patterns that beg for therapeutic intervention. Such help, while available, cannot begin without the person first admitting she/he has a problem and the desire to invest time and effort, and perhaps financial resources, to explore the problem and decide on new action steps.

Breaking a pattern of negativity cannot be done with a sledgehammer. A person who consistently abuses alcohol when problems become overwhelming cannot be helped by mere overt criticism of the behavior. It is necessary to get at the underlying problems and help the person develop new and improved coping mechanisms, which will have potential for making a positive impact on the person's thinking, behaviors, and, most importantly, their attitudes. Otherwise, there is a void left behind with the perpetual risk of relapse at the slightest provocation.

The force of habit can interfere with a person's ability to forge revised patterns of responding to internal and external stimuli. Whereas one person who faces unforeseen problems may turn to a friend or begin therapeutic treatment to help them cope more effectively, another may succumb to negative behavior, which may, in turn, result in significant consequences. A person's resilience plays a role in the person's ability to withstand pressures and resolve conflict without suffering or causing damage to self or others. Such resilience can be fostered through therapy (Kreuter 2013a).

The therapist who encounters a client with maladaptive schema should first understand the various complexities of the person's life as well as the triggers of such negative behaviors or debilitating thoughts. In addition, assessment of the person's past experiences encountering difficulty and how they handled each will provide excellent and valuable clues as to the person's patterns. From such in-depth understanding, the therapist can provide coaching points and ask targeted questions of the person designed to elicit thought-provoking responses, which can lead to greater internal awareness of their past maladaptive schema. From such new awareness, the process of change can occur. This is the "hard work" therapists speak of with their clients and where the power of talking therapy comes in. Through the trusted therapist–client relationship and some trial and error, newfound strength and resolve becomes possible. The power of change is always in the hands of the client. Helping the client to first realize this power, then to harness it, increases the potential for improvement. Puff (2012) wrote:

> As humans, we are very good at grasping at objects and feelings that make us feel good and resisting that which causes pain. Unfortunately, in the process of holding on to things and thoughts, we create attachments, which cause us to miss out on what is happening right now. (p. 1)

Adapting to Generational Change

As the generations change, new ideas and new idealisms shift towards what is viewed as furtherance of modernism. Applied to the workplace, this change may take the form of the way a worker responds to the job and also how a person allocates his time and effort towards his chosen career. An older person may struggle with what appears on the surface to be a lack of dedication or motivation on the part of a subordinate. However, a deeper perspective of this issue may reveal that what is different is the dynamic of how a career issue impacts on the thoughts, actions, behaviors, attitudes, and conduct of the younger person as compared to the older person. In light of this potential schism, judgment should be deferred until all the data are gathered and not until direct dialogue has taken place between the two individuals.

A younger manager, for example, may have carved out a work–life–family balance schema that fits his life quite well. Moving up in the company, while very much a goal, does not consume the manager. Instead, the manager views that the time devoted to work should be judged by only the quality and not also the quantity of effort. This view can certainly clash in the mind of the principal when there is more work needed to be done and not enough willing workers to take on the additional tasks. However, today many people have addictions such as "…immersions in exercise, religion, eating, work, and sex…" (Gergen 2000, p. 15). Any form of extreme behavior can lead to serious consequences and also symptoms such as fatigue, stress, or burnout.

The Challenge of Dealing with Endings and Trauma

Whether it is a meal or life, we as human beings must face the ultimate reality, which is often a challenge dealing with endings. Especially when we are depressed or emotionally upset, the temporary reprieve that we achieve appears in hindsight to be unfulfilling. It must be examined and weighed for what it truly is. Does it address the problem or is it a fleeting salve? Societal approbation is associated with such escapism, particularly substance abuse. Thus, a meal, or a sexual encounter, provides a respite, a way to forget, but it ends as does everything else. Death and taxes are truly inevitable and, so too, are a person's problems. But what if the problem does not have a solution, or at least a solution that is, at best, uncertain and not immediate? There are those who cannot accept, or refuse to accept, endings of "happiness" that return to the seemingly everyday problems of life (the "ordinaries"). When those endings predominate or when they weigh like a cloud and intrude into a person's day, they almost become a person's very being and her self-fulfilling prophecy. Sad or happy, seeing the glass as half empty or half full does, in fact, have meaning. It equates to whether we are generally a positive or negative thinker. Perceived attempts to escape the seemingly pervasive problems of life are, in fact, paradigms themselves. Such is a way of coping, which is not dissimilar to superstitions or magical thinking because they cannot affect real change. It is not having the problem that is the problem, but it is the way we deal with our problems that make all the difference in the quality of our lives.

There comes a point where, in order to shake off the doldrums, despair must yield to decision, decision must yield to action, and action leads to lasting results in order for there to be effect. There is no guarantee. "…for modernists of the twentieth century, it is through powers of reason that one establishes knowledge. As individuals sift the evidence, propose hypotheses and antitheses, and evaluate the outcomes of their deductions, they build repositories of knowledge within" (Gergen 2000, p. 99). There is hope and perhaps expectation. And that is the true meaning of paradigmatic thinking, a person who has been able to take action and break through the mental and emotional ties that bind.

Trauma, as an experience, can alter a person's perception of their world, impacting their behavior as they try to move forward with living. Therapists who treat clients with trauma often have a challenge in helping the client regain stability and positive momentum. "Therapist's today have a language for trauma's impact on the mind. They recognize that the mind's primary defense against agony is dissociation and that the primary motivation for dissociation is stability" (Epstein 2013, pp. 72–73). Dissociation is a type of defense mechanism. According to Brown (2012), dissociation is described as:

1. The splitting off of a group of mental processes from the main body of consciousness, as in amnesia
2. The act of separating or state of being separated
3. The separation into two or more fragments (p. 1)

The brain does not archive different memories of experiences in the same way. "One of the distinguishing qualities of trauma is that it cannot be held in normal memory. Because the feelings associated with it are by definition unendurable, they never make it into the part of the brain that makes sense of emotional experience" (p. 148). It is for this reason that bad memories can haunt a person, impacting his or her life.[2]

Cognitive Flexibility

"Our mind is flexible and can accommodate in different situations. Our mind has the ability to adapt to fit in new knowledge." (University of South Alabama 2014, p. 1) The ability to switch between thinking about two different concepts and to consider such concepts simultaneously is considered cognitive flexibility. This flexibility is a component of executive functioning. It involves the ability to restructure knowledge in multiple ways that depend on the changing situational demands, defined as the level of difficulty or complexity (Spiro et al. 1995). Cognitive flexibility can be seen from a variety of viewpoints, one of which is a switch in thinking, whether that is specifically based on a switch in rules or broadly based on a need to switch one's previous beliefs or thoughts to new situations. Some people can multitask; others can adapt very quickly their mental considerations of a situation. In reality, these people can consider various viewpoints and move from one to another for purposes of conforming to keep equilibrium with the views of others or to define their position, stand their ground, and fight if necessary.

Constructivism involves the "…authentic, realistic experiences for each individual. It encourages the use of multiple pathways and multiple purposes when approaching problems" (University of South Alabama 2014, p. 1). "The theory of cognitive flexibility leads to case-based learning" (Graddy 2001, p. 2). In this type of learning, the person is exposed to different cases to review for the purpose of obtaining a broad understanding of a particular topic. Kreuter often provides career coaching to management-level professionals to initiate research into deeper nuances of their work so as to benefit from a wider span of knowledge and to explore extant research prior to reaching conclusions based on a more narrow study or investigation. Also, the process of immersing oneself into the variety of available perspectives informs a person's thinking, which serves to influence the person's ultimate conclusions. Investigation and exploration should normally precede action. Retrospective consideration could be given to actions that have been taken. Planning on predicting outcomes may be useful as precursors to contemplated action.

[2] Post-traumatic stress disorder is one example.

Negative Schemas

Negative schemas are exacerbated by a reluctant psyche unwilling to work through adversity, to do the things that are necessary for change and improvement to take place. In a way, the person digs the proverbial hole deeper and deeper since it is the misery of being a malcontent that becomes the familiar bedfellow. This continuation of nonpurposeful energy becomes self-feeding, resulting in absolute morass. The unsolvable dilemma, then, is the challenge to tilt the person into an alternative way of thinking. This, of course, is made much more possible through willing engagement of the therapist, coach, mentor, and friend, but is also possible through intervention. Where the person is not fully engaged in the arduous steps towards transformation into an improved, functional schema, any attempt to instill change will most likely fall on deaf ears.

There is no better accountability than to oneself. Integrity can be considered when measuring a person's awareness of their negativity and their desire for change. For example, a person who feels deeply inside that she/he is in the wrong career, or a toxic relationship, or living where they know she/he is not happy, etc. can become quite lethargic in terms of working on their internal negative bias towards their own life. Negative thoughts only breed more negative thoughts, resulting in a pattern of downward spiraling of emotional energy. This syndrome can envelope most aspects of a person's life, sending him or her into a state of emotional chaos or a state of emotional dormancy where the will to achieve is self-quarantined.

Even attempts to change result in false starts. The weak will is unable to overcome the internal desire for complacency. In the process of working towards change, a person can run into considerable roadblocks, which suppresses momentum, making progress unlikely. What is lacking is courage. Such courage allows the will to benefit from a new sense of internal energy, enough to push through previously established limitations. Once a person gets the taste of new success, further progress can be sought.

Life is a building process, which incorporates striving towards accomplishments. Self-improvement is compounded by little steps towards greater accomplishments. This taste of change can breed a new hunger for seeking even loftier goals. To sustain this momentum, a trusted champion may well be needed to encourage the person to stay the course.

The role of the champion (therapist, coach, mentor, or friend) is to hold the person accountable for their actions and choices. Through open and honest discussions and listening, the champion can instill new concepts, fostering greater likelihood of actual positive change. The impact of new approaches, an experimental process, allows for dynamic dialogue and the necessary fine-tuning. It is very important that the person being helped feels the ownership of the problem and the progress, even though instigated by the champion. This avoids unnecessary dependency. Success, regardless of how small, should be positively regarded. Failure, a necessary step along the continuum of change, is part of the process and can be dissected to provide for even more powerful guidance for the future. By omitting negativity attached to failure, but, instead, asking the person to take ownership of the problem thereby creates an environment where she/he can freely address what happened, why it happened, and how to prevent recurrence. It is the lesson in the failure that can further be analyzed, providing even more value. It is important for the client to realize that it is okay to have a problem, but not okay to do nothing about it. Action is the key to success. Calm nonfeasance does not get the job done in most cases. Problems can dissipate over time and many have a half-life aspect to them, but the impact of problems may be a continuous problem. At times, clients feel that the problem is gone, but the problem may not be resolved deep within them. In order to truly resolve the problem, the issue must be looked at a deeper level.

Lazarus (1999) maintains that without the prospect of hope, the individual is left to the uncomfortable arousal state of despair and hopelessness, whereby a person does not possess the capacity to foresee any desirable outcome. Goals, pathways, and agency in Snyder's (2002) view of hope are referred to as the "trilogy" for understanding the concept:

> Goals are viewed as mental representations directed toward "positive goal outcome" or the avoidance or delay of "negative goal outcome." Pathways are described as an individual's ability to link one's present reality with an "imagined" future. High-hope individuals have a "highly articulated" or clearly defined pathway to achieve their goals. They also possess an ability to adapt in the event that a singular pathway fails to lead to a desired outcome. Finally, agency is described as "the perceived capacity to use one's pathways to reach desired goals." (pp. 250–251)

Hope: A Theory, a Process

Hope can be defined as "a positive motivational state that is based on an interactively derived sense of successful (a) agency (goal-directed energy) and (b) pathways (planning to meet goals)" (Snyder et al. 1991, as cited in Snyder 2000, p. 8). Hope theory can be subdivided into four categories according to Hanson (2014): "goals, pathway thoughts, agency thoughts and barriers" (p. 1).

Goals provide direction. Pathway thoughts refer to routes we take to achieve our desired goals and the individual's perceptions on how to create these routes (Snyder 2000). Hanson (2014) described agency thoughts and barriers as:

> Agency thoughts refer to the motivation we have to undertake the routes towards our goals. Barriers block the attainment of our goals and in the event of a barrier we can either give up or we can use our pathway thoughts to create new routes. (p. 1)

In essence, we have the innate ability to modify our thoughts to open up to avenues of thought, which can either bring about new barriers or help us find ways to break through them. A shift in paradigmatic thinking brought about because the person (coached or not) desires to try a new approach, which leads to a discernible break though will be motivated to adopt the new paradigm and absorb this new approach forming a new pattern.

Hope attained can lead to the sense of achievement of a goal. Goal attainment has been found to be associated with positive emotions (Snyder et al. 1996). When we meet an objective, we can and should feel positive about ourselves. One attainment can lead to further achievement through a willingness to think positively about one's own efforts with realistic notions of what changes are possible given the particular barriers in the person's life. Coaching or therapeutic intervention play a role in encouraging the person to fortify their self-esteem, which keeps hope alive and the person dynamic.

The Societal Paradigm of Rejection

Overcoming rejection and the persona that leads to acceptance of the societal-created imperatives creates the necessity to overcome it. Overcoming the reliance for one's self or self-worth, in whatever part, is based on the acknowledgment of others.

Society creates structures of authority and power. It can be said that society could not exist without it; otherwise, anarchy would reign. But with that structure necessarily follows control bestowed by society mores, for example, the appointment of judges in New York and the election of our governmental officials. Or, on a micro sense: a boss and her employee; a parent and child; or a teacher and her pupil. And with authority comes power and the power to choose or decide. There is nothing wrong with that.

Relationships, by their very definition, can lead to rejection and have the inherent risk of rejection, which can happen with or without forewarning. Was there a person who you admired from afar, who you got up the courage to talk to or ask out, but who "rejected you?"

However, a maladaptive offshoot of power and authority is the individual's reaction to it. Whether by upbringing or perceived necessity, people are overly dependent on what can amount to no more than the subjective whim of those with authority to determine their self-esteem or sense of worth. Even as a child, not being chosen for the baseball team can be especially hurtful. Being passed over for a promotion can seem humiliating.

Some people respond to stimuli in an antisocial manner. According to Agnew's (1992) *general strain theory,* the manner in which a person responds, including responding antisocially, "…is determined by conventional social supports, intelligence, self-esteem, and temperament" (Ruback and Thompson 2001, p. 52.). "General strain theory has defined measurements of strain, the major types of strain, the links between strain and crime, coping strategies to strain, the determinants of delinquent or nondelinquent behavior, and policy recommendations that are based on this theory" (Florida State University 2013, p. 1). "While control theory rests on the premise that the breakdown of society frees the individual to commit crime, strain theory is focused on the pressure that is placed on the individual to commit crime" (Agnew 1992, p. 49).

People cower before those invested by other men with authority, whether they believe it is deserved or not. People most often act in their self-interest, to protect their own turf. And why should they not? If a mistake is made and it is between you and your boss as to who will take the blame, assuming equal responsibility, would you expect your boss to step up and accept responsibility? Or would you be expected to be thrown under the proverbial bus? And why should you not be? Because it is not "fair" or not "right." What does that even mean? That is a conclusion based on perhaps your mores, but that is not necessarily societal or more importantly the practicality that will govern the situation (our governing mores). It is a dog-eat-dog world. What is "fair" and what is "right" is relative, often quite relative. There are also multiple definitions of truth.

"If there were any doubt that self-esteem is the dominant motive of man, there would be one sure way to dispel it; and that would be by showing that when people do not have self-esteem they cannot act, they break down" (Becker 1971, p. 75). "We come into contact with people only with our exteriors—physically and externally; yet each of us walks about with a great wealth of interior life, a private and secret self" (p. 28). We often put on a game face or appear brave when, in fact, we might be very frightened. Much is built upon the notion that we are on this earth to achieve as much as possible. Some who have no trust or belief in the afterlife are susceptible to going to extremes to achieve wealth and/or fame during their lifetime. There is no thought of leaving behind a better world because of the proverbial rat race. "…the great increase in bitterness and frustration in the modern world is largely due to the eclipse of the sacred dimension, to the expectation that all satisfaction has to happen here and now" (p. 192).

> And to draw one's power from the source or creation itself can't fail to give one more self-reliance in the world of men: one no longer needs to live in the power of others, of mere mortals, of acquaintances, friends, even parents, and heads of state. By leaning on this power, the person can get his own footing; he can get begin to search his own mind and soul for decisions, choices, judgments; he no longer has to lean reflexively on the directives of the world of men (p. 193).

Becker (1971) continued: "From a behavioral point of view, what we call 'mind' is merely the style of reaction of an organism to its environment" (p. 5). "The development of mind, then, is a progressive freedom of reactivity" (p. 7). Living is all about moving from one reaction to stimuli to another. Learning is what we gain in the form of insight based on the outcome or consequences of our behavior (the way we have reacted in the past). Adaptation is the process of altering such learned behaviors due to awareness of the negativity of the outcomes. Therefore, improvement in life is the positive change applied to a given type of stimuli, easily remembered and applied to the next similar exposure.

Being able to apply one form of learning to different stimuli is to gain capability beyond the past level. When that happens, the person becomes better able to cope and deal with difficulty. Recently, Rex (see the case study of Rex in Kreuter 2013a) lost his cell phone and had an immediate reaction of stress and panic. But when he reasoned that there was a good chance he would recover his phone the next day, he relaxed and went on with the day. While he initially labeled the occurrence a "crisis," he soon realized that it was just a phone and that there was nothing to gain by panicking. This type of learning to strategize using the best available thinking and acting can alleviate some or all of the negativity associated with a challenging event in life. Expecting to face such challenges becomes part of the fabric of living a full and authentic life.

Expressive writing is one way to embark on a therapeutic opportunity. Reaching deep inward to pull out hidden concerns, thoughts, fears, etc. can lead to self-discovery. "The labor of writing poems, of working with thought and emotion in the encasement (or is it the wings?) of language, is strange to nature, for we are first of all creatures of motion. Only secondly—only oddly, and not naturally, at moments of contemplation, joy, grief, prayer, or terror—are we found, while awake, in the posture of deliberate or hapless inaction" (Oliver 1999, p. 5).

So let us approach from a different perspective. We too often rely on others for what we think about ourselves. In his book, Kreuter (2013a) noted that we in a sense set ourselves up to fail sometimes. By over-relying on the opinion of others, we exacerbate that and denigrate our self-worth. And therein lays a problem. What are the causes? What are the solutions?

Perception

Perception is the organization, identification, and interpretation of sensory information necessary for humans to comprehend their environment. We all perceive the world (in its entirety and our much smaller circle) in a unique way. "As human beings, we attempt to make sense of all our experiences" (Spinelli 1989, p. 1). Spinelli viewed reality as "…inextricably linked to our mental processes in general, and, in particular, to our in-built, innate capacity to construct meaning. That view is the starting point to phenomenological enquiry" (p. 2). Perception, then, becomes the key to our ability to understand the universe and what is happening to us. Thus, the way an individual perceives the world will be different from the way others perceive it. It is for this reason that a 100 people witnessing a crime will report somewhat differing facts. Further if you poll people after a film if they enjoyed the experience, some will say yes while others will say no. But ask about the reasons and it will seem almost as if some people saw an entirely different film. What causes such differences?

We experience phenomena or phenomenal reality through interpretations, which are themselves subject to modifications over time. With new life experiences, further education, and trial and error learning, our abilities to perceive will adapt. When a person's perception is in the clear minority, it may be unfair to label him or her as simply incorrect since, for him or her, the perception is based on his unique viewpoint. This is not to suggest that holding the minority viewpoint equates to being wrong when the opposite might prove to be true. There is ample room for diverse opinions on countless subjects. Variety, it has been said, is the spice of life. Understanding the varied ways people interpret experiential phenomena will help practitioners in helping professionals understand their clients better and help them to overcome difficulties with respect to the complex challenges of everyday life. "Today common sense tells us that people differ in their reasoning abilities, that emotions are powerful forces in people's lives, and that it is important to be aware of a person's true intentions" (Gergen 2000, p. 13).

"Each of us, as a representative of our species, develops, both through maturational processes and through social experience, increasingly complex mental frameworks (or 'schemata', as some developmental and cognitive psychologists might label them) through which we interpret the raw stimuli which bombard our senses" (p. 9). Spinelli further suggested that if we return to an object (a painting) previously experienced, we would possibly interpret it differently since "…your experience of the painting would not (could not) be the same as it was in the first instance, since in returning to it you would now be adding to your previous 'schema' for that painting and, through this fresh experience, you'd be altering its previous context and relations" (p. 9). The same holds true of a perceived issue someone may have about another person, which, after the passage of time, may dissipate. Of course, the matter of a grudge needs to be understood as having the potential for having a very long-term shelf life. The story of the Hatfield's and the McCoy's is a notable historic example of the phenomenon of a lasting feud over an allegedly stolen hog. But, as a key towards unlocking the mystery as to why a person may be stuck in neutral, over a particular issue, we can consider the function of habit coupled with an unyielding sense of righteousness towards a rigid, perhaps long-standing perspective. In general, people can be very stubborn, holding on to what they believe as if it were part of their DNA to have such beliefs. There is, though, so much to gain by being willing and open to considering new paradigms as worthy of voluntary replacement of old ones. If something new works so much better, why would we not adopt it? Such a habit drives the way a person views a thing. Such a view is not likely to change absent sufficient counterbalancing stimuli. When the view long held becomes toxic, it is said to be negative, even hurtful to the person and to those nearby or affected.

The phenomena of the ways in which a person responds to stimuli can be studied from numerous perspectives. The psychoanalyst would consider the person's background (upbringing, medical history, mental and physical limitations, prior experiences, past trauma, etc.) in order to blend this intake data with the psychiatric interview and one or more sessions of treatment. "The introspectionist, for example, examines the responses of the subject to external stimuli, reduced down to sensations, feelings and images" (Spinelli 1989, p. 185). Therefore, there is a certain reality to a situation or circumstance that cannot be doubted in terms of actual existence, but the reactions to the situation or circumstance can be measured and evaluated in terms of appropriateness and effectiveness. For example, feeling fear in the case of being confronted by a charging bear in the woods would seem quite normal and predictable followed by some measure of considered response (i.e., running away, dropping a backpack, picking up a gun, screaming, etc.), whereas pretending the bear is not there (ignoring its reality or the presence of a threat) would seem foolish and inappropriate, leading to probable injury or death. The bear, on the other hand, processes nothing like the human does. The bear is either:

- Curious, but not particularly hungry;
- Hungry and desiring of a readily available meal; or
- Angry and wanting to protect its territory or it is young.

In writing about psychological fears, Tolle (2004) said, "This kind of psychological fear is always of something that might happen, not of something that is happening now. You are in the here and now, while your mind is in the future. This creates an anxiety gap. And if you are identified with your mind and have lost touch with the power and simplicity of the Now, that anxiety gap will be your constant companion" (p. 43). We worry about things that have not happened, may not ever happen, or may happen in a long time from now. "Usually, the future is a replica of the past. Superficial changes are possible, but real transformation is rare and depends upon whether you can become present enough to dissolve the past by accessing the power of the Now" (p. 60).

The memories of the past can become ingrained in our minds, chiseled into the active mind, and ready to influence future behavior. "All negativity is caused by an accumulation of psychological time and denial of the present" (p. 61). Tolle (2004) suggested that "people should live in the present moment instead of dwelling in the buildup of what he terms 'psychological time' which is identification with the past and continuous compulsive projection into the future" (p. 56).

In the case of Greg, he dwells largely in the past, recalling mostly negative life events, feelings, etc. When challenged to consider adoption of new attitudes and outlook, he frequently rejects the new idea of transforming to any new paradigms because of the ingrained maladaptive schema that infiltrates his conscious mind. In doing so, he negates any possibility of developing new positive energy in his life. This, then, becomes a syndrome where his psychological time becomes the equivalent of his living not in the moment, but in the past. As such, he easily and most unfortunately replicates the ineffectual mindset that disables him from making any discernible progress in his life. As a highly educated person, he is able to grasp the new concepts on an intellectual level, but is entirely unable to apply the concepts to his life. He is aware that he is doing this, but is not able to alter his negative pattern.

The Power of Will

The importance of existential analysis, according to May (1983), is in its capacity to have man understood as a being (p. 91). "The distinctive character of existential analysis is, thus, that it is concerned with *ontology,* the science of being, and with *Dasien,* the existence of this particular being sitting opposite the psychotherapist" (p. 91). Individuals are responsible for their own existence. "Man is the being who can be conscious of, and therefore responsible for, his existence" (p. 96).

A characteristic of man's existence (*Dasein*) is the capacity to transcend the immediate situation (p. 143). Progressive beings are always in a state of growth, a dynamic element of sorts. Problems for some are roadblocks to success, but to others are opportunities to invent grand solutions, opening up new pathways of how we see the universe, one problem solved at a time. Allport (1955) referred to this process as "becoming." May viewed this process as "emerging" or "transcending." To be better able to emerge from one state to a theoretically improved one, a person must be aware of himself as well as how and where he fits in with society. Having a feeling of disconnection will destroy a person's mood and mute their determination to carry on with the business of living a dynamic life. With self-awareness, higher consciousness can be tapped. Freedom is implied in the process of human transcendence. Through freedom, a competent and clever person can work on potential solutions to problems and draw upon their own background, run ideas by peers, and also glean helpful information from the Internet through what is today known as the "Infosphere." With new information, new choices emerge. Courage is that which is needed to embark on a new path. Using the power of intellect and the vitality of a renewed spirit, one can strike out and break through his or her own envelope, leaving the confinement of the status quo in the dust.

According to May (1983), "the 'will to power' is built into every individual because it is inseparable from life itself" (p. 70). This implies that individuals attempt to work through their potential throughout their life's endeavors, which, in a very real sense, forms a basic unalienable right. This power can mean the difference between a person giving up amidst the pressure of adversity or rallying and trying new concepts and approaches until some improvement is achieved. Mankind would not have been able to transcend the perceived limits of space flight or reach the depths of the oceans if the initial setbacks were allowed to curtail the zeal of achieving what had never before been accomplished. Pioneers of all types, throughout history, have brought us new discoveries and opened up new pathways for others to travel behind them. Internally, each of us can become our own pioneer, pack up the wagon with our thoughts, beliefs, dreams, and fears and move past the stuck place where we were towards the freedom of a new experience.

Therefore, it is not being in psychological rut that is the problem, but remaining voluntarily in that rut that can consume one's vitality and shut off the inner strength to even try to surmount the perceived problems. The person who pulls the covers over his head in the morning instead of rising cheerfully to take on the new day loses some velocity in his life. Repeating this behavior can lead to laziness and lower the active potential of the person. In a less requiring life such a person can afford to be lazy, but does this then create a syndrome of reaching down to a low point where the world passes quickly above? Bitterness and apathy become the bedfellows of laziness and lethargy, propelling the person into the abyss of despair and lonely struggle merely to survive. Death may even appear to be a better option. But can this be altered through therapy? Perhaps it can, but first we must understand the problem.

Where Tillich suggested the need for courage as a way of opening up the way to simply being, Nietzsche determined that the process of being injured leads to strengthening. A defeated person will not see a setback as a form of strengthening, but as a force where they become weaker. A thriving person will take on the challenge of a setback and continue moving forward regardless of the pressure against them. May wrote about creativity and Sartre added that individuals are subject to the results of the choices that they make in life. Through the additional element of our becoming as postulated by Allport, perhaps the summarization of prior intellectual thought is that the individual may do better by first sensing their past as representative of who they were and then reaching a complete resolution of where they are at the particular moment (the present) and reconciling that position as just what it is and without lamentation of what is not. Then, adding in creative thought with the notion that we must assume responsibility for our actions, the person can consider the future and the person they wish to become when they reach that point, whether in the form of the proverbial 5-year plan or expressed in their own unique way.

"Creative people also have an ability to persist in spite of repeated rebuffs." "Creative people must retain the capacity to keep going, even in the face of very little external validation of their worth" (Andreason 2005, p. 32). Using Kreuter's analogy of the three-points-in-time technique used effectively with incarcerated females, any rational person should be able to improve their sense of grounding and use their ability to plan for the future to make better choices today in order to ensure a superior outcome in the future. This analogy led the women in a discussion from their points of view as to where they were in their lives in the past, where they are in their lives at the present moment, and where they plan to be in the future. For example, making a decision to begin a fitness regimen along with healthy dietary changes, the person will doubtlessly be in a much better position in a year to achieve better health. This result may then extend to other areas of the person's life (career, relationships, etc.). By making an effort every day towards one's goals, achievement is more possible than remaining frozen and complacent.

By setting goals, a person can feel more in sync with the world. In May (1983), we read:

> Kierkegaard, Nietzsche, and the existentialists who followed them perdurably pointed out that the two chief sources of modern Western man's anxiety and despair were first, his loss of sense of being and, second, his loss of his world. The existential analysts believe there is much evidence that these prophets were correct and that twentieth-century Western man not only experiences an alienation from the human world about him but also suffers an inner, harrowing conviction of being estranged (like, say, a paroled convict) in the natural world as well. (p. 118)

Goals and the process of goal-setting can be a daunting task. With the aid of a therapist or coach, a person may be better able to break through resistance in the form of lack of confidence, while building a renewed sense of courage to forge ahead and break through their negative schema or ineffective paradigms. Shifting into "high gear" would be a less eloquent manner of referring to this process, but the idea comes across that with increased effort greater results naturally follow or can be predicted. We must also be ever mindful that even with superior and sustainable effort, good results are never guaranteed. This is because life is not so structured that one person's efforts can impact others in any meaningful way unless the world is either prepared to act in concert or motivated to act. Thus, a person can do all they can and still fail miserably, but the therapeutic alliance should be to coach the person that they are, at the very least, improving their potential and that results will speak for themselves. Otherwise, clients will perceive being lifted up only to experience let down. It is precisely the inherent risk that can be used as motivation to help the person try so hard that they accept the challenge of failure and make failure less of an option through their mindedness, determination, and behavior. It boils down to pure attitude, which if shifted more positively, will guide the person to truly transform into a person of possibilities rather than a nonpurposeful being. Thus, there are two forms of being: just being and being determined.

The determined person then has choices: to be consistent, to give up, and to redouble effort when effort fails. The person who finds a path to success should remember that path, follow its code, and pass the keys to others. Perhaps if we establish an altruistic goal of leaving behind wisdom, we will seek to achieve more. The mistake is to focus merely on wealth building at the expense of self-development. Two famous quotes of Henri-Frederic Amiel (1821–1881):

- "To know how to grow old is the master work of wisdom, and one of the most difficult chapters in the great art of living."
- "I'm okay today. I'll be okay tomorrow. And the next day after that I'll still be okay. But in a year you will see me, I'll be amazing."

The will to succeed does need fuel. This fuel can come from encouragement or from inner will. One way to understand this is to establish a very small goal, prepare oneself to take the few necessary steps in order to achieve the goal, reach the goal, and then set a loftier one. This has been referred to as taking "baby steps." For an adult who has had years of apathy, the technique can be made more adult by suggesting that the easily achieved small goal sets the stage for the higher goals, thus, creating a roadmap for success. Winning over the confidence of the client is a prerequisite to the person becoming sufficiently engaged in the process of seeking improvement.

In Hamlet, Polonius said, "To thine own self be true…" In the movie "A Few Good Men" (Reiner, Brown, and Scheinman, Castle Rock Entertainment 1992), Jack Nicholson famously challenged Tom Cruise: "You can't handle the truth." We first have to find our truth before we can determine whether we can handle it, let alone change it. Even hurtful truth is better known than kept from us. All information is potentially useful. It is for this reason that only a friend would tell another friend something personal about them that, while maybe difficult to be said, would be very instructive for the person to be aware of. Once aware, the issue can be considered and, possibly, dealt with. That is the critical beginning of the journey to a paradigm shift from maladaptive behavior. What is the "truth"? How often do you feel you can truly be yourself?

We are each born into a certain identity with a DNA and experience-based mix of influences on our emerging personality. As a cliché, we are who we are. This does not mean we cannot change our attitudes, behavior, and how we respond to stimuli. We always have the capacity to change, perhaps not the willingness or drive. Montgomery (2013) wrote about compass therapy as a way of interpreting personality rigidity. "Compass Therapy interprets personality rigidity as the way in which people unconsciously try to minimize anxiety by becoming inflexible, opting for stereotypic mind-sets that offer false security and impair actualizing development" (p. 1). People are oblivious to their own way of being because they do not view themselves the same way others view them. "Nevertheless, these trends and patterns are formidable barriers that arrest growth toward loving self, others, and God, constituting a hidden dimension of sin within the human condition" (p. 1).

"A rigid personality trend strands individuals in a lifestyle characterized by too much dependency, too much aggression, too much withdrawal, too much control, or a combination of these trends" (p. 2). Refusal to address one's own shortcomings only relegates the person to repetition of actions that simply do not work as well as they should. Montgomery (2013, p. 3) provides a good overview of how psychologists have viewed manipulative trends (defense mechanisms):

- William Reich—observed that manipulation tenses body musculature, terming it character armor
- Karen Horney—described manipulation as a tragic waste of human potential
- Carl Rogers—viewed manipulation as a struggle for authenticity between an idealized self and a real self
- Joseph Wolpe—described rigid trends as maladaptive behavior that can be unlearned
- Eric Berne—construed the self-fulfilling nature of manipulative trends as negative life scripts
- Albert Ellis—noted that a maladaptive mindset is held in place by a set of irrational assumptions
- Aaron Beck—referred to manipulations as exaggerated cognitive processes

The Value of Authenticity

There is an inner authenticity and an outer authenticity. How positive is the correlation between what we say and do as compared to what is occurring inside us? This is referred to as our outer authenticity. But do we even know ourselves? Are we fully or even partially aware of our inner selves? "Philosophers throughout history have held the idea of authenticity in high esteem, but few psychologists have taken it seriously until recently when positive psychologists turned to understanding human flourishing" (Joseph 2013, p. 1).

As Joseph (2013) said, "No one is fully authentic all of the time in their outer presentation" (p. 1). Shakespeare referred to people as being actors: "All the world's a stage" (*As You Like It,* Act II Scene VII). The need for someone to act instead of just being themselves is influenced by circumstance. Even lying can often be rationalized in cases where it is done as a human kindness.[3] We may feel compelled to

[3] An example is not telling a woman with dementia over and over again that her husband of over 50 years had died, which would only re-traumatize her.

smile on the outside even though we are not happy internally. We hide, in essence, our true feelings in order to protect them from being exposed. The frequency of such "acting" can begin to form a pattern in how we respond to stimuli. By putting on an inauthentic persona often and achieving better results from this way of being may lead to greater willingness to pretend even at the expense of our relationships. Joseph (2013) wrote:

> It is unpleasant and damaging to us if we are trapped in jobs or relationships where we rarely get the chance to be ourselves. If we are trapped, we need to change the situation when we can so that we can be free to express ourselves authentically. (p. 1)

A person who is very aware of themselves, but who chooses to act in an inauthentic manner is making a conscious choice or has developed a phobia of self-disclosure. While not quite the same as lying to fool people for improper financial gain, the ramifications of repeatedly acting inauthentic can mount. The problem becomes larger when we no longer are in touch with our own inner self or when we become inauthentic within. We see this in a confused person who responds to stimuli in diverse and unpredictable manners, even to the point that they surprise themselves. In this situation, a person may start to feel as if they no longer know themselves. Siamese twins born with two heads will have separate and distinct personality structures. Thus, a person who has two or more mechanisms of responding where there is a lack of awareness of both or all will exhibit odd behavior and have trouble forming lasting relationships with others.

Therapeutically, it is important that a confused or troubled person be evaluated medically as there are a myriad of conditions that can lead to confusion. For example, decisions made at a time following severe sleep deprivation or done during a low-blood-sugar event may not be the same decisions that would have been made absent such factors.

Being in harmony with others leads to greater happiness. This would have to apply at least with respect to the harmony within a single person. "Happiness is when what you think, what you say, and what you do are in harmony" (Mahatma Gandhi, 1869–1948). Helping a person come to terms with the pressures of the outside world requires first guiding them to seeing what is really going on in the inside world. When a group of runners, for example, start out in a race, they appear to be running in harmony even though each is a separate person and feeling the impact of the challenge uniquely. Yet, each has the opportunity to feel as if they are part of a collective, a form of harmony with the present community, sharing a common goal. But, inside, the person is alone in their thoughts and in control of how they respond to the outside. If the person feels as if she/he has his or her "act together," there is greater harmony within leading to greater potential to be authentic when presenting to others. Where there is internal schism, the person may act incongruently with how the inner feelings and thoughts are occurring. There is a likely connection between how authentic a person feels and his sense of self-esteem. By maintaining a solid sense of self, a person is better equipped to respond appropriately to stimuli, using proper filters and with a balanced level of disclosure and sharing of opinions.

It also seems that in many situations, it is easier said than done, but the case examples in this book illustrate how people who have shifted their paradigms for what they believed to be a happier existence have either resulted in difficulties or improvements in their lives. Rollo May (1975) proposed a theory that "creativity occurs in an act of encounter and it is to be understood with this encounter as its center" (p. 77).

Shifting Paradigms: Questions and Responses

The following questions were asked of people regarding the process of paradigm shifts and what blocks career growth:

1. What are the top three behavioral aspects of people, in general, that holds them back from becoming more successful?
2. What is the most difficult habit you have encouraged someone else to break?
3. How did you help the person break that habit?

Responses

Akram Soloman (Personal communication, February 12, 2014):

Question 1:

a. Fear of leading
b. Lack of confidence
c. Insecurity

Question 2:

Feeling as if she was unqualified and could never become a leader

Question 3:

Coached the person that "everything can be broken down to component parts so that she could gain confidence to become a future leader." He added: "Nothing in life is hard once you break it down into small pieces"

Jeff Jacobs (Personal communication, July 11, 2013):

Question 1:

a. A sense of self-worth or self-esteem
b. Competence greater then confidence
c. Fear and anxiety of failure

Question 2:

"Betraying a confidence"

Question 3:
"I helped the person to see how destructive it was to the other people"
Anonymous (Personal communication, September 15, 2013):
Question 1:

a. An inability to learn from failure
b. Not being honest with oneself when it comes to one's shortcomings and consequently not working to improve them
c. Fear of success and not being able to handle it

Question 2:
"My wife was pessimistic about certain aspects of life"
Question 3:
"I helped my wife to see the glass as half full and not as half empty, helping her to greatly reduce her negative thinking. I did it by gently, consistently pointing out the many positives in her life both professionally and personally—she is much improved. With that said, she has helped me an enormous amount to overcome my issues and problems. Lastly, I would be honored to be quoted as a reviewer of your book. I greatly look forward to it"
Arlene Kaminker (Personal communication, September 7, 2013):
Question 1:

a. Being a negative person (half-empty glass)
b. If you cannot accept blame for something done wrong
c. Not having the ability to adapt to new environments with regard to interactions with people

Question 2:
"Obsessive non-productive thinking and talking repetitiously about an issue"
Question 3:
"I was able to help them to stop obsessing about the same issue"
John Enger (Personal communication, October 25, 2013):
Question 1:

a. Ego
b. Pride
c. Fear

Question 2:
"To get out of their own way; the self must be set aside"
Question 3:
"By helping seek more than just the physical world. Helping them see and embrace the spiritual. We are as much spiritual as we are physical. Releasing anger and hatred—of self and others!"

Habitual Behavior

The occurrence of human behavior can be described in the following terms:

- Purposeful actions, including those forced through coercion and threat
- Subconscious motivation and instinct
- Raw, habitually driven conduct

As a person emotes and responds to the world, what is behind the response may not even be discernible to the person. "It can be difficult to distinguish willed, conscious behavior from that which is habitual or automatic" (Mlodinow 2012, p. 12). Urges certainly play a role as in risky behavior, which, when done in a patterned manner, may lead to a certain degree of self-destruction, such as imprisonment or disease. Urges are formed from early development of values. White (1966) wrote:

> Piaget traced the evolution of the child's moral judgment between the seventh and fifteenth years. He demonstrated a trend from a literal belief in rules, almost as if they had an independent physical existence, to an attitude of relativity, in which precepts were perceived in relation to the social purposes they were designed to serve. (p. 397)

We can look at smoking as a bad habit, but behind the basic instinct of pulling a cigarette out of the pack and lighting it, what else is the person doing at that time? Could it be that it is the programmed connection between doing some activity in particular and also smoking? The cigarette may be nothing more than a prop used to stay busy while staying busy doing something else. Some people fidget. Kreuter works with a young man who constantly clicks his pen during meetings to the point of being distracting. He has done this in meetings with clients, which may leave a negative impression of the man's professionalism. When confronted, the man admits to not even being aware of the pen-clicking, but the behavior is very noticeable to others and quite distracting. When Kreuter has confiscated the pen, the man seemed edgy as if to convey that there is something missing now in the equation, rendering thought more difficult. He said: "I need to have something to hold onto." This is the type of maladaptive behavior that forms the thesis of this book. How can this man's "habit" be moderated? Before even trying to delve into curative possibilities, it is first necessary to consider whether it is more of a problem for the pen-clicking man or for everyone else in the room.

Habitual behavior can become more serious than simple idiosyncratic behavioral patterns (annoyances) such as the way a person gets ready in the morning or long rituals prior to swinging a golf club. Phobias plague certain people who may avoid elevators, flying, walking under ladders, living through Friday the 13th, and numerous other concerns. Maladaptive patterns, when engrained, may become potentially debilitating, as seen in disorders such as obsessive–compulsive disorder (OCD). OCD is an anxiety disorder in which people have unwanted and repeated thoughts, feelings, ideas, sensations (obsessions), or behaviors that make them feel driven to do something (compulsions). According to the National Institute of Mental Health (2013):

> Everyone double checks things sometimes. For example, you might double check to make sure the stove or iron is turned off before leaving the house. But people with obsessive–compulsive disorder (OCD) feel the need to check things repeatedly, or have certain thoughts or perform routines and rituals over and over. The thoughts and rituals associated with OCD cause distress and get in the way of daily life.

As another example, a person who worked in Kreuter's company spent inordinate amounts of time parking his car, which, when finally parked, had to be equidistant to both the white lines painted on the parking lot. He would get out of his car and closely examine the relative distance between the right and left sides of his car and would painstakingly move his car back and forth until it was parked, in his mind, just right. While this person was able to perform in his job function adequately, his behavior led to his being ostracized by coworkers who thought he was simply "weird." Likely, there were other aspects of his behavioral patterns that would easily match the manner in which he parked his car.

As a collective, when inner compelling behavior takes over an excessive portion of a person's life, problems in life may emerge. These problems, unaddressed, may become larger and more pervasive, leading to erosion of self-confidence, limiting career growth, negative consequences, and difficulties in social situations and relationships. Whereas the outward signs are very obvious to others, they may be less evident to the persons themselves.

Does any part of our behavior result from automatic thoughts, ones that cannot be filtered or controlled? We can observe a child eating an ice cream cone, but that does not mean we have to also have one. But what about the person who sees a woman's purse on the store counter and during a moment when the purse in unattended, it is swiped away by the onlooker who waits patiently for an opportune moment to make a score? Such a person can be correctly labeled a thief and may also have a sociopathic personality unable to distinguish right from wrong. "The second primary symptom of psychopathy is the missing or deficient sense of morality" (Guggenbuhl-Craig 1980, p. 95). In a prison program run by Kreuter, he listened to the story told by a female inmate that if she saw an item of valuable property lying around that she "had" to steal it. The woman explained that the theft was not in any way optional. She felt compelled to do it as if an inner voice and force had overpowered her, leading her into action. Compulsion leads to compulsive behavior, a psychological condition in which a person does a behavior instinctively or habitually and, often, repeatedly, having an overwhelming feeling that they must do so. When questioned about whether she first considered the possible consequences of stealing, she indicated that such rational thoughts did not enter her mind in the slightest. Thus, the evidence presents that a developed pattern of negative behavior may be rooted in personality. This phenomenon may be serious enough to make it virtually impossible to attenuate even following arrest and incarceration for crimes. It is as if the consequence and the compulsion are decoupled instead of entirely related. Even reaching the person's cognitive capacity to understand the connection with the grip of the power of compulsion remains strong, keeping the person from being able to break free of such power.

In another perspective, that of sensation seeking, how is behavior impacted by mood? Findings from a study of college student drinking conducted by Cyders et al. (2009) suggest that: "Whereas sensation seeking related to increases in the frequency with which college students drank alcohol, positive urgency predicted increases in (a) the quantity of alcohol students consumed at any given drinking episode and (b) negative outcomes experienced from drinking" (p. 1).

Urgency in the above-referenced study is the negative or positive mood the person was in, leading up to the sensation-seeking behavior. The study concluded that:

> It appears that although sensation seeking is a risk factor for participation in drinking behaviors, risk for increased quantity of consumption and its negative outcomes may be more a function of dyscontrol stemming from high positive mood for college students. (p. 2)

Episodic dyscontrol syndrome (EDS) is a pattern of abnormal, episodic, and frequently violent and uncontrollable social behavior (Elliott 1984). There is an absence of significant provocation; it can result from diseases and disorders of the brain or from abuse of alcohol or other psychoactive substances. The growing problem of underage drinking suggests that maladaptive behavioral patterns in young adults may increase and result in greater impact on society to the extent that individuals become a drain on resources or resort to criminal behavior, including driving while intoxicated.

The person seeking help who admits to habitual behavior has reached the starting point wherein change is possible. In Kreuter's prison example, where he ran a program for female inmates with a history of money addiction, he created an exercise to help them include a preventive image prior to committing crime. The exercise involved asking each woman to imagine a stop sign with the picture of either a person they loved or some other manifestation of choice, such as their very freedom. Then the inmates were instructed to imagine being in a place where there was an opportunity to steal an item with everything being as it might have been in prior experiences except for the stop-sign metaphor. Through the use of the device, they were each asked to picture the stop sign with the image of what they would risk losing in between themselves and the item that might have been able to have been stolen. Therefore, they were asked to consider whether they wanted the item that badly that they were willing to "go through the stop sign" in order to reach the item. This exercise provides a momentary delay in the behavior, which provides for a conscious consideration of risk brought to a real and practical level.

The above therapeutic tool was developed by Kreuter following an inmate describing in detail how, if she saw a woman's purse sitting on a store counter unattended, she "had to try to steal it." The demeanor of the woman suggested that this projected behavior was ingrained in her and not something born of conscious thought. Such ingrained images can derive from childhood experiences, trauma, or how someone was taught, which would impact his ability to eliminate the negative behavior. The dilemma was how to replace this ingrained notion with something better or to eliminate the urge entirely. The metaphor offered was designed to make the inmate think twice not only about the impending behavior, in this case criminal but also to add a thought about consequences in a unique and personal way.

Transitions can lead to changes in behavior. But how does a person know what to do or how to act when faced with a new situation? Personality appears to influence behavior in situations where individuals make a transition from one context to another, especially where the new context provides a higher degree of behavioral freedom (see, for example, Caspi and Moffitt 1993). Instinctual behavior based on the person's temperament guides the individual to behave in new situations where there is less information on proper ways of behaving. Additionally, some individuals are less confident in social situations; therefore, to the extent possible, they may try to avoid such encounters. In doing so, they are less exposed to what could be growth opportunities for them.

Living in the Moment

One paradigm shift that should not be given short shrift is living in the moment. It is very easy to be drawn into the pull of the past or worry about the future. But why and to what end? Anxiety can lead to negative impacts on health and well-being. Oliver (1999) wrote about anxiety:

> I am burdened with anxiety, anxiety for the lamb with its bitter future, anxiety for my own body, and, not least, anxiety for my own soul. You can fool a lot yourself but you can't fool the soul; that worrier. (p. 14)

Being drawn into the past is adversely comforting. It is one thing to "learn from the past" constructively, but another to wallow in it. "New" takes getting used to. One may not succeed with the new, but already knows what happened with the old. It is one thing to plan for the future, it is another to fritter away the present. But many people do both to the detriment of the present.

We often either live in the past either through actual or recreated memories or try to live in the future to the extent of longings, even dreams. While it is not possible to literally live in the future, there is a definitive attempt to consider what the future has in store at the expense of actively living out the actual day at hand. Mondays of the new work week are a good example where the person may feel sluggish and lament over the long week ahead, looking forward more to the next weekend than to what life experiences may present during the current week.

People suffering from anxiety because of the hectic pace of their lives may be able to calm their concerns by changing their focus from the pressure of the future towards activities they can handle on the present day. "Anxiety strives to become fear, because fear can be met by courage" (Tillich 2000, p. 39). By changing focus to the currency of a situation, the person's energy is more concentrated on what is currently going on as opposed to spreading his energy among multiple concerns, some of which cannot reasonably be addressed at the moment. The common fallacy is that by worrying about something, we are, effectively, handling it. However, in reality, there is no impact on these concerns whatsoever, but there is a casualty suffered by the person, which is an increased level of stress. In the long run, such behavior can lead to depression, physical problems, and emotional pressure. Today's modern technology also has become the vehicle for a fuller emersion into our world. "New technologies make it possible to sustain relationships—either directly or indirectly—with an ever-expanding range of other persons. In many respects we are reaching what may be viewed as a state of social saturation" (Gergen 2000, p. 3).

The feeling and/or the expression of the feeling of dread or worry can consume a person so much so that their daily living becomes ineffectual. A person looking for a job or a better job can become so overwhelmed with self-inflicted pressure that he begins to fail doing things in his present existence because his focus and concentration is on the future. But can these people be helped? Is there anything truly wrong with thinking about the future?

One technique that might help a person "lost" in the abyss of the future is to develop a strategy or plan to consider what he needs to do or even what he can do now, which will likely help him to achieve a future objective. In doing so, the focus turns more towards proactive management of life as compared to an endless cycle of worry and stress without any discernible progress being made in his lives. Maturana and Varela (1987) wrote:

> We tend to live in a world of certainty, of undoubted, rock-ribbed perceptions: our convictions prove that things are the way we see them and there is no alternative to what we hold as true. This is our daily situation, our cultural condition, our common way of being human (p. 18).

The planning phase may actually require looking ahead, for example, at a type of job or position desired. But, the technique to bring the active mind back to the present is to consider what needs to be accomplished in order for the person to qualify for the position desired. It may be the need to complete a matriculated course of study or it could be obtaining a new or updated certification. More basic, there may be a need for the person to learn how to use a computer or brush up on math or other skills. Even more simply, the person may need to "look the part" required of the future position and go out and refurbish his wardrobe.

Of equal importance is the benefit of a person seeking ongoing coaching or mentoring. By maintaining a dialogue with a trusted person, the issues become more centered in the present moment assuming the guide or mentor or coach helps the person center his or her thoughts of what is at hand that needs to be done rather than just chat about some possible future event.

An added dilemma is a person who is locked up in a lack of self-confidence who worries incessantly about likely failure should something happen, such as being hired for a job. This type of feeling can paralyze the person, rendering him lacking the ability to transform. Instead of being excited about the new possibilities, the person dreads what may happen, which can then debilitate the person and weaken his resolve to do all they can to earn the position. Such negative thinking about the future takes on a certain self-fulfilling prophetic quality to it, rendering the person lost in their own life.

Changing the paradigmatic thinking of a person consumed by notions of failure in the projected aftermath of a future event can help the person to become more effective in the management of his life. Once a person becomes fully grounded, she/he can then embark on proper planning for the future, defined as activities in the present or near present. The rest is helping fortify a person's sense of inner will to succeed or to be more determined in his or her quest for success however she/he may define it.

One challenge is the formidable hurdle of the relative obstinacies of the individual who is so rigid in his or her views such that any recommended change becomes a struggle within the therapeutic relationship. Defensive postures include stating reasons why new approaches will fail and sighting past failed attempts as the primary excuse. False starts also become problematic as the person may not have adequate determination to withstand the pressures associated with the struggle, which can involve setbacks. Like peeling an onion, there are many layers to a person and many levels of maladaptive thought behind any negative pattern. Unlocking repressed strengths will help a person develop resilience against giving up.

Technique for Moving Past Being Stuck in Neutral

Consider, for example, Scott, a middle-aged man who has become a veritable hermit in his own life. He does not have a steady job of any type, though he is highly educated and holds a professional license. Scott is under the care of a psychiatrist and takes several medications for anxiety. Scott admits to being "fearful" of taking steps to secure employment because he is extremely worried that he will fail on the job. This fear debilitates Scott, occasionally keeping him from following through with job applications. He is afraid to be hired because of his fear of being fired for incompetence. He has been receptive to coaching and will push himself towards help, but vocalizes an almost constant mindset of high anxiety. Scott's affect is certainly dour and he exudes low self-esteem. He speaks of his endless bouts of downward spiraling of his mood. It is possible that his internal worry actually instigates the occurrence of the reduced mood.

Kreuter, as Scott's coach, introduced Scott to the imagery of a crossroad between four choices where the middle point cannot lead to anything positive happening. That point, however, represents momentary safety, though it will be guaranteed to lead to a negative result if Scott remains stuck on it. In comparison, moving in one of the available directions yields only the potential for a positive result. "There is a point at which a life becomes unsatisfying. Regardless of the reasons, a person begins to place too much emphasis on: what already exists; and what he believes" (Rappoport 2013, p. 1). The choice of movement is doubtlessly superior than remaining static.

By requiring the person to remain static in one place until there is psychological movement can be useful to teach the person that he is able to construct a new direction in his life and that staying frozen (nonmovement) can be more damaging than taking the risk of positive movement. This is a way of increasing substance in a person's life. What was once held as a permanent belief can one day lose his or her muster. "The beliefs lose their dynamism. They turn into dead stars" (p. 2). Dynamic people need to be proactive and strive to continually renew their internal energy through adventurous creativity. Even seemingly boring projects can take on new meaning through a positive attitude.

In this exercise, Scott was asked to imagine himself in the middle of four possible directions. The middle represents neutrality, where there are no pressures and he feels safe. As a contrast, Scott was asked to compare how he felt about the safety of being in a neutral state and how he might feel should one of the other destinations prove to lead to improvement in his life. He is aware that three of the four choices of direction will not lead to a positive change in his life, but one of the choices will. This exercise demonstrates that life does not include guarantees, but only potentials. Rappoport (2013) recommends the use of imagination as a simple device to "wake up the psyche" (p. 3). "Imagination awakens abilities beyond the five senses and beyond structured consciousness" (p. 3).

The Self and Internal Will to Achieve Transcendence

Humans, like all animal species, possess an important will to survive. Our ability, however, to thrive is somewhat dependent on our self-image and the power of our will. "The self image has its point of reference in one body, one consciousness, one continuous series of personal memories; it cannot be separated from our enduring sense of personal identity" (White 1966, pp. 138–139). The dynamic will is always searching for what increases happiness and decreases unhappiness. We want things to be better. This despite the adage—the enemy of good is better. Perhaps we desire only those things that can actually be incorporated into our lives. "…the will does not strive for something it does not have, for some object outside itself, but wills itself in the double sense of preserving and transcending itself" (Tillich 2000, p. 27). Thus, the dynamic person looks for growth opportunities in life.

Sometimes, there are stumbling blocks in the process of striving for improvement. Persons who engage in therapy might be more capable of examining their inner world in ways that will help them cope better with the influence of their outer world. In client-centered therapy, "…the client can let himself examine various aspects of his experience as they actually feel to him, as they are apprehended through his sensory and visceral equipment, without distorting them to fit the existing concept of self" (Rogers 1995/1961, p. 76). This requires a trusting relationship with the therapist.

We all have a certain way of acting, called our propensity. It is a natural way of behaving in a certain situation, influenced by how we were born, how we are raised, and what our experiences are in life. As such, each time we face a challenge or crossroads in life, it is our natural propensity that largely determines how we act. With respect to phobias and superstitions, May (1977) found that "…it can be done constructively, as is shown in therapeutic sessions in which the individual learns to view his dangers realistically and at the same time develops confidence that he can meet them adequately" (p. 64). We can even experience anxiety when we are unable to act in a consistent manner. Anxiety can be rationalized in terms of fears. We can override our tendencies and ignore their strong impulses, but it would seem foolish to presume they are not there. Some natural tendencies, such as proneness towards anger, can lead to problems such as physical violence, relationship problems, or health issues. Curbing the tendency towards angry outbursts, for example, may require significant personal effort, counseling, and reshaping maladaptive behavior. May (1977) spoke of some of his patients: "I noticed that some patients did not repress their sexual, aggressive or 'antisocial' urges (in Freud's sense) in any discernible way" (p. 128). The start of the process of change begins with acceptance and willingness to find new ways of responding to stimuli. The following poem by Kreuter (2013b) depicts the concept of natural tendencies:

Propensity
Obstacles in my way
Illusions of my mind
The light ahead blinds like darkness
I see the road ahead but it curves in all directions
Crossroads confuse and repel my progress
Motivation ebbs like tide subdued
Failure becomes the option of choice
Determined spirit finds the way around despite the odds
The opening in the wall invites consideration
The renewal of purpose grips my life
I follow my intensity, which drowns calmness
The fallback is the propensity to settle for less

A Cognitive Therapy Perspective

Charles H. King, Ph.D., ABPP, psychologist and diplomate of the American Board of Professional Psychology in a personal communication with Laurence Steckman (2014), offered some insights on the subject of this book. The term "maladaptive schema" would be referred by cognitive behavioral therapists as "irrational belief systems." Schemas are cognitions with the pattern of thought described as the "cognitive life view." Paradigms are "entrenched belief systems or automatic thoughts."

The philosophical revolution stated by Kuhn's research on paradigm shifts involved setting aside Freudian concepts in favor of, first, Skinner's learning theory and later social learning theory, creating much in the way of a professional controversy. Various therapeutic tools employed to help people shift their thought process are designed to help people to "talk sense to themselves" in order to influence a change in behavior. When clients have difficulty articulating their beliefs and stay at the feeling level, the cognitive work of the psychotherapist is difficult. Schema-focused therapy is more eclectic, accepting a variety of techniques whereas many cognitive behavioral therapists feel limited to the social learning phenomenon and in general are not as open to the unconscious as a construct. The unconscious is difficult to measure empirically creating struggle for the therapist.

Schema-focused therapy "appears more empathic and less therapist-oriented than Cognitive Behavioral Therapy, which is often very directive and didactic with less emphasis on support and the therapeutic relationship." The cognitive behavioral therapy (CBT) therapist does not "re-parent" but can be a role model for rational thinking, self control, and modeling coping behaviors with less emphasis on transference. "The therapist attempts to identify maladaptive cognitions and works to alter these by disputing irrational beliefs." When "schema surrender" occurs, the client "gets stuck cognitively" and with "schema avoidance" the client tends to "stay stuck in their stuff." With schema overcompensation, the person's thinking makes it possible to externalize the schema by blaming others.

Through the process of challenging and disputing, "Old cognitive patterns are broken and old maladaptive 'tapes' are discarded." Dependency is discouraged with an emphasis on having the client do his own disputing and changing, thus being less reliant on the therapist to remain long term in this role. "Cognitive behavior therapists use imagery as in vivo work where the client ventures into the world and tries out new behaviors." The process however usually begins with imagining and visualizing coping behavior in the treatment session. Healthy coping strategies are "rewarded." Structured homework is given to encourage clients to reinforce improved thought patterns in their lives, "substituting rational beliefs for irrational ones."[4] "Different thinking and different behavior patterns result in feelings of peace and a sense of well being". Creative thinking results in the clients "thinking in ways they never dreamed of with the homework designed to generate achievement of cognitive and behavioral goals." The clients are encouraged throughout treatment to make a commitment and to try not to "bail out" when old dysfunctional patterns reemerge (personal communication, Charles H. King, January 24, 2014).

Synopsis of Chapter

- Man has always been in a search for peace within his world.
- Paradigmatic thinking is when a thought, idea, model, belief, or notion presents to a person as a rigid perspective of truth applied to a problem in the world.
- All transformation requires a sense of honesty with the self.
- Humans have a right to choose their attitudes.
- Breaking a pattern of negativity cannot be done easily due to the force of habit.
- The therapist must first understand the various complexes in a person's life prior to treatment for negative schemas.

[4] The cliché "no pain, no gain" applies well, helping the clients work against "low frustration tolerance and discomfort anxiety."

- Cognitive flexibility allows a person to switch one's beliefs or thoughts to new situations.
- Negative schemas are exacerbated by a reluctant psyche.
- The role of the therapist, coach, mentor, or friend is to hold the person accountable for his actions and choices.
- We experience phenomena or phenomenal reality through interpretations.
- Individuals are responsible for their own existence.
- The need for courage is connected with the process of being.
- Being in harmony with others leads to greater happiness.
- Transitions can lead to changes in behavior.

Chapter 2
Paradigms and Maladaptive Thinking

What seems to be is, to those to whom it seems to be.

—William Blake (1757–1827), poet

Introduction

What is a paradigm? How does a paradigm apply to a shift in paradigmatic thinking? Kuhn advanced the concept of the societal paradigm. While adopting the concept of a framework that is generally recognized as part of a paradigm, we, however, are analyzing the construct "paradigm" from a different perspective—from the individual's point of view. Rather than a "community" or "societal" paradigm, it is the individual's "pattern" or "archetype" that takes precedence; the individual's "philosophical or theoretical framework" that the individual applies to a given circumstance and particularly to a given challenge or stimuli.

We include the issues that affect the ability of an individual to develop the necessary knowledge, skills, and courage to make a shift from maladaptive thinking or at least manage it better. Given this context, we view a paradigm as the boundary or confine of action or reaction, particularly, but not exclusively repetitive, including thoughts or thought processes, to stimuli that is perceived by the actor (or reactor) to be similar or the same as previous stimuli. The most important aspect of the definition of paradigms is the "boundary" or "confine"—the limitation on our ability, or flexibility, of thought process *if it* results in maladaptive thinking and the inability to change it. This is based on schemas.

The concept of schemas was first introduced by Jean Piaget:

> Piaget called the schema the basic building block of intelligent behavior—a way of organizing knowledge. Indeed, it is useful to think of schemas as "units" of knowledge, each relating to one aspect of the world, including objects, actions, and abstract (i.e., theoretical) concepts. (McLeod 2012, p. 2)
> Piaget emphasized the importance of schemas in cognitive development, and described how they were developed or acquired.

E. A. Kreuter, K. M. Moltner, *Treatment and Management of Maladaptive Schemas*, DOI 10.1007/978-3-319-06817-6_2, ©Springer International Publishing Switzerland 2014

> A schema can be defined as a set of linked mental representations of the world, which we use both to understand and to respond to situations. The assumption is that we store these mental representations and apply them when needed. (p. 2)

The concept of maladaptive, as commonly understood, has negative connotations. "Maladaptive schemas" can, depending on the particular situation, be seen as a foundation or personality or as building blocks for maladaptive thinking. They can also equate to the maladaptive thinking itself. In the context of this book, maladaptive thinking are thought processes injurious to the person insofar as they intrude upon or inhibit the person from making a paradigmatic shift away from that thinking. Maladaptive thinking are thought processes that for the individual do not reflect his/her "true" inner self or results in a failure to succeed, which creates palpable frustration or anxiety, if not depression and thus, if responded to affirmatively, compels an impetus to change. At first blush, the thought of an affirmative response to a feeling as deep and abiding as depression may appear to be inconsistent with that attitude. But that is the point. It is the very issue that tugs at one's mind and heart that necessitates affirmative action and is the launch pad for change. After all, if the issue does not create anxiety, or worse, depression, and is not recognized by the person as creating that feeling, then there is no reason to change. That issue is often recognizing exactly what his/her truth is. His/her truth was, for example, homosexual, not heterosexual. His/her truth was not religious even though she/he was brought up religious. The way of thinking, especially, but not exclusively if it becomes a way of life, is maladaptive for the person until she/he overcomes or modifies it. As Mark Twain put it, "A man will do anything, no matter what it is, to serve his spiritual comfort … A man cannot be comfortable without his own approval" (Twain 1917, p. 17). As we discuss below, however, the concept of truth is not theoretically easily categorized or realized. Perhaps somewhat ironically, the truth in the above examples is more easily understood by the individual—it is the action to change if not overcome that can be the challenge. Change and modification to make the individual "more fit," resulting from stimulation mainly because of self-motivation promoted by self-actualization is the essence of the individuals' thinking that underlies this book.

What it took in the individual situations discussed in this book to overcome the maladaptive thinking, and the assistance required (if any), varies upon the circumstances, and perhaps most importantly their drive, their will, and perhaps their respective levels of risk tolerance. The time that it takes to change, whether the steps are "large" or "small" are likewise situation dependent, and ultimately defined by the person's perspective. That perspective stands in marked contrast to a societal perspective or view. In fact, the societal perspective—the current mores—can act, depending on the person's thinking, as a deterrent to the person from realizing his/her truth, and thus either be maladaptive in and of itself, or a challenge to overcome. In short, the thinking that results in reaction to the stimuli, however relatively great or small the person perceives that stimuli to be, forms the essence of paradigmatic thinking.

The authors suggest that the individual's paradigm is bounded by multiple sides and societal mores and pressures have a significant effect. How we are raised and what we are raised to believe in have a significant effect on our behavior and internal processing of information.

Paradigms are a belief system—we engage in them because we perceive (even if we do not affirmatively think about it), that they do something for us—they have meaning. This is not always a conscious process, which explains why they are sometimes challenging to treat. People engage in paradigmatic thinking even though they may perceive that it is not good for them. For example, a person who eats, smokes, drinks, or takes drugs when under pressure (a stimulus) may well realize that the action is not "good" for him or her, but does it anyway. In this sense, the paradigmatic thinking is maladaptive—it is a coping mechanism that does not address the underlying issue(s), it is *a way of not dealing with reality*. Smokers, for example, may feel while the health risks of nicotine use are well-known, they are not currently diagnosed with emphysema or lung cancer and they probably will not die from a smoking-caused disease today. Denial is a major factor in a person's general reluctance to shape-up or to adopt a new regimen. Realizing that a behavior or situation is detrimental to the person's being and changing is the shift from maladaptive thinking that is explored in this book. In order to change from maladaptive thinking, we need to achieve that understanding.

Implicit is the critical understanding that we rely on paradigms. This is the starting point to understanding how to change them. We indulge in paradigmatic behavior for one of two reasons: we cannot or do not care to control it or we expect it to lead to a certain result. In turn, paradigmatic behavior is predicated on our reaction to stimuli.

If we do not rely on a particular paradigm, and, concomitantly, if we do not believe that the paradigm has value or will "work" (to whatever extent and a subjective concept) there is no rational reason to act in accordance with that paradigm. Put otherwise, if, for example, achievement of a specific goal is the end game, it is not rational to engage in a process that one perceives will not achieve that goal. Doing so engenders more than a gratuitous expenditure of energy and time. It feeds into the falsity of the paradigm. This is not to say that people do not sometimes begin down a path only to discover that it is not working—and it is not always clear when an objective may or might not be achieved which would necessitate a change in the process to achieve that goal. The willingness to engage in changing thinking when a paradigm is not working toward an individual's self-fulfillment and the ability to effectuate that change is also critical.

Failure in and of itself is not indicative of maladaptive thinking at all. Rather, maladaptive thinking results from a paradigm that causes the individual frustration, or worse, affirmatively deters the person from achieving his/her trust or goal. An inability may be attributable to a physical factor (or factors) that affect the mental process, with which we do not discuss in this book. Or the lack of result may stem from a manner of perceiving or thinking that can be changed.

Superstitions

Accepted paradigms may themselves be maladaptive or at least not rational. Superstition is a primary example. Superstitions are commonly understood to be actions taken without a definable cause and effect, an action that is predicated on a belief that has no factual foundation.

Superstitions are not predicated on logic. Because they are not logical they can morph into or lead to maladaptive behavior. Superstitions, and superstionistic paradigms, abound in society. Past success is no guarantee of future results. However, that is precisely what a superstition is supposed to "guarantee" or help realize, despite the fact that there is no logical (read objectively caused) nexus between the two. The athlete engages in his/her ritual; the person thinks the way she/he does in order to attempt to preordain or at least influence an outcome in his favor. That "achievement" may be positive—as in making the dispositive play in a game—or negative—as in not throwing a home run ball that can lose the game, or not fumbling on the one-yard line. It may be positive as in doing well at a presentation because she/he has worn the "lucky" clothes, or negative by not getting stuck in an elevator. In softball, players may put their hats on backwards to extend a rally. She/he expects that some external force that has no connection, let alone necessary connection, to the desired result will intervene to assist in achieving that result—by the very fact that the result has happened (or, as the case may be, has not happened) previously. In reality, people tend to hang on to what they think works, such as carrying around a lucky rabbit's foot or finding a four-leaf clover. There is a pervasive, although perhaps implicit, underlining expectation that is the foundation of a superstition. Absent that expectation that the desired result will be either accomplished or at least because of the superstition, there would be no reason to engage in the superstitious behavior or thought pattern.

Superstitions are emblematic of the tension between expectation and reality. The ability to do away with superstitions would be a paradigm shift to rationality, but that does not mean, as we discuss below, that they do not have some benefit. For example, there is the athlete who has a particular pregame or routine prior to stepping up to home plate. The athlete who engages in his ritual expects that he will achieve something positive as a result. But will she/he actually perform better? What happens when reality intercedes and overrides the superstition? The routine changes when the batter slumps, and the new routine maintains when he hits well, until perhaps the next slump.

Triskaidekaphobia is a primary example. It is not only the fear of the number 13, but is the "…the irrational fear of the number 13" (triskaidekaphobia.info 2014, p. 1). At the outset, we ask whether there can be a rational fear of the number 13, or any number or the false attribution of a specific number as having lucky qualities, such as the number 7 with triple 7 being three times as good. Slot machine manufacturers feed into the subliminal notions of superstition. It is one thing to fear something tangible or that is founded in a tangible action, such as a barking Doberman Pinscher as it sprints toward you with its teeth showing after you climb over the fence to retrieve a lost ball. But is it rational to fear a symbol or a concept, one that was instigated, if not imposed, by society, i.e., some other person's or people's "belief," and passed down through centuries?

Why the number 13? It has possible historical roots: "Some attribute it to the Bible, where the Last Supper was attended by 13 people, and some speculated that the 13th person at the table was Judas Iscariot, who later betrayed Jesus. However, there is no reference to support this theory. Another belief is that the phobia of number 13 is caused by it being an irrational number and 12 being the number of perfection. There are 12 months in a year, 12 zodiacs, 12 hours in a clock, and there were 12 tribes of Israel…." (triskaidekaphobia.info 2014, p. 1). The purposeful absence of Floor #13, resulting from triskaidekaphobia, exemplifies the issue (in which case those denizens on the "14th floor" are, in reality, on the 13th floor, but it is apparently the number, not the reality that matters). The roots of fear of Friday the 13th go far back. Roach (2004) stated:

> Dossey traces the fear of 13 to a Norse myth about 12 gods having a dinner party at Valhalla, their heaven. In walked the uninvited 13th guest, the mischievous Loki. Once there, Loki arranged, the blind god of darkness, to shoot Balder the Beautiful, the god of joy and gladness, with a mistletoe-tipped arrow. "Bolder died and the whole Earth got dark. The whole Earth mourned. It was a bad, unlucky day," said Dossey. (p. 1)
>
> As for Friday, it is well known among Christians as the day Jesus was crucified. Some biblical scholars believe Eve tempted Adam with the forbidden fruit on Friday. Perhaps most significant is a belief that Abel was slain by Cain on Friday the 13th. (Roach 2004, p. 2)

Whatever the cause of triskaidekaphobia, its implications are real and severe. "It's been estimated that [U.S.] $ 800 or $ 900 million is lost in business on this day because people will not fly or do business they would normally do" (Roach 2004, p. 1). Let us pause to consider the loss of such an extraordinary amount of economic activity and what that signifies about paradigmatic thinking. Add to that the following observation:

> Of the more than 300 million people in the United States, an estimated 10.5 million suffer from obsessive–compulsive behavior, and about a quarter of them have phobias related to superstitions that cause them to change their lifestyle or engage in avoidance behaviors says Karen Cassiday (clinical director and owner of the Anxiety & Agoraphobia Treatment Center in Chicago)
>
> In addition, 21 million Americans suffer from generalized anxiety disorder…. Of this group, Cassiday estimates a whopping 75 %–85 % may be superstitious. (Kawamoto 2012, p. 1)

Superstitions, as a way of thinking, have very serious deleterious consequences. The behavior has no apparent casual connection to the result (and is thus defined as "irrational"). The behavior, which is apparently widespread, can properly be, but not necessarily be, characterized as maladaptive. Nevertheless, superstitious behavior has an apparent significant effect on, and acknowledgment and acceptance by, society. But, after all, a result by way of action (or inaction as the case may be) is the underlying predicate for superstitions in the first place.

In the authors' view, Stevie Wonder's song "Superstition" encapsulates the concept of superstitious paradigmatic thinking. The essence is the line: "When you believe in things that you don't understand…." (Wonder 1973). There are many things that we "don't understand," and may never understand. It is the human condition to expect to understand and then create paradigms to compensate when we do not or cannot. Moltner wrote, “We are taught ‘rationally’. People are preoccupied by what can be proven. But science, even logic, cannot always disprove … there is not always an answer to everything” (Kreuter 2013a, p. 161).

However, do superstitious paradigms necessarily constitute maladaptive thinking? Let us return to the baseball player who has a certain long-used, pregame ritual. Postulate that he is having a breakout season, so he maintains the pregame ritual throughout the season. And the season ends up being his best. There can be no evidence that the pregame ritual, which occurs a certain amount of time before he plays up to 162 games, had any casual effect on his physical play. Or can there be? Did the ritual have a salutary effect on his mental state—which is arguably a, if not the, foundation of his physical play? Did he become more relaxed, more comfortable within himself, more confident which in turn was reflected in his play? Consider this issue when we discuss confidence and its effect below. Is there, or might there be, in that situation, a casual connection after all? Or is that just an attempt to rationalize? Some professional players will not shave their hair once the playoffs begin until they either win or lose.

Contrast that to triskaidekaphobia. It may be argued that avoidance with the number 13, analogously to the ballplayer’s pregame ritual, provides a person with comfort. But comfort to what end? Is the comfort that a ball player achieves any more or less “rational” than the comfort that a person who has triskaidekaphobia achieves? How does the tremendous economic loss factor into the equation? Should we be analyzing, in this instance, paradigmatic thinking on a macro-level instead of an individual level? Mr. Wonder sang that “Superstition ain’t the way.” But it is the paradigm, the way, for many a person in many a situation. There is a distinction between an objective, “logical,” connection and a potential causal connection.

On the other hand, the number 13 has not had a deleterious effect on the careers of certain sports figures. “In honor of Friday the 13th, the most unlucky day on the calendar, ESPNW takes a look at the athletes past and present who have proudly sported the number” (Rykoff 2011, p. 1). She lists, among others, Wilt Chamberlain (who, Ms. Rykoff observes, was an All-Star, you guessed it, 13 times and the authors daresay one of the greatest basketball players of all time), Alex Rodriguez (the authors would be hard-pressed to conclude that his current issues were caused by the number 13 on his jersey), and Dan Marino and Kurt Warner (both of NFL fame).

In more extreme circumstances, however, superstitions become flawed coping mechanisms that have become a false foundation to action or reaction: “One of the mind’s most fundamental approaches in dealing with the unknown and the uncontrollable is the belief in pure magic” (Serban 1982 p. 51). Serban (1982) opined:

> People like to believe that every event is produced by a specific cause either self-evident or beyond their knowledge—yet possibly discoverable. This approach represents a great relief to the mind and provides a sense of confidence in mastering situations. The more logical, rational, and scientific man’s thought has become, the more need there is to explain the unexplainable. But because science is unable to penetrate the ultimate mystery of life and nature, people continue to rely on their own beliefs.
>
> Two sets of magical beliefs are used in the attempt to adapt to reality: those that protect an individual against unknown dangers, and those that rescue him when he is overcome by danger.

> Most magical beliefs are recognized as superstitions. Superstitions, as magical safeguards against the hazardous character of life, can become an integral part of a person's daily life. (p. 51)

Serban (1982) further opined:

> Some people never succeed in making this transition [from "mythical, prelogical thought to casual, logical thought"], either because social reinforcement supports their mythical beliefs or because they are simply reluctant or unable to cope logically or realistically with particular areas of life for which they do not have explanations. (p. 54)

Or, the authors would reiterate, fear: "[t]he phobic individual simply attempts to avoid the anxiety-provoking situation" (Serban 1982, p. 73). Thus, one irony is the person who adopts a superstition may well recognize that it is not rational, but continues the superstitious paradigm despite that realization because, as we observed above, it "works" or because she/he perceives that it will ward off an undesired, if not dangerous, result.

Faith as a Paradigm

Faith is also a paradigm. Compare to the definition of superstition, the definition of faith. "…the Bible defines faith as 'being sure of what we hope for and certain of what we do not'" (Hebrews 11:1). Thus, in the biblical vernacular, faith is a *channel of living trust*—an assurance—that stretches from man to God. In other words, "it is the object of faith that renders faith faithful" (Christian Research Institute 2010, p. 1). The commonality between superstitions and faith is the lack of proof upon which each rests.

What then is the difference, or where is the line drawn between "magical thinking" (Serban 1982, p. 11), superstitions, and faith? Is it akin to beauty in that it is in the mind of the beholder? "The difference between faith and superstition is that the first uses reason to go as far as it can, and then makes the jump; the second shuns reason entirely—which is why superstition is not the ally, but the enemy, of true religion" (Harris 1953, p. 1). Gibson (2009) writes:

> The difference between superstitions and religion is not only the difference between meaning and randomness, and between faith and anxiety, but also the difference between belief in a personal, benevolent God and fear of a pitiless Mother Nature, waiting to be appeased—or exploited—by mumbo jumbo. "Superstition" by definition "stands beyond" us, whereas religion is part of the human experience and interacts with it.
>
> Superstition offers the illusion of control by manipulating nature or revealing her occult intent. If the spells are recited properly, all should be well. It's a big "if," however. Religion gives the promise, rather than the illusion, of hope. God does not always respond as we would like; loved ones die, livelihoods are lost. Mystery is deepened and hopefully, with faith, leads to peace rather than disillusionment. Accidental similarities between religion and magic should not lead anyone to confuse the difference in their content. Nor should the focus on witchcraft in places like Africa blind the rest of us to the lures of superstition that continue to cloud our own beliefs. (p. 2)

One of the authors spoke about this topic with a friend, John (a pseudonym). He believes that, at the bottom, the difference lies in the "depth of conviction" (Personal communication, John December 21, 2013). Faith: "purpose and meaning gives depth to the individual." Once one gives away the control to ones faith, she/he can find inner peace. But for the authors, regardless of faith, or perhaps thanks to it, one still must find one's own purpose. States John: "I have found 'inner peace and that's where I'm resigned'" (Personal communication, John 2013). With faith, one cannot prove, or disprove. Superstitions are provable, or disprovable, and sometimes even quantifiable, but faith is neither. He views superstition as the suspension of reality, an inability to see reality. Faith, on the other hand, is "a submission to belief when common sense tells us otherwise." That is potential of faith, but how does that specific aspect differ from superstitions? My faith, John states, teaches not to know everything but to accept. Acceptance—what a basic but challenging paradigm. But don't people accept superstitions? Or is it the depth of conviction that creates the distinction? Its foundation in reality, but its conflict with desire if not need, is a critical paradigm. States John, with faith one has been taught all one can, considered as much as one can, and nevertheless accepted what one cannot prove. No scientist, no one, can come up with the spiritual side because it cannot be seen. But to the authors that is the beauty—because it does not have to be proven, nor necessarily, as stated by John, even understood intellectually.

A distinction must be made between spirituality and faith as not necessarily the same as religion. Structures are products of man, the spirit is for "mine and mine alone," John posits. He continues that it is not for anyone to give or take the spiritual, because one cannot. We suggest that men and objects can help, but we agree that no one can give or take. A spirit cannot be rectified like a car part or a broken bone. It can heal and change with assistance, but ultimately one must prevail for one self, if not necessarily on one's own.

Superstition, to John, is an unaccepted casual connection. The authors agree, at least in part. We suggest that the difference lies in the words "false concept of causation" that characterizes superstition. Faith, to John, is an "accepted connection." Faith is supernatural and metaphysical. Faith relates to the intangible, the unknowable, the untouchable. Superstition is the here and now (read temporal), superstition is "in the natural."[1]

Faith is generally viewed as an attempt to achieve a positive moral purpose, while superstition is viewed as a means of warding off negative consequences or bringing primarily material benefit. Superstition is connected with "bad luck," while faith embodies the higher moral ground and the spiritual side. But there are gradations of faith. Not only in the level of belief but also in the moral ground that it occupies. Cults are generally considered to be a warped form of faith, with concomitant negative connotations, because they are not within the mainstream thinking of what society accepts as religion. In a cult, believers may be swayed by a charismatic leader

[1] John further posits that "science" is also acceptance: For example, 2+2 equals 4, does it not? But it is man who defined 2+2. Galileo can teach a man anything, but man must find it within him or herself to accept it (or not).

out of a search for something to grab hold of or champion. It is societal values that inform the determination of what a cult is. This is not to place a judgment value on the societal determination. Rather, it is to say that such exists and is influential in terms of what is "acceptable" and what is not.

Societal Influences

This brings into play the effect of societal mores on an individual's paradigms. The impact of societal mores on an individual's paradigmatic thinking thus invokes another aspect of Kuhn. More specifically, the concept of societal mores, what is "accepted" and what is "outside the mainstream" fits directly into the theme of certain of the shifts that we discuss. We discussed how we have adapted Kuhn's theory of paradigms from a societal perspective to the study of individual patterns of thought. However, as the concepts of superstition, religion, and cults demonstrate, there is, in many instances, a component, often strong, of current societal mores that can impact upon the individual's paradigmatic thinking. Here, we observe how the shift in societal mores impacts on the individual's paradigm.

For example, we will discuss a person's shift from heterosexual to homosexual. One of the poignant points that he makes is that being gay was considered taboo and there was not a strong cultural support system. In *United States v. Windsor,* __ U.S. ___, 133 S. Ct. 2675, 186 L Ed. 808 (June 26, 2013), the US Supreme Court, by a 5–4 vote, found a section of the federal Defense of Marriage Act unconstitutional. For the purposes of this book, the focal point is the effect of that decision on the public mores. In his dissent, Chief Justice Roberts referred to ".... Congress's decision to retain the definition of marriage [between a man and a woman] that, *at that point,* had been adopted by every State in our Nation, and every nation in the world" 133 S.Ct. at 2696 (emphasis added). "That point" was 1996, not even 20 years ago. The opinion specifically leaves to the individual states to decide whether to adopt same-sex marriage and the benefits and obligations that go along with it: "The significance of state responsibilities for the definition and regulation of marriage dates to the Nation's beginning; for when the constitution was adopted the common understanding was that the domestic relations of husband and wife and parent and child were matters reserved to the States...." 133 S.Ct. at 2680 (from the syllabus, quotation omitted). Societal mores will thus again play roles in this instance in each state's decision. In turn, each state's decision will be the product of the influences of the citizens and institutions of each state on the legislature and the governor who has and will make the decisions arising from that case.

> State legislatures have been deeply involved in the public debates about how to define marriage and whether the official recognition of "marriage" should be extended to same-sex couples. Eighteen states and the District of Columbia currently have laws that allow same-sex marriages.
>
> A federal judge in Utah ruled in December 2013 that the state's ban on same-sex marriage is unconstitutional. The New Mexico Supreme Court ruled in December 2013 that same-sex couples in the state are allowed to marry. The Hawaii and Illinois legislatures

> adopted same-sex marriage legislation in November 2013. In October in New Jersey, the State Supreme Court refused to delay a State District Court decision requiring the state to recognize same-sex marriages and the governor announced that the state would drop its appeal, so that New Jersey now allows same-sex marriages.
> New Mexico and Utah's court rulings make it nine states where same-sex marriages were made legal this year, joining Hawaii, Illinois, Delaware, Minnesota, and Rhode Island (all through legislation) and California and New Jersey (through court decisions). (National Conference of State Legislatures 2013, p. 1)

On January 6, 2014, the Supreme Court "ordered a temporary stop to same-sex marriages in Utah" (Kendall 2014, p. A3). On March 22, 2014, the US Court of Appeals for the Sixth Circuit stayed an order of a Michigan federal District Court that allowed same-sex marriage in Michigan until the appeals court could decide whether to grant an injunction pending an appeal of that order (Eligon and Eckholm 2014, p. 1). The state's positions are quickly evolving. The federal government has also stepped in. On Friday, January 10, 2014, the US Attorney General Eric Holder stated:

> I am confirming today that, for purposes of federal law, these marriages will be recognized as lawful and considered eligible for all relevant federal benefits on the same terms as other same-sex marriages. These families should not be asked to endure uncertainty regarding their status as the litigation unfolds. (Savage and Healy 2014, p. 1)

Notice too that the change in nomenclature from "gay" to "same sex." We should ask whether that is in accord with evolving societal mores. Query also whether there is an analogy to the nomenclature change from Miss or Mrs., pursuant to which a woman could be identified as married or unmarried, to Ms. which, like a man, would not identify a woman as married or unmarried, with evolving concepts of equality of women.

The Mechanism of the Paradigm Shift

Another critical aspect of this analysis is the shift itself—the shift to positive thinking and action away from maladaptive or negative thought. In this context, we speak of shift with reference to how permanent it is or whether it could be attenuated. Once the shift has been achieved the goal is met, but it must then be maintained. Maintenance is as much a part of the shift as obtaining the goal itself. Is an incentive necessary to maintain the shift? Or has the shift become the new norm? The goal and its achievement become an integral part of life, on a daily basis, but sometimes it requires a fight against sliding back. The "incentive" normally takes the form of the internal feeling of success by moving toward or obtaining a goal. Although the cliché: "Never say never" is, for good reason, apropos in the world in which we live, there are shifts that are as close to hermetically sealed as possible. And then there are the shifts that must be affirmatively, consciously maintained lest one lapse back into maladaptive thinking. It normally takes a reasonable period of time adopting a new thought process for it to sink in as a permanent change. Time not only heals all wounds but it oftentimes cements the shift. The longer that one is able to maintain the shift, the better are the prospects that the shift will have permanency.

A shift away from maladaptive thinking, but a regression back into it, while not a permanent shift, does not mean that there has been no achievement. On the contrary, the authors argue that there have been two achievements—first, that the person made strides toward the shift and, second, that the person was able to, for whatever period of time, overcome (or forego) the maladaptive approach. Those achievements provide the foundation for hope in the future that she/he will be able to do so again, perhaps for even a longer period. The hope of a shift became a reality, even if not a permanent one. And, just as clearly, the reasons for the regression back into the maladaptive thinking have to be explored. But just because one cannot obtain, or has not obtained, the ultimate or permanent shift does not mean to give up or suggest that she has obtained "anything." On the contrary, she/he has.

In the end, only we can determine when we have gained a sufficient understanding to realize whether we can effect real change—but we must be confident that we have in fact gained an understanding and that that understanding is the "truth," at least for that particular objective.

In the preface, we discussed the source of paradigms and changing behavior, that we cannot or do not care to control it or we expect it to lead to a certain result. In turn, paradigmatic behavior is predicated on our reaction to stimuli. We are surrounded by stimuli. In fact, we are reacting to stimuli virtually every second of every moment when we are awake. Depending on the relevance we attribute toward the stimuli, our reactions vary as to both intensity and conscious thought that we give to it. Stimuli cause reactions, borrowing from the laws of physics. Our reaction can be conscious or subconscious, to varying degrees, to the point of being rote or a habit. Habits are a type of paradigmatic thinking and may be subconscious.

Moltner recently was advised that due to a hip condition, certain exercises that he enjoyed would have to be eliminated—just like that, one day he could do them and the figurative next day he was told that he could not. Physical therapy has been prescribed (to strengthen the muscles around the area), but that, the doctor has advised, will not "cure" the condition, only surgery might. The condition, while far from debilitating at this time, is at varying times uncomfortable or painful, and, more importantly, as far as he can infer from what the doctor has advised, will likely continue to be limiting. Moreover, he infers, since the condition cannot heal on its own, it can only get worse with age. His objective is to avoid surgery. All of this will necessitate a shift in exercise habits. And he has already begun to do so. He has begun to swim, in particular, and exercise on the elliptical machine. The reason: There is no reasonable other choice. Exercise is necessary mentally as much as physically (yes, half the battle is getting to the gym and into the pool, but once there the enjoyment and the endorphins do kick in—it is remembering that feeling that is an incentive to go) and the exercises that he used to love he can do no longer.

Habit itself implies a certain permanency of how one acts, and to effectuate change new habits will have to succeed the older ones. Some habits are harder to break then others. We daresay that many on the show *The Biggest Loser* became overweight due to their habit of eating too much. Now those who have lost weight may well have the challenge of keeping it off. But if they are able to develop positive habits such as exercise and "eating right," they are likely to succeed. The decision to achieve a meaningful weight loss is itself a paradigmatic shift. It takes as much mental fortitude as physical fortitude. Whether the weight stays off is a matter of permanency of the shift. Many such examples abound such as the smoker who must kick the habit or face serious medical consequences and the alcoholic who has recovered. Changing any negative habit, however major or seemingly minor, requires incentive buttressed by intestinal fortitude, which is one of the primary factors to obtaining and maintaining a paradigmatic shift. As Mark Twain suggested, "[h]abit is habit and not to be flung out of the window by any man, but coaxed downstairs a step at a time" (as cited in Gooder 1992, p. 34). This implies that habits are negative, but not necessarily so. The habit of going to the gym, for example, is not one that we daresay most doctors would say to kick.

The Role of Thinking

If one awakens each morning with the expectation of failure based on the results of the past and fear of failure that she/he expects in the future, a therapist or coach may advise the client that the road ahead is the only important direction. The past becomes more distant with each new mile travelled. One must never look back because that could cause you to stumble.

A person's mode of thinking begins at birth and becomes ingrained. Piaget's theories on cognitive development have resonance here.

> Piaget believed that newborn babies have some innate schemas—even before they have had much opportunity to experience the world. These neonatal schemas are the cognitive structures underlying innate reflexes. These reflexes are genetically programmed into us. (McLeod 2012, p. 3)

"Assimilation" is applying the schema to a new situation (McLeod 2012, p. 3). As the authors observed above, schemas are the way people see and react to situations. According to Piaget, "accommodation" is when the person's schema fails to work and, therefore, must be changed to adapt to the new situation (p. 3). Repetition breeds acceptance. As typically found, the more ingrained the harder to change. Further, it is usually the case that the harder to change, the harder to shift. Factors, including societal stimuli and "mores" reinforce these patterns. The patterns become our road map to resolution of issues and thus our confines and paradigms. Fear of change often endures because there is no guarantee that the change can be accomplished; the alternative, however, is being stuck in the quicksand of maladaptive thinking. There is also a fear of success where a person is apprehensive about moving into a career position of higher authority where much more will be expected.

The Impact of Dependency

Another reaction to stimuli results for many of us from dependency. The world is people made. People build the icons and houses of worship, make the laws that they follow (or bend or ignore), decide who is be promoted or rewarded and how much, decide who stays and who goes, whom to honor with an award (that people create and name), and to whom the accolade does not go. Implicit in this schema is a dependency on others, to whatever extent. To be dependent on the approval (read whim) of others to fulfill one's sense of self or happiness puts you as a person into someone else's hands. And that creates a chance that the proverbial rug will be pulled out from underneath you.

Put differently, there is a societal paradigm of reliance. We begin our life, and go through at least our first years having to rely on others. We all have to rely on somebody at some point (as the song goes, "we all need someone to lean on"; Withers 1972, Sussex Records). The times in which we are raised either urge us to rely or urge us to challenge, the 1960s and Woodstock being one example. As we age, the societal expectation is that we should and will become less reliant, until we reach a certain age when we may again be reliant others (e.g., social security, aides, our family), although not necessarily as reliant as we were when we were infants and children, although that is dependent on one's physical and mental condition.

There are different types and levels of reliance, such as financial and emotional. Why do we rely on anything or anybody? Our upbringing teaches us to rely (and trust), for example, on those persons of authority. Teachers, police, and politicians are examples. In a micro-sense, a child relies on his/her parent, and an employee on his/her boss. In an orderly society, in a society of laws, people are expected and required to respect authority with which society imbues certain persons in order that society function. Nevertheless, history proves that the fabric of society, societal mores, can be changed by historic figures such as Dr. Martin Luther King, Jr. or Nelson Mandela, or abused by governments. Our focus here, however, is not macro; rather, it is on the potential individual consequences of reliance and the potential effect on one's paradigmatic thinking.

With authority comes the power to choose or decide. There is nothing wrong with that. But that is different from dependency. A maladaptive offshoot of power and authority is the individual's reaction to it. Whether by upbringing or perceived necessity, people are overly dependent on what can amount to no more than the subjective whim of those with authority. And people allow others to determine their self-esteem or sense of worth. Put differently, we too often allow others to overly influence what we think of ourselves. In Kreuter's (2013a) earlier book, he made several observations that we, in a sense, set ourselves up to fail sometimes. By over-reliance on the opinion of others, we exacerbate the potential for denigrating our self-worth and setting ourselves up to fail. Measuring our self-worth based on the opinion of others is a recipe for disappointment, and probably worse. And therein lays a problem that can be characterized as maladaptive submission to authority.

People too often cower before those invested by other men with authority out of habit or perceived lack of choice. People most often act in their self-interest, to protect their own turf. If a mistake is made and it is between you and your boss as to who receives blame, assuming equal responsibility, would you expect your superior to step up and accept her share of the responsibility because it is the "right" thing for her to do? Or would you be expected to be thrown under the proverbial bus? It is a dog-eat-dog world. What is "fair," what is "right" is relative, often quite relative. What may be wrong for the individual is who she/he is relying upon, and whether that dependency is engendering maladaptive thinking.

How does necessary reliance transmogrify into maladaptive behavior in relying on others for a measure of self-worth? What happened to landing on one's own two feet?

Ralph Waldo Emerson (1841) wrote extensively about self-reliance, parts of which we quote here:

> To believe your own thought, to believe that what is true for you in your private heart is true for all men—that is genius. Speak your latent conviction, and it shall be the universal sense; for the inmost in due time becomes the outmost….
> There is a time in every man's education when he arrives at the conviction that envy is ignorance; that imitation is suicide; that he must take himself for better, for worse, as his portion…. (p. 1)

One man may justifiably ask if that time truly does come in "every man's education." Emerson (1841) continued:

> Trust thyself: every heart vibrates to that iron string. Accept the place the divine providence has found for you, the society of your contemporaries, the connection of events. (p. 2)

"Accept[ing] the place the divine providence has found for you," is arguably antithetical to the self-reliance of which Emerson writes. Emerson's use of the word "acceptance" implies passiveness. Self-reliance, however, implies constant activeness and awareness of oneself and one's surrounding. Those who have overcome maladaptive thinking, have a motivation that is fortified by action that in turn is predicated on self-awareness and understanding, and in many cases self-reliance. Even on a "theoretical" level, Emerson's statement in the context of his essay on self-reliance raises thoughts. Compare Emerson's statement to John's or Kim's view of religion. They view religion as providing or supplementing an inner strength, a means to finding an inner comfort. It is an active, not a passive, acceptance. This is not to be critical; rather, it is to promote discussion of the role that religion plays in self-reliance. Emerson's is a challenging thought in light of the context of his essay in which, for example, Emerson continues:

> …. I am ashamed to think how easily we capitulate to badges and names, to large societies and dead institutions. (p. 3)

Emerson exhorts us as human beings to realize our challenges and rise to them:

> …. I do not wish to expiate, but to live. My life is for itself and not for a spectacle…. Few and mean as my gifts may be, I actually am, and do not need for my own assurance or the assurance of my fellows any secondary testimony.

> What I must do is all that concerns me, not what the people think…. It is easy in the world to live after the world's opinion; it is easy in solitude to live after our own; but the great man is he who in the midst of the crowd keeps with perfect sweetness the independence of solitude. (p. 4)
>
> It is easy to see that a greater self-reliance must work a revolution in all the offices and relations of men; in their religion; in their education; in their pursuits; their modes of living; their association; in their property; in their speculative views. (p. 13)

Compare Emerson's exhortation in this sentence that "a greater self-reliance must work a revolution … in their religion" to his concept of acceptance noted above. Emerson further writes:

> Another sort of false prayers is our regrets. Discontent is the want of self-reliance: it is infirmity of will. Regret calamities, if you can thereby help the sufferer; if not, attend your own work, and already the evil begins to be repaired…. (p. 13)

This is another critical concept in shifting from maladaptive thinking—the pull of the past, wasting our time and energy on the mistakes that we made, on that which we could have or should have done differently, of the opportunities (in whatever context) that we perceive that we missed, or that which we had, but let go which on 20–20 hindsight and in the context of our current reality and challenges look so much better. But all of those that have the same reality—they are a past that, if cannot be changed, we must learn from and otherwise let go. "Those who do not remember their past are condemned to repeat it" (Santanya 1905, p. 284). Let us learn from our past, but not drive ourselves crazy over it is too often more easily said than done. There can be a false comfort in dwelling on the past which is used as an escape mechanism, which is a maladaptive schema in itself. The ability to take action when we can to ameliorate or correct our mistakes is one thing. The ability to otherwise accept and move on is another and an important concept of self. The concept that it is never too late is not always true.

It is never too late to change maladaptive thinking, but there are some actions and their consequences that cannot be changed. Thus there is a line, sometimes fine, between recognizing the potential of making a mistake, encountering an analogous situation and thinking ahead to avoid a mistake previously made, and letting the fear of making mistakes become a maladaptive schema that negatively affects one's life. What can be changed is how a person deals with her perceived mistakes.

The concept of mistakes can arise in situations major or small. The significance of mistakes varies to a person individually and on whether the person believes she/he made a mistake that affects his or her own life or the life of others. For example, one of the authors knows of a person who made a career change out of finance because that person was uncomfortable with having an effect on other people's finances. That person successfully perceived and changed a maladaptive schema. In continuing on his concepts of self-reliance, Emerson further writes:

> Insist on yourself; never imitate. Your own gift you can present every moment with the cumulative force of a whole life's cultivation; but of the adopted talent of another, you have only an extemporaneous, half possession. That which each can do best, none but his Maker can teach him…. (p. 15)

Again, we note Emerson's reference to a deity and ask how that comports with self-reliance. We are not taking a position as to whether it does or does not. That is an individual's choice. To sum it up:

> Nothing can bring you peace but yourself. Nothing can bring you peace but the triumph of principles. (p. 18)

What are those individual principles? They are the person's truth. In Shakespeare's Hamlet, Polonius said, "To thine own self be true…" (Act I, Scene 3). In the movie *A Few Good Men,* when Tom Cruise demanded from Jack Nicholson "the truth," he famously challenged Mr. Cruise that, "You can't handle the truth." We first have to find our truth, before we can determine whether we can handle it, let alone change it. That is the critical beginning of the journey to a paradigm shift from maladaptive behavior.

> A theory of truth is essentially an explanation of the nature of truth and a set of laws that "true" things obey. Electricity is the property that all electrical things share. What is the property that all true statements have in common? Why is a theory of truth important? Because that is what, ultimately, our cognitive life is all about: truth. Whenever we analyze a scene, whenever we analyze a statement, whenever we recall a memory, whenever we do anything with our brain, we are on a quest for truth. Our cognitive life is a continuous struggle for truth: Is that stain in the distance a tree? Is she home tonight? Will my flight take off on time? Why did the Roman Empire fall? Our mind, ultimately, is an organ to identify truth. The meaning of our life is truth. (Scaruffi, undated, p. 1)

There are many theories of truth. Following are some of them:

The Correspondence Theory

> … the label is usually applied much more broadly to any view explicitly embracing the idea that truth consists in a relation to reality, i.e., that truth is a relational property involving a characteristic relation (to be specified) to some portion of reality (to be specified). (David 2013, p. 1)

The authors note that pertinent to this exploration is that:

> You may think it is easy to figure out what is so. [However there is] overwhelming psychological evidence that there is no such thing as "pure" perception or "pure" linguistic description … some people have rejected the correspondence theory because they say we simply can't discover what is so in any "objective" way. (LaFave 2005, p. 1)

The Coherence Theory of Truth

> A coherence theory of truth states that the truth of any (true) proposition consists in its coherence with some specified set of propositions. (Young 2013, p. 1)

The coherence theory is also described as follows:

> The "coherence theory of truth" defines truth as coherence with the system of beliefs in one's mind. (Scaruffi undated, p. 2)

The Pragmatic Theory

> …. TRUE IDEAS ARE THOSE THAT WE CAN ASSIMILATE, VALIDATE, CORROBORATE AND VERIFY. FALSE IDEAS ARE THOSE THAT WE CANNOT. That is the practical difference it makes to us to have true ideas; that, therefore, is the meaning of truth, for it is all that truth is known as. (Scaruffi undated, p. 2)

Constructivist Theory

> …. Rather than assimilate a body of knowledge about one's world and environment, constructivists believe we "construct" meaning based upon our interactions with our surroundings. (Warrick undated, p. 2)

Consensus Theory

> A philosophical viewpoint based on the assumption that truth is a matter of social agreements, including the agreements reached by the scientific community, of reality. Compare correspondence theory of truth. (Oxford Dictionary of Sports Science and Medicine 2007, p. 1)

Functionalism

> …. Lynch argues that there is a plurality of "truths", rather than a single all-encompassing theory of truth. For example, truth in ethics and truth in justice and truth in mathematics obey different laws. The nature of truth is difficult to find because there isn't only one nature of truth. One needs a different theory of truth for each domain, and that is precisely what ordinary humans employ in their daily lives. (Scaruffi undated, p. 3)

A Person's Personal Truth

In one study:

> Moral identity was investigated phenomenologically as it was experienced both by those who adhered to their stated moral convictions as well as those who did not. More specifically, 16 adult, unmarried, pro-life women who had experienced an unwanted pregnancy were interviewed, 8 of whom had carried and 8 had aborted…. Those who carried saw their moral beliefs as serving their self-interests, but those who aborted did not. Connection with a higher purpose was found in those who carried…. (Broderick 2009, p. 1)

We first pause to note how many theories of "truth" there are (and the above are not all of them). The "truth" is thus not readily generally definable. Of these theories of truth, the authors contend that the coherence theory best captures the essence of changing maladaptive schema to the extent that it emphasizes the truth to one's self and moral purpose, closest to what we perceive as Broderick's thesis. Finding one's personal truth, and taking steps toward it, is the essence of the shift away from maladaptive thinking.

The first issue in ascertaining one's truth is what it will take for one to care to attempt to find it. Some people do not perceive a need or desire to change. They may want "more," but do not feel the need to seek it. This could be because the proverbial glass is always half full and they are thus satisfied with themselves. Or it could be because they do not have the drive to change or a fear of change and thus accept, perhaps passively, their lot. That does not mean that those people are not happy; rather, it means that they do not believe that the time and effort to achieve greater happiness is worth it, if they have seriously considered it. The people who have made paradigm shifts who we interviewed for this book unequivocally gave considered thought to what their reality was and the internal truth that they sought and achieved. But what if you have realized your truth but cannot reach it?

There are times when people arrive at an intersection of life points. In general parlance, the word "crossroads" is used to describe the point of decision—one can choose to go one way or the other. But we refer to the point where the person's truth meets reality and the person's reality prevents further movement, which is a sort of reality traffic jam. For example, a person might be miserable in his or her job. She/he recognizes the truth that not only would she/he be happier doing something else (recognizing what that something else is). Yet she/he has a family to support and the financial consequence of change is too great, and entails risk particularly in these precarious economic times. She/he is at an intersection, not a crossroads. If she/he were, in fact, at a crossroads, then she/he could make a decision concerning the right road to travel. But here the intersection is clogged by the financial reality of his or her situation and, we will assume, an inability despite efforts to move. She/he is virtuous for maintaining what she/he does to support her family, but there is not yet a practical resolution to his or her travails. This brings back into play the concepts of incentive and confidence: Incentive to make the change while fulfilling her financial responsibilities and confidence that she/he can make the change. It also brings into play the notion, as Kreuter (2013a) explored in his case study of Rex, of taking small steps to the ultimate goal. To evaluate what the risks of change are, decide whether change is financially viable (in this situation), and then attempt to take incremental steps to effectuate that change. There are no guarantees of success. The risk/reward of change must be evaluated, and the reality faced and dealt with.

Confidence

The New York Rangers goalie, Henrik Lundqvist was quoted as saying with regard to two Rangers losses, "Yeah, it wasn't pretty, but you have to realize those were two strong teams playing with a lot of confidence and we were still trying to find ours" (Caldwell 2013, p. A27).

In a more general vein, a lack of confidence can be a form of maladaptive thinking. What is confidence? How much is, or should, confidence be based in reality? Is there a dichotomy between how others perceive how confident you are and how you perceive yourself? How can one shift from not confident to being confident?

In society, confidence is thought to be a critical element in success, be it in the cutthroat world of business or interpersonal relationships. "A study of more than 500 students, academics and workers, published in the *Journal of Personality and Social Psychology,* show that those who appeared more confident achieved a higher social status than their peers" (Furness 2012, p. 1). The authors of one study regarding self-esteem concluded, in part, "[w]ith the exception of the link to happiness, most of the effects are weak to modest. Self-esteem is thus not a major predictor or cause of almost anything (again, with the possible exception of happiness.).... One could argue that self-esteem deserves credit for so-called indirect effects, even if other variables are more directly related to the outcome.... The seeming benefits of self-esteem could be a product of other factors that overlap with self-esteem, of subjective bias, and of reciprocal causal relationships" (Baumeister et al. 2003, p. 37).

A common thread in many of the case studies in this book is the concept of confidence, albeit in different contexts and to varying degrees. The question becomes how people can shift from being "nonconfident" to being confident and how to effectuate that shift. There are a number of issues to be addressed including how much is or "should" confidence be based on objective reality, how much does the input of others contribute to confidence. Ultimately, however, only you can achieve your own confidence, as necessary with counseling. Of course, one must recognize the need for assistance in order to seek it, and be open to accepting such assistance which, in turn, assumes that the counselor is effective for the purpose.

First, what is "confidence?" What does it mean to be confident? One perspective of confidence, and we daresay how it is generally understood, is the belief, more than an unfounded feeling, that you can achieve an objective. Compare confidence to self-esteem. "Self-esteem is the general opinion a person has about himself or herself. Having high, but realistic self-esteem is essential to good mental health" (Heitz 2013, p. 1). From these definitions, we can perceive the difference between self-esteem and confidence—self esteem is "how you feel about yourself overall" while confidence is "how you feel about your abilities and can vary from situation to situation" (Roberts 2012, p. 1). Nevertheless, there is a relationship, "Self-esteem is the disposition to experience oneself as being competent to cope with the basic challenges of life, and as being worthy of happiness. Thus, it consists of two components: (1) self-efficacy—confidence in one's ability to think, learn, choose, and make appropriate decisions; and (2) self-respect—confidence that love, friendship, achievement, success—in a word, happiness—are natural and appropriate" (Branden 2013, p. 1).

Having confidence does not necessarily mean that one will obtain a goal. But having confidence and self-esteem (or either) can open one up to taking rational risks, to perceiving an opportunity when someone who is not confident or does not have self-esteem might not, and therefore, not pursue it. Nevertheless, both confidence and self-esteem may run into the brick wall of reality. But the person who has self-esteem, or confidence in a particular situation, has more internal presence and perhaps more drive to climb that wall, maneuver around it, or maybe even attempt to smash through it. "High self-esteem has value in causing people to persist longer in the face of failure, at least when there is no viable alternative task or goal to pursue and when no cues suggest that persistence is not a good strategy. When there is an alternative goal or information that persistence may be a poor strategy, high self-esteem is associated with knowing when to quit. Thus, in performance contexts, high self-esteem people appear to use better self-regulation strategies than low self-esteem people" (Baumeister et al. 2003, p. 15).

The authors suggest that past experience and one's perception of the current situational reality play a defining role in confidence. If an unemployed person has unsuccessfully attempted to find work for a year she/he is less likely to be confident in finding work. This is supported by statistics of those who drop out looking for jobs. The editorial entitled "Out of Work and Hope" (New York Daily News 2013, p. 20) opined:

> America is now a country where the official count of joblessness is dropping largely because so many people have stopped looking for work. Under the government's statistical rules, those who have thrown in the towel are no longer counted as unemployed. Perversely, this drives the rate down.
> … the labor force participation rate is, a solid measure of the country's connection to paychecks, is at a near-historic low.
> Over the last three months, three people have stopped looking for work for every person who's found a job….

In its editorial on the issue entitled "Jobs and the Fed," the *Wall Street Journal* (2013) opined:

> …. The labor force participation rate ticked up to 63 % from 62.8 %. This is still near a 35-year low, but it's a relief to see even a small reversal of the post-recession trend of millions of workers fleeing the job market. (p. A14)

Confidence brings into play many concepts. For example, confidence is related to expectations. The more confident someone is in an outcome, the higher the expectation that the outcome will be achieved. "Confidence consists of positive expectations for favorable outcomes. Confidence influences the willingness to invest—to commit money, time, reputation, emotional energy, or other resources—or to withhold or hedge investment. This investment, or its absence, shapes the ability to perform. In that sense, confidence lies at the heart of civilization. Everything about an economy, a society, an organization, or a team depends on it. Every step we take, every investment we make, is based on whether we feel we can count on ourselves and others to accomplish what has been promised. Confidence determines whether our steps—individually or collectively—are tiny and tentative or big and bold" (Kanter 2004, p. 7–8). "The context that creates expectations affects outcomes" (p. 10). "It is human nature to set expectations based on assumptions about whether conditions seem to be improving or deteriorating, about whether the game can be won or invariably lost" (p. 8). See also quotation by Lundqvist above.

"Objectively," confidence also brings into consideration the ability one has to exert control over a situation, or a person's perception of it. If, for whatever reason, you believe that a desired outcome will happen then you are confident in it (even if you are not confident in yourself). Your confidence varies on how certain you are, and, in turn, your analysis of the facts upon which your conclusion is predicated. This again brings into play expectations. Moltner discussed the pervasive role of expectations in our lives (Kreuter 2013a, pp. 147–163). The confluence between confidence and expectations is yet another example. On the other hand:

> Overconfidence leads people to overshoot, to overbuild, to become irrationally exuberant or delusionally optimistic. That's what induces people to become complacent, leaders to neglect fundamental disciplined investors to turn into gamblers. (Kanter 2004, p. 8)

And,

> [ ] under confidence is just as bad, and perhaps worse. It leads people to under invest, to under innovate, and to assume that everything is stacked against them, so there's no point in trying. (p. 8)

Another factor is the "truth." Is one's confidence concerning a particular situation predicated on objective fact, subjective miscalculation, or false bravado? Then again, the veneer of confidence, even without factual foundation, can have salutary benefits. The idiom "bulls—ing" ones way through something is exemplary. Even if the empty veneer of confidence is perceived by the other, that other person might appreciate the portrayal of confidence—after all, "perception is 99 % of reality." It is somewhat akin to those who, perhaps outwardly only, go around without a care in the world. Whether it is cloudy or raining, the outwardly sun is consistently shining. For some, most things are emotion-laden. John's philosophy is to simplify, to move, if not throw away, that which clutters ones existence; in short, to bring things to their essence.

Subjectively, confidence can be based upon something that is without objective proof if not emotion-laden. For example, we spoke of superstitions versus religion. Each brings to the individual a form of confidence. Take the scenario of one who sees an attractive person and wants to speak to that person or ask him/her out. But she/he does not do so because she/he fears rejection and does not even talk to the other. The result is the same as speaking with the other and him/her saying no, so why not do so anyway? A lack of confidence could be whether based on personal factors or being uncomfortable given societal mores. But the result is still "no." Another example is confidence in the face of authority, such as lawyers to a judge or an employee to a superior. There is a fine line between being perceived to be not confident and respectful. Confidence affects how others perceive you, and how much they believe they can try to take advantage of you.

There is often a dichotomy between how others perceive you and how you perceive yourself. When we speak of this dichotomy, we first have to understand why it matters what other people think. Does a person's confidence derive from the opinion or approval of others? "Should" it? Why can others build up one's confidence, or tear it down? Confidence underlies the shift from maladaptive thinking by each of the individuals in this book.

Gradations of the Shift

There are gradations of the shift in maladaptive thinking. There is the shift that is completed. There is the shift that once made requires the individual to actively work to maintain it; in other words, even after the shift is achieved, in many instances, the shift is not completed because there remains the prospect of reverting back to the maladaptive thinking. There is movement away from maladaptive thinking toward a positive goal(s), but not free from maladaptive thinking. For example, overcoming the habit of drinking or smoking represents a shift. But does that shift withstand life's pressures or is there a reversion. Taking steps, "small" or "large" to obtain one's goal, such as applying for a job is a shift. But does the shift maintain in the face of a downtrodden economy and consistent rejection?

There are physical and tangible goals and there are mental and emotional ones, but the foundation of the shift comes from the meaning ascribed to the goal. Meaning is individualized, but the ultimate point is that there is meaning. Whether meaning may be categorized as tangible or intangible is not necessarily the issue. Nor does meaning necessarily reflect complete meaning in all aspects of life.

These gradations can be seen in the people who we have interviewed for this book. Rex has made movements toward his goal and affirmatively changed his behavior and attitude. He is currently very free from maladaptive thinking, but admits to the need for ongoing coaching in order to maintain his positive momentum. Therefore, in addition to his changed thinking, such change must be affirmatively maintained. The shift in Scott is complete (heterosexual to homosexual), and has been for years. That is not only a physical shift, but an emotional one as well. We can safely assume that the period of challenge in having made that shift, particularly given his marriage, has passed and the shift will be maintained. For Jennifer, one part of the shift—reconciliation—has been made. For her, and her spouse, the shift must be maintained. This is an example, unlike Rex, of when there is no definitive line of when, if ever, the shift is fully considered complete. As discussed, the authors dispute whether there could be underlying or continuing anger or regret on Jennifer's part. In comparison to Stephanie (a pseudonym), who went through the amicable divorce, has apparently completed her shift, not only in divorcing, but in moving on from the maladaptive feelings that led to the divorce in the first place. That the divorce was her initial decision undoubtedly played a role in her ability to complete the shift. These two situations are in contrast to Susan (a pseudonym) who, by virtue of the nastiness of the divorce and continuing aggravation, has understandably not yet fully completed the shift, but has taken significant and affirmative steps toward it. Samantha's (a pseudonym) eyesight is much better than her doctors thought it would be, but she still fights through the tears.

"Lifestyle imbalance, where the management of everyday life stressors with adaptive coping mechanisms and strategies is not in place, is seen as a fundamental factor in the failure to maintain change over a long period of time" (Weegmann and Cohen 2002, p. 121). Working with clients who have relapsed into addictions and other maladaptive patterns by helping the client become more aware of the relapse process is an important element in the relapse-prevention efforts. "Examining the patterns of the individual's previous relapses would help identify the latter, increasing awareness or insight would also involve looking at the individual's general strengths and weaknesses as well as general coping strategies" (p. 121).

We cannot speak of shifting paradigms without the context of what does success mean with regard to the truth and how the paradigms impact upon it. Success, as is the truth, is a very individualized concept that may not be that difficult to obtain. Success can be as broad as a career change, or as meaningful as viewing the want ads. As Kreuter described with Rex, the movement toward a goal can also be a success. What meaning the individual ascribes to the success is critical because that can define whether she continues or veers off the path. Why the goals change (e.g., boredom, believing it is not attainable, expectations not met) is also relevant. It is only when the goals are set that we can know if we have met it and thus have succeeded. There may be a change in goals and thus a change in the paradigms necessary to meet them.

A shift has gradations and may be subject to regression, but the fact that a shift has been effectuated demonstrates success.

Synopsis of Chapter

- Paradigms can be analyzed from the individual's perspective.
- Maladaptive thinking has many causes.
- Societal concepts and mores impact upon an individual's thinking.
- An individual overcomes maladaptive thinking when she/he finds is his or her truth.
- The concept of truth has many definitions.
- Each individual must define truth for him or herself.
- Confidence, self-esteem, and self-reliance are critical elements to effectuating the shift from maladaptive thinking.
- A shift has gradations and may be subject to regression, but the fact that a shift has been effectuated demonstrates success.

Chapter 3
Shifting Maladaptive Spirituality

"The universe has no restrictions. You place restrictions on the universe with your expectations."

—Deepak Chopra

Introduction

The term "spirituality" has no precise definition. For the purpose of this discussion, it means searching for the sacred, but can include tenets of humanistic psychology, ethics, mystical, and esoteric traditions. The construct of spirituality means something beyond earthly human control and worthy of veneration. It is different from organized religions, which encompass attendance and participation in various forms of practice normally taking place at venues such as, for example, churches, synagogues, or mosques.

Having a spiritual essence ingrained in many people through the active practice of an organized faith is far from universal. One of the areas of a person's life that can become maladaptive is a person's spirituality. Therapists must be able to help clients resolve their vocalized spiritual concerns and issues regarding their spiritual sense in order for them to feel complete, leading to restoration of their psyche. Ignoring it, when an issue, would be like overlooking other important aspects and issues of the whole person, such as his or her sense of family or sexuality.

Some people seek counseling from a Rabbi or a Christian counselor or other sectarian therapist/guide, or choose therapists with such a specific background or orientation, to help them with their specific or general dilemma or concerns.

Spirituality forms the basic underpinning for many people, guiding them on how to act and how to respond to their universe, their problems, and their hopes and fears. For example, to Christian believers, "Religion with man consists in a life according to the Divine Commandments, which are contained in a summary in the Decalogue" (Swedenborg 2008, p. 148). The Decalogue is another name for the Ten Commandments—a set of biblical principles relating to ethics and worship, all carrying binding authority. According to a Christian faith-based viewpoint: "Spiritual life is acquired solely by a life according to the commandments in the Word"

E. A. Kreuter, K. M. Moltner, *Treatment and Management of Maladaptive Schemas*,

DOI 10.1007/978-3-319-06817-6_3, © Springer International Publishing Switzerland 2014

(p. 135). Spirituality (more or less) is a component of our consciousness. For those who do not look upon themselves as spiritual beings, such people simply avoid any self-reference to them as having a belief in an acknowledged God and, instead, view the present world as "the" world and the only world. As such, they consider themselves as self-reliant insofar as there is no deity that guides them. They believe that they are fully conscious of their internal capacity for understanding the world and trust in themselves to respond to stimuli with no reference to any external entity. As such, they are fully conscious of their fate as resting in their own hands. In John Locke's (1632–1704) philosophy, consciousness is a property of the human mind (Chappell 2004, p. 1). Locke defines consciousness as, "…is the perception of what passes in a Man's own mind" (1975/1690, E II.i.19:115). It is, therefore, entirely personal in every regard, leading to sharing and communication by choice.

A spiritual person brings into life that aspect of his or her internal belief system. Thus, faith, that which cannot be seen, becomes a powerful force, guiding thoughts, actions, and responses to stimuli. For some believers, prayer is always successful, unlike our human endeavors or acts, though true belief requires complete trust in how prayer is answered. "An act can only be successful or unsuccessful when it is over; if it to begin, it must be, in the abstract, right or wrong" (Chesterton 1994/1910, p. 20). Thus, people rely on their own resources to act correctly in a given situation, and a person of faith may also add prayer to the act of acting. Some preachers will suggest praying through the day as a way of allowing faith to intersperse with one's free will.

Persons of faith are not always as spiritually connected as they used to be or wish to be. Their faith becomes dislodged in their life because of an event, which is an example of prayers not being offered or answered, or maybe they just slipped slowly away from their God and lost the continuity of prayer in their lives. When this happens, a negative schema can exist, whereby the disconnection between person and faith becomes increasingly a powerful negative force in life, leading them to backslide into negative behavior (sin) or feel lost, panicky, alone, or ignored (depression and anxiety). The schism created in the life of a person who once had, but has now lost faith, can result in a lack of connectedness. Some people who feel lost may develop heightened feelings of abandonment and disconnection with the world, and may turn to destructive behavior (drugs, sexual perversion, or crime). Those who abandoned the practice of their faith years ago, but turn back to their God in some manner, may find resolve useful in recreating positive energy in their lives. Thus, regaining a lost spiritual essence may help a person resolve troublesome aspects of his or her life—which is itself a coachable point or an appropriate issue for a psychotherapeutic encounter.

The Bible (or any other religious text) requires much effort to fully understand and to apply to modern life. In order to assist a person who is lost in this way, the following essays may provide a new road map to help a person with spiritual concerns or issues or people who have fallen into maladaptive schema as a result of such perceived issues.

Running–Walking Metaphor

During a recent half-marathon, Kreuter noticed while running on the streets of Yonkers, New York, as he was headed north, the majestic Palisades' mountains. The mountains appeared to be moving in the opposite direction though; obviously, they were static. He realized that based on the speed of his pace, whether running or walking, the seeming opposite movement of the mountains was faster or slower. So too, the movement of our lives follows a similar approach. We progress through our lives at a sometimes fast and sometimes slow pace, but the world around us may appear to be moving opposite to us. Sometimes our movement is rather static, or even engenders a feeling as if we are moving in a backward direction. We can use this as a treatment metaphor to explain how humans are meant to keep moving forward and that the world around us is either static or moving in the opposite direction. It is useful to help a person recover from trauma or from a mistake—to move ahead and allow the past to move away—to not live in the past or the future, but the present. While, therapeutically, it is perhaps best to get issues out into the open where they can be responsibly handled, the forward-looking mindset enables a person to avoid becoming imprisoned by the patterns of the past—something soon-to-be-released prisoners have great difficulty doing. Living in the moment may derail any attempt to forage into the past, but that could serve to bury a pervasive problem with the potential to resurrect one day. Some individuals who feel stuck in a rut psychologically may say that the reason they cannot think positively about the new day, as well as the future, is that either something always goes wrong or there will doubtlessly be failure to encounter along the way. In essence, such individuals bring onto themselves negative consequences because they sabotage any potential for the light of the new day to shine brightly on an otherwise dreary outlook. Therefore, it is the negative outlook where the main problem resides and festers into a lasting syndrome.

While we can take a great lesson from the past, we can never properly live in the past. Thus, even though we recognize the movement of the past, we do best by living in the present and looking ahead, not behind. We recommend against wasteful worrying about the future. Kreuter (2013c) wrote the following poem for a dear friend who has been experiencing great difficulty with a child:

Mother Am I
How can I help you feel better?
I am lost inside your pain.
When you were born I saw you as perfect?
I felt perfect in motherhood.
What changed?
Growing up I dried your tears.
I fed and clothed you.
I listened when you were upset?
I laughed when you were happy?
What changed?
Now you are in distress.
I share every moment, but I am not you.
The torment is different in many ways.

Some of your tears I cannot dry.
I am unable to feed your hidden hunger.
How can I change?
In the between time I think of you.
The silence between the notes is deafening.
My heart aches as if crushed by stone.
Can you perceive my devotion to you?
Can we both adapt?
Will you always know a mother's love?
Can you dry my tears one day?
In your struggle I will always have hope.
Yet the distance can heal in some way.
Love can always grow.

Attitude Counts

What is attitude? Does a person's attitude matter? Attitudes can, in a way, be chosen. For example, a person can wake up in the morning and make a determined effort to face the day in a positive manner as opposed to a negative one. In a way, we can "open up our attitude drawer" and make a selection for the entire day. Even when faced with difficulties expected during the new day, a positive attitude can go a long way towards shifting the person's energy and making the best of whatever is happening. An individual facing challenge stated, "I am very determined to take the right actions just to take care of what's right in front of me" (Personal communication, Roland Provence, December 22, 2013). In Roland's world, daily survival becomes the direct challenge in his life. He struggles, but also recognizes that living his life involves making decisions throughout the day, each concurrent with an attitude. He reminds himself constantly of his internal power to choose his attitude, and has come to understand how important a power this is. When he stays positive better results occur in his life compared to when he is dour, cross, or bitter, when he reports that the life around him turns negative. He has come to the point where he accepts the notion that what you sow is what you reap. Roland applies that well to his life. While it may not make his daily struggle any different, he feels better about being alive and, therefore, feels more welcome and courageous towards facing the new day head-on.

Positive people may accomplish more than negative people. Happiness, itself a relative term, may be dependent on attitude and personality. An article (Schutz et al. 2013) comparing relative levels of happiness to personality type found that, "People who are considered 'self-fulfilling'—meaning they have a high positive affect and a low negative affect—are more likely to be happy, have less depressive symptoms and have higher life-satisfaction, than other personality types" (p. 1). Researchers have identified exactly what kind of personality type is most strongly linked with life satisfaction and happiness. Positive affect is defined as reacting more intensely to positive things, while negative affect is defined as reacting more intensely to negative things. For the study, researchers created four categories of personality based on these concepts of negative and positive affect: "self-fulfilling" people with high positive affect and low negative affect; "self-destructive" people with low positive affect and high negative affect; high-affective people with high positive and negative affect; and low-affective people with low positive and negative affect.

The researchers, who are from the University of Gothenburg, Linnaeus University, and the Network for Empowerment and Well-Being in Sweden, also found that these "self-fulfilling" people were more likely to use certain strategies to boost their moods (p. 9). Specifically, effective happiness-boosting strategies included receiving support from friends, self-acceptance, self-control, and seeking support from the proactive practice of one's religion/faith. (Other strategies examined by researchers included partying and clubbing, passive leisure activities like surfing the Internet, active leisure activities like exercising, and mental control in the form of telling yourself to stop being unhappy.) Other research has shown links between life outlook and happiness, as well as social connectedness and happiness. The Harvard Grant Study, conducted over a period of 75 years, showed that love and social connections are crucial to leading a happy and successful life (Gregoire 2013, p. 1).

Introspection and Attitude

Attitudes are a part of our personal identity, the sense of our self as a person. A person, according to Locke, is, "…a thinking intelligent being, that has reason and reflection, and can consider itself as itself, the same thinking thing, in different times and places" (Perry 2008, p. 39). One technique, useful in self-judging and reforming negative patterns, is to review at the end of the day the events of the day and, specifically, what attitudes came into being. This is reflective-thinking, a form of introspection. Consequences of portions of a person's thinking can result in negativity. When that happens, there is potential to consider projective replacement of that attitude with a different one and the consideration that the predictive outcome had that attitude been present.

Handling the Ravages of Discouragement

Perhaps the most potent challenge facing a person struggling to overcome a problem is discouragement. Discouragement is a loss of confidence, or dispiritedness. When perceived, the person may shut down his effort to triumph over difficulties. In contrast, the ideal of encouragement is where a person is championed towards achievement by others. Some professional athletes do better when cheered on by the crowd. What about the case of a person trying to climb a mountain when that person is alone? Who can cheer him or her on? In such cases, the internal will of the person is the lone resource for encouragement.

When people feel discouragement, they tend to shrink their efforts to a low point and enter a feeling of depressed mood. It is not only their confidence to overcome a particular problem that is adversely affected. Their self-esteem becomes challenged and they may start to exhibit signs of withdrawal, moodiness, fatigue, and gloom. Pulling them out of such a morass is not easy. The onset of feelings of discouragement can come from only a few harsh words, such as, “You’re no good.” Failure noticed by others becomes the deepest form of failure and can be felt as complete failure. What follows is the destruction of a portion of the person’s resilience to withstand negative energy. In a way, the person can become slowly beaten down by the onslaught of repeated discouraging blows to their ego. As we have discussed, while this should not be the case, it oftentimes is.

Sometimes, a setback in the form of failure can actually benefit the person who desires to be as perfect as possible. Therefore, she/he looks upon failure as a part of the process of success, or as the learning process to achieve success. Some are relatively immune to the negative comments of others about their failures. Early on in the US space exploration programs, National Aeronautics and Space Administration (NASA) experienced many failures, using test pilots to try out new rocketry until it succeeded in landing a human on the surface of the moon and returning him safely to Earth. Other even more ambitious missions followed. Many of them succeeded; some failed, resulting in loss of life. But without explorers, how would mankind reach new destinations and develop new capabilities? Individuals, too, can break through previous impenetrable barriers (like the sound barrier) and crash through paradigms through sheer determined effort.

Helping a person cope with the agony of defeat as a motivator to rise like a phoenix from the ashes is to encourage a person not to give up. While some efforts may appear to be futile or pipe dreams, is it ever fair for one person to tell another where the limits are? Reality is the sense of proportion that comes with being rationale and is best approached as a study of all facts that can be known and a fair assessment made of all perceptible risks. Once that work is accomplished, trying and redefining one’s boundaries may be the optimal course of action. Foolishness may take center stage when a person attempts to do something that is, at face value, extremely likely to fail and lead to injury. For example, a person who feels that she/he can fly and jumps off a tall building only to crash to his or her death would be seen as foolish or mentally disturbed. However, a person who walks across a tightrope and succeeds is seen as heroic and brave. What draws the line between an act of bravery and an act of foolishness?

True support of a person is to first understand what she/he wishes to accomplish and how she/he intends to prepare. Then, we must act in accord with offered support and cheer him or her on despite what may amount to our own internal fear of his or her failure. Once we come to terms with ourselves, we may be better able to separate our internal fear and being afraid to watch someone else fail. But we must be careful not to destroy another person’s dream solely because of our own fear. That would be unduly discouraging. In a counseling situation, acknowledgement of the sovereignty of a person’s right to choose (assuming an adult of competency) is the starting point that must be established prior to reacting to stimuli of watching a person do something or being made aware of a person’s intent to perform some feat.

In a discussion about the potency of discouragement with Rex (Kreuter 2013a), he said a few things worth noting that point to how one specific person shifted his thinking as a way to counter what would likely have led to his feeling discouraged:

- "It is better to do something than to do nothing."
- "Love is a currency."
- "Things turn around when I'm in communion with God."
- "So many things in the framework prove everything is manageable."
- "Persist in prayer beyond our limits."

Rex's mother said to him: "You are wonderful just the way you are." Rex felt good. He made eggplant parmesan for his roommates and they responded well to him. Socializing has become very important to Rex.

A Matter of Choice

James (1908) talked about the concept of choice—both a live choice and a dead one.

1. A live choice has some emotive appeal to the chooser. This is an internal and subjective appeal, not a rational or forced appeal.
2. A dead option or choice is one which has no appeal to the chooser in question (p. 135).

"The great world, *the background*, in all of us, is the world of our *beliefs*. That is the world of the permanencies and immensities" (p. 135). An option is forced when there is an either-or situation that does not comport with what the person would want to do. Most forced options involve such a choice. An avoidable option is when a person is asked to choose either A or B, but that can be evaded by not choosing at all. Opposed to this are trivial options—options which do not really make much difference in the world or ones where you have the option all over again in the near future (Corbett 1980, p. 1). However, whether something is material or trivial is a matter of opinion and, therefore, ambiguous. James would say that we are born with our beliefs, but are we? Can we choose to not believe something previously believed? Perhaps we can retrofit our attitude about something or see it through the lens of an altered perspective, which can have the impact similar to us changing our belief. The difference, as James pointed out, is that we cannot rationally exempt proven knowledge or belief from our systems through will. To do so would require artificial modification of thoughts we hold firm. The issue of our free will enters into the picture when we examine our choices. We may be easily influenced by popular thought or by political leaders or by the press, but each of us has our own internal code that may override such messages. Being skeptical is also part of our exercising of our will. President Ronald Reagan had a saying: "Trust but verify." It is the verification process that makes the difference between being overly influenced and being considerate of our optional choice to believe or not to believe. Accepting personal responsibility for our choices equates, as James would say, to taking responsibility for our fate. "Believe, and you shall be right, for you shall save yourself. Doubt, and you shall again be right, for you will perish. The only difference is that to believe is greatly to your advantage" (James 1882, p. 75).

In daily life there are numerous opportunities directly or indirectly linked to the feeling of discouragement. It could be the loss of an important client for a professional, receipt of an unexpectedly large invoice, or a letter denying insurance coverage for a past procedure. When too many discouraging things happen in a relatively short period of time, a person can start to take on symptoms of overwhelming helplessness and, even, depression. Worsening of this state can lead to development of maladaptive thinking and withdrawal from some challenging, but worthwhile, life endeavors (i.e., the syndrome of giving up). In isolation, perhaps any one form of discouragement would not be enough to derail a person's life, as she/he might take the issue in stride (acceptance) and just move on (cope and deal). But, for some, even one discouragement could lead to a setback or downward spiral of mood and affect, in essence creating a negative turning point affecting the person profoundly.

With the help of a guide, discouraging news can be handled by keeping a solid perspective about the importance of the particular matter, why it happened, what it actually means, and then by inventorying what negative consequences follow along. People tend to take on forms of catastrophic thinking when something bad happens. A medical test is thought to result in terrible news even before the test has been read by a physician. A person may be worried about the total loss of his or her business just because of the loss of a single customer. More is often made of less. Could it be that there is a human tendency to expect disappointment? Humans think about the future, which, for some, can bring on stress and worry, and for other, a sense of hope. Perhaps a workable strategy is to take on the fullness of life, inclusive of its inherent ups and downs and the occasionally occurring disasters. Problems will occur. Calamities will always be possible. Humans are perpetually vulnerable to the risk of exposure to accident, natural disasters, or other unfortunate happenings.

Shifting Spiritual Emphasis

We began this chapter by discussing spirituality and spirituality-directed counseling. The Bible, Torah, the Koran, the Bhagavad Gita, the Dhammapada (the Path of production, collections of aphorisms that illustrate the moral teachings of Buddha), or other religious texts can form the basis for such counseling. Some people discover or rediscover their spirituality during their life. John Lennon stated during an interview in 1967: "I don't and never did imagine God as one thing. But now I can see God as a power source, or as an energy" (Gregoire 2013, p. 1).

Examples of Metaphor Useful in Christian Counseling[1]

Sometimes the use of a metaphor can trigger a change of mindset in the person who has had a lapse in his or her faith. The following examples are included in this book to show how a therapist or a religious counselor can augment the process of helping a spiritually troubled person through the use of imagery and metaphor.

[1] These views are Kreuter's.

The Ultimate Bench Strength

Having God on the team means the confidence of certain defeat of all adversity. Acquiring God on your team requires only a commitment to love, honor, and obey Him, as well as adhering to those other tenets of God's legislation commonly referred to as the Commandments. It is a long-term contract with spectacular back-end loaded benefits, such as, in Christian teaching, everlasting life in an incorruptible body.

Christians are quite fortunate to have solid bench strength when praying directly to the Father is either difficult or not what works for you in a particular circumstance. On the bench is found the beloved Son, Jesus Christ. Also, Christians can always call upon the Holy Spirit to either pinch-hit or act as a closer. Balancing the line-up of an all-star squad are the saints who each have a designated specialty. Of course, there is Mary, the Mother of God, to intercede for us.

The game strategy is a simple one—prayer. It works for the spiritual self. One cannot, though, demand a specific action, no more than one could have demanded that Mariano Rivera throw a strike at any moment of the game. One need not even worry about probabilities. Faith and trust in the Living God is all that is needed to see the game through to its proper conclusion. Human minds cannot determine the optimal conclusion, but God and the team can, through their collective bench strength. There can be no failure. Even when people drop the ball or strike out while swinging foolishly at a bad pitch, God is lenient and patient and helps them shake off the dust and get back in the game.

God is more than a coach, far more powerful than a manager, and trumps ownership through His Divine authority over mortal subjects. The essence of God's game plan is to love, and inspire to love Him and others as Him. Thus, God smiles approving, each time people lend a helping hand to others who have dropped the ball, struck out, or fallen away from the power of the bench.

Importantly, God does not keep score. Were He to do so, people would all be traded or dropped from the line-up. Instead, the roster is comprised of people just like us: sinners, selfish souls, and thoughtless folks. But this is precisely the reason God heads up the team and finds purpose in saving people from certain devastation. He is, therefore, the constant crusader and the optimal manager of the team.

Fruit of the Womb: We are God's Creation

Referring to birth, Buber (2000/1958) said, "He has stepped out of the glowing darkness of chaos into the cool light of creation. But he does not possess it yet; he must first draw it truly out, he must make it into a reality for himself his own world by seeing and hearing and touching and shaping it" (p. 37). As a metaphor for creation, one can consider a loom. A loom is a device used to weave cloth. Weaving is done by intersecting the longitudinal threads. The fruit of the loom is cloth made of fibers of many types. Similarly, in Christian teaching, we are like disconnected fibers having been woven by the Creator—God. Born of the womb, people share a common entry to the world with Jesus, but not the same origin. Jesus was the perfect cloth, unable to be stained, torn, or destroyed. Christians, however, were designed to start a Christian life unstained by virtue of Baptism, confirmed, then sent on their way to face the temptations found on the long road ahead. As such, to Christians, believers are given the beautiful gift of choice, whereas Jesus only had one choice—to bring salvation to the wicked and pay the ultimate price for the sins of Man by enduring the excruciation of crucifixion. We display the figure of the suffered Christ on the cross of salvation as a poignant reminder of the singular intention of the father—God to save His people from devastation.

The loom is used to interlace thread. God weaves character through situational challenge and varying degrees of opening one's eyes, as well as understanding. The finished product (the human person) is comprised of perfect design because the weaver is perfect. Because of the difference in origin, our fibers are not same as those used to bring Jesus into the world through the womb of Saint Mary. One's fibers are designed to have potential for failing, which also sets up numerous opportunities for success. Such success is based on individual gifts and the choices one makes in life. Without this granular dichotomy of choice, human existence would be disingenuous as a true gift. In any gift, the recipient is free to make choices as to use. God's ultimate brilliance was to provide a soul along with complete freedom. God provides influence over lives in the way one's sense perceive movement in the world as well as the silent voice speaking to us. We can ignore or override the voice if she/he is blessed to hear it and, if done, it equates to tragedy, both for them and for God, who surely laments each time we sin or turn our back on the messages, or even the gift of life itself.

The main processes and motions of the loom are shedding, picking, battering, and taking-up operations. All of these motions turn yarn into cloth. God's methods are similar. Shedding is the removal of sin from the lives of Christian believer's lives through confession and absolution. Picking is the selection of those saved from the unsaved. Battering is the process of living a human life, confronting the daily challenges, and reading the more sternly written passages in the Bible, which are well designed to point out that spiritual death is the fruit of a sinful life. Taking-up is God's guided process purifying the souls post-mortem through the purgatorial deliberations and the Heavenly arbitration, whereby Christians may be further blessed with a new body to be refused with their intact soul to be forever in harmony with the Lord. Once done, the renewed cloth can no longer be corrupted. Unless they go through the loom of God or birth through the womb of our mother, life is purposeless. God does not waste material. It is in this regard that they must care about every person and even every other form of life because their human discernment is not capable of knowing who is godly and who is not. We judge usually on superficial grounds. If God, the weaver, were to do this they all would have been deposited into the waste basket and burned up.

Thus, when God battens their fibers through the formed patterns of their unique existences, he does so with the purest love and care. Once created, we progress through life as humans with potential for use as a conduit of love or a catalyst of hate. God does not make this choice, but most certainly provides influences. It is for this reason that communion becomes the essential renewal of the weaver's promise. With God inside, Christians are more prepared to withstand stainable activity. It is like adding a new thread to the existing design, which, in a way, acts to repair spiritual damage of sinning. Believers all need these new threads.

Commentary—Roland Provence (a devout Christian living in Sarasota, Florida) (*note—the references are to author Kreuter*)

I spent last eve and part of this morning absorbing and taking notes on your dynamic piece "spiritual writing." It stunned me. Your words land much like the writers of Catholic apologetics that I had briefly read recently (Fundamentals of Faith, Peter Kreeft's Socratic logic). Oftentimes, I feel as if I were a piece of cloth being expanded and repaired as a catholic man. I got quite a lot of love and understanding from reading it. Have you thought of becoming a man of the cloth (Smiles)? Well, you seem to be made of strong fiber in my opinion.

Firstly, it is difficult as humans to let go of EGO (my point of view), so life is difficult, but not impossible to come back and be a part of "the fabric of Life" no matter what. Therein is just some of the 2000-year tradition of the Catholic Church. I still hear Fr. Fausto's words, "Welcome Home," after absolution. The bottom line is that we all need a SAVIOR or we stay lost. I am glad that your piece included the actions that are necessary: confession and Eucharist. Even writing a small commentary after reading your piece is difficult. How so Roland? This life is a long process. Writing is a birthing process.

I like the phrasing that makes the distinction that we are the same as the Son of Man yet not of the same origin. After two or three readings, it hit me re: the existential dilemma of being human, a sometimes thinking animal.

"The beautiful gift of choice" is a burden and a show of the loving Creator. What comes up for me is Our loving Father–Creator sent Jesus (Himself) to save his kids (us) because he hates evil and sin. Ron, the Ironworker always remarked on how humanists tend to forget and gloss over sin and evil with relativistic ethics, the story of the 70s. Well, yes, the beginning is just to hate evil.

The word "devastation" is on target with the enormity of the effects of sin over a lifetime. And yet, this enormous God, when we let Him, moves us and places us back into the fabric of living again. He does not throw us away if we surrender the ego. Again, that it just a point of view based on my painful experience as one dot in the universe, seeing that others in the family of humanity are battered emotionally and tested similarly.

God is more than just the Dream Weaver interlacing the threads of our existence. Fr. Martin remarks how sweetly interdependent we all are in this fragile life on Earth. There is a Perfect Designer as the Deists and Physics boys are showing. Yet, why not see the God-man Jesus? It hurts. That is why it costs. Make the leap and you are never the same. For me, your writings of the situational challenges as part of the perfect plan are "bang on" regarding my own life view now. The Zohar (Kabballah) writes that we as souls are tested so that we can grow in the Light. Revealed more than 2000 years ago, the *Zohar* is a spiritual text that explains the secrets of the Bible, the Universe, and every aspect of life.

I like the phrases: God's Ultimate Brilliance, and how you work the reader towards that encounter. We tend to forget to be in awe of God's plan. For me, I often have to give up how my mind interprets how things ought to be. The lines of us as fibers with the potential for failing is so, so accurate. Hubris, I discounted it, often to my peril. It is remarkable to me how you see The Watchmaker, the Architect of the Universe, yes, God processing us. God as being at the loom: shedding, picking, battening—I liked your usage of those expressions to get your points across.

I considered - Taking us from yarn to cloth. Best of all, I enjoyed seeing the writing of my friend Eric, concluding in this writing, that the battering of our fibers occurs so we become a channel of love versus hate. Those are the gripping words of your piece for me.

Eric, this writing impressed me and, again, stimulated my view that you take the challenge of writing about the faith, which is difficult, and you do so with passion. Yes, it strikes me as though again we are kindred spirits. Thank you for sending this piece.

Spirituality

People decide whether they want it or do not want it. St. Augustine said, "Please God, make me good, but not just yet" (Morton 2013, p. 1). This can be applied to say that people can seek to become positive, but may not be ready to abandon their negativity. Such abandoning is a process with notable attached and ongoing requirements: physical, mental, emotional, and, also, spiritual. The metaphor about the glass being half empty or half full is of one's view of life. Akin to an hourglass, one can perceive the sands of time slipping away to never be felt, seen, or heard from again—a wasting away, or, the grains of sand falling onto those already placed, can be viewed as building on what has already been accomplished thus adding to the foundation, building on what has already been built to form a greater, if not yet complete, whole.

"I think it fair to say that no theory of psychology will ever be complete that does not centrally incorporate the concept that man has his future within him, dynamically active at this present moment" (Maslow 1961, p. 59). Capra (1996) wrote:

> Ultimately, deep ecological awareness is spiritual or religious awareness. When the concept of the human spirit is understood as the mode of consciousness in which the individual feels a sense of belonging, of connectedness, to the cosmos as a whole, it becomes clear that ecological awareness is spiritual in its deepest essence (p. 7).

As part of the evolutionary process where humans transitioned from Southern apes (Australopithecus), the brain grew in response to the need for "...supportive families and communities, and the freedom of the hands to make and use tools..." (Capra 1996, p. 293). As language developed, so did abstract thinking, "…bringing forth an inner world of concepts, objects, and images of ourselves" (p. 294). In time, man began to create and to express the inner psyche through art, etc., leading both the development of wonders as well as horrors in terms of aggression exacted on people by people. Capra (1996) wrote about the fluidity of life:

> Out of ignorance (*avidya*), we divide the perceived world into separate objects that we see as firm and permanent, but which are really transient and ever-changing. Trying to cling to our rigid categories instead of realizing the fluidity of life, we are bound to experience frustration after frustration (p. 294–295).

In Capra's view, "To regain our full humanity, we have to regain our experience of connectedness with the entire web of life" (p. 296). Perhaps, we can view a troubled person having lost the connectivity within his or her own life and that of his or her existing universe (the world immediately around him or her). As commonly perceived through the lens of the egocentric viewpoint, people live in bubbles or cloisters of small groups. Even within the individual mind, the vast cavern of thoughts can sometimes overwhelm a person, causing schism between what is done and what ought to be done in order for the person to live happily and adjust to the stressors of everyday existence. As Maddi and Costa (1972) wrote, "Perhaps the most basic of the convictions shared by Allport, Maslow, and Murray is that man has internal processes and structures that have a causal influence upon perception, thought, feeling and action" (p. 16).

Humans have the unique ability to determine what is right and what is wrong. Halbertal (2014) referenced the Aristotelian conception as, "…man's defining quality is his ability to distinguish between truth and falsity" (p. 138). Moses Maimonides (1135–1204) believed that human perfection is attained through intellectual activity and that the fulfillment of the active commandments was a means rather than an end (Halbertal 2014, p. 139). In the practice of many faiths, helping people cope and deal with their corporeal needs is, obviously, more urgent than initiatives geared towards perfecting the person's soul.

> On an elementary level, there is but one desire which issues from the biopsychic unity of the person, namely the desire to discharge inner tensions, whether they pertain to the sphere of hunger or of sexuality. This is impossible without contact with the outer world. Hence, the *first* impulse of every creature must be a desire to establish contact with the outer world (Reich 1972/1945, p. 271).
> As Halbertal (2014) wrote:
>> Because man is also a material creature, he needs an orderly, well-structured society that can provide him the necessities of life. To that end, there must be polity ordered by law, whose purpose is to deal with bodily needs. That purpose is served as well by the development of moral qualities, both because they make possible the existence of a proper society and because they allow man to control his other impulses, a precondition to a life of inquiry and contemplation (p. 138).

The philosophy of Maimonides can be applied to the concept of negative schemas in that the person who is troubled by the impact of negative thinking can be led to a process of reconsideration of his or her very purpose on earth and the ultimate dispensation of all that she/he will mean to the world upon his or her passing. While dramatic, the essence of the therapy borrowing from Jewish tradition is to help the person to see the connection between his negative patterns and how continuation of them will lead the person astray, thus losing his direct path to reach their goals. It is the blind of thought who are most likely vulnerable to the distortion caused by twisted thinking. A guide is very important to help a person going off onto patterns of distortion to slow down, recognize his actions, attitudes, impressions, beliefs, and feelings, to then redirect, reposition, reorient, and transform himself into a more enlightened, better able, and more effective being. In Maimonides' writings, most men do not live fully human lives (p. 78).

A person can be in conflict in terms of his attitude concerning his sense of reality. Hegel (1977/1807) wrote:

> The various modes of the negative attitude of consciousness, the attitude of skepticism and that of theoretical and practical idealism, are inferior shapes compared with that *of pure insight* and its diffusion, of the Enlightenment; for pure insight is born of the substance [of Spirit], knows the pure *self* of consciousness to be absolute, and enters into dispute with the pure consciousness of the absolute essence of all reality (p. 320).

Reality is that which actually exists as compared with an idealistic notion of the state of existence of a thing. Thus, the way a person interprets his or her own reality must be first understood on his or her terms as he or she applies it to his or her life. Once she/he is helped to gain insight, the process of treating maladaptive thinking can commence. Pure insight is the rationally courageous project of an individual thinker (Harris 1953, p. 332).

The construct of courage has important meaning for the psychotherapist. "… Every existing person has the character of self-affirmation, the need to preserve its centeredness. The particular name we give this self-affirmation in human beings is 'courage'" (May 1961, p. 77). "So I know, here and now, stripped of all delusions, that I am affirmed, that there is meaning in the absurdity of life. Meaning which brings happiness" (Ratzinger 1986, p. 15).

Synopsis of Chapter

- Spirituality acts as a basic guide for many people in how they act and respond to their universe.
- Consciousness is that which occurs inside the mind.
- For some, the internal belief system is brought about through spirituality.
- An event or slowly slipping away from faith can disconnect people from their spirituality.
- A loss of connectedness can create a schism in a person's life.
- Attitudes can be chosen and are part of our personal identity.
- Not everyone is ready to abandon their negativity.

Chapter 4
Schema-Focused Cognitive Therapy

Life isn't about finding yourself. Life is about creating yourself.

—George Bernard Shaw

Introduction

A person may say she/he is not a pessimist, but an optimist with experience. Pessimism, when applied inwardly, can lead to negative thought, which can extend to patterns. Schema Therapy is used to help people change maladaptive patterns in their lives. Some of these patterns may have lasted for many years. "Schema Therapy (or more properly, Schema-Focused Cognitive Therapy) is an integrative approach of treatment that combines the best aspects of cognitive-behavioral, experiential, interpersonal, and psychoanalytic therapies into one unified model" (Pearl 2013, p. 1). Dr. Jeff Young, who developed the schema-focused model, studied people who had not benefited from other forms of treatment "...discovered that these people typically had long-standing patterns or themes in thinking, feeling and behaving/coping that required a different means of intervention" (p. 1).

Usually beginning early on in life, these negative patterns of thought interfere with the person's ability to reach goals set for his life. For some, lowering their sights may be an understandable response due to trauma or repeated negative attention during the formative years. Perhaps the most basic negative schema is the mantra: "I'm not important" or "I'm not good enough." Instead of "Why not me?" the person thinks herself/himself into believing "It will not be me." Some civic or religious leaders have used the constantly repeated idea that the person is important in their speeches to rouse the crowd into repeating the phrase, thus building resilience into their minds, encouraging a "can do" attitude (the Rev. Jesse Jackson, for example). Negative thinking can occur later in life, perhaps triggered by a bad experience. Schema therapy attempts to break these negative patterns and replace them with positive thinking. Staying positive is a great start from which thinking can develop, which can enable the brain to alter its patterns.

E. A. Kreuter, K. M. Moltner, *Treatment and Management of Maladaptive Schemas*,
DOI 10.1007/978-3-319-06817-6_4, © Springer International Publishing Switzerland 2014

In Kreuter's (2005, 2006b, 2007b) work with female prisoners, the same concept was used to encourage transformation of the mindset of the prisoners from a common sense of failure to a shift in their energy, focusing on their potential for future success. This process is accomplished through catalyzing a change of will and creating a transcendent sense of determination. A simple breathing exercise provides an example: asking the client to choose a color representative of good and one for bad, then, asking them to breathe out "bad" and breathe in "good." This exercise is more than a metaphor. It involves active participation in the mind of the clients with a physical response showing them that they do have control over how they think. Through the process of encouraging them to consider what is positive in their lives, they are placed in a better position to begin the process of rebuilding their lives. There are questions raised by some inmates, of course, concerning their future, expressing negative recurring thoughts of how it will likely be on the "outside" where they will be stigmatized and labeled like wearing a scarlet letter around their necks. By showing them that it is primarily important for them to have a renewed sense of themselves as worthy beings, they are better able to accept the notion that others may view them with disdain or suspicion. Certainly prospective employers may hold their past against them, but that is the reality of having a prison record. Despite the formidable challenge, they still can face their future brightly and avoid judging themselves on a constant basis. Doing so would be tantamount to continuing the punishment long after release. Again, it is attitude that makes the difference in the person being able to make a successful transition to life following incarceration.

Even those who never experience imprisonment can act like they have been or are in a form of psychological confinement. Living a life mostly apart from others can bring a person into a state of being a recluse. Similarly, a person who feels frustrated about not being able to find employment, for example, may become self-isolating refusing to remain actively engaged in the community. Such a person may begin to act like a hermit, possibly using sleep, drugs, or alcohol as means to escape reality. As such, the practice of interacting with others in public may dissipate as a skill, requiring relearning. Regardless of the reason for the schism between being a fully functional and happy person in society and having grown psychologically apart from society, there are answers to the persistence of the problem of negative schema. Those answers can be found in the brave willingness to enter into a process of delving into the abyss of the self in order to first uncover then to resolve blockages in life. It is a process that brings with it some emotional pain and perhaps frustration as the necessary trial-and-error method is followed.

Schema-focused cognitive treatment begins with assessment of the various patterns involved followed by clients getting in touch with their emotional awareness of these patterns in daily life, then, ultimately, replacing negative thoughts with positive ones (Pearl 2013, p. 1). Pearl outlined types of negative patterns of thought:

1. Abandonment/instability
2. Mistrust/abuse
3. Emotional deprivation
4. Defectiveness/shame

5. Social Isolation/alienation
6. Dependence/incompetence
7. Vulnerability to harm or illness
8. Enmeshment/undeveloped self
9. Failure
10. Entitlement/grandiosity
11. Insufficient self-control/self-discipline
12. Subjugation
13. Self-sacrifice
14. Approval-seeking/recognition-seeking
15. Negativity/pessimism
16. Emotional inhibition
17. Unrelenting standards/hypercriticalness
18. Punitiveness (pp. 2–3)

In treating a client for negative schema, the relationship between the client and the therapist may have a strong impact on outcomes reached during treatment. As a way of encouraging the client to open up, the propensity of the therapist to listen and allow some silence may stimulate the client to contribute more information, useful in later analysis. "Something introduced by the analyst (rather than by the patient) is likely to be experienced as belonging to the analyst's agenda, not the patient's" (Casement 2002, p. 97).

Casement (2002) found that "…it is sometimes appropriate to respond to the quality of an initial silence, taking this also as a communication that can at least be acknowledged" (p. 97). This period of reflection can lead to the client's deeper connection to where she/he is at that moment. In the existential approach, determining where the client is (psychologically) is vital to the process of treatment. Periods of silence can simulate this identification and communication with the therapist. Should the therapist be impatient or try to take over the treatment session, then "therapy" might be corrupted.

The Mentoring Dilemma

Coaching is closely related to the act of mentoring, whether done individually or under the auspices of an established group. A short list of things effective mentors do is as follows:

- Listen carefully.
- Teach by example.
- Offer encouragement.
- Empower.
- Share ideas.
- Provide helpful advice.
- Assist in the creation of workable strategies.

- Lead by example.
- Involve everyone in the process.
- Suggest to others to consider alternative solutions to problems and to choose the optimal solution wherever possible.
- Monitor the progress of others.
- Offer positive reinforcement.
- Guide when there are shortcomings.
- Offer constructive criticism.
- Motivate.

Within the mentor/mentee relationship, there may be a problem involving either reluctance or resistance on the part of the mentee. The reluctant mentee may avoid being completely open with his or her mentor. In this situation, the depth and quality of the dyad is stifled. Equally obstructive to the value of the relationship is when the mentee does listen to the active advice of the fully committed mentor, but does not make any effort to consider adoption of the information—not because of any worthy challenge to its soundness, but due to a negative attitude towards any outside help. Reluctance and resistance, therefore, can exacerbate an already maladaptive schema. In a poem titled *Reluctance* by Robert Frost (1874–1963) (2014/1915):

> Ah, when to the heart of man
> Was it ever less than a treason
> To go with the drift of things,
> To yield with a grace to reason,
> And bow and accept the end
> Of a love or a season. (p. 1)

Masking the Pain

Too often, the person who is down creates for herself/himself a psychological mask. The purpose of a mask, in general, is to create a disguise to conceal one's identity. This is done creatively and dramatically in the hit show *The Lion King* where the human actors hold or wear masks that make them appear to be animals. The masks provide just enough illusion to transport you into belief that the characters are transformed into beasts. People also carry around masks to conceal their true selves, whether their feelings or their fears, without resolving the underlying issues. We recognize this in sayings such as:

- She/he is keeping up a good front.
- She/he is putting on airs.
- Despite the tragedy, a person is acting bravely.

In some cultures, a man who loses his job may continue to dress for work and leave the house at the regularly established time only to walk around the city or sit on a park bench brooding. An analogy can be drawn to masking physical pain. One of the authors has back issues. His doctor prescribed an anti-inflammatory drug, but clearly told him that while the drug might alleviate the pain it would not cure the underlying issue. The drug could address (and perhaps only temporarily) the symptoms, but he was not led into the false belief that it would cure the problem. The cure, if there was to be one absent surgery—and that might not necessarily work—could be physical therapy to strengthen the back muscles and constantly doing the physical therapy exercises at home.

Drinking alcohol to excess is a psychological mask. In one of Kreuter's prison groups, the topic of the label "alcoholic" came up. Many of the inmates suggested that the very label hurts their motivation to overcome their having made poor choices whether done under the influence of alcohol or otherwise. So, too, perhaps a negative person must not be labeled as being merely "negative" because of absent self-esteem; this label also could undermine his or her will to find ways to climb out of the morass and begin to thrive again. So too, using illicit drugs is a psychological mask. They may provide a perceived temporary respite from the problems, too often at the expense of the person's ultimate health, but drug and alcohol abuse do not address the underlying issues. With reference to the analogy of using a prescription drug to mask physical pain, drugs and alcohol are worse for they do not even address the symptoms. They may help avoid, for whatever time, thinking, or being able to think, about the problems. They may provide an "escape" or moments of facial satisfaction, and thus provide the perceived respite to which we referred, but they address nothing (the person would be better off going for a jog or swim or even watch a favorite TV show. Such activities would similarly provide a respite, a temporary avoidance, but in a healthy way, certainly at least for the jog or swim). In fact, studies have shown that physical activity helps depressed people. "There is evidence from four prospective epidemiological studies that those who become or remain active or fit are less likely to suffer clinical depression" (Fox 1999, p. 412). After the drug or alcohol state is lifted, the problems are still there and maybe even exacerbated by the realization that they have not gone away and drugs or alcohol will not make them go away.

Prescription antidepressant medication is better than alcohol or drug abuse, but it, like the anti-inflammatory, addresses symptoms (on a longer basis than drugs or alcohol) but not the problem. Exercise can augment therapy. Mutrie (2001) reviewed various controlled studies on the effect of exercise on depression and concluded, in part, that the effect is on the same scale of success as psychotherapeutic intervention. For problems, especially psychological ones, they do not go away by themselves. Analogous to the constant work required to strengthen back muscles, the negative person must recognize that he has a problem that she/he has been unable to resolve, and seek solutions that address the problem, including strengthening his or her resolve to fight the negativity.

Negative people may also be trapped in a viscous cycle of maintaining their negative aura because it may lower expectations people have of them to succeed in life and they have for themselves. It becomes, then, to the person a self-fulfilling prophecy to "wear" a mask of negativity because she/he believes that any effort to overcome its impact will have little or no effect. As a result, staying in a negative zone becomes inviting as it excuses the person from taking chances where failure is an essential option. The price paid, of course, is the chance for success is snuffed out due to the person not even trying. Such logic is very counterintuitive and becomes self-feeding. Some may refer to this as laziness, but, if examined more closely as a mask, the person could be a good candidate for coaching to stimulate greater willingness for entering a process of trials. Without taking some chances, there is a guarantee of nonachievement of success. The shift in schema is to recognize the inherent value of risking failure as a way to attain potential success.

Gentle persuasion, or therapeutic assistance, may help the person to take down the mask and allow for the person to begin experiencing the actual feeling of the trials and tribulations of ordinary life, which may, legitimately, involve challenges. Confrontation, a less gentle technique, may wake a person up who has been living a long-term existence buried under a false façade. This confrontation can be some through questions (Socratic) with encouragement of the person to ask himself if the mask is at all valid. Once the person starts to decommission the mask reality seeps in and the person can now begin to engage with coach or therapist to explore his responding to actual stimuli in his life. Through such experiential work, the cognitive, behavioral, and emotional issues will have a chance to rise to the surface where they can be first noticed, then understood, and then, finally, addressed. Clarity involves replacing negative energy with positive energy, false auras with the reality of personal identity. Only with the awareness of who the person actually is can repair work be done, thereby reclaiming the whole person.

Like an onion being peeled, the layers of complication must be allowed to drift away, leaving the person exposed to resolve conflict and handle opportunities more fully engaged in a more authentic self-image. Pride of accomplishment can then occur when the person, stripped of falsity, begins to transcend into a truer person. Shakespeare wrote: "To thine own self be true" (Polonius, in Hamlet, Act 1; Scene 3). We can adapt this philosophy and apply it to everyday life and use it to provide keys to a hurting person to shake off false shields and become true to herself/himself, necessary before she/he is ready to become authentic when presenting to others.

Altering Patterns of Behavior

Behavior can be influenced by events and by personality. Patterns, when the term is expressed in relation to behavior, are repetitious following a predictable manner. Jung (2010/1973) developed the concept of the archetype. "The archetypes are formal factors responsible for the organization of unconscious psychic processes; they are 'patterns of behaviour'" (p. 20). To alter behavior, a person needs to be catalyzed effectively, which can start with a new determined mindset. It can also be guided through therapy or from the instigated reformed thinking brought about through a relationship with a coach.

The attitude of a patient can either support or block the potential for lasting change. If unblocked, the psyche goes through a process of renewal. "Any essential change of attitude signifies a psychic renewal which is usually accompanied by symbols of rebirth in the patient's dreams and fantasies" (p. 23). In turn, the general level of happiness in a person's life can be improved through such psychic renewal, which equates to dynamic movement. The benefit to the person's confidence is that it is boosted as a result of the improved attitude. This boost will likely lead to renewed optimism and the person becoming more creative and successful in his or her life. Tolle (2004) wrote about living in the present moment, called the "Now": "Find the 'narrow gate that leads to life'. It is called the Now. Narrow yourself down to this moment. Your life situation may be full of problems, most life situations are—but find out if you have any problem at this moment. Not tomorrow or in 10 minutes, but now. Do you have a problem now!" (p. 63). "When you create a problem, you create pain. All it takes is a simple choice, a simple decision: no matter what happens, I will create no more pain for myself. I will create no more problems" (p. 65).

Is Negativity Created or Genetic?

Some suggest that at birth, it would seem that we have a "clean slate"[1] upon which to build a life, which is impacted by experiences, thoughts, dreams, and our genetic makeup, as well as the unfortunate impact of trauma due to injury, accident, or ingestion of pharmacological substances. Development of a negative mindset seems more likely to be the product of selection of responses to stimuli, which are influenced by our intellectual and emotional intelligence, education, mentoring, and the consequences due to human error.

On the other hand, others argue that the slate cannot be clean because we are, at least initially, a product of our genetic makeup. If a person's parent or grandparent has or had a very negative attitude, for example, does the child or grandchild necessarily inherit this trait, disposition, or learned responsiveness? And does the offspring then proceed to model to some degree the behavior pattern of the elders, the "role models" in his or her midst? It seems very plausible that each capable person can nevertheless "personalize" his or her system of acting, which, as a composite, forms the person's schema.

If we consider stress as a component of the environmental background of any individual, then stress is one influence over the mindset of the person. According to Gaisler-Salomon (2014), "…it is undeniable that stress experienced during a person's lifetime is often correlated with stress-related problems in that person's offspring—and even in the offspring's offspring" (p. 1). Progeny of parents or grandparents who have suffered extreme pressures may have inherited certain predispositions, which may include how stressful situations are handled. Adopting

[1] The term "blank slate" can also be used in and refers to the epistemological theory that individuals are born without any fixed mental content. Those who favor the tabula rasa theory believe that a person's personality, emotional behavior, and intelligence derive from her/his experience and perception (the nurture argument).

this notion to the thesis of this book, perhaps it is at least worthy of consideration when doing an intake of a new client or for a coach or mentor to gather background on a new protégé for the purpose of examining this potential genetic component. Gaisler-Salomon (2014) refers to his study, conducted with peers, on experiments with rodents to make his point: "When rats or mice are out under duress, particularly during early development, their second and third generation offspring exhibit behavioral irregularities" (p. 1). They speculated that the genetic material encoded on a molecule involved in the way the body responds to stress is passed through: "…ova, or eggs of the stressed females in significantly concentrations" (p. 2).

Therefore, there is at least the potential for available clues to understanding the behavior of a person by looking into his or her genetic roots, but, even if discovery is made that parents or grandparents exhibited negative schema in their own lives, the current client cannot be "let off the hook" or excused from doing all he or she can to repel negativity and transcend towards a more productive, happy life. A woman, in Kreuter's prison group, explained that, although she recognized that she was an alcoholic, she did not want the label of alcoholic because it then could form the basis for an excuse for her behavior, which she rejected. Instead, she preferred to take full responsibility for her own plight and past and learn ways of coping notwithstanding the presence of the disease of alcoholism, whether genetically influenced or not.

As the late Dr. Eugene I. Taylor explained, we are not to be reduced to laboratory rats in that we are to be properly understood in more humanistic terms. Thus, while the research into genetics is extremely important, we must apply it to determine ways to treat the present suffering and credit the sufferers with at least a fighting chance to break through their paradigms and transition their mindset into more effective and positive directions. The therapist would normally "meet the client where they are" in cases where the new client does not wish to delve into the past, inclusive of the potential for clues to their present behavior which might be linked to a possible genetic component.

Neural Path Therapy

Neural pathways strengthen with use and weaken with disuse. Certain events can provoke a hardwired neural response, but a person is able to create new neural paths with a thought. In doing so, automatic triggers do not dictate our responses to painful events. Thus, the nervous system can be trained to short-circuit the response that lead to painful thoughts and emotions.

"Chemical imbalances exist because the neural pathway systems of the brain sometimes lead to emotional pain, i.e., anxiety and irrational conclusions" (Social Anxiety Institute 2013, p. 1). "Cognitive-behavioral therapy for social anxiety disorder causes literal changes in the brain which are measurable and 'seeable' using modern brain imaging equipment, such as MRIs and CT scans" (p. 1). "Social anxiety cannot occur unless events, situations, and circumstances in the persons' environment 'push' or 'lead' the person to develop it" (p. 2). "Because we develop social anxiety over time (although some people feel it hits them all at once), the brain is learning how to be socially anxious—this is cognitive structuring" (p. 2). "Anything you learn, regardless of what it is, becomes a part of the vast neuronal associations in the brain, which contain over one billion nerve cells" (p. 2).

Cognitive learning therapy works by learning and practicing new strategies and concepts so new neural pathways begin to form. Medication used to change neural pathways or associations is only temporary. Thus, learning new associations or pathways helps a person to extinguish social anxiety. Repetition through practice and trial reinforces the new associations. For example, a person who has a fear of public speaking can develop techniques to help ease the anxiety such as using small talk to warm up the crowd and getting comfortable in the particular setting prior to delivering technical material or other ice-breaking devices. Also, breathing techniques and movement around the room will serve to dissipate the nervous energy. Cognitive therapy teaches a client how to learn appropriate methods and strategies, which results in changes in brain neurology, leading to changes in brain chemistry. "Learning, for example, is a psychological phenomenon" (Grigsby and Stevens 2000, p. 14). "Theories of learning specify the cognitive and behavioral processes involved in acquiring a new skill or new information, whereas theories of synaptic plasticity concern themselves with what takes place in the brain while a person is learning" (p. 15).

> Today the medley of our outward lives has made a perplexity of our inward lives" (Derr 2001, p. iii). "We learn that the path we take is our free choice and that we can change our paths if we so desire. (p. iv)

New pathways can be created in the brain following new experiences. ".... When we realize we need to change the way we're coping with life's dramas and traumas, we can harness the power of neuroplasticity in our brain to create those changes. But we need to learn how" (Graham 2013, p. 50). "Two practices of choosing new experiences that science shows to be powerful catalysts in rewiring our brain are *mindfulness* and *empathy*" (p. 50). "Mindfulness—the steady, nonjudgmental awareness and acceptance of experience—leads to self-awareness and to shifts in our perspectives that allow us to see clearly what's happening and how we are reacting, to respond to triggers and traumas with for more open-mindedness, and to face the process of necessary change with far more flexibility and tolerance" (p. 51). "While mindfulness and observation—reflection create the self-awareness and expanded brain capacities that allow us to create the changes in our behaviors critical to resilience, the other essential catalyst for brain change—empathy—requires skillful interacting with other people to generate the connection and self-acceptance we also need for resilience" (p. 69). "The body stores somatic memories of previous stress and trauma, such as the tension in our arms if we have had to protect ourselves from intrusion; a clenching in our fists or jaw from when we wanted to strike out or speak out in self-protection but learned it wasn't safe to do so; the collapse in our gut when we have been shamed or humiliated" (pp. 218–219).

Research shows that "…our bodies cannot be anxious and relaxed at the same time" (p. 221). Exercises, such as ones involving breathwork, can attenuate the experiences of tension and relaxation, resulting in greater tolerance within the autonomic nervous system (p. 221). "When we seek out new experiences in relationships that frame both our strengths and our vulnerabilities as part of being human, we create new circuits in the brain that encode these new views of ourselves (new conditioning)" (pp. 160–161). "Evolutionarily and culturally, we are hard-wired and conditioned to look first for what's wrong, what's negative, and what's potentially dangerous in any situation" (p. 161). Rick Hanson (Hanson and Mendius 2009) refers to the process of pausing to let positive experiences sink deeply into the mind and body. "All emotions are, in essence, impulses to act: e-motion. When processed and expressed well, all emotions lead to resilient action" (p. 252).

> 'Switching the channel' by redirecting your attention to more positively optimistic thinking helps shake the brain loose of the old habit. You can learn examples of more positive thoughts—specific content—from role models, teachers, coaches, therapists, and friends. (pp. 326–327)

Normal people have moments of seemingly abnormality in their behavior. Understanding such behavior in terms of the whole and complex person, the therapist can help a client resolve small issues before they develop into major concerns. "It was while tracing back the abnormal to the normal state that Professor Freud found how faint the line of demarcation was between the normal and neurotic person, and that the psychopathologic mechanisms so glaringly, observe in the psychoneuroses and psychoses could usually be demonstrated in a lesser degree in normal persons" (Graham 2013, p. v).

Kernberg (1985) classified character pathology according "…to the degree to which repressive mechanisms or splitting mechanisms predominate" (p. 13). Kornberg referred to lower-level character disorders as: "…severe character pathology typically represented by the chaotic and impulse-ridden character, in contrast to the classical reaction-formation types of character structure and the milder 'avoidance trait' character" (p. 12).

As written by the Late Eugene Taylor (2009):

> Most of us live our entire lives oriented to the demands of the external environment without ever understanding that there are other worlds within. Some accident, a temporary illness, possibly a vision or a near-death experience, a certain poetic sensitivity, a religious quest, or simply an active urge to understand more about ourselves may push us beyond the immediate barriers that prevents us from even acknowledging the reality of the unconscious. (p. 129)
>
> As a way of reaching the unconscious, Jung's approach was more imaginal. He drew and painted what he could not intellectually articulate and later encouraged his patients to enter into such artistic productions, not to exhibit in the art galleries, or simply to develop their artistic sensibilities, but as a mere process activity. (p. 129)

Stanley Cobb (1887–1968), a neurologist who is considered the founder of biological psychiatry in the United States, "…insisted that the psychiatrist have a basic understanding of neuroanatomy and cerebral function" (White 1984, p. 217). Cobb saw psychoanalysis as one approach to the incredibly complex relations of mind, body, and environment (p. 218).

Treating Maladaptive Schemas in Prisoners

The cognitive component of empathy requires the therapist to "...maintain a sense of self that permits the therapist, while being deeply affectively connected, to make the complex clinical judgments that must be made" (Kaplan 1991, p. 47). In group therapy, to help the clients best, the therapist should develop a process of "...weaving individual issues into a group dynamic in order to provide guidance to at least the majority of participants" (Kreuter 2007b, pp. 159–160).

As a way of dealing with the inherent manifestations of guilt, Yalom (1980) stated: "In attempting to facilitate a patient's awareness of responsibility, the therapist soon discovers an uninvited presence in the therapeutic arena. That presence is guilt, which often trespasses into the process of existential psychotherapy" (p. 276). Kreuter (2007b) developed a suggestion, which he used in his volunteer counseling work with female inmates to help them deal with their guilt: "My suggestion is that such guilt be painted on the walls of their cells every day so that when the inmates are released from prison, such harmful feelings of guilt do not prohibit them from re-entering society as transformed beings, newly capable of making a contribution to society" (p. 160).

"By taking on the role of life coach, a therapist can instill change in the client" (Kreuter 2007b, p. 160). "The transferable helping skills, which trained and experienced therapists bring to the coaching relationship, are extremely valuable in facilitating successful change and growth for coaching clients" (Williams and Davis 2002, p. xiii). Ellis (1998) wrote: "Life coaches assist people to discover what they want in life and unlock their own brilliance to achieve it. Life coaching is about people generating their own answers, not looking outside of themselves for solutions" (p. 1).

The Gestalt Approach

Gestalt therapy stresses the construct of immediate experience. "Phenomenology seeks the truth or source of knowledge by concentrating on immediate experience, shorn of assumptions or presuppositions" (Clarkson 1989, p. 15). "It's phenomenological orientation implies a disciplined focus on experiencing what is obvious in a given situation without prejudgments or expectations" (p. 15). "The Gestalt approach originated in the existential-humanistic tradition of psychology" (p. 3).

Differentiated from Freudian psychoanalytical thinking, which viewed humans as biologically determined and motivated by sexual and aggressive instincts is the

Pavlovian school focusing on conditioned reflexes and learned behaviors. Behavior modification and cognitive-behavior theory stemmed from Pavlov's work.

The third force in psychology began in 1968 based on the work of Abraham Maslow. From this new theory evolved Gestalt. Using psychodrama, the client is placed in a central position to play out his or her life drama, empowering the client to do his or her own healing (p. 4). "The principles of Gestalt psychological theory were largely based on experiments in perception, which emphasized the holistic, organismic and biological theory of human functioning and growth" (p. 5).

Individuals can Block their Ability to be Spontaneous

> Egotism in Gestalt is characterized by the individual stepping outside of himself and becoming a spectator or a commentator on himself and his relationship with the environment. This neurotic mechanism gets in the way of effective action to get one's needs met, and disturbs the good contact with the environment (p. 61).
>
> The mind itself has recourse to other measures also in its endeavors to deal with excessive excitation. One of these is the blocking of stimuli, preventing them from entering. The mental apparatus has its limits in its ability to cope with stimuli both from the outside and from inside. (Berg 1959, p. 106)

Kreuter (2006c) applied the theory of learned helplessness to his case study of a commercial airline pilot, the victim of crime at the hands of a female psychopathic predator. The daughters of the predator were also part of the victim cohort. Kreuter (2006c) wrote:

> Each daughter grew up tormented by their mother's frequent antisocial behaviors. This led to erosion of their skills under the inescapable (i.e., they lived in her house) and unavoidable (i.e., their mother had jurisdiction over their movements) punishment (i.e., being subject to their mother's irrational conduct). Therefore, a direct result of the adverse contingency (i.e., aberrant behavior of the mother) is the inability of the daughters to compensate. They stayed in the mother's home until each was able to emancipate. Because they were never able to fully understand their mother's psychological disorder, they lived in a world of denial that their mother was suffering from mental illness and was just an evil person. (p. 78)

Forming a Lasting and Effective Coaching or Therapeutic Bond

Within any approach to treatment, it is important to form a meaningful and appropriate relationship with the person providing help. Essential towards this goal is for the person to present candid and forthright information, as well as thoughts during the process should the discussions not result in the therapist adding insight. There is certain up front time requirement or investment when the coach or therapist is gathering data. This time is critically necessary for the helper to understand sufficient background information about the client before any true insight can be properly shared. Too often, people have an unreasonable expectation of going in for a quick fix. Some therapists may dislike clients who enter therapy for very brief periods, referring to this as "binge therapy." While of course the client is in charge of the decision about starting and stopping therapy and how often sessions will be needed, the therapist also plays a role in determining whether they can help the client. There will be a sense of a "click" in the therapeutic relationship or the coaching relationship when things go smoothly. The person will look forward to the next session and present new data, which will then be used by the coach or therapist to blend with past discussions in order to build a bond suitable for leading to sharing of insight.

The effectiveness of therapy or coaching occurs when the client feels that identified issues in his or her life are beginning to become more clearly understood and problems more manageable. This may entail a trial-and-error process with reporting results of replaced behavioral patterns and revised thought patterns. Thus, engaging a cooperative client will make the job of the coach or therapist that much more dynamic and ensure the highest potential for success.

The coach or therapist should develop a sense of confidence to inform the client when the sessions seem to be dragging or old material keeps coming back with no real effort made on the part of the client to try new approaches. The resistance itself may become material for treatment as well as the person's attitude, if negative. The confident coach or therapist is able to influence the client through honest dialogue and clear focus on the client's main issues when the patterns become apparent. Regardless of the orientation of the therapist or the methodology of the coach, the purpose of therapy is to first listen, then to talk, finally to help. "One of the primary goals of successful therapy is the formation of a meaningful and strong therapeutic alliance. This bond between the therapist and client is essential for creating an environment of openness, acceptance, and trust[2]" (GoodTherapy.org 2012). This process is hampered if there is an awkward bond or no bond in the relationship. This does not mean the goal is to create a lasting dependence, but a bond in the form of the fertile agreement to work together towards the goal of the client resolving issues. While this process cannot and should not be rushed, there is prudence in establishing reasonable objectives that the client may have so that the therapist or coach can gear the treatment sessions towards meeting those goals, assuming all goes well in the sessions and no new crises occur.

The bond is enhanced by active listening and interjection of appropriate comments. It is also aided by the therapist or coach avoiding unwarranted sidetracking, which only serves to exhaust the time of the sessions, which might become annoying to the client. As well, a wandering client or a verbose client who merely rambles may need to be corralled before the bond can develop. While therapy is a talking cure, some clients who just like to vent cannot listen and improvement of their listening skills may be desirable.

[2] http://www.goodtherapy.org/therapy-for-trust-issues.html.

Synopsis of Chapter

- Schema therapy can help people change maladaptive patterns in their lives.
- Schema therapy is an integrative approach, combining the best aspects of various modalities.
- Negative thinking can occur later in life, triggered by bad experience.
- The relationship between the client and the therapist may have a strong impact during treatment.
- False impressions can be changed through intervention.
- The client must accept personal responsibility for his life.
- Encouragement is the key to helping a client become more confident.
- Psychological masks hide one's true identity and must be removed.
- Negative people may be trapped in a cycle of maintaining their negative aura.
- Removing the layers of complication, a client is able to become more authentic.
- Behaviors can be influenced by events and by personality.
- The attitude of the patient can support or block the potential for lasting change.

Chapter 5
How Do We Define Success?

For success, attitude is equally as important as ability.

—Walter Scott

Introduction

As we begin tackling the problem of maladaptive schemas and shifts in paradigmatic thinking and developing management and treatment strategies to enable those being helped to achieve greater success in their lives, we need to consider what success even means. Why speak of shifting paradigms without the context of what success means and how the paradigms impact upon it? Success is a very individualized concept and, we will shockingly say, may not be that difficult to obtain. A survey of the topical headlines in *Success Magazine* (Success.com 2014) shows the following:

- The Impossibles: Making the Impossible Possible
- 5 Ways to Break Out of a Decision-Making Trap
- Make Productivity a Habit
- 8 Steps to a Prosperous 2014
- Maximum Leadership: Improve Yourself
- From Pooped to Pumped: Tackle Your To-Do List
- Top of Mind: From To-Do Lists to Storytelling to Mentors (pp. 1–2)

Success can be as broad as a career change or as meaningful as viewing the want ads. In the description of Rex (Kreuter 2013a), the slow movement toward a goal can also be a success. Further, bouncing back from setbacks, disappointments, temporary discouragement, etc. can become an indicator of a person reaching momentum toward success. It all begins somewhere.

For Rex, the necessary change in his mindset was to realize that his job, at least for now, is to get a job.[1] As such, he has something to do each day—search for

[1] The early coaching of Rex by Kreuter was to view the value of his time as a considerable and predictably renewably daily resource. Encouraging Rex to formulate a plan as to how he would

E. A. Kreuter, K. M. Moltner, *Treatment and Management of Maladaptive Schemas*,
DOI 10.1007/978-3-319-06817-6_5, © Springer International Publishing Switzerland 2014

meaningful employment. In doing so, his mission is to continue to take care of himself (physically, mentally, psychologically, and spiritually). He also attends daily mass at his local church and has a warm relationship with the resident clergy. By staying positive, Rex avoids depressive feelings and their associated debilitative impact. He must do so concurrent with the threat of long-term unemployment and the fear of homelessness.[2] While he has been able to tap into certain forms of financial relief, the continuation of these sources is uncertain. Though food stamps are available, there is no governmental help (federal or state) with rent, clothing, transportation, etc.

What meaning the individual ascribes to the inner vision of success is critical because that vision can define whether she/he continues or veers off his or her chosen path. A change in attitude (e.g., boredom, believing it is not attainable, expectations will not be met) is also relevant. These attitudes impact on goal-setting and eventual behavior. It is only when the goal is, or goals are, set that we can know if we have met it and thus have succeeded. There may be a change in goals and thus a change in the choice of paradigms. Some people have confusion about what they really want out of life and do not have a clear notion how to establish goals. For them, the starting point of psychotherapy or coaching is to help the person to consider the various opportunities in life and weigh these against his or her existing capacities to obtain them within a reasonable period of time, and then, to help the person put together a reasonably achievable plan of action and continue to work with them to monitor progress. It is typically important for a person stuck in neutral to have a caring sounding board to interface with in order to cipher what is going well and what is not going well. When coaching, Kreuter offers the metaphor of tuning a car or piano—it takes some tinkering and trial and error to get everything right, but, in the end, the effort is worthwhile.

Mistakes, worrying (which by definition is about the future), being subjected to another's judgment or control, and how to change those paradigms are necessary to meet the goal or goals. In fact, it is the error or the slipup that becomes potent to incorporate into the discussion with the helper who can dissect the steps leading up to the negative result and then work backward with a careful eye on finding the exact decisions, action, attitude, behavior, etc., that can be assigned responsibly for the resulting negative outcome. It is in this process of situational dissection where the negative schema can be extricated from the person's behavioral repertoire and replaced (in theory) with a superior methodology for application in a future similar situation. This process can seem tedious, but it is effective and, with the very cooperative client, can reshape negative patterns of responding to stimuli with improved dynamics. Just as a hitting coach in baseball observes the player striking the ball along with the movements of the player's body and "tinkers" with the dynamics,

---

"spend" his time led to Rex developing a proactive routine, including daily trips to the local library where he used the available computer to search for job postings and to submit his resume. This new routine got him out of his little dwelling and into the world where his comfort level being around people grew.

[2] Rex was homeless in the past.

suggesting variations to the player for use in the practice session to see how they work. Professional golfers are known for changing their swing entirely following coaching by a respected expert.

By staying dynamic, the person avoids getting into a rut, becoming stale, and losing interest. Kreuter knew a golfer who, after a terribly disappointing round of golf, threw his expensive bag of golf clubs into a lake, thereby giving up the game he once loved. We can say that this type of behavior is tantamount to a temper tantrum, but it seems sad that the person chose to act out and give up instead of giving herself/himself the opportunity to humbly admit failure, seek a coach, and work on improvement of her/his game. Maybe golf is not everything, but walking away from one important domain of life following perceived difficulty can lead to choosing an attitude of quickly walking away from issues rather than facing them. We create our own dilemmas, which interfere with our progress toward achievement of success.

Success: An Overview

There is not a single definition of the term we call "success." It varies perhaps at the same rate as that of differences in fingerprints. We are born into a certain environment. Barring tragedy, we can take advantage of opportunities and we also must suffer the consequences of challenging aspects of our life or, more colloquial—living the cards we are dealt. But can we alter the predestined notion of such cards? Kreuter has seen many crippled individuals participating in marathon events using hand cycles and metal feet. It is not how we handle the good that counts as much as how we handle the bad.

Definitions of Success

The following are components of the construct of success:

- Psychological and philosophical commentaries on success and the importance of success in people's lives.
- Practical issues in defining success—an individual's needs and its role.
- Societal pressure to succeed and how society measures relative success.
- Different cultures/different expectations? Success in societies, e.g., industrializations, difference between "big cities" and small towns, between "industrialized societies" and "third-world" countries.
- Individualism and success—building on Descartes' "I think therefore I am."
- Specific success stories, such as biographies of modern heroes, sports superstars, etc.
- If success has an application that fits all.
- Success is individualized.

Skinner (1971) wrote:

> Any evidence that a person's behavior may be attributed to external circumstances seems to threaten his dignity or worth. We are not inclined to give a person credit for achievements, which are in fact due to forces over which she/he has no control. (p. 44)

The way witnesses respond to our achievements goes a long way toward motivating our future behavior. The great runner, Bill Rodgers, explained during a talk before a marathon that in the early phase of his international running career, while running in China, he reached the 24-mile mark, but felt he was struggling and would not finish anywhere as well as he wanted to so he dropped out only a few miles from the finish line. He said that had there been spectators along that part of the course who knew who he was and had they cheered him on to finish he might have mustered up the courage and will to complete the marathon. "When someone behaves in a way we find reinforcing, we make him more likely to do so again by praising or commending him" (p. 44).

In the school system and in some forms of extracurricular activities, social promotion becomes the standard with high-performance taking second position. "And while positive reinforcement is important, far too often schools go the other way with happy-clappy pablum that preaches that everyone is excellent and no one is a failure" (Wooster 2013; p. 1). Fostering excellence may require a delicate balance between praise and criticism. Perhaps we can look at the benefits of pure participation as being paramount to instilling the notion in our youth that winning is the only goal. At a local high school race, Kreuter saw two young girls cut the distance short by a material amount at a place on the course where the race officials would not likely notice. The two girls who cheated came in first and second by only a short interval of time. Thus, it was extremely likely that had they not cut the corner out of the course they would not have done as well. Seeing the two girls acting happy and proud with their shiny medals and colorful ribbons was pathetic. Kreuter did advise the race officials of the situation. This experience (for them) could very well lead toward encouraging them to find success in life through cheating.

In one of Kreuter's prison groups, a woman recounted her story that when she was 5 years old she was in a candy store with her mother. The little child grabbed a piece of candy from one of the lower racks and placed it in her pocket. Looking up at her mother, she saw her mother smiling and nodding with approval. Following this, the mother began to tutor her daughter into the fine art of shoplifting, which led, eventually, to incarceration of now less innocent child turned adult. As a workshop exercise toward transformation of mindset, Kreuter asked the woman (now in her 40s) to close her eyes, pretend she was again a 5-year-old girl, once again in the same candy store, but to imagine right after grabbing the candy that her mother immediately scolded her, requiring her to apologize to the store owner, and to learn a lesson about stealing. The woman stated that had this actually happened, she would not likely have entered a life of crime.

We can blame the mother of course, but it is the valuable example of the replacement of a consequence within the structure of therapy or coaching toward the goal of reformation of mindset that can turn a person into a dynamic and successful person. Using adversity to make the point makes the situation much more poignant for the troubled individual.

Pioneers believe that they can break new ground because of their belief in themselves and in the possibilities of success. Shubber (2013) wrote an article about space travel, which referenced a 1954 quote by Wernher von Braun (1912–1977), the father of rocketry for NASA: "We have, or will acquire, the basic knowledge to solve all the physical problems of a [manned] flight to Mars" (p. 1). An interesting website published by a private company (MarsOne 2014; p. 1) is seeking to colonize Mars with about 1000 qualified persons. They include the qualifications to be an astronaut, which, more or less, could be adapted for use as a list of attributes for success in various domains on planet earth. The qualifications (characteristics and practical applications) are as follows (p. 2):

Characteristics	Practical applications
Resiliency	Your thought processes are persistent
	You persevere and remain productive
	You see the connection between your internal and external self
	You are at your best when things are at their worst
	You have indomitable spirit
	You understand the purpose of actions may not be clear in the moment, but there is good reason—you trust those who guide you
	You have a "can do!" attitude
Adaptability	You adapt to situations and individuals, while taking into account the context of the situation
	You know your boundaries, and how/when to extend them
	You are open and tolerant of ideas and approaches different from your own
	You draw from the unique nature of individual cultural backgrounds
Curiosity	You ask questions to understand, not to simply get answers
	You are transferring knowledge to others, not simply showcasing what you know or what others do not
Ability to trust	You trust in yourself and maintain trust in others
	Your trust is built upon good judgment
	You have self-informed trust
	Your reflection on previous experiences helps to inform the exchange of trust
Creativity/resourcefulness	You are flexible in how an issue/problem/situation are approached
	You are not constrained by the way you were initially taught when seeking solutions
	Your humor is a creative resource, used appropriately as an emerging contextual response
	You have a good sense of play and spirit of playfulness
	You are aware of different forms of creativity

Success can be as feared as failure. A person receiving a promotion at work may want the increased compensation, the larger office, and the new title, but may, internally, be fearful that the requirements of the higher position are actually more than the person feels capable of. Staying silent about that issue could lead to problems, which could be disastrous. Personal integrity and humility would require admission of such fear and, if acknowledged, could lead to a mentoring opportunity. Through a process of internal examination of confidence and abilities, a person is better able to work toward success in a more sensible, ethical manner.

Incremental progress toward goals enables a person to gain confidence and encourage continuance of effort and renewed commitment. When there is a stumble, it is important to encourage the person to identify the problem or error, make mental corrections, and return to the mission. The setback can be very instructive and enable the person to take stock in the situation, examine the problem, weigh available options, and make new decisions as to the best way to continue.

Situational guidance plays a useful role with a mentor walking the mentee through a recent scenario in order for the mentee to see clearly how her/his actions, conduct, behavior, or attitude had a causal effect on the outcome. Following such identification and acceptance of personal responsibility, reshaping of the identified negative schema into a more positive future way of responding is possible.

Setting Your Own Goal, Not an Artificial One

In a competitive environment, we can establish goals based on the perceived performance or demonstrated capabilities of others. An example is a professional golfer who wants to win more tournaments than anyone has before or a club member who wants to card the lowest score for a full round. Most record holders will cheer a person who finally surpasses their long-held mark, as they know full well that records were made to be broken.

We can measure our goals using the achievements of others. We can also create internal goals to become better than we currently are by trying harder, training more, or using coaches and mentors. Blockages toward furthering our goals can be worked out in therapy or other venues. But goals have deeper meaning when they are personal and have more to do with a person's self-perception of their present capabilities juxtaposed against his or her notion of what capabilities she/he would like to have and, finally, awareness of what it will take to obtain those capabilities.

Performing at the peak of your abilities can be defined as "doing your best." That may be true for that moment. It may draw criticism that you could have done better if you made more of an effort. A teacher may tell a student that his or her grades could be better if she/he studied more. The implication is that more time devoted to practice, rehearsal, or study will necessarily translate into improved performance. That may generally be very true. We must also, though, consider the inner will of the person who may not desire to make such an effort because the goal that someone else subtly sets for them (i.e., advice that performance will improve with greater effort) may not be internalized as the goal for that person. It is for this person that "the enemy of good is better." The struggle so often endured is when another person inflicts his or her will on someone trying to push them further than the person wants to go. Unless that person requests being pushed, should the pushing take place?

If each of us comes to terms with who we are right now and takes complete responsibility for driving our own future then goals that are set may be more likely to be met because of the likelihood that a more sustained effort will be deployed trying to reach self-determined goals. Confusion can be avoided by separating the goals established inside the personal will and those suggested by the outside environment. A person may decide that his or her career is adequate and acceptable, while others may feel that person could do better. There is something potentially corrupt in such implied criticism. Unless solicited, it would seem that each of us has the sovereign right to decide what we want out of life. Once determined, some help from others will doubtlessly be necessary, but it is the issue of goal incongruence that requires a closer look. Too much exposure to criticism for not doing what others want may, if the person is not strong enough to withstand it, undermine a person's self-perception of their own abilities, which could interfere with their own progress. However, the person who understands, and takes to heart, the importance of establishing his/her own goals and putting aside the distraction created by unwanted suggestions of others, will presumably have the internal strength to not be thrown off target.

Thus, there may be an artificial component to a troubled person who is unable to make progress in his or her life. This component may be a hidden element of goals infused into the person's mindset by others who think they know better and who feel justified in communicating this information. It may also require some sifting on the part of the therapist or coach to determine if the problem has more to do with how the information is passed on versus what that information entails. Confidence can be shattered when trusted allies challenge our own progress because of a usurpation of our own authority for the establishment of goals.

Synopsis of the Chapter

- Success can be broadly defined.
- Success may not be difficult to obtain.
- Attitudes impact goal setting and behavior.
- Mistakes or setbacks are often necessary in order to progress toward a goal.
- Pioneers believe in themselves and in the possibilities of success.
- Success, like failure, can be feared.

Chapter 6
The Source of Paradigmatic Thinking

Success each day should be judged by the seeds sown, not the harvest reaped.

—John C. Maxwell

Introduction

We indulge in paradigmatic behavior for one of two reasons: we cannot or do not care to control it or we expect it to lead to a certain result. In turn, paradigmatic behavior is predicated on our reaction to stimuli. We are surrounded by stimuli. In fact, we are reacting to stimuli virtually every second of every moment when we are awake. Depending on the relevance of the stimuli to us, our reactions vary as to both intensity and conscious thought that we give to it. There are innumerable examples and we will give some. Our reaction can be conscious or subconscious, to varying degrees, to the point of being rote. It can be planned, our thought put to varying degrees.

What are paradigms and why do we rely on them in the first place? This is important in understanding how to change a paradigm. Paradigms are a belief system—we engage in them because we think that they work (or we don't think about it at all) or have meaning. If we do not believe that they will work, we would not engage in them. They are coping mechanisms, a way of dealing with reality. In order to change, we need to understand which paradigms work, which do not, and why.

"In addition, the psyche pursues a definite aim according to its interpretation of the world and along the lines of an ideal behavior pattern dating from early childhood" (Adler 1998/1927, p. 37). "The ever-present psychological goal that determines all our activity also influences the choice, intensity, and activity of those particular psychological faculties that give shape and meaning to our picture of the world" (p. 39). Adler (1998/1927) wrote:

> In our examination, we must ferret out the subject's earliest childhood experiences, because the impressions of early infancy indicate the direction in which a child has developed as well as the way in which she will respond in the future to the challenges of life. In her response to these challenges a child will make use of all the physical and mental equipment she was born with; the particular pressures she felt in the days of earliest infancy will color

E. A. Kreuter, K. M. Moltner, *Treatment and Management of Maladaptive Schemas*,
DOI 10.1007/978-3-319-06817-6_6, © Springer International Publishing Switzerland 2014

> her attitude toward life and determine in a rudimentary way her view of the world, her cosmic philosophy. (p. 68)

> In child development, an important phenomenon shows clearly the process of preparation for the future play. Games are not the haphazard creations of parents or educators. They should be seen as educational aids and as stimuli for the child's psyche, imagination, and life skills. Every game is a preparation for the future. The manner in which a child approaches a game, his choice of game, and the importance he places upon it show his attitude and relationship to his environment and how he relates to his fellow human beings. Whether he is hostile or whether he is friendly, and particularly whether he shows leadership qualities, is evident in his play. In observing a child at play we can see his whole attitude toward life; play is of the utmost importance to every child. (p. 77)

> The envious person will be interested solely in taking things away from other people, in depriving them and putting them down. At the same time, he will tend to find excuses for his failure to reach his goals and blame these failures on others. (p. 84)

> It is a feature of the age of technology that human beings are treated like machines and expected to follow laws of life much as machines obey the laws of physics. In the latter case, such laws are universally applicable, but in the case of human beings, they lead eventually to isolation, loneliness, and the destruction of human relationships. (p. 185)

Why are we here? What is our true and lasting purpose?

One of the age-old questions people ask is why are we here? That question may never be answered or a person may discover the true destiny of his or her life and seek to fulfill it as best as possible. When we are born, we are not assigned any particular role in society, though past societies have tried in some way to do this. In many respects, we are left on our own recognizance to live our lives and make sense of what is out there in the world. Our responses can be positive or negative. We may seek to carve out a life or life's circumstances may confront us and either create choices or limit them. For example, a young person may become involved with a group of tough friends in the neighborhood who resort to crime as a way of managing their time and freedom. As a way of fitting in, the youth goes along with the plans of the group as established by the perceived leader. These plans, if carried out, may result in arrest, conviction and incarceration, or relegation to a juvenile detention facility. Once labeled with a bad start, a young person who might not have otherwise become criminal minded suddenly is swept away and then becomes a repeat offender. A child of a wealthy family may enjoy the many fruits of the rich environment, including fancy cars, exotic vacation trips, and exclusive education. This privileged upbringing may lead to status within the social network. Some will thrive in such an environment; others will rebel and turn rogue, disappointing their parents. Becoming the black sheep of the family may be a matter of choice, but it also may be influenced by exposure at an early age.

Dr. John Enger wrote a beautiful and emotionally touching story of the life and death of his first grandchild, Madison. She died at age 3. Instead of living the rest of his life in a state of grief, Dr. Enger decided to create a book about the concept of our uniqueness and purpose in life. "Each of us is created with a specific purpose and we are to use our breaths to leave positive prints on this world" (Enger

2013, p. 52). Even the life of a small child leaves a lasting impression on others, as did Madison. As a former police lieutenant, Dr. Enger became an expert in the forensic science of collecting and reading fingerprints left at crime scenes. He used the scientific aspects of fingerprint differentiation to describe a life lesson: to live your life knowing there is a profound reason why you were born. "Regardless of how you came to be born or what circumstances you've grown up in, your life has a purpose" (p. 54).

The fingerprint, then, just like our purpose in life, is unalterable, though we may not use our lives to reach our potential and find that purpose. "Your fingerprint, or purpose, never changes. You may or may not want to fulfill your calling but the calling does not change. You may or may not work diligently in your purpose but your purpose doesn't change. You're here for a reason. There is a reason why you are alive…to make an impression" (p. 63).

When a man begins to question a life in the ministry, for example, the Catholic Church, he is first offered guidance by an experienced priest. He may be asked to spend some time in quiet contemplation, listening to the whispers to determine what God is saying with respect to the future and the future in the Church. So, too, any major life decision may be best considered through the lens of patience and discernment brought about through listening to the quiet voice inside.

A life led with distinction does not have to mean achieving fame or fortune, just purpose. The process of living involves etching or using life's experiences, trials, and tribulations to make the best of life and to work for us in life toward a productive existence. "Don't leave a smudge; and indistinct print" (p. 65).

The Value of Freedom

Despite whatever problems a person may be experiencing, the value of freedom can never be understated. Freedom comes in many forms. "Freedom of behavior is a pervasive and important aspect of human life" (Brehm 1966, p. 377). As a reaction to one's freedom being reduced, taking steps to re-establish the former level of freedom is the usual motivation. Such motivation is referred to as "psychological reactance" (p. 377).

As a metaphor for the temporary shift from being physically contained to being suddenly set free, the actual story of a pet tropical parrot who escaped to the outside is offered.

Pluto's Flight to Safety

My name is Pluto. I am a 12-year-old parrot. I live in a really cool iron cage with toys and a water bowl and tasty food. I have a play gym near my cage and get to play on it often. I am an expert climber. I can fly, but don't very often except when I am bored or want to see where everyone is. My cage is near a window so I can watch the outside birds. I am an inside bird. I've never been outside except when carried in a box to the nice lady who trims my nails. The outside looks exciting, but also scary.

It was a usual Saturday: Dad was cleaning my cage and Aaron was watching television, looking at his computer, reading a book, and having a snack. Dad placed me on my play gym, which is so much fun. After finishing my cage, Dad left the room and I was a bit bored. I decided to fly around and see if I could find Mom. I circled the room and soared past Aaron, enjoying the cool breeze under my wings. Flying is so much fun. But something was very different. After flying past Aaron, I kept going and then the house looked so different. All these strange trees! I picked one nearby and perched on a long branch.

Is this part of my house? Where is Dad? Where is Aaron? Where is Mom? I am so very scared. But the cool breeze is nice and there is so much green and so very places to climb. I must be outside. There's Dad and Aaron, but why do they look so concerned? They are so far away. But this is fun. There's my play gym. But where are my water bowl and my tasty food? Why is my play gym in a strange place? I see Dad and Aaron climbing toward me. I guess they want to play. This game is fun. I'll just jump over to another tree branch and see if they follow me. Dad and Aaron seem to be struggling to reach me. Maybe I can get my neck scratched. Dad is pulling the branch lower, bringing me so very close to Aaron. I can see his hand reach near me so I climb on and now I am back in my own home. It is time for a bath and some tasty papaya. That was a fun adventure.

Tomorrow I think I will go outside again and explore the neighborhood. Each day I watch the outside birds flying all around. I want to play with them. Where do they go at night, I wonder? Is it safe to be outside? Maybe I'll just pretend to go on little trips, but stay as an inside bird. I have my family and my water bowl and my tasty food and my play gym. The outside birds seem to be happy flying all around, but who takes care of them or scratches their necks or feeds them or plays with them? I have Dad, Aaron, and Mom. They are my family. Aaron lets me sit on his shoulder while he does homework. I like to visit Mom while she does online shopping with Dad's debit card. There is no pace I'd rather be than in my own home where I am safe and happy.

The bird, like a person, when tasting something (freedom) in life for the first time, finds the experience appealing, the desire of it being high, and the repression of it can form negative impressions. Imagine a person born blind suddenly regaining his or her sight, but only for an hour or a day and, then, losing sight permanently again. How frustrating. In Kreuter's volunteer experience with incarcerated females, the inmates who were serving their second or third sentences seemed much more embittered and internally angry at the world and at themselves.

Awakening to New Opportunities

Each day presents a clean slate in the sense that whatever negative energy filled the prior day may not necessarily need to repeat in the future with the future described as the present day. What catalyzes new forms of energy is making the choice of a new and improved attitude—one more positive. In a very real way, we choose our attitudes. Waking up grumpy and staying that way for the entire day is optional. The shift toward a divergent attitude can be planned the day before or occur spontaneously. It can be suggested and influenced by a coach or therapist. While it sounds overly simplistic, perhaps a client who realizes the inherent power of attitude who takes a chance and adopts a better attitude then realizes that the day turns out to be more effective than it likely would have been otherwise. Proof is in the outcome, but the test is the trial to act differently, be different, to think differently, and become partly transformed within the existence. Remaining status quo only guarantees same old.

Even the new challenges present us with new opportunities to find creative ways to triumph, make the outcome as good as possible, or diminish the consequences of negative outcomes. Failure, itself, provides a unique backdrop where a person can learn from error, overcome deficit, open up brave new fronts, and face the saboteur inside. In the new light of the new day, we can decide to be a new person with fresh resolve to approach common problems in an uncommon way. We own our perspective. Accordingly, we can modify it.

The Social Networking Phenomenon

Holmes (2013) offered suggestions for feeling more positive. "It's impossible to go an entire year without navigating through some challenges—but despite any setbacks, many are approaching 2014 with an optimistic outlook. Almost 50% of Americans believe their fortunes will improve in the new year. Is 2014 going to be the year of positivity?" (p. 1). The ways to improve happiness and positivity cited by Holmes are as follows:

1. go outside,
2. log some time with your nephews (or nieces, siblings, or neighbor's kids),
3. meditate,
4. play with your pet,
5. unplug every once in a while,
6. say thank you,
7. read more books, and
8. dance (or sing) it out (p. 2).

Facebook, texting, Twitter, Snapchat…we are bombarded with information daily—and not all of it is good. Studies have shown that spending time on social media can actually make us feel lonely and bad about ourselves. Turn off that computer and let yourself be happy (p. 1).

Goldsmith (2013) wrote about the negative impact on mood due to being plugged in to social networking. According to German researchers, witnessing friends' vacations, love lives, and work successes on Facebook can cause envy and trigger feelings of misery and loneliness. A study conducted jointly by two German universities found rampant envy on Facebook, the world's largest social network that now has more than a billion users and has produced an unprecedented platform for social comparison. The researchers found that one in three people felt worse after visiting the site and more dissatisfied with their lives, while people who browsed without contributing were affected the most. "We were surprised by how many people have a negative experience from Facebook with envy leaving them feeling lonely, frustrated or angry," researcher Hanna Krasnova from the Institute of Information Systems at Berlin's Humboldt University told Reuters.

Social networking, as a modern phenomenon, is likely to continue to influence the ways people connect with each other. Everyday activities and thoughts are shared as much as significant events on various Internet sites. The ease of access on laptops, tablets, and cell phones makes these sites very easy to use and, perhaps, addictive. People may be derided if they do not have a Facebook page or if they don't "Tweet." "The wealth of social information presented on Facebook is astounding. While these affordances allow users to keep up-to-date, they also produce a basis for social comparisons and envy on an unprecedented scale" (Krasnova et al. 2013, p. 1).

Seeing friends and neighbors, even family, achieve success or on a fabulous vacation can spark internal feelings of negativity. Do we really enjoy reading about someone winning the Powerball Lottery? Is the statement said to another—"I'm so happy for you"—sincere or does it mask a hidden jealousy? "From a provider's perspective, our findings signal that users frequently perceive Facebook as a stressful environment, which may, in the long run, endanger platform sustainability" (p. 1). The achievements of others can ultimately become measurements with which to consider our own success in life. But they should not. We should not measure our lives against anything other than what we believe and accept as our own values, reasonable expectations, and actions to take positive steps, like those people in this book, to improve ourselves and find our true selves. We should not, but we do. The question is why waste the time being jealous or stressed out over someone else's success? Unless we view someone else's success as a motivator to do better, there is no salutary benefit, let alone positive reinforcement or encouragement, from doing so. But that is human nature, and one might say that it is a form of maladaptive thinking that calls for change.

The answer, we suspect, is often an innate dissatisfaction with one or more material aspects of our life and the frustration of not changing it (them). We then allow our emotions, read jealously, to override rational thought concerning those who, from our perspective, are successful, who have what we do not—the proverbial banging our head against the wall.

Synopsis of the Chapter

- Paradigmatic behavior occurs because we either cannot control it or we expect it to lead to a certain result.
- Reactions to stimuli can be conscious or subconscious.
- Paradigms are a belief system and are coping mechanisms.
- Individuals do not always use their full potential in life.
- Freedom is important to cherish despite problems in one's existence.
- Each new day presents new opportunities to be positive and triumph.
- Failure provides an opportunity to learn from the error.
- Social networking can lead to feelings of inadequacy and negativity.

Chapter 7
The Problem of the Static Paradigm

The complexity of things—the things within things—just seems to be endless. I mean nothing is easy, nothing is simple.

—Alice Munro (New York Times October 11, 2013, p. A1)

Introduction

While perhaps life is not always designed to run in the fast lane or we do not design our lives that way, it is also very true that staying in the status quo (non-movement) is likely counterproductive. A static paradigm, then, can be defined as a state of stillness of mental attitude comprising largesse within the domain of the mind. It stifles determination and motivation and equates to being non-dynamic."Adler's conception of personality was based on the idea of dynamism, that is, life cannot be conceived without movement" (Taylor 2009, p. 162). Stasis can be defined as the state of stagnation or inactivity. Stasis is fine when we are talking about the level of oxygen in the atmosphere or the good health of our children, but not so when the subject is a paradigm of such importance that fixation serves only to harm the ability of a person to move outward from ineffectiveness into a world of exploration filled with new, exciting potential.

Fixations can lead to problems. Cummins (2013) wrote:

> …the dangers of *target fixation*—focusing so intently on the goal of one's desire that bad choices inevitably follow. Sometimes the results can be deadly. More often, it ends in lost opportunities, wasted time, and goals never achieved. Target fixation is different from the admonition to keep your eyes on the prize', that is, to not allow minor distractions or set-backs keep you from pursuing your true goal. (p. 1)

Each morning on the way to work, Kreuter observes the multitude of unhappy faces on the weary travelers taking the train into Manhattan from the northern suburbs. Moltner notices similar sights on his subway ride to lower Manhattan. Why are they looking so miserable? Do they hate their jobs or only despise their commute or, perhaps, are they just exhausted? Or is it a combination of some or all of the above? Life

E. A. Kreuter, K. M. Moltner, *Treatment and Management of Maladaptive Schemas*,
DOI 10.1007/978-3-319-06817-6_7, © Springer International Publishing Switzerland 2014

itself can be an exhausting occupation. We have considered whether this "morning look" wears off by midday, but, come lunchtime, a short walk through the bustling streets of midtown or downtown tell us otherwise. There is a look of frustration, perhaps, or even upset. Not everyone wears this outward appearance either equally or in an obvious way. We are sure that we are misreading many such looks, but it is there as a piece of phenomenological evidence to at least consider. It is this phenomenon that served as one of the influences of Kreuter's (2013a) book on resilience.

The cultural anthropologist might chalk it up to the impact of living or working in a bustling, civilized city or the necessary suffering in order to afford a certain lifestyle. The overworked lawyer treks daily to the city in search of new cases while working the existing backlog. Files accompany him home, perhaps on a computer tablet or an overstuffed bag. While a break would be welcomed, such hope attaches a sense of fear because without backlog there is diminished need for his very position. Work piles up, but the contrasting thought that haunts is what if there was insufficient work? In such a case, there may be no job. So the hunt continues and the proverbial rat race endures. The civilized professional warrior lives on to fight another day's battle with the goal of dragging home metaphorical fresh deer-meat. And all during this type of lifestyle, the person may consider family pressures and the desire or need to exercise juxtaposed to possible health concerns. In all, the patterns of thinking may deviate from either positive for the individual or suitable for a productive life.

Humans do not usually go about their lives in a straightforward trajectory. Things happen to sway us from our chosen paths. For example, temptations interfere with conservative thinking. Danger may act as a calling or something we run towards instead of against simply as a way of confronting fear or done out of boredom. Calliet (1955) wrote: "Why then, may we ask, does human thinking so often go astray?" (p. 131). He further said: "It is nonetheless true, however that this splendid instrument we call the human intellect may be put out of tune under the distorting influence of a will led astray" (p. 135). The human will is prone to temptations and poor decision-making. "Knowing oneself is integral to growing up. But, to the extent that we live in a blaming system, we do not want to know the truth about who we are and, therefore, resist growing up" (Karen 2001, p. 110).

A school teacher loves introducing young minds to the beauty of mathematics, science, and the arts, but the day is filled with struggle just to get to and from school then to make ends meet after expenses and taxes. What is all this about, she may ask while hanging on for dear life on an overcrowded subway line? The challenge of ordinary life may extinguish the fun out of life if we are unprepared and find insufficient antidotes to counteract the external pressures.

We can get completely absorbed inside our own paradigm of existence never taking time to climb to the surface and breathe in fresh perspective. Are we doing enough to make sense to achieve happiness in the long run? Because we continue in this manner does not itself mean we are missing anything. It is only when there exists some form of psychological pathology in our lives that call for examination of the elemental as well as complicated structures of our lives. For example, if someone is unhappy with his or her present career why would she/he not consider a drastic change? It could be that fear of change stops him or her or she/he feels economic pressure to not give up what she/he has out of fear of not finding suitable work in another field. One creative response to career apathy could be to investigate and then study an alternate career while maintaining an income in the present occupation, then seeking a new position using the newly gained knowledge. Perhaps not easy, but who can say not possible? Indeed, the very point is to offer one's thinking to be open to the possibilities. Instead of viewing a situation from the perspective of what is not possible, it is wise to see the other perspective of what is achievable.

Life, for some, is simple and rests on basic survival. Along with the relative simplicity of the lifestyle of the homeless person, albeit clearly challenging, including misery and constant struggle to survive the elements and the anxiety over how to meet his or her basic needs, the homeless occupy their time searching for what they need to sustain life or for whatever small comforts they may be lucky to find or be given. The discarded old coat may equate to survival of the onslaught of the next winter. Consider, for example, noticing a seemingly homeless man sitting on the ground outside a store with a cardboard sign reading: "Hungry, please give me food or money. God bless you." We may take pity on this person or ignore him as the vast majority of the passersby will do. Or, we can take a few minutes out of our hectic day, move past our own focused personal struggle and buy this man some nourishment. Then, two choices prevail: We can quietly hand over the food and continue on with our day or we can provide the gift and add a smile or a kind word of encouragement or concern. Kreuter has done both. There is a certain inner peace that comes over one's being each time you extract your thoughts from just your own world and consider what it must be like to be in a much more difficult environment. Seeing something in the person who is down on his or her luck more deeply humanizes the person and creates an opportunity to look upon and interact with him or her on an equal platform despite the obvious differences. When our own negativity is transferred onto the already suffering person, it becomes easy to minimize his or her humanity and discount any morsel of responsibility we may have felt in considering whether or not to step in and provide some form of help.

Kreuter's dear and long-time friend Peter always gives a certain man small sums of cash. This man, who routinely sits in a wheelchair on a particular street corner in Manhattan, is missing his legs. He sees this wheelchair-bound person regularly as the person's corner is near Peter's exclusive club. Peter has explained to me that he has taught his two children never to look down on another human being. Peter's actions inspire and instruct, showing that regardless of how busy we happen to be we must always consider others. Peter is generous not only with his money but also with his kind spirit as he offers the legless man a connection through his warm overture acknowledging the importance of the man's existence in a non-condescending manner. This may sound like a sermon of ethics. It is not meant to be. Instead, the underlying message is that when we help someone less fortunate and do so dynamically we spark an improved outlook in our own lives. We can take this newfound positive energy and catapult ourselves into a new way of thinking. When we become less selfish and less self-centered, we open up to the larger world. In doing so, we realize how vulnerable we all are. This sense of vulnerability carries with it a paradigm shift towards greater humility. With a more humble sense of self, we can better cope with our own adversity and find ways to cope taking a lesson from those we have witnessed living on the edge. While we have no wish to join them in their specific plight, we can help. One does not need to be impoverished to understand what impoverishment means or what it may feel like. Similarly, you do not need to suffer disease to be able to find a way to donate to research to cure that disease. With deeper understanding and compassion for others, negativity dwelling within may well dissipate.

Perhaps the idea of working towards being a selfless person is this type of shift from the negative schema of selfishness to the overtly aware person who does something every now and then to respond to persons outside of our own immediate lifestyle. It is the act of caring about another that reverberates back to the self. If we have the determination to help others, we should be able to muster the internal resources to help ourselves.

Our worldview is often clouded by suppositions based on false information (i.e., fear that debilitates). All of our views engender feelings whether expressed or kept hidden from either public or even our own awareness. We get locked up, refusing to consider options regardless of the source of suggestion. "As different as peace, relationships, and healing may appear to be from one another, they're all based in the same principle: the 'language' of belief and the feelings that we have about what we believe" (Braden 2008, p. xvii). Life continues along based on that certain coded mantra we each construct, expressed in our speech patterns, behavior, and handling of situations. Where some may see us as dynamic, others may, instead, consider us as quirky or even unstable. Those with a contrary perspective may view us as rigid. When we vocalize a different perspective, we may be seen as argumentative or as a troublemaker. "Today we are at a pivotal time when three major ways of knowing—belief, faith, and science—are being tested against the reality of our world" (pp. 49–50).

Relativism

As a construct, points of view have no absolute authority, truth, or validity in themselves, but have relative value ascribed according to changing perceptions. Therefore, we can apply the concept of relativism to negative schema through the connection of how we feel internally about our own set of truths, whether we find ourselves valued, and how we do not respect the perception of others. According to the *Stanford Encyclopedia of Psychology* (2003):

> Relativism is not a single doctrine but a family of views whose common theme is that some central aspect of experience, thought, evaluation, or even reality is somehow relative to something else. For example standards of justification, moral principles or truth are sometimes said to be relative to language, culture, or biological makeup. Although relativistic lines of thought often lead to very implausible conclusions, there is something seductive about them, and they have captivated a wide range of thinkers from a wide range of traditions. (p. 1)

Transformation of Paradigms

How do we alter our internal views of a particular topic? And if such views are steadfast, ingrained over time and especially having survived the onslaught of challenge, are they too rigid to withstand serious and lasting modification? According to Kuhn (1922–1996), from a societal perspective, when enough significant anomalies have accrued against a current paradigm, the scientific discipline is thrown into a state of crisis. During this crisis, new ideas, perhaps ones previously discarded, are tried. Some sense of desperation may even apply during this process. Eventually, a new paradigm is formed, which gains its own new followers, and an intellectual "battle" takes place between the followers of the new paradigm and the holdouts of the old paradigm. In this book, we apply the ideas expressed by Kuhn towards internal paradigms and personal paradigmatic thought along with the internal struggle that may take place when we consider the potential for shifting our paradigms. Just as there is a process followed by an entire culture with respect to shifting paradigms, at the individual level, there is a process, sometimes even a subconscious one.

Think of a paradigm shift as a change from one way of thinking to another. It is a revolution, a transformation, a sort of metamorphosis. It just does not happen, but rather it is driven by agents of change (Artemisia 2011, p. 1). As Puff (2012) stated:

> Our thoughts create our realities. Therefore, if we want to change our behavior, our way of thinking, or our lives, awareness is the first step. Unfortunately, many of us go through life oblivious to our actions and thoughts. The good news is that once we're aware, we can change them. (p. 1)

Agents of change helped create a paradigm-shift moving scientific theory from the Ptolemaic system (the earth at the center of the universe) to the Copernican system (the sun at the center of the universe), and moving from Newtonian physics to relativity and quantum physics. Both movements eventually changed the worldview. These transformations were gradual as old beliefs were replaced by the new paradigms creating "a new gestalt" (Kuhn 1970, p. 112).

"It is Kuhn's premise that science does not build upon itself in a linear progression, but by leaps and bounds; and, such progressions are not dictated by empiricism alone, but by a mixture of elements contained within a paradigm" (Johnston 2013, p. 1). Kuhn used the duck–rabbit optical illusion to demonstrate the way in which a paradigm shift could cause one to see the same information in an entirely different way.

According to Kuhn (1996), paradigms refer to normal science inclusive of "… research firmly based upon one or more past scientific achievements" (p. 10). Such achievements are reflected in modern textbooks and form part of what Kuhn referred to as actual scientific practice. Kuhn's work "…counts as one of the most influential twentieth-century works of philosophy and history of science" (Stix 2012, p. 1).

Socrates (469–399 B.C.E.) defines thinking as the conversation of the soul within itself (Ambuel 2007, p. 8). "A paradigm is a model for comparison, but the term is ambiguous in a way instructive for the discussion that will follow" (p. 8). Stix

(2012) added: “Kuhn wasn’t against progress; he just thought that progress wasn’t ‘to’ something. It was progress away from what didn’t work very well, but that there isn’t any kind of permanent goal” (p. 4).

The Role of Expectations in Paradigmatic Thinking

In his chapter, "Expectations versus Reality…," Moltner (2013) wrote about the pervasive influence of expectations, both conscious and subconscious, in our daily lives. Whether we are walking across the street with the subconscious expectation that we will make it to the other side or we embark on a course of action with the conscious expectation of achieving a particular goal, expectations are pervasive, if not paramount, in our thought process. Expectations play a similarly important role in paradigmatic thinking and shifts from maladaptive thinking.

As a general proposition, we expect our paradigms to result in something that we want or need, be it tangible or psychological. Human nature is presumptively geared to seek pleasure or fulfillment. Therefore, it would be counterproductive to our intrinsic force to engage in thinking that runs contrary to these precepts. Such thinking is an essence of maladaptive thinking. That is not to say that such thinking does not occur. Of course it does, but that is the challenge that is to be overcome.

Expectations play an informative, if not controlling, role in the process.

For example, the invocation of superstition is an end to a means and carries with it the expectation of satisfaction of that means. Thus, the ball player’s pre-game ritual, the decision to not walk under a ladder, pick up the face-up penny, or not (supposedly) have a 13th floor, all result from an expectation that the act will effectuate something positive or avoid something negative, however defined. Indeed, the common thread of the experiences of those people in this book who have met that challenge and overcome their personal maladaptive thinking is a conscious expectation of being able to change their thinking and with it a particular aspect of their reality (read essence) for their betterment. The recognition itself of the “maladaptive”—read contrary to the truth of the individual—thinking and the subsequent conscious decision to attempt to change not only that thinking but also that reality of his or her life was done with the expectation that the individual’s life and personal essence would be enhanced or more fulfilled.

The attempt at change itself, before the change was made, was done with a directed purpose—a purpose directed ultimately to a goal the foundation of which was three expectations (or, perhaps, hopes that became reality): (1) the yearning and individual necessity to achieve the outcome; (2) the effect of the outcome, i.e., the result of perceived achievement on the person’s life; and (3) the determination to maintain the outcome and not regress into the prior “maladaptive” thinking. Each of these stages carries with it the excitement, and challenges (if not burdens), of the expectations that come with it. And, they carry with it the permutations of expectations that are discussed in that chapter including hope, subjectivity, objectivity, and outside influences. As we will discuss when discussing the individual shifts, an individual's expectations in engaging in the attempt to make a shift and his/her expectations in effectuating the shift underlay what they did.

The Mask of Negativism

Like an onion being peeled, the layers of complication must be allowed to drift away, leaving the person exposed to resolve conflict and handle opportunities more fully engaged in a more authentic self-image. Pride of accomplishment can then occur when the person, stripped of falsity, begins to transcend into a truer person. Shakespeare wrote: "To thine own self be true" (Polonius, in *Hamlet,* Act 1, Scene 3). We can adapt this philosophy and apply it to everyday life and use it to provide keys to a hurting person to shake off false shields and become true to themselves, necessary before they are ready to become authentic when presenting to others.

Overcoming Fear to Overcome Negativity

There is, perhaps, no more potent emotional commodity than pure fear. Fear is a rather unpleasant emotion, which is typically the result of a belief, real or false, that someone or something is dangerous and about to inflict harm or at least poses a threat of harm. Fear equates to worry. It can last for a moment or much longer. There is a saying: "Just because you are paranoid does not mean someone is not out to get you." We like to tell people who share their feelings of fear not to worry, that it will pass, or that they have nothing to worry about. In essence, the person's fear becomes discounted. Yet, the feeling, which properly resides uniquely inside each person, may not be easy to abandon even with strong evidence for doing so.

In contrast to a deer, for example, who may be enjoying a flavorful berry only to be annihilated by a single gunshot to the head from a camouflaged hunter, there was no fear prior to the killing because likely, the brain of the deer would not have had time to process the feeling of fear in the moments before death. Were we able to interview a strolling deer and ask if the deer felt vulnerable to being hunted down, it is not likely the deer, absent a cerebral cortex, would have been able to understand the concept of such vulnerability. So, fear could not be instilled even with forewarning.

In the human, fear is learned at a very early age. A child who touches a hot stove quickly realizes doing so results in a painful burning sensation; therefore, the learning is to avoid touching hot surfaces. Recently, Kreuter was with his son at a large campground with paintball gear. Unlike his son, 14 at the time who admitted no fear, Kreuter certainly felt trepidation. After being outfitted with the proper protective clothing and the heavy artillery, they set out into the woods. Kreuter soon found himself behind a sturdy tree looking into the woods for the "enemy." This was not an easy task given the fog and the fact that Kreuter is nearsighted, plus the all-important face mask was fogging up from all the heavy breathing brought on by increasing anxiety. Once shots were fired, Kreuter considered that this must be the very rough equivalent of what it feels like to be a soldier inserted in active combat. Then, of course, the thoughts turned to the logic that much more experienced paintball enthusiasts would probably know how to maneuver and soon that pristine yet foggy mask would be covered in splatters of paint. The feeling was actual fear and the memory of that fear lingers, causing disinterest in ever repeating such an outing. Therein lies the issue—fear creates a negative consequence: the unwillingness to try again.

We can extend this concept into the realm of everyday life where there might be a public-speaking opportunity, an invitation to take over management of a group of coworkers, or the news of an illness. The person might begin to process fear and become quite negative in his or her attitude, which could lead to a withdrawal of some sort from opportunities or anger and resentment towards a medical report. Such negativism creates a barrier to interpersonal growth.

A young woman, who spoke at an event sponsored by an organization for children's cancer research, said at the podium that "cancer was the best thing that happened to me because it made me realize how precious life was." This young woman startled the audience, but for her, she was testifying to her resilience and her quest to stay positive regardless of her life circumstance. She was a true survivor, one who bravely chose to share her awakened vision with others.

Fear can be overcome by facing it head-on and through the guiding help of a coach or therapist. Unlocking the root of any fear becomes the challenge. Scott Carpenter, the second man to orbit the earth, interviewed shortly before his death in October 2013, said that one of his remaining quests in life was overcoming fear. For him, the challenge existed inside his persona. For others, they may need assistance to get to a place where they have the willpower to begin the work necessary to develop the tools to combat their fear. Once an individual recognizes that fear is holding him or her back she/he is in a position to consider what could be done to overcome his or her fear. But it is the negativity that must be challenged first. The maladaptive notions involved with catering to a person's fear are, to some extent, a problem rooted in attitude and behavior. By bringing these feelings to the surface, they can be better understood, dissected, and replaced with a progression of more positive feelings, attitudes, and growth-oriented behaviors. Kreuter (2009) wrote:

> Creative writing, in particular poetry, can be a useful tool for the therapist who addresses the needs of the "driven professional." Such professionals, who may be identified by their singular career-mindedness, sometimes find that their drive undermines possibilities for greater satisfaction through activities unrelated to their fields. (p. 165)

Changing False Impressions

Often, we engage in ideas or impressions of the world around us. This can be due to fear or from lack of confidence. The impressions may strike us as very real, especially those occurring in the small hours of the night or the ones that wake us up from otherwise restful sleep and serve to torture us until we have to officially "wake up" to face the onslaught of another day. Likely, the planned or feared event(s) of the day occupies the mind and provides ample fodder for dreams the night before. We rise to consider the consequences of the day going badly and whatever shred of confidence that might still remain has been lost. Grumbling, we get ready and leave the relative safety of our home environment to face the challenges in the world. Such thinking contributes to an unwitting act of sabotage perpetrated on the self.

Planning and preparation are the best antidotes to combat such self-defeating images and serve well to remove the fear of failure. Some healthy anxiety is good when we are facing a real challenge and this anxiety should have been the fuel to ignite our effort in the planning and preparation phases. No prizefighter enters the ring for the title fight without ample preparation and training, though both fighters probably have at least some fear of their opponent.

When we face these negative impressions, we would do well to slow ourselves down, reconsider our involvement in activities and our management of time and put forth some effort in planning what is ahead. It is like a budget of time. We know or should know what is required, and we know or should know what it will take to accomplish the task at hand. All we then need to do is meet the goal by spending the time wisely.

If we have low energy, we may need to consider our diet. If we are sluggish, an exercise plan to help drive our energy so we can have better focus and stamina should be considered. Physical exercise also feeds the mind and counterbalances the pressure we feel inside our heads.

Asking someone for coaching can help improve focus and steer us from straying too much. The key is that when the stakes are higher the effort must be commensurate to the task. Missing the boat on such realization can spell disaster. But, even if disaster does occur, we can learn and maybe the next time we can be better prepared. Sometimes a knock on your butt can do more for encouragement than a compliment. We must never take life for granted nor our own ability. The most professional and seasoned golfers practice their skills so as to remain sharp. Therefore, we can take a lesson from the pros and practice until we blister (physically or metaphorically). Once we learn that training is sometimes meant to hurt, we can muster the internal resources to carry on despite wanting to stop.

Comparing the use of time between what we know we should do and what we otherwise might want to do is healthy. When we find ourselves making such a comparison, we should use that moment to reconsider why we are in the position we are in and use that to redouble our commitment to be the best we can be. Alternatively, we might be better off realizing that maybe we really do not wish to continue on the present course. At some point, most people hang up a part of their active life due to age or infirmity or because they lose the zest for the same level of challenge and excitement they enjoyed in their younger days. The mental will has, however, a lot to do with when that day arrives and can remain active after physical activity subsides. Through power of mind and determination, we can continue our mental will by removing the toxicity of negative thought and find new energy to continue propelling ourselves forward.

In Kreuter's (2013a) case study of Rex, his progress in life has been mixed with some work experiences and some misfortunes. Recently, he landed a full-time job with a national retail chain and thought this was finally the break he has been looking for. During a workday, he needed to make a quick cell phone call to find out about his last food stamp allotment as he still relied on that until his income kicked in. He stated that he had not been told that it was forbidden for employees to use cell phones while at work. He was seen by a supervisor and immediately dismissed. While this was very unfortunate for Rex, his manner of handling the issue was mature and resilient. The following are his words describing the situation as where he was emotionally and mentally:

> It has been a mighty tough week for me. Fr. Mike came through by connecting me with St. Vincent de Paul society. I will be meeting with case workers for rental assistance and help with possible job at Target today at 4:30 pm. I had to make a choice and embrace humility as opposed to forcing myself to risk day labor and not get out for money for Saturday. Local church assistance is far more responsive during crisis than Catholic social services that are bogged down with Federal and United Way requirements. I am living as a man of choice. I chose to put getting through the bureaucracy (my needs) for food stamps over the employer for 3 minutes. I received a dismissal from the lower management. They take things very seriously at Wal-Mart. Some writing for spiritual growth: It ain't what you don't know that gets you in trouble; it's what you think you know that ain't so! It is a relief to receive the help from the Church members. Yes it is in our moments of decision that our destiny is created. I did in fact make the right choice in prioritizing my going to handle food stamps. My morning had begun trusting not just believing that my times are in the hands of God. We serve a merciful God. Speak to you soon. (Personal communication, Rex October 8, 2013)

While Rex continues to struggle and find his way through the trials and tribulations of ordinary life, living in a state where there is no welfare for a single, healthy male, he continues to adopt a positive attitude, which replaced the prior negative attitude that kept him from even trying to improve his chances for steady and adequate employment. This positive attitude paid off in his obtaining a new full-time job in which he is thriving. As a believer, Rex relies on his faith in God to help see him through. He also accepts full responsibility for his plight and blames nobody. The absence of any bitterness helps him think clearly and use his psychic energy towards resuming his search for work and asking his church for help when he needs it most. Even the experience of being fired for using his cell phone has increased Rex's resolve to learn better how to live in the modern world and cope with rules, even to anticipate them when they are not first explained. Perhaps he should have realized using his phone could be a serious violation of policy, but he made a choice, as he mentions above. The positive aspect of this experience is that Rex is more capable of accepting apparent injustice even when it adds to his misery because, in doing so, he remains positive. Thus, his example should prove powerful for coaches and therapists to help their clients who are facing tremendous hurdles to first look at themselves for answers how they can improve and why a positive attitude is more beneficial in the long run.

Even when you are knocked down, repeatedly, the next best thing to do is pick yourself up and keep moving forward. Ants who build a pyramid-shaped structure of sand, in an area heavily trafficked by feet, only to find their newly built fortress demolished by a passerby, commonly just start the building process anew. Perhaps they suffer heavy casualties, but the remainder carries on. In human warfare, the beach landing at Normandy is an incredibly powerful example of people who had the heart and internal fortitude to mount a group effort despite knowledge of the bloodshed to come. The success of the unit was paramount to the survival of any one soldier. It may seem pointless for the ants to attempt rebuilding over and over again (due to the lack of a cerebral cortex, the ant cannot understand the logistics of building in harms' way). Perhaps after many rounds of defeat they might take the hint and move on, but the point is their sheer determination against horrendous odds of survival (their structure and themselves). People can take a lesson from the army of ants and consider their actions, the results of their actions, and how they can improve their lot in life by both determination and by making superior choices in ensuing opportunities. Rex sees life this way. He has researched employment prospects in other states and would relocate if he could be more secure elsewhere.

Perhaps, then, one of the most important aspects of the help we can give other human beings is encouragement to develop themselves to become better, brighter, more aware and increasingly capable to withstand the mighty challenges ahead. In addition, helping people expand their sight horizons to consider a wider range of possibilities may lead to their discovery of better choices. Those who improve can claim a measure of success. We must not take this positive feeling away from them. It is when people judge others negatively, but they do not have the self-esteem to withstand the onslaught or it comes from an authority figure that they may be propelled into a state of negative schema. We, in essence, push them into the abyss because of judgment. This judgment takes on many forms, including patronizing those who are trying to better themselves in such relatively small ways. As an example, Kreuter was in the courtroom observing the sentencing of the perpetrator of crime against a victim whose life he was studying. Prior to that case being heard, a man was being questioned by the judge about what efforts he had made since his last court appearance. The man's attorney handed the judge a stack of completion certificates for courses the man had taken. Though the man stood proudly before the judge, the judge rudely barked to the man: "Anyone with a printer could have made up these certificates." While the man's attorney proceeded to provide further proof of that the courses were, in fact, taken and completed, the man's demeanor changed from pride to an expression of obvious sadness. It appeared as if the man's confidence was shattered even though the man knew the truth. In this way, we need to be mindful of the importance of validation of the achievements and efforts of others regardless of how small we may deem these to be by our own selfish definition. People can be overly cruel. One antidote to such cruelty in the world is to coach people to sustain their increased feelings of self-worth and insulate themselves from the thoughtlessness of others. Doing so builds strength and character while also helping the person become more resilient.

Habitual attitudes play a role in creating false impressions. "Jung considered that habitual attitudes were nearly always carried too far, so that the thinker neglected his feelings, while the intuitive paid too little attention to the facts given by sensation" (Storr 1983, p. 18). "A man's attitude to reality is something extraordinarily persistent, but the more persistent his mental habitus is the less permanent will be his effective achievement of adaptation" (Jung 1983/1961, p. 59). "It is merely incumbent on us to choose the master we wish to serve, so that his service shall be our safeguard against being mastered by the 'other' whom we have not chosen. We do not create God, we choose him" (p. 246).

Converting Daunting Goals to Manageable Segments

One of the dilemmas faced by people who attempt to reach goals that are perceived to be difficult is the haunting notion of the amount of time needed to complete the goal or the relative effort necessary. As happens, there comes a point in the process for many where the process becomes overwhelming. Some do not even start the process because of the projected difficulty. As a way to manage this negative schema, breaking down the challenge into segments, using mental discipline, will help lead to completion. As an example, let us examine the challenge of running a marathon—26.2 miles. First-time runners may be quite concerned about the daunting nature of such a distance. Pre-race jitters are common. Once the race begins, the runner may feel incapable of making it to the end and may even question why she/he signed up in the first place.

A technique to use the power of mind to reduce the task is to first break the race down into 26 1-mile races (no disrespect to the extra two-tenths of a mile). In this way, the requirement is just 1 mile at time. A second technique is to consider after reaching the first mile that 1 mile is over and 25 remain. By looking forward to the crossover point where there have been 13 miles covered and 13 to go the level of internal confidence begins to set in. In a recent marathon (his 70th), Kreuter used this technique successfully and imagined a line initially rising from the lower left corner of a graph to the upper right corner, with the left representing the miles completed and the right representing the miles ahead. For each mile thereafter, the equation begins to look much more favorable with the line's positioning methodically changing with the left side increasing and the right side decreasing. At the 20-mile mark, the method would be to consider 20 completed and only 6 to go—mentally positive thinking and the line graph looking tilted upward from left to right. It is at this point where a lot of distance runners hit the "wall." The wall, of course, is imaginary. What is really occurring is that one's physical energy and perhaps internal drive mechanism is depleted.

By using a mental strategy, the challenge (any challenge) can be broken down into manageable components. Using the metaphor of the graph, the runner can feel positive inspiration from the positive movement of the line, feeding new psychic energy into the person. While it will not necessarily translate into added physical capability, it can and does bring out newfound resilience and determination inside the runner who may not have tapped his or her full level of strength. Most marathon finishers leave behind only a portion of the physical, emotional, and spiritual "fuel" on the marathon course. It would be unrealistic and, frankly, irrational to risk one's health by straining to traverse the mileage faster than physically possible. Training is meant to push through the envelope, leading to a higher level of fitness and ability to run faster and longer. Testing that to the maximum capacity of the marathon course can and does lead to injury. Kreuter has seen many individuals pulled from the course with serious injuries, rendering them incapable of completing the race. How unfortunate. Running within one's capability is more sensible. Of course, it also could mean that slower finish times are likely when the runner refuses to push through perceived barriers. But finishing is an accomplishment.

In November 2013, Kreuter ran the Philadelphia Marathon. At mile 20, he started talking with another runner, Sean (actually both were walking at that point). As it was Kreuter's 70th marathon and Sean's first, Kreuter was able to impart much of what he learned running long-distance events for the past 15 years. In doing so, both Kreuter's and Sean's reality shifted. Kreuter's thoughts turned away from his personal experience of discomfort and Sean's thoughts converted from self-doubt to learning about his own well of resilient strength. Sean experienced a similar level of emotional energy that Kreuter experienced after his first few marathons, especially the first. Sean wrote to Kreuter the next day:

> Sorry for the delay. I feel great although my legs are very sore. I will be running my next marathon on 4/2 at the Shore in NJ. You were right. I'm hooked. Even while I'm writing this message I'm getting that emotional feeling again. It's Amazing! I'm glad you said it's normal lol. Everyone I've spoken to about the race I had to mention you. As I said before, I believe things happen for a reason and for you to have been there for me at the end, and live just 20 minutes away is just mind boggling! There was something you said that I wanted to remember….I just can't seem to think of what it was. Not sure if it had to do with running or something. If you can think of it please let me know. My time was 5:50.55! The 1st 10k my average speed was a little over 10 minutes/mile. I need to pace myself better. (Sean Baresi, Personal communication, November 19, 2013)

In a latter message, Sean wrote:

> I took the medal to work and everyone was pretty amazed especially because I hadn't trained for it at all. Now I have a goal—to complete 26.2 miles in less than 5 hrs. I will start training in the gym and strengthen my core. As far as applying it to life, I've already done that. Feeling tired is a thing of the past now. I pushed myself that day like I never had before. And to have finished that race proved to me that I can do anything. Mentally it did something though I can't quite explain it. You were an inspiration for me during the final moments of the race and I'll never forget that. I hope we never lose touch because special people are hard to find. (Sean Baresi, personal communication, November 22, 2013)

Running with a purpose and with conviction also brings the need to run with pain and discomfort. Willingness to suffer the consequences of some activity that is self-determined makes such suffering much more palatable.

While running the West Palm Beach Marathon in December 2013, Kreuter spoke with several runners who explained their rationale for running such a distance. One person has run this particular race each year for the past 10 years without any training regimen. He indicated that he runs the race annually because it is near where he lives. Interestingly, he does not consider himself to be a runner and even said he does not like running. Yet, he runs the marathon distance. When asked what it does for him he said that it gives him a sense of accomplishment not otherwise achievable in his life. A woman said that it was her first marathon and she was a cancer survivor, having completed treatment several years prior. She felt she needed to create her version of the proverbial "bucket list" during her chemotherapy and included running a marathon among the list. Her resilience was evident and she said that her thoughts of her past illness changed her outlook on life. Now that she was running the marathon she felt uplifted by the notion of her own accomplishment.

People can choose to listen to their inner hearts and follow their dreams or become less motivated to quest for every possible yearning in their lives. Bloch (1993) wrote about this choice using marathon running as an example:

> Some people spend their whole lives dreaming of doing something—climbing a mountain, visiting a faraway country—and die with their dreams unfulfilled. Running a marathon is a dream that can be fulfilled—all that's required is an application of effort. It can happen at virtually any time in life; you just have to be willing to put in the time and effort to prepare for it. (p. 38)

"Exercise is good for your brain as well as your body" (Bloch 1993, p. 35). Neuropsychologists have found that exercise can lead to the formation of new blood vessels in the cerebellum, which is at the base of the brain from which messages are transmitted controlling muscle activity. The brain increases in size due to the increased oxygen and glucose. Running helps people think more clearly, enhancing problem-solving ability and creative thinking. In addition to vigorous physical activity, visualization techniques can help a person get through difficult situations. "You can create vivid pictures in your head to inspire yourself to realize your best efforts during the race. Visualization can be calming, inspiring, motivating, or focusing—whichever you feel you need" (p. 148).

Kreuter has often advised aspiring young accountants, interested in pursuing licensure as a Certified Public Accountant, to combine their study regimen with an exercise routine, such as walking or running on a treadmill. Through the intermix of cerebral strain with movement of the body, the combination offers the person a counterbalancing approach to the process of study and the arduous task of absorbing large amounts of new information for later regurgitation on a comparatively difficult exam. Similarly, Kreuter has asked the young CPA aspirants to visualize their CPA license with their name on it in order to fortify and sustain their motivation towards their studies.

Finding ways and techniques to get through challenging situations equates to resilience in the individual. As in life, facing the long road ahead in a marathon can require mental tools in order to stay on course. "Another way to help keep going during the rough parts of the marathon is to say words or phrases over and over to yourself as a sort of mantra" (p. 148). Nervous people may develop jitters when in a stressful situation. Others may feel the rush of adrenaline, which can lead to decreased oxygen flow to the brain (the flight or fight response). While helpful in sports, it can result in a sudden inability to speak, causing the person to feel as if she/he were experiencing a cardiovascular event. In reality, it is probably the anxiety brought on by the challenge. Therefore, finding ways to cope and deal with the challenging situation can help alleviate the pressure, creating the environment where the challenge can more easily be met. Exploring the inner causes of the anxiety can enable the person to avoid creating a negative pattern whenever faced with a similar challenge, something that could hamper the person's career and their life.

The experience of pain with the knowledge of why the pain is occurring results in greater acceptance. It is for this reason that completion of a challenge knowing this form of pain will certainly be encountered along the continuum can actually be craved. Some refer to this as the "runner's high" or the person having a "running addiction." So be it. The point is that any challenge can be more accepted when the purpose of doing it is well understood and demanded juxtaposed to the predictability of agony or strife along the way. One runner at the start told Kreuter "No matter what your finish time is it will be faster than the people who stay home sitting on the couch." Kreuter often says: "Life is not a spectator sport." Running for a cause also provides an extra ingredient of motivation, inspiring a less-than-fully-fit runner to accomplish the task. Kreuter noticed in the 2001 London Marathon that numerous runners (including him) were running for a cause. In his youth, Kreuter participated in the annual March of Dimes Walkathon, which involved 20 miles of walking back in the 1970s, but has since been reduced to about 5 miles for some unknown reasons.

Applying this strategy within a therapeutic or coaching environment allows for the client to cite a particularly troublesome issue and set one or more goals necessary to resolve at least part of the problem. The process of walking through the issue, breaking down the problem into segments, allows for potential solutions to those issues to be debated and, finally, adopted. Resolving each segment eventually brings to the surface a synchronous way to resolve the entire problem.

The key to forging a successful segmentation of the dilemma is maintaining a consistent positive attitude with focus always moving forward. Life is not and should not be lived in the rearview mirror. Similarly, problems are not resolved looking in the past except as a tool to review past methods of handling issues and a fair determination of what worked and what did not work. Returning back to the running metaphor, the following summarizes one possible scenario of how the power of mind can help a person overcome challenges:

Miles completed	Miles remaining	Mindset
1	25	Overwhelming concern
2	24	
3	23	
4	22	
5	21	
6	20	
7	19	Where the battle of internal will occurs
8	18	
9	17	
10	16	
11	15	
12	14	
13	13	At midpoint where the cross-over begins

Miles completed	Miles remaining	Mindset
14	12	More completed than left to do
15	11	
16	10	
17	9	
18	8	
19	7	
20	6	Transition from concern to confidence
21	5	
22	4	
23	3	
24	2	
25	1	The final mile, growing excitement
26.2	0	Satisfaction of a completed challenge

Application to Strategy of Losing Weight

Steps

- Form new commitment to lose 50 pounds.
- Start diet and exercise program.
- Lose 5 pounds the first week and feel positive.
- Weight loss stabilizes and mood shifts to self-doubt—strategy deployed to go 1 day at a time and consider every meal and use of discretionary time.
- Lose 20 pounds and feel the battle of internal will.
- Lose 30 pounds and feel the transition taking hold.
- Lose 45 pounds and experience the soon-to-be attainment of the goal.
- Lose 50 pounds and experience satisfaction of the achievement.

The number of pounds one seeks to lose, so long as it is material and promotes the person's health is not the issue. The process, the will to achieve, and accomplishment is.

Inclusion Versus Exclusion

One aspect of a negative schema is a person excluding him or herself from a life experience because of an internal feeling that she/he is not worthy of inclusion. Inclusion is when a person is either invited in to the inner circle of an activity, a group, a club, or a meeting or when a person voluntarily joins an existing group expressing sincere interest in joining and is then accepted. Exclusion is the exact opposite, resulting in a person either not being asked to join or not feeling comfortable requesting participation. Being excluded one or more times can lead to a feeling of rejection.

Why Treatment?

A person who realizes that his or her life is not going as well as perhaps it "ought" or who has discovered within himself or herself one or more distinguishable patterns of maladaptive thinking may consider entering into a relationship with a trained therapist or experienced coach. The person also comes to the realization that she/he cannot handle the situation or deal effectively with his or her problems on his or her own. One goal of such engagement is to ferret out the underlying causes for the negative schema. Another is to create replacement modalities of thought so as to live life more happily and effectively. Both the treating professional and the client have a role in the process. As Grof (2000) said:

> What all the traditional schools of psychotherapy have in common is the effort to understand how the psyche functions, why the symptoms develop, and what they mean. This theoretical knowledge is then used in developing a technique that the therapist employs in his or her interaction with the client to correct the deviant psychodynamic processes. (p. 179)

Trust must be developed within the dyad. Considering the nature of highly confidential information shared in therapy, the client is more likely to share deeper thoughts if she/he feels comfortable that there is a high degree of trust in the therapist or coach. If that trust is developed, the trusted person (therapist or coach) is expected, of course, to have the wisdom to be able to guide the client past the intake stage and through the process of treatment with an end goal in mind. This end goal (or goals) should be discussed in the very beginning of treatment so the client remains focused and keenly aware of what brought him or her into treatment. Additional issues may arise during the course of treatment and these, in tandem or in conjunction, may also need to be treated. However, the client can become disheartened if treatment wanders into multiple directions solely out of interest in the issues by the therapist, but without making a connection to the original presented issue(s). Responsibility for any such detouring is primarily in the hands of the professional, but the client may also bear some measure of responsibility for introducing new or modified material during the course of treatment or expression of interest in exploring new issues. People raise new problems, and the scope of the issues that they came to see the therapist for and the scope of them should become clearer as therapy continues. In a way, the professional is somewhat vulnerable to having new issues crop up, which creates a burden necessary to deal with. This added burden may be easily fit into the existing treatment plan or it may require acknowledgment of the need and predictability of additional time. Working diagnoses may change dependent on newly offered information and response to inquiry.

The time it will likely take for therapy to have a positive and lasting impact cannot be accurately predicted. While it is important to forge an understanding with the client there cannot become an absolute requirement for the professional to predict the number of visits necessary for improvement; there should be some discussion along the continuum of treatment as to how the progress is to be measured and by who the measurement is to be made. Some clients see their therapist for many years, but this may be their choosing to do so, seeing their therapist as a consultant as well as a mental health professional. Of course, the ability of the client to afford such long-term care becomes essential to consider.

The client brings in to therapy certain material or food for thought and discussion. "The specific contribution of the therapist is that she/he has a conceptual framework large enough to provide a meaningful context for anything that emerges in the process" (Grof 2000, p. 204). In addition to verbal reporting of past or recent events, thoughts, and emotions, the client may also bring in exhibits or materials of interest pertinent to the discussion. The therapist cannot know in advance what these exhibits may be unless prearranged in a prior session, but it would appear to be necessary for the therapist to consider them in the context of treatment albeit they themselves may open up new veins of thought within the general framework of understanding the person.

Vaughan (1979) in speaking about transpersonal psychotherapy[1] wrote about the way a transpersonal therapist follows the clients to any domain or level of the psyche where their process takes them. The inclusion of concepts helps the therapist form a more complete composite of the person and the underlying potential causal roots. By excluding new information or tangential concepts, such as the emotional history and makeup of the person who presents a dilemma about some current event, a treatment may be too narrowly focused and while there may be success treating one or more symptoms, the driving force behind them may lurk underneath ready to manifest in the form of another problem later on, thus hurting the client. It is precisely for this reason that the implied contract (relationship) between the treatment professional and client be delineated at the outset and refreshed as treatment occurs. Therapy can be considered to have been effective when the maladaptive thinking of the client subsides. Otherwise, the treatment professional may unwittingly be subsuming the client's intentions for what she/he hopes to get out of the process of treatment, something perhaps best left to the client, assuming she/he is competent to do so.

Who is in charge of the therapeutic process? "Although the client's cooperation is an essential part of the therapeutic process, it is the therapist who is seen as the active agent and the source of knowledge necessary for successful outcome" (Grof 2000, p. 179). Grof argues that the selection of one or more techniques of the various and divergent schools of thought are influenced by the therapist's basic training and orientation towards a particular philosophical school.

[1] Transpersonal psychology is a field centered on the spiritual aspects of human life. Started by Abraham Maslow and Victor Frankl in the 1960s, the field uses psychological methods and theories to understand subject matter dealing with spirituality.

Treatment modalities can be done in isolation or in combination. The orientation and training of the therapist or the experience and training of the coach will have a major impact on how the treatment progresses. Modalities include, but are not limited to:

- Psychotherapy
  - Existential–humanistic–transpersonal
  - Freudian
  - Family
- Gestalt practice
- Poetry therapy
- Expressive painting
- Dance therapy
- Music therapy
- Psychodrama
- Sand play
- Eye movement desensitization and reprocessing (EMDR)
- Meditation
- Exercise regimens
- Yoga
- Other forms of healing

Grof (1992) created a special category of non-ordinary states of consciousness, called holotropic. He suggested an approach to therapy referred to as holotropic strategy of psychotherapy. This approach "…suggests that in our everyday state of consciousness we identify with only a small fraction of who we really are. In holotropic states, we can transcend the narrow boundaries of the body ego and reclaim our full identity" (Grof 2000, p. 2). Such states are characterized by changes in perception within the senses. An example is closing the eyes to perceive the environment absent the sense of sight. "We can reach profound psychological insights concerning our personal history, unconscious dynamics, emotional difficulties, and interpersonal problems" (p. 3).

Grof created a technique using holotropic breathwork: "It induces very powerful holotropic states by a combination of very simple means-accelerated breathing, evocative music, and a technique of bodywork that helps to release residual bioenergetic and emotional blocks" (p. 183). Breath has been used throughout human history to link mind, body, and spirit. Certain yoga exercises focus on breathing and the use of controlled breathing can be incorporated as part of a meditative practice. Runners can control their heart rate through the slowing down of their rate of breathing.

In holotropic therapy:

> …symptoms of emotional and psychosomatic disorders represent an attempt of the organism to free itself from old traumatic imprints, heal itself, and simplify its functioning. Effective therapy then consists in temporary activation, intensification, and subsequent resolution of the symptoms. (p. 179)

The premise of holotropic therapy is to externalize the symptoms of the client so that healing can take place through awareness and the process of willing change, leading to transformation.

On the other hand, Reich (1972) wrote about the negative consequence of therapy:

> The clinical basis upon which Freud postulated his theory of the death instinct is the so-called negative transference, i.e., long after it had been clinically established and theoretically formulated by Freud. This formulation means that some of our patients react to our analytic work of interpretation not by showing signs of improvement but by developing stronger neurotic reactions. Freud assumed that this intensification was tied in with an unconscious guilt feeling or, as he called it from then on, a "need for punishment" which compels the patient to resist the therapeutic work and to persist in his neurosis, i.e., in his suffering. (p. 289)

What Stands in Our Way?

Upon waking up, the events of the day or the near future may flash in high-speed mode through our minds, causing some trepidation. Worry may morph into abject fear, which can debilitate, sending the emotionally vulnerable person into a tailspin. This, in turn, may lead to a troubled person giving up on some aspect of life, perhaps a job search. Is it the world that is in the person's way or is it something specific about the person?

Regardless of whether it is the person or the world that stands in one's way, and it may be both, the hard reality is that it is the person who must deal with it and overcome it. Akin to the confident person whose confidence, compared to the nonconfident person, would drive that person to climb, find a way around, if not smash through a wall that impedes, the person whose negative thought patterns are ingrained will likely have a much more difficult time energizing him or herself to overcome the obstacle. After all, if the assumed result of any material action is failure, why act in the first place? When perceived failure is constant, the expectation of failure is confirmed within the mind's eye. The expectation to fail becomes that person's reality because the person perceives nothing but failure.

Moving Through Impasse

Is the blockage real or perceived? Humans come in every shape, size, and thought process. Difficulties, too, are perceived in dramatically different ways. Reasonably, the road ahead of everyone is fraught with at least some unknowns, if not, danger. As such, the challenge is to proceed through the minefield of life and work through as many of the challenges as possible. Moving through is the process that carries with it a complex series of ups and downs. It is the impasse that provides the discussion point of why this creates so much angst for some and not for others.

An impasse is a situation where there is no possibility of progress. Patience is the first step in solving the problem. The next is in recognizing that having a problem is not the problem, but is the opportunity to solve a problem and do so creatively. Thus, the impasse requires that the identified problem gets worked until it is solved. Solving part of the problem is often an effective method of solving the other parts, eventually leading to a whole solution.

Guarendi (1971) wrote about ways to deal effectively with anger:

> By its nature assertiveness is an animal tough to tame. If allowed a long leash, it can be trained into pushiness. Through an ever more sensitive vigilance for any offense, however slight, I can assert myself into obnoxiousness. In teaching others to walk on me, I can teach them to walk around me. Sometimes, it is healthier, for both the slighter and the slighted, to let some things pass. (p. 64)

Driving or walking to the edge of the Grand Canyon would lead to a clearly definable impasse, one that only illogic would say is solvable. But most problems can be at least partially resolved through determination and maintaining a positive attitude.[2]

When the person develops a history of feeling defeated at impasses or becomes unable to develop strategies to effectively deal with them, then the aura of negativity becomes evident in the person's life. Confidence affords a person with the fortitude to continue moving forward despite obstacles. Lack of confidence has the opposite effect. Persons who lack confidence shudder away from challenge and, when faced with it, back away and accept defeat. An example is when a person at work receives an opportunity to accept a challenging assignment, requiring some out-of-town travel, meeting new people, and working outside the person's comfort zone. The nonconfident person may turn down the opportunity or offer an excuse as to why he or she cannot accept. What could have been an upward career move could then become a weight keeping the person down.

Impasse equals dilemma. Dilemma requires a difficult choice to be made between two or more undesirable alternatives. Dilemma leads to the need to make decisions and choices. For a person that has a serious level of negativity, dilemma will not be welcomed and could produce anxiety. Anxious people do not react well when a clear mind is most needed. Working with a therapist or mentor, a person with such difficulty could try to understand the phenomenon of dilemma-induced anxiety and work on potential transformative approaches to future dilemmas. The serious-minded person wanting to change will be willing to try the introduction of new methods and strategies. Then, the aftermath of trial and error can be explored and the new approaches fine-tuned, ultimately, leading to a new person with new capacities. While this may sound overly simplistic, why does it need to be more complicated?

The level of how much a risk-taker the person is comes into play. High risk-takers will be much more willing to take chances as long as the payoff of a right decision is comparatively high. Low risk-takers will be unwilling to take many or high-stakes chances regardless of potential outcome.

---

[2] Perhaps it is for this reason that people attempt to perform feats such as crossing large elevated distances on a high-wire.

When to Hold and When to Fold?

A classic decision in a poker game is when to fold and when to hold the cards, continue wagering, and play (or hope) for winning the pot. Circumstances in life often lead to decisions of choice where maintaining momentum (sticking with the chosen course of action) or ceasing one's own progress (changing course or just stopping altogether) are two such choices. When faced with this sort of issue a crisis may unfold. Some people when at a crossroads are unable to decide which direction to turn. Adopting a frozen position may seem easiest when fear of the unknown is seen as more potent than the potential benefit of making a good choice at the risk of making a poor one. What considerations occur in a person's mind when faced with one of these choices?

Looking ahead helps a person perceive issues well before deadlines and ahead of the time when problems turn to crises. We can call that planning. Planners consider where they are currently and compare to where they want to be in the near future (or even long-term) and what steps need to be taken in order to get them there. With the exception of unpredictable elements, such a person figures on achievement of goals with appropriate effort. Progress can be measured along the way and increased effort expended when acceleration is not only possible but also desirable.

Those who are merely spontaneous, do no planning, and are otherwise more reckless on their activities are unlikely to be as successful as planners. They may hold on to long or fold too quickly out of sheer reactive emotion or by snap decision-making. Also, procrastination, the bane of the person incapable of reaching decisions, can toll progress.

Synopsis of Chapter

- Fixations serve to harm the ability of a person to move outward from ineffectiveness into a place with new potential.
- We can get absorbed inside our own paradigm of existence, ignoring fresh perspectives.
- A sense of vulnerability carries with it a paradigm of humility.
- During a crisis, new ideas may be tried.
- A paradigm shift is a change from one way of thinking to another.
- Overcoming fear is often a prerequisite to overcoming negativity.
- Fear can be overcome if faced head-on through the guiding help of a coach or therapist.
- Planning and preparation are antidotes to combat self-defeating images.
- Taking on problems in manageable segments will help a person solve problems.
- The key to successful management of a problem is to maintain a consistent positive attitude.
- Setbacks can be useful to propel a person's will towards a successful comeback.
- Various treatment modalities can be used to forge a positive relationship between the client and the treating professional.

Chapter 8
Catalyzing the Hidden Inner Strength Toward Exploration

It is our attitude at the beginning of a difficult task which, more than anything else, will affect its successful outcome.

—William James

Introduction

We have a certain core strength that often remains unused or underused. This strength, once harnessed, allows us to explore new possibilities, leading to potential discovery of new paradigms to replace ones deemed antiquated or no longer relevant to our present life. But how can this hidden capacity be unearthed and allowed to ferment and positively impact on our life?

Most of us have allies of one form or another. These may be family and friends, or coworkers who like us and in whom we place much trust. We may presently be in a therapeutic relationship or have one or more life coaches. Alternatively, we may be completely devoid of such exterior help, but have significant tools with which we can deploy to open up our own horizons to new avenues of thought, which we can refer to as the process of exploration. Willingness to open up to another person requires a sense of creative wonderment. In doing so, the client may become aware of internal issues that may, at the outset, be viewed as disturbing, but, after methodically dissecting the cause and reforming one's thought process, the person should be better able to face the challenges of everyday life more effectively than before treatment.

An astronaut explores outer space or lands on the moon not only to learn about that particular region but also to help explain the origins of the earth. So too, we can become an explorer of first-rate courage and enter willingly into the abyss known as ourselves. Deep within the core of who we are is the energy to become who we wish to be. Like the butterfly has origin in the caterpillar, we can climb out of our mostly self-imposed cocoon and metamorphose into a future entity. Some concrete examples may help to explain this process better.

We might have struggled for many years with one or more forms of addiction. We might have been previously unsuccessful in upgrading our skills sufficiently to

E. A. Kreuter, K. M. Moltner, *Treatment and Management of Maladaptive Schemas*,
DOI 10.1007/978-3-319-06817-6_8, © Springer International Publishing Switzerland 2014

land a better job or to enter a new and exciting field. We may have had difficulty attracting a mate or may desire to cultivate a new set of friends. Maybe we are just plain bored with life and desire something new or perhaps we lost a spouse of many years and feel renewal of spirit coming upon us that makes us wish to embark on the journey of falling in love again. Such possibilities exist, but we are so capable of sabotaging our own success that we stumble at the first difficulty or feel so unworthy of even trying to break out of the morass. A catalyst will doubtlessly help to encourage us to get out there and try new things. That may be called hard-core coaching. Such help can also be provided by a qualified psychotherapist.

As long as there is recognition of the present state of life being unsatisfactory, there can be dialogue and challenge suitable toward identifying possible newness in life. In his last book (Kreuter 2013a), Kreuter explored how Rex was able to triumph over long-standing adversity mostly of his own making. He went from being chronically unemployed to finding a good job, one suitable to his past skills, and he did so on his own merit. Yes, Kreuter acted in the role of coach and humbly so, but Rex did the work, came to amazingly beneficial realizations, and transformed not only his way of expressing himself but also his outlook and level of determination. He was unlocked, but he always had the key. Only we have our own key. True, there may be insight from outside observing the connection between the lock and the key, but without the person's ready willingness to apply the key and unlock his or her own inner secrets, there can be little hope for lasting or significant transformation. While Rex continues to struggle with life, his attitude remains extremely positive. When he experiences a setback, instead of simply lamenting, he picks himself up, dusts himself off, and considers his options from that point. He does speak of being bitter when things happen in his life outside his control and he is knocked down in life, but he recovers emotionally from this and rallies to find new pathways in his life. As a prayerful man, he uses his faith to stay grounded and accept his circumstances, but not as a way of avoiding responsibility for finding creative solutions to his life's dilemmas, and instead as a way of living a good and, for him, Christian life, but one where he accepts full responsibility for his circumstances.

What is needed is not a fancy or lengthy embarkation, but an earnest, guided exploration into waters never previously navigated. Simply put, it is navigating into the waters of the deep dark self, a place hidden from view to all, even the person to whom it belongs. It is not easy to wake up the sleeping giant known as our soul. We may be afraid to take risks or be too lazy to do the work needed to awaken this inner conscious. Kreuter offers a new idea: we have a major soul that is known and knowable and a minor soul that is mostly hidden away in the recesses of our subconscious. This is not meant to clash with the spiritual perspective where the soul is the repository of things divine; rather, Kreuter is suggesting the location of the soul as the place where inventories are maintained about what we want out of life, how we can best achieve what we want, and insights into what holds us back. However, getting a chance to wade through this inventory is not easy and may take many years to encounter unless we are guided where to look and what to do once we find it.

One way to achieve a life goal is to plot out a strategy of action steps, and then following the plan until success is achieved. But what if we stumble along the way and feel our own resources are so depleted that we cannot continue or find ways to break through the impasse?

Peterson (2013) reported that "Keeping a purpose in your life, going for a goal, and interacting with other people through work—be it paid employment or as a volunteer—staves off depression and even death, researchers have concluded" (p. 1). Many people plan for the financial aspects of retirement, but do not consider what they will do with their time. Thus, for some, retirement is first becoming tired of working, and then it is becoming tired of not working. People get bored.

"The energy by which the work of the personality is performed is called psychic energy" (Hall and Nordby 1973, p. 59). Jung differentiated his use of the word "libido" by expanding the definition to describe more than Freud's definition restricting its use to refer to sexual energy. Jung included "the appetites of hunger, thirst, and sex, as well as the emotions. Libido is manifested consciously as striving, desiring, and willing" (p. 59).

Change Yourself Rather than Others

There are some situations where it is a futile effort to change those around us. But, it may be possible to change our own approach in dealing with situations. By adapting to the environment, those around us may respond more favorably if they perceive that you are treating them fairly. The key objective is being able to evaluate the situation thoroughly and assessing where the problem lies. The next step is contemplating what changes are necessary for there to be an improvement in harmony. Finally, insert a change in the mix and then evaluate the results. As an example, a manager who has had difficulty with his or her team because the team members feel they are overworked, not listened to, and otherwise uncared for changes his approach by becoming more inclusionary, has more departmental meetings, assigns meaningful tasks and appropriate responsibilities to members, and takes time to listen more attentively, which leads to improved workplace morale.

We like to think that when we are in charge, we get the right to demand that those under us will change when and how we want them to. But, for example, that may cause workers to rebel subtly causing diminished productivity and an erosion of harmony. When there is pressure to change your attitude because the other person is in a more powerful position to force the issue, such change is done only as an appeasement and is purely transient. The world is full of manipulation and manipulating dialogue.

When we consider the aspects of our everyday life that do not proceed as planned, we can become either baffled or confused as to why. Looking inward at what we can do to alter our own approach and attitude may lead to humble realities becoming known to us, which, in turn, may lead to the development of new and improved patterns of living. Responding to stimuli does not have to be consistent with previous negative patterns once we choose to change. It is the willingness to make these changes that starts the process. Therefore, a fitting entry point for coaching or psychotherapy might be to examine what blocks us from this process of change. Through the active engagement with a trusted person, we may be able to identify and take responsibility for flaws in judgment and perception.

Shifting from the hustle and bustle of everyday life to the stark simplicity of witness and appreciation for nature's hearty, but vulnerable, creatures shifts the mood toward a positive appreciation for life. On a recent trip to the Bahamas, Kreuter (2013) wrote the following short story, titled "The Starfish":

> Today I held a starfish in my hands, a beautiful, simple, perfect starfish. And it made me wonder. Why does a starfish exist? What is its purpose on earth? How is it connected to all other creatures on earth? I can't fathom the answers to these questions? Oh, I'm sure I could "Google" the answers, but I think so many questions would still remain. I just want to say thank you, starfish, for existing and adding to my delight on this day. And for helping me to appreciate life in all its forms.

Forced Paradigm Shifting

As an example of a paradigm shift, today, young adults do not necessarily view home ownership as a way to build a nest egg for their future or as a prudent use of resources. This is quite different from the paradigm common to earlier generations and can be attributed to several factors, including the burst of the housing bubble and the increased unemployment rate. These factors led to more adult children of baby boomers choosing to rent rather than own. People today are also marrying later in life and delaying the start of families. Nisen (2013) found,

> In America, men and women are waiting longer than ever to get married for the first time. In the 1950s, women married at age 20 and men at 23. The median age at first marriage has been rising rapidly ever since. We're now at an all-time high of 27.1 for women and 29.1 for men. (p. 1)

As such, the need for a large living space has decreased. We also see empty nesters (parents whose children have grown and left the home), leaving the couple (or a single parent) to manage perhaps a large house with more room than is needed. Of course, there is a parallel or offsetting paradigm shift of a young adult not being able to leave the parental abode due to lack of sufficient income to fully emancipate. Some young adults may need to return to the parental home following loss of employment or after their own divorce. What shifts is the preconceived notion that we become an adult, complete our education, find immediate and lucrative employment in a chosen career, and commence a life independent of that of our parents, perhaps in a distant city or country. Economics certainly plays a superior role on forced shifting of paradigms.

Lack of an Independent Mindset

It is said that merely following the crowd is a surefire way to lose money. This wisdom is borne out in the investment world where people do not have an individual plan, but place their surplus wealth in popular investments that have already risen in value. They think just because something has a proven track record, this trend will continue indefinitely. What can happen is they will not perceive a downturn, hold on to their investments, and experience a severe drop in value. This phenomenon is similar to the gambler who observes bells and lights going off in the casino or people cashing in winning tickets at the racetrack so they "hop on" and make bets hoping to be one of the lucky few who "hit it big." Once losses are sustained, they may dip in to their pockets or, worse, credit, and wager more in desperate hope of making back their losses. This behavior is an excellent way to deplete one's personal wealth.

Contemplative Time is Good for the Creative Soul

We are so busy being busy and always thinking how busy we are that little or no time is allocated to just sitting back and thinking in order to examine perspectives and consider options. A lawyer I met explained that he rose early every morning and swam for 30 minutes, saying it was "good thinking time." A motivational speaker explained that people would do well planning time in their schedule to just think. Donald Trump is famous for saying "You have to think anyway, so why not think big?" (BrainyQuote.com 2014). Forming a plan for the day is a good way to establish a method of disciplined time management, but if the schedule is chock-full of activities with meetings butting up against other meetings with no time to breathe, how will creative thinking occur? In business meetings, there is usually a power differential where some have taken over the aura of the meeting, but are these people really able to listen? Communication requires both speaking and listening. Otherwise we drown out all sources of input. Because of their ego, they may be reluctant to allow other, particularly less powerful, persons to have the floor to assert their ideas. This only creates apathy on the part of creative individuals who may start to disconnect their loyalties and look elsewhere for career development in venues where their ideas will be respected.

Activity Does Not Equal Momentum

Though a person seems very busy, such activity does not always equal results; therefore, the achievement of positive momentum is not a guarantee. In flying aircraft, the landing gear is retracted once the pilots determine that the aircraft has reached a positive rate of climb. In a way, some people experience drag on their lives in the form of static movement in the progression of their life. This is evidenced by lack of career progress despite years of faithful service, limited emotional bonding between long-married couples, and a lack of enlightenment later in life threatening the attainment of self-actualization. Instead, the person with such "drag" may become depressed or even feel like there is no longer a point to life and, as such, she/he exists in a sort of bubble, waiting out Father Time. She/he does not look forward to illness or death, but is less and less fearful of the concept. The suicidal ideation of some could be triggered by a sustained period of largess in their mental state brought on by the complete lack of momentum in their lives. The authors feel that people who have lost such momentum in their lives can, in fact, be helped.

Turning Strategy into Execution

It is important to develop good strategies leading to doing the right things right. Once plans of action are in place, properly executing these plans becomes critical. Often good ideas die on the vine because of a lack of plan to execute. Plays called in the huddle by the quarterback are only effective if carried out well. Any misstep from the moment of the snap can derail the called play, resulting in a loss of yards or even an interception or fumble. Good strategy coupled with good execution is a recipe for success. We can ensure our own luck by taking responsibility for following through with our plans. It is also wise sometimes to let go of unfinished ideas.

Strategic thinking must be reassessed regularly taking into consideration new developments and changes in the applicable landscape. Many operating budgets in corporate America have failed because they are not revised to deal with changes that take place both in the economy and within the company. It is for this reason that a rolling 13-month budget becomes important, which allows a company to constantly forecast the next year and into the successive year.

Set Yourself up for Success and Monitor Progress

Success can be measured and goals can be established. Without goals, defining success is nebulous. Goals need to be realistic and weighed carefully against expectations. In Kenneth Moltner's chapter titled Expectations and Realities (Kreuter 2013a), he expounds on the important and often overlooked differences between these two constructs. When we establish and define success, we are well advised to consider the realities inherent in what we wish for or strive to attain. A new college enrollee wants to be a psychiatrist and may very well achieve that lofty goal. But does she/he realize what being a psychiatrist means and what effort is involved in attaining this goal? Is the defined goal based on a full analysis of the meaning of being a psychiatrist, which involves both earning a doctorate in psychology as well as a medical degree with psychiatry as a specialty? While the stated goal is very laudable, is it possible to know so far in advance that this is actually what the person wants?

Adding validity to the previous example is when the young person carefully works backward from the terminal goal, creating a roadmap of the steps needed to be taken and done well leading to the ultimate goal. Thus, the freshman exerts a superior effort knowing that his or her grades will count mightily in the eligibility for admission to medical school. The planning for the future requires performance many years before. The discipline necessary now has a direct and tangible impact on the success toward the future goal.

Patterns of behavioral responses to external events can be examined to identify specific flaws in a person's thinking. A process of detailed dissection of actual life experiences and the outcome as reported by the person provide fertile material, leading to challenge. It is at this juncture where excuses may be brought up, defending why the person acted the way she/he did.

Anger is also a potent human emotion that can interfere with a person's progress toward accomplishment of his or her goals.

Sigmund Freud long ago said something similar in regard to matters of the mind: Anger and its companion, aggression, need to be vented; otherwise, they will reach a boiling point and wreak havoc on their vessel, the human psyche. Freud called this release catharsis (Guarendi 1971, p. 88).

It is sometimes better to be quiet than to make an outburst or fight. "Silence is a giant first step toward self-control. 'I'm sorry' is a giant first step toward damage control" (p. 100). In Kreuter's (2003b, 2004, 2006a, 2007a, 2009, 2010, 2011a, 2012a, b) case study of a commercial airline pilot whose career was destroyed by a psychopathic predator, Robert, the pilot, described how he decided to become an airline pilot at an early age. He enjoyed television shows about flying and marveled at the constant stream of planes seen out his bedroom window. As he lived near an airport on Long Island, New York, Robert was able to observe flights in a regular pattern. He started noticing that the planes always intersected a particular spot on his window screen. Robert created a chart of the time interval between spotting planes and discovered a rhythm to the stream of planes. He even wondered whether the same crew was on different flights on successive evenings.

When Robert and his family were returning from vacation in upstate New York, they passed an airfield that was giving gliding rides and lessons. His father took Robert to the airfield, and Robert went up with the instructor for a ride on the glider. He was immediately fascinated with the feeling of weightlessness and desired to take lessons. His family allowed him to return to the airfield regularly by bus, which was more than 2 hours each way so he could take a series of lessons.

From these experiences, Robert's fascination with flying grew. He read all he could about becoming a pilot and, when he was old enough, took lessons to fly small planes. He earned his pilot's license (his "wings") at age 16, earlier than his friends earned licenses to drive cars. Robert worked his way up to flying the Boeing 737 commercial aircraft for US Airways.

Pilot Robert had a plan, stuck to it, and succeeded in achieving his boyhood dream. It was his unswerving effort that led to his achievement, not just wanting to be a pilot. In essence, he became a pilot by following a process. Thus, if we accept life as a process, we can more easily accept the notion of a long-term investment of time and energy in order to accomplish a life goal. As a metaphor for willingness, to sustain the necessary energy is to get to the end zone still carrying the football, where success is not a myth. Because new circumstances in life often interfere with our missions, dreams can be shattered, plans ruined, and our hopes smashed. But, if a person with such defined missions, vibrant dreams, and substantial hopes can work through difficulties and challenges, there is a likelihood of achievement.

How Hard Do You Push?

To catalyze someone, you may need to push very hard, sometimes, to the point of being blunt. Bluntness, which subsumes honesty, particularly by a trusted mentor should be valued. The truth that creates the tolerance for bluntness must be established. However, this is not the same as telling someone what to do or what you would do if you were him or her.

To set up the freedom to "tell it like it is," you first need to establish a verbal contract with the other person. This contract can include agreement to confront the other person when something is said or planned, which the catalyst deems to be inappropriate. The challenge can then freely take place and, perhaps, debate ensues, but the external viewpoint is able to be told by a trusted person, giving it much more likelihood of being seriously considered. Without such an agreement, often trying to provide guidance to another person has little chance of being effective because of a cloud of resistance built inside the person's head. Until this cloud is lifted, there is too much chaos taking place. The person is under metaphorical siege by his or her own mindset. Until the unhealthy thoughts are "breathed out" and new, healthier thoughts "breathed in", there will not likely be a way in to catalyze much change. Therefore, recognizing a situation where a person has such a large amount of chaotic material (such as thoughts or fears) inside his or her head can lead to helpful ways and exercises for the person to free himself or herself up, readying the person for therapeutic intervention. It is tantamount to help a person rise above noise and confusion. The confusion blocks listening and prevents willing adaptation of new concepts, no matter how sensible these may seem.

"All inner resistance is experienced as negativity in one form or another. All negativity is resistance" (Tolle 2004, p. 188). "The ego believes that through negativity it can manipulate reality and get what it wants" (p. 189). "Once you have identified with some form of negativity, you do not want to let go, and you do not want positive change" (p. 189). "Negativity is totally unnatural. It is a psychic pollutant, and there is a deep link between the poisoning and destruction of nature and the vast negativity that has accumulated in the collective human psyche" (p. 189).

How Do We Define a Core Belief?

As a famous example of a core belief, "We hold certain truths to be self-evident."[1] When challenged, we staunchly defend our core truths and are usually reluctant to change our belief systems. While the global use of "truth" consists of national ethics or a way of life, such truths, on the individual level, are at the core of our being. The basic elements of truth are that we have been convinced of its consistent value, unimpeachable righteousness, and high level of applicability to us.

[1] From the United States *Declaration of Independence* written by Thomas Jefferson et al., written June–July 1776, ratified July 4, 1776.

When confronted with an alternate perspective, we may or may not keep an open mind. If we are receptive to at least listening to the new perspective, we might be surprised at its potential viability. Adapting a new perspective requires a change in attitude. For such change to become fully accepted, we need to apply it to the constructs of our lives. “A person is both actuality and potentiality” (Maslow 1961, p. 54).

Embracing new ideas intimately is essential to forge true transformation. Adapting a core belief by replacing it or modifying it with something new is an act of bravery and shows good resolve to become better at some aspect of life.

Making a change in a core belief can lead to consideration of other core beliefs, especially those most closely associated to the one now permanently altered. An example is a person deciding to give up fattening foods in order to improve his or her overall health, possibly in response to an alarming medical test result. Once the person’s diet is altered and the person’s health is improving, additional change in related areas may be considered.

The person may decide to also give up smoking at the same time she/he is giving up certain fattening foods. The reason may be that she/he has altered that attitude, wanting to transform him or herself into a healthier being. She/he realizes that controlling one vice while maintaining another makes no sense. It would be like repainting one room in the house, which, after doing so, makes the adjacent rooms look shabby relative to the newly painted room.

Changing the Direction of One’s Life

For example, Mary, a newly divorced mother of two teenagers, feels that she is stuck in a rut. Between holding down a full-time job as a retail store manager and taking her daughters to soccer practice, games, and school events, she has no time to work on herself. She feels depressed and lost most of the time, not interested in very many aspects of her life.

Mary opens up to only a few close friends and has not considered therapy as an option, but her dour feelings are increasing so she knows something must be done. Mary’s best friend suggested that she call Mark, who helped one of his coworkers break out of his morass, leading to his opening up new avenues in his life. After weeks of ambivalence, Mary finally contacted Mark and arranged to see him. Almost at the outset of therapy, Mark began to challenge Mary about her previous lack of motivation to re-create the dynamics of her life.

Burnout

“The symptoms of burnout overlap considerably with those of depression, except that in most cases, burnout is work related. So burnout is an eight-hour-per-day depression, and its context-specific nature suggests that learned helplessness might indeed be operating" (Peterson et al. 1993, p. 257). "Burnout involves maladaptive passivity" (p. 257).

Workaholics sometimes find that their lifestyle is not sustainable. Gerry (2013) wrote of the experience of burnout associated with career: "…it was a classic case of burnout. Multiple chronic stressors over an extended period of time left me totally drained and no longer performing at my best" (p. 1). To offset the characteristic signs of burnout (including domestic problems, deteriorating health, fatigue, and unhappiness), creating a counterbalancing life outside of work will help. In addition, learning how to relax or taking up an interesting hobby or sport will serve to break the chronic pattern of work stress and help the person to unplug. Setting limits will help set the stage for time to develop such a counterbalancing life.

Some people are hardier than others, and therefore, more resistant to illness and also able to bounce back better from setbacks—part of everyday life. Hardiness, conceived by Kobasa (1979), is an individual difference spanning several dimensions: commitment, control, and challenge. People committed to their goals are excited and fully engaged in the project. Believing in one's control over outcomes enables a person to devise solutions to dilemmas encountered in life. Such people are determined and find creative ways around roadblocks. They are undaunted when the going gets rough. People who appreciate being challenged see them as growth opportunities. If the challenge is high, the attainment of a related goal must also be worthy of the required effort. "With choice comes opportunity and responsibility. If you want to reimagine your life, you have to be the one who chooses. You get the opportunity to do it, and you accept the responsibility for the outcome" (Leider and Webber 2013, p. 100).

We tend to lose our balance in life because we sometimes respond to our life experience with extremes of emotion—fear, sorrow, anger, and even joy. Creative "Righting" (a term coined at the Creative "Righting" Center in New York City) is based on the simple belief that reading and writing are beneficial to one's psychological health and emotional balance (Reiter 2009, p. 3).

Writing as a therapy opens up locked emotions in a person. "Through the use of poetry the therapist can open up a channel within the interiority of a person" (Kreuter 2006b, p. 41). Becker (1971) suggested an inherent contradiction between the inside of a person's body—his or her thoughts and feelings—and the outside. Although we experience mostly on the outside, all objects in nature have some interiority.

In work with prisoners, they can be offered "…an alternate to modern remedies as drugs, binge therapy, or self-help" (Kreuter 2006b, p. 42). Schneider (2004) suggested that people can be coached to "…recognize that the capacity to tolerate ambiguity, discord, and strife is one of the hallmarks of maturation and that without such a reserve, there is almost no chance to thrive" (p. 40). "When we write from the heart, we impact mind, body, and spirit" (Reiter 2009, p. 4). In describing the case of a cancer patient (Alysa), "Through the ritual of daily writing, Alysa has the opportunity to give expression to the emotional dimension of her life. Writing simultaneously expresses and contains her intense emotions, achieving the important purpose of self-regulation" (p. 75).

"Emotions are how we feel about what we touch with our imagination, from the dread of a loud scary noise in the dark to those fifteen minutes of fame when you know you're at the top of your game and everyone else gets to see. Emotions are what move us and motivate us" (Hughes et al. 2005, p. 11).

Synopsis of the Chapter

- Each of us has one or more core strengths that may remain unused or underused.
- Deep within our core is the energy to become who we wish to be.
- A way to achieve a life goal is to plot a strategy.
- Keeping a purpose in life staves off depression.
- It may be possible to change our own approach in dealing with situations.
- Responding to stimuli does not have to be consistent with negative patterns.
- Activity does not equate to having momentum in life.
- Contemplative time is beneficial to the interior (soul) of the person.
- Success can be measured and goals can be established.
- Patterns of behavioral responses to external events can be examined, looking for flaws.
- Making a change to a core belief can lead to consideration of other core beliefs.

Chapter 9
Case Examples of Clients Who Shifted Paradigms

Do not follow where the path may lead. Go, instead, where there is no path and leave a trail

—Ralph Waldo Emerson

Introduction

> In general, case studies are the preferred strategy when 'how' and 'why' questions are being posed; when the investigator has little control over events, and when the focus is on a contemporary phenomenon within some real-life context. (Yin 1994, p. 1)

Rex: Transformation of Being

At the 2013 Annual Conference of the National Association for Poetry Therapy held in Chicago, IL, USA, Dr. Kreuter and Dr. Reiter conducted a presentation on resilience based on Kreuter's (2013a) book titled: *Fostering resilience for loss and irrelevance,* with a foreword written by Dr. Reiter. The presentation ended with Gloria Gaynor's "I will survive." Dr. Kreuter described the case study of Rex, which is an important component of the book. After working with Rex for 13 months, the case study was completed and the book published. In that time, Rex's attitudes, paradigms, and behaviors had modified, enabling him to be better suitable for seeking employment and living his life more happily. Dr. Kreuter explained to the group that his role in the dialogue with Rex was one of coach and not one of therapist. Reiter et al. (2009) wrote:

> What gives us the power to renew ourselves? Our resilience shows itself in our creativity. Interestingly enough, within the human body itself, there are "poietic" organs, such as the lymph system, where there is a continuous creation of new blood cells. This poeisis is creativity on a biological level…. On a psychological and spiritual level, creativity enables us to transcend our limitations. It kindles the imagination, fuels our dreams, and plants seeds of hope that are vital for our renewal. (p. 14)

E. A. Kreuter, K. M. Moltner, *Treatment and Management of Maladaptive Schemas,*
DOI 10.1007/978-3-319-06817-6_9, © Springer International Publishing Switzerland 2014

"...Writers work to complete an internally derived inspiration, which is considered to be a source of both spiritual and creative energy; for these writers, the internal completion of the task may be more important than the sharing of a finished product" (Edwards 2000, p. 3). Referring to the novelist/poet John Updike (1932–2009) and Ursula Le Guin (1929): "The pervading philosophy of Updike includes the notion that life is inherently empty, and that we must make meaning through those hopes and fantasies that stand in tension with the harsh reality of the world. Le Guin would see emptiness as opportunity, since out of emptiness comes all that is created" (p. 22). "We assume we are capable of understanding the objective world we live in, yet we also strive to reorder that world" (Zebrowski, Jr. 2000, p. 165). "From a Taoist viewpoint, the movement of Heaven's energy, via the human imagination, through the writer's body and into the earthly substance of the printed page, might be seen as the union of essence (*Jing,* the essential components of the physical body), energy (*Chi,* the energy that flows through all bodies), and spirit (*Shen,* the mind of the Tao)—the three Treasures of the Tao" (Edwards 2000, pp. 17–18). Tao is a metaphysical Chinese concept signifying a path or doctrine, dealing with the natural order of the universe.

It is said that everyone on the planet who is alive has a right to be here. The sense of being brings with it an opportunity to consider our place in the world, now and where we would like to be. For Rex, in a spiritual sense, for a believer, being alive means something because of his sense of an acknowledged God. In one person's view, "A Franciscan reminded me we are here now in God's presence not in an imaginary theological construct of the future. It is God's love that gives us a sense of aliveness" (Rex, personal communication, November 11, 2013).

Rex contributed a new poem:

BUILDING A NEW LIFE
Where I was?
Being at the effect of my circumstance
Being at the effect of my reactive mind
What I went through?
Panic
Outbursts
Where I am now?
I am a man of choice
No longer controlled by the reactive mind
New possibilities
Increased resilience
One goal—financial self-sufficiency
The "should" statements
Decreased
The "could" statements
Increased
Undue self-criticism
Not from God
Not healthy
Not productive
When I foolishly put myself down
I do not

Have to put myself down
For putting myself down
Correcting my behavior
Not condemnation
Progress through routine efforts
Momentum through constancy
Greater noticing of the self
I monitor my progress
I assess
No longer isolated
Rehabiting my routine
A whole new world
Suddenly
Appeared
I want to keep improving
Myself
Momentum shall not halt
It is better to avoid
Seeing any crisis
As unbearable
It is never more
Than 100 %
Awful
Routine
A sign of success
The day divided into segments
I can manage
No need to be super human
Discretion and appropriate behavior
The keys
I will use my time
More effectively
Power imagery
Gives me confidence
I no longer
Feel lost
There are no pros to drinking
I conned myself
Thinking it would help
Cigarettes no more
They are bankrupt
I no longer blame employers
For my plight
It is never too late
To become who I
Might
Have been
Now I am a part
Of the fabric of life
Back on the game-board
A player in my own existence
Transformation is dumping old reactions
Now I bask in the light
Of God's love

About a year ago, Rex was with some friends and had a few drinks, which, for him, was counter to his then professed abstinence from alcohol. Though he felt he was fine to drive, he was pulled over by the police because Rex was driving at night with the lights off. The police conducted a field sobriety test after Rex refused to take a breathalyzer test. The police felt that he stumbled during the test and took away his driver's license and arrested him. He was appointed a public defender and prepared for trial. He was convicted and sentenced to 3 months in the county jail. Rex was released on March 3, 2014 after serving about 2½ months. He was released early because of some essays he wrote as part of the rehabilitative program run by the facility.

Kreuter was able to correspond with Rex by mail. Some excerpts of Rex's letters:

- "I want to give you a tremendous shout out of praise of thanks to you for your inspiring and consoling letter you sent me. I often read it to refresh me during my stay here. It broke the sense of isolation and tension that I adopted the first 2 weeks."
- "I have been nicknamed 'Pops' by my cellmates as I have fulfilled that role of calming them when they get upset with one another."
- "I will say I have grown here to see my natural ability to relate to jail persons as sons of God, able to give."
- "I have greater confidence as I ask questions and do not act like I know everything."
- "Your friendship and prayers these past 2 years prepared me to move through this experience with a greater strength and resolve than I could have previously projected."

In a second letter, Rex wrote some additional thoughts:

- "By practicing being present daily, I am inspired to write."
- "The intense culture of the drug offenders and street people amidst the corrections' guards (each with his own 'pet' methods of lineups and shakedown) has kept me in action using my freedom."
- "I did the time; the time did not do me."
- "I used my time to cleanse my heart and mind and, yes, get closer to God."
- "Weekly mass gave me structure and purpose."

In the first 2 weeks since Rex was released from jail, he has reached a very stable place within his emotional and mindset. His new resolve is towards making the most of every day and doing all he can to secure full-time employment. His attitude is good and he has no bitterness. His communication style has become very adaptive towards his surroundings, which serves his need to properly convey his thoughts to others.

Rex discussed the need to be persistent. This is one of the first topics discussed in Kreuter's previous coaching of Rex (Kreuter 2013a). To emphasize the concept, Kreuter asked Rex to imagine a stream of water where he was on one shore, but needed to cross to the other shore. While crossing seemed difficult, if not impossible, Rex was asked to notice a series of rocks that he might be able to use to step on and traverse his way to the other side. In his imagining, Rex then developed a more solid notion of possibilities and the need to continue on despite the apparent difficulties and challenges.

An additional element of transformation suggested to Rex was for him to begin to create a journal of his daily life issues and how he resolved each. In doing so, he will eventually create personal manual of how he lived his life and faced obstacles for Rex to later give to others who might benefit from learning how Rex handled his issues, so they too could find solutions to their own lives. Thus, the stumbling blocks he faces fuel the persistent and creative energy to find potential solutions try them and find what works. Once he breaks the barriers in his own maladaptive schemas, which he is doing admirably, he positions himself well to pass on what he has learned to others.

Gloria: Career Dilemma

Gloria, female, age 55, is seeking to reestablish her career with a stable company within 1–1½ years in order to obtain health and other employment benefits. She has been "working on her resume" for months, but has been having difficulty planning ways to meet her goals. She has been steadily working in her own consulting business, but due to injury, has seen her client load lessen. She is concerned about the future.

We discussed spending some time pursuing credentialing and joining new professional organizations plus committing to writing several business articles in her local professional organization's monthly journal. She was very receptive to all ideas presented, which were delivered as direct challenges to her. During the discussion, Gloria displayed the feeling of fear twice, each time rooted in self-limiting career growth concerns. In essence, she could not get out of her own way.

Within the dialogue, it became apparent that a fantastic career opportunity might be very obtainable for Gloria with only the need to communicate her interest to a few key people well-known to her inside the organization. Gloria reached a shift in her own self-perception of her skills and of her emerging interest in the organization, one she has volunteered for over the past two decades. What she was blocking was how fitting this potential career position could be for her and how convenient it is upon analysis.

Gloria's paradigms were surrounded by distorted perceptions of her value juxtaposed to the "other people" whom she felt would be out there and be better candidates for the position. She was completely ignoring her own tremendous value and her strong history with the organization. In essence, the job she would love was present under her own obstructed eyes. By questioning her about the possibilities of approaching the organization about a position, she slowly shifted her mindset from one of casualness to one of commitment to contact those inside the organization whom she trusted to inquire about the possibilities of her working there. Her shift had to so with her internal belief that she was valuable as a volunteer, but that they would not want her as a full-time employee. She became transfixed on her own negativity, which served to mask this first-rate career possibility. Now, she has a dynamic plan of communication and something to consider that may very well meet her career needs long into the future.

The shift for Gloria, while on the surface subtle, is nonetheless remarkable because it provides an example of how the puzzle pieces of life can be reassembled through the guide of a catalyst, but with the work of the client.

Margaret

Margaret is about 60 years old. She struggled for many months about a suspected fraud in her husband's company. When she was challenged to review the facts juxtaposed to the original questions, she altered her approach to the struggle. During the inquiry into her claims, it was brought to light that what was really bothering her was that she felt deeply wronged by another female for having an affair with her husband. As her husband was aware of Margaret's concerns, the situation slowly resolved once Margaret was able to confront her husband for the suspected indiscretion. Once out in the open, they were able to continue on as a couple. The impact of the affair on Margaret was significant, but given her age and that her husband was older and now infirmed, it became pointless to do anything more than move quickly past her own pain and continue her marital relationship, focusing more on what future they could still have together.

Shawn the Lawyer

The following case study is an example of an individual who experienced a shift in thinking at middle age. Though stuck in a negative groove for decades, Shawn was able to make a determined shift, and started to change his life.

Shawn, currently a single, 43-year-old male, living in southern California, is a licensed attorney in several states, with some positive case experience, though he continues to struggle to earn an adequate living. His life has been one of confusion and struggle. Shawn suffers from a sleep disorder where he sleeps for unusually long periods of time, often resulting in missed appointments and a lack of steady rhythm in his life. Shawn is fairly athletic, a good tennis player, and in reasonably good physical shape.

When Shawn was in his 20s, he was interested in becoming a filmmaker. He was able to write a script, arrange financing, and encourage a celebrity to play a role, and, ultimately, created a finished short film. The completion of his film did not lead to a film career for Shawn, which served to diminish any effort on his part to embark on a career path with steady income potential. As a result, Shawn spent the next two decades bouncing from job to job without achieving any reasonable level of success as he later reflected on it. Kreuter began to work with Shawn and started him on a walking regimen, which resulted in Shawn ceasing his smoking habit and increasing his cardiovascular health. He then reached an extraordinary decision to apply to take the Law School Admission Test.[1] Shawn did pass the exam and was admitted to a law school in California. He completed his training and then passed the Bar Exam.

Though Shawn attained this level of achievement, his sleep issues continued to hamper his efforts to enter the practice of law except for managing to work for individuals on very small cases. His debts mounted and the pressure for him to find a permanent solution to manage the economics of his life steadily increased. Interestingly, none of these pressures kept Shawn from maintaining his sense of fun or diminishing his interest in socializing or athletics. He manages to stay one step ahead of creditors and lives a very modest lifestyle.

Shawn is a case of a person who did shift his thinking at the midpoint of his active life, but has not been able to reach any level of sustained success. While his thought process is improved since before he started law school, he continues to search for answers. Shawn's thinking is, perhaps, still maladaptive in that he could be considering basic employment at a much lower level in order to prevent complete economic chaos in his life, but he has been reluctant to do so. Management and treatment of this type of situation could start with helping Shawn come to terms with the inherent realities in his world and challenging his choices and decisions. The sleep disorder may be genuine, but it also could be a symptom of Shawn hiding behind a diagnosed disorder as a way of letting himself off the hook. It may be that Shawn needs to hit a lower form of "bottom" for him to actually shift his mindset.

Paulette

Paulette presents as a 35-year-old Caucasian female currently living with her mother and two daughters in a small three-bedroom house. Paulette is diagnosed with generalized anxiety disorder and depressive disorder, not otherwise specified (NOS),[2] as evidenced by her anxiety, panic attacks, and depression. Paulette reports a past relationship with her stepfather as most important in her life as a young girl. When Paulette was a teenager, her mother committed a crime that Paulette later discovered to be the murder of her beloved stepfather. While her mother was incarcerated, she lived with her grandparents. Paulette later fell in love with the father of her first daughter, who was later killed right in front of her. Several years later, Paulette began a relationship with the father of her second daughter who helped raise both girls as if they were his own. Paulette's youngest daughter maintains a long-distance relationship with her father. Paulette's oldest daughter currently suffers from substance abuse and addiction, which has caused a lot of problems within the family, including conflict, stress, and financial strain. Paulette's youngest daughter, now a

[1] Shawn's IQ is reportedly over 140.

[2] Generalized Anxiety Disorder—DSM-V, code 300.02; Depressive Disorder—DSM-V, code 311.

teenager, was recently sexually abused by a boy she knew and is being bullied in school. For Paulette, this increases her anxiety and ability to cope with the stressors in her life. Paulette's relationship with her mother would best be described as tense due to her feelings of frustration when communicating with her, but she is entirely dependent on her mother financially.

Since the initial session, signs of resilience have been present with Paulette, which could be seen through her desire and dedication towards improving her life. Her therapist has been working with her for about a year and she has made improvement in her ability to apply coping skills and techniques when her symptoms are present. One session in particular stands out when she came to see the therapist directly after an initial psychiatric evaluation. Paulette was visibly upset and in the middle of a panic attack. After some breathing techniques, Paulette and her therapist were able to rehash her appointment and work through the psychiatrist's comments. Paulette was scared because the psychiatrist wanted her to stop all her medication; medication which Paulette has been reliant on for many years. Deep breathing and active listening, eye contact, and supportive feedback decreased Paulette's anxiety and enabled her to develop a plan for moving forward with medication management through her previous psychiatrist. Paulette's resilience lies in her refusal to give up and her constant desire to learn and grow as a woman.

Greg

Greg is aged 55, single, no children, and lives alone in a small apartment in a major city. Greg worked as an attorney for several law firms, but is currently unemployed and takes multiple medications for various ailments, including depression.[3] Greg is a fearful person and has lost his confidence, especially when it involves seeking employment. Given his legal training, Greg remains sharp-minded and reasonably articulate. Because he has been sedentary, Kreuter suggested that he begin a walking regimen, which Greg has done. The daily routine of walking became a metaphor for pursuing movement (improvement) in his life endeavors and has brought about a more positive outlook. Even after reverting back to not working, he has shown good internal resolve to start again and shows an increased willingness to try.

Greg reported that he maintains a "Scale of Good Days." This scale involves him keeping a tally of the number of consecutive days that he feels generally good. In a recent conversation, Greg reported a feeling of "going back down after 25 good days." Upon exploration of what may have triggered this reversal of momentum, Greg stated that he woke up after 9½ hours of sleep, with a feeling of fear over his

[3] One medication he takes in *Provigil* (400 mg/day). Greg reports that this drug helps counteract the "drugged-out effect" that he sometimes experiences. Because his mood is generally low, he only hopes for feeling more stable as opposed to being helped to feel much better. He has been diagnosed as having the symptoms for which he is currently diagnosed: major depressive disorder, recurrent severe without psychotic features (DSM 296.33) and anxiety disorder NOS (DMS 300.00). He has had these symptoms on and off for the past 40 years.

ever-worsening financial pressures.[4] He admitted having "bad thoughts of anxiety and panic." Greg is in the regular care and treatment of a psychiatrist and has disclosed having these feelings in his sessions. The psychiatrist has recommended that Greg undergo electroshock therapy on an in-patient basis. Greg is strongly considering this option as he feels "desperate" to do something to help himself.[5] As an alternative, Greg located a local hospital that provides these treatments on an out-patient basis and has discussed this option with his psychiatrist.

Greg does not give himself adequate, if any, self-affirmation. This contributes to his ongoing problem. Because he does not validate himself, he is not out in the world where he could receive some validation for his work. By staying out of the mix, he has fewer sources of validation. Greg may be recreating a pattern of unworthiness that he learned in his past, perhaps from childhood. Greg is resistant to do much of anything to improve his life or decrease his symptoms, except rely on psychotropic medication, which he also admits to using excess sleep as a form of "sedating" himself from the impact of the outside world.

Recently, Greg reported feeling "better," but when asked how he spent the day, he said he just "stood around the apartment." When encouraged to walk outside, he sometimes agrees and does it or he provides some form of excuse, such as "it is raining" or "my legs hurt." Kreuter suggested that Greg investigate his qualifications for Social Security Disability (SSD), which even his psychiatrist agrees he may be eligible. However, Greg resists making efforts to apply because he fears, if he applies, it would "label" him "mentally disabled." Kreuter encouraged Greg to discuss this apprehension with Greg's psychiatrist. When he does push himself to walk, he goes further than he otherwise would want to out of feeling "embarrassed" if he did less. It is, therefore, Greg's internal maladaptive schema, which requires ongoing management and treatment.

Recently, Kreuter spoke with Greg at a time when Greg was feeling depressed. He made the following statements:

- "I have a difficult time working in a public environment."
- "I can't understand why I can't look for a job."
- "Doing anything takes an extreme amount of energy."
- "I am a neat freak, but there is a dirty pot sitting in my sink for the past 2 weeks."
- "It bothered me that the pot was sitting there."

Eventually, Greg put the pot away indicating that "it was no big deal." Kreuter asked Greg: "How do you feel?" Greg responded:

- Tired
- Depressed
- No inertia
- Lethargic

[4] Greg is currently living off his savings, including steady depletion of his retirement funds. He receives Medicaid, which covers his medical expenses, but, otherwise, has no income. He estimates that in 1 year he will have exhausted his assets.

[5] Greg reports having tried this treatment in the past with very little improvement in his symptoms.

Kreuter encouraged Greg to contact a local law firm that specializes in helping mentally and physically disabled persons apply for SSD. Before providing Greg with the contact information of the law firm, Kreuter spoke with the firm, which felt very certain that it could help Greg. Greg did agree to contact them and reported that he made an appointment. When Greg told Kreuter he had made the appointment, Greg felt a sense of fear and indicated with a self-deprecating statement: "I am a lazy bum." He further said, "I don't make the right choices with my time."

One of Greg's problems is that he thinks about his low energy levels and speaks openly about his lethargy. When asked about his current energy level, Greg responded:

- "Not tired."
- "Not enthusiastic."
- "Not tired" (an interesting repetition of first comment).
- "Disgusted."

When asked if he felt anything positive, he said that he did post a resume to an online site, but said it was a minor step and was "ridiculous." When asked if his negative feelings are optional, he said:

- "Not optional."
- "Going through 40 years, ingrained at this point, I take some steps, but then fall back."

There is incongruence between his statements, indicating that he is confused by his own state of being. This could be partly due to his medication and partly due to his long-standing repertoire of self-defeating behavior. It is his psychic energy, just as much as his lack of physical exercise, which prevents Greg from finding the will (energy) to move forward with his life. Kreuter asked Greg how he reconciles the contrast between feeling ingrained and not seeing himself as a disabled person. He responded:

- "Laziness."
- "Lack of will power"
- "Fear."

When asked if anything was under his control, he said, "No." When asked who controls him, he said, "I do." When asked if he wants to be a different person, he said, "Yes." When asked what he could do today to make himself a different person, he said:

- "Not binge tonight."[6]
- "Filing for SSD would be a flashing sign that I am disabled."

[6] Greg reported that he periodically overeats (binges). He indicated that he has made this known to his psychiatrist.

When asked if he thinks he is mentally ill, he said, “Yes.” He routinely refers back on his long history of feeling depressed. When asked how many bad days he has had in a row, he replied, “5–6 weeks.” He added that he “feels the inertia of depression.”

As a way of providing him with a new tool to use as a method of increasing his psychic energy, Kreuter conducted the following exercise (*The Power of Unlocking the Chains*) with Greg:

Kreuter asked Greg to close his eyes and stay in a sitting position, then perceive that he was wrapped in chains with closed locks, keeping him restrained. Kreuter asked “How do you feel?” Greg responded “Like my usual self.” Then, Kreuter asked him to consider having an enlightened thought: “Wait a minute, I have a key in my pocket and I can reach it.” Then, Greg was instructed to imagine himself actually unlocking the chains and removing them, leaving them in a pile on the floor and stepping away. Kreuter pointed out to Greg that the dilemma is when you lack a process to solve the problem. The solution is to consider how to unlock the locks and remove the chains (barriers) to gain insight or move towards positive thinking.

Greg was initially resistant with respect to reaching for the key, saying “it is too much effort to get the key.” Kreuter added supportive guidance coaching Greg to find the deep well of energy inside his being to retrieve the key and perform the task of unlocking the chains. Even when Greg persisted with his opposition by saying “there are so many, it’s taking a long time,” Kreuter used the technique of remaining silent to see what Greg would say and do next. After 20 seconds of silence, Greg reported that “most of them are off,” and, eventually, “all of them are off.” He was instructed to keep the key and use it whenever he encounters a difficult situation. By applying the simple exercise, Greg might be somewhat stronger and find new will to resist the former negative schema where he falls back on his perceived disability. In this case, it is clear that the schema needing change is making Greg’s failure possible. What he needs to do is to use power of mind.

Greg did well with the exercise despite several times citing how difficult the problem is, which, for him, reflects accurately how he sees the real problems in his life, both imagined and unimagined. Through the use of the simple device in the exercise, Greg has at least one more tool to shift his mindset from one where he is trapped to one where there is an awakening of possibilities, leading to solutions both on mental and emotional levels.

Negative Schema Within Marital Discord

Introduction

Divorce has become prevalent in our society. See *Marriages and Divorces–Number and Rate by State* (estimated as of July for 2009; Divorcestatistics.info 2014). In this part of the book, we explore four different perspectives of marital discord. In one, the parties separated but reconciled. In the other three, the parties were divorced. In two of the situations, the parties divorced amicably. One couple had one child. One couple did not. Both resolved their issues on their own. They obtained a non-contested divorce. In the final case, the parties have two relatively young children. It was litigated extensively with, in the authors' view, an apparent emotional drain on the wife.

Maladaptive Schema in the Form of a Toxic Relationship

Consider the plight of married couples or people with significant others in a committed relationship who feel stuck in their respective relationships with no apparent solution. According to Carter (2011) "...unhealthy relationships can turn into exactly that—a toxic internal environment that can lead to stress, depression, anxiety, and even medical problems" (p. 1). Habit and fear of change or feeling trapped may contribute to these people's decisions to stay together or they do so for other reasons such as children or finances or even fear of being alone. Months and years go by with no apparent improvement in the relationship. Yet there is a noticeable, albeit subtle, impact on the people involved. They start to slowly wither in terms of their inner strength and desire for life. They may become bitter. Some will turn to affairs outside the marriage to work out their internal frustrations or to have their emotional/sexual needs met. The consequences can be large. "In a long-term study that followed more than 10,000 subjects for an average of 12.2 years, researchers discovered that subjects in negative relationships were at a greater risk for developing heart problems, including a fatal cardiac event, than their counterparts whose close relationships were not negative" (p. 1).

Finding answers require determining what the questions are. Beneath the rubble of a toxic relationship are the people involved who just might be much better off separated or enrolled in a program to help them deal with their problems as a way to salvage the relationship. The way of life experienced on a daily basis by people in toxic relationships can lead to internal anger, work-related problems, health problems, depression, and other manifestations of high stress. Working through the difficulties may involve consideration of bold choices, made alone or actually with the other person.

As an example of a shift from a maladaptive lifestyle to one of growth and renewed energy, the following is Kreuter's personal story of his first marriage and ensuing divorce and remarriage:

I had been married almost 9 years with three beautiful children, but the marital relationship was becoming unacceptable for both of us. We tried marriage counseling, which helped in a way to lead us both to the realization that maintaining the marriage was going to be much worse on us and the children, but that ending the marriage would free us both to continue on with our lives while also continuing to care for our children. The negative pattern was apparent. I would come home after a long day at the office and the long commute home and immediately plug in to either do more work or take care of the yard or deal with the children. I was perpetually occupied. My relationship with the children was strong, but I was unhappy, feeling unfulfilled. My wife and I had divergent dreams and our aspirations were vastly different. I began to consider that getting married at age 22 was much too young. The shift in my thinking came in the form of a simple question posed to my then wife: "Do you want to continue to stay married?" Her answer was a very polite, yet emphatic "No." Thus, we decided then and there to take steps to orchestrate a calm separation, since it seemed to both of us to be the optimal solution to our never-ending problem and would be in the best interests of our own children whom we were jointly committed to. The separation was accomplished and the children continued to be nurtured, albeit the transition was not easy for them. What was necessary for me was to change my mindset from feeling trapped to feeling able to establish new momentum of my own life and find a way to do it nicely and respectfully while maintaining adequate harmony in my former home. What resulted from the joint decision to move the relationship in a different direction was interpersonal growth and renewal of psychic energy. It took courage and determination to make the transition successful and as easy as possible for the young children and for my soon-to-be ex-spouse. The 2 years following the physical separation were the most challenging as these were the years when I had to figure out a new time management system to be able to have as much time with the children as possible and adjust the family finances. Emotionally, I needed to adjust to being alone much of the time and how it felt to bring the children back to their mother's home after visiting with them. I took them on extended trips whenever possible. After several years and some dating, I met a wonderful woman who I married. We have been happily married now for almost 21 years. As an additional element of the shifting mindset, I was able to maintain a very strong relationship with my ex-wife through honest dialogue and genuine concern. This relationship continues to be very healthy. The divorce was not of the bitter variety, but one of choice of how people should live. Perhaps individuals who are unable to reach a comfortable compromise in their relationship may be better off separating, if for no other reason than to preserve their health. Being married did not, ultimately, remove my sovereignty over my own life or the life of my ex-spouse. While it certainly caused pain all-around, this pain did not last and proved to have been a very effective mutual decision. Perhaps because neither of us used anger or warred over money, the separation was less complicated.

Stephanie

Stephanie (a pseudonym) is in her mid-40s, and lives in a metropolitan area. She divorced her husband amicably approximately 10 years ago.

She met her husband through an online dating service. She was then in her early 30s, he was a couple of years older. She was first attracted by his looks. The description he gave did not matter that much. They exchanged e-mails, she gave him her phone number, and he called. They shared a common background, having grown up in the same area and with a similar upbringing.

When they met, she was attracted to his smile, the way he carried himself, his self-confidence, and sense of humor. Being with him was always fun—going to concerts, sports events, new restaurants, traveling, going away for a weekend. She enjoyed trying new things with him, things that she would not do. He was adventurous and spontaneous. He had a lot of interests and, she reiterated, exposed her to new things. "It was fun." When asked what made him different from other men, Stephanie said that he was a "little edgy," "just fun." Three months after meeting, the relationship was exclusive. Most people said that he was not the type to marry; he, however, said that he wanted the same things as she did—children and marriage.

She found out after the fact that she did not know what was real and what was not. She did not know the person, the intimate details. It boiled down to trust. There was no trust issue when they were dating. There was "no reason not to trust him."

After they married, it was still fun. However, questions about finances and other women, who he said were just friends, arose that did not make sense to her. While it appeared that he had a successful business, he claimed business debt but would skirt the issue when she asked. Instead of explaining, he made her feel like she was crazy. Stephanie verified that the indebtedness was not from the business but rather, she concluded, from a gambling issue, and had obtained some evidence that supported her concern about other women. She felt insecure because what was going on did not make sense. But when she again sought to discuss the issues, he again made her feel as though she was crazy. He did not communicate well with her even though she expressed growing concerns.

They had discussed having children but he said that he was not ready, even though he originally said that he wanted children. They tried couples therapy at which point he said that he was ready to have children, but there were infertility issues. The marriage was so rocky at that point, as she put it, she was "so out of it," they did not go forward with fertility treatments. She had lost trust and, therefore, did not feel secure in the marriage.

When they would argue, he would leave sometimes for 24 or 48 hours. Then he would call or she would call. She felt sick that he would leave. One time, after having been married for 1½–2 years, they separated for 2 months because of an argument. They got back together by talking and building back some level of trust. The last time that he walked out was the last time that she wanted him in her life. She did not feel sick. When he came back she told him that she wanted a divorce. He said fine, if you feel that way, and walked out. He took his belongings and she did not let him come back. She had built up her confidence which she had lost, which in turn made her doubt herself.

The divorce resulted from lack of trust. Stephanie kept emphasizing the trust issue. Trust is the key. Without trust, one loses faith. When pressed on what trust means, Stephanie said that trust brings comfort that one knows the other is telling the truth. The lying and the lack of sharing undermined the relationship. She felt as though she did not know this person, she did not know his intimate details.

Once she lost trust, not having children made it easier to end the relationship. With children, she said, she would have been more hesitant to break up the family. Without trust and children there is "no one else to be responsible for but you."

She filed for an uncontested divorce. She did not want anything of his and he did not want anything of hers, so there were "no real negotiations." It was "clean" because neither were the type of people to fight over materialistic things. There was no attempt by him to try to reconcile during the divorce. Nevertheless, he did not want to sign the papers. She advised him through an intermediary that if he did not sign the papers she would go after his business. He signed shortly thereafter. She made herself busy during that time so as not to have to think about it. They were divorced 6 months later because of a lack of trust.

They are more friendly now, speaking every once in a while. He will always have a special place in her heart. She now has a renewed opportunity to find greater happiness in a future relationship.

Susan

Susan (a pseudonym) is an intelligent, attractive professional in her mid-40s who is going through a bitter divorce, including a bitter custody battle over her children. The proceedings have lasted years.

Susan grew up to believe that she was a victim in an urban culture with the perception that suffering was ingrained into the fabric of its society such as its literature and music. She was raised in a high-pressure environment where what she did was never good enough, that she had to do more, her parents were not happy with her doing "fine." Her parents were divorced.

If one acts like a victim, Susan said, she will be treated by life like a victim. When one has a victim mentality, then one arranges to act like a victim. As a result, the circumstances of one's life develop in a way that confirms this expectation (or perhaps the individual's focus always remains on negative developments, so they consistently experience themselves as a victim). Susan realized that is what happened to her. She created suffering. Nevertheless, there can be a benefit to being the victim. One can receive compassion or pity. And it could provide an excuse if one fails. Even more importantly, one always gets to be "right" about their view of the world and themselves. Over and over again, people get a confirmation that she/he is treated badly by life and life is hard. Susan has gotten over the victim mentality "to some extent." She decided that she has a choice. When one realizes that the price she/he is paying to be "right" is too high (resulting in hardship, loss, conflict, suffering, and isolation), she/he can make a different choice. People realize it is more important to be happy than to be right.

The theme of creating a new story came up consistently in our conversations. Looking at her past, Susan said that she would find support for her "story" to confirm her story. One needs to decide what "it's about" and live life in that way. "All interpretation is invented," Susan said. And, while one needs a reason to change, a person must have the willingness to change at any time to "create a new story." Create yourself "every second and you can go back." There is a cost–benefit analysis—do not do anything unless there is a benefit, she warned.

On marriage: She came to realize that she would have to do it herself; however, it is "hard to do it on your own." Her husband was worse than no help. The day she and her husband married, he felt an entitlement that he did not have to try anymore, he did not care. He made no effort. After many years of carrying the burden and feeling used, sad, and resigned, she realized that this suffering was optional and she could make a different choice. She filed for divorce because she recognized that she was making a choice to stay in an unhappy situation, while her husband was just being himself. As soon as you accept responsibility for your life situation instead of shifting the blame to others, you recognize that you have this amazing power to change this situation.

In terms of marriage, generally, "marriage depends on expectations." There may be no issue in the marriage for so long as people complement one another, but people will not change their ultimate dynamic. There are different levels of partnership, so why burden one person with being a partner in everything, which is what a marriage entails. She knows people who have children but are not married and are happy. And it is hard to stay romantic. In some cultures, Susan noted, having an affair is expected. "Change it or learn to love it," Susan said, whether it is a marriage or a job. Meditation and transformational courses helped her through the bitterness of her divorce.

Susan believes that it is important to understand that there is a whole area out there that we do not know exists. Frequently, solutions to the problems that we are facing are found in that area, but we cannot see them without a paradigm shift, as we are only looking in the familiar area. In order to make a change permanent, Susan stated, "You have to act in accordance with what you're saying." It is not just declaring who you are, but it is taking actions and taking responsibility for your declarations and the actions. You can say that you are not a victim but you have to do something to show it. Your actions have to be consistent.

Jennifer (From Separation to Reconciliation)

Jennifer (pseudonym) is a professional, intelligent, confident, attractive lady in her early 30s. She graciously agreed to be interviewed about her separation from her husband and their reconciliation. Jennifer and her husband have known each other for much of their lives, and have been married since they were in their 20s. They have two children and live in the New York metropolitan area.

Jennifer and her husband had lived a plane ride away from the New York area. When Jennifer first moved with the children to the New York area, she explained that her husband was continuing to work for his employer in another state with the intention that he would soon find employment in the New York area and rejoin them on a regular basis. Until then, there would be the "long-distance relationship" that many a couple endures until they physically live together.

There was, however, an issue that arose before the move that caused a deep schism between the couple that boiled to the surface after Jennifer and the children moved, which was a contributing factor that led to the couple's separation. In fact, ultimately a separation and custody agreement was drafted, signed, and for months effectuated, including the children's visitation with the father in the state in which he lived. Jennifer explained that the husband had not been faithful. Moltner, who conducted the interview, assumed that the husband had a physical extramarital affair that caused the separation. However, Jennifer advised that the affair was not physical and that her husband and the other women had never met in person. Rather, the husband communicated with other women online, which ended up possibly putting Jennifer in harm's way because one of the women began to repeatedly reach out to Jennifer after the relationship had ended with her husband. In fact, Jennifer had a long conversation with this woman trying to help her. Although Jennifer did not state that the woman threatened her, Jennifer was understandably concerned, especially with relatively young children, that the woman expressed that she knew personal facts, which had not been shared by her.

Jennifer described her husband's online communications as breaking a trust and that "she was better than that." Her father had cheated on her mother, and her mother knew. Jennifer was "not going to be my mom."

Jennifer was introspective. She said that she understands herself well. If something benefits her, she said, she does not consider the effect on the other person. She stated that she did not know that she had faults (Moltner interpreted that as major faults), that she does so many things, and did not make "big" mistakes. She felt like it was "all on her," and she emphasized the need to make time for herself. She also felt the need to make "the other person happy." She did not say the need to make her husband happy; rather, it is (as it should be) a two-way street—both need to make the "other person" happy. Not surprisingly, Jennifer felt distance before the separation. "If I treat myself poorly," Jennifer said, "so will you [treat me poorly]." These points were a poignant precursor to our post-reconciliation conversation.

A few months later, Jennifer advised Moltner that she and her husband had reconciled, that he was moving in with her and the children in the New York area. Moltner assumed that it was primarily for the children's sake, but Jennifer corrected that assumption.

Jennifer began the next conversation by saying that one has to understand that both people have faults and why his online communications occurred. She said that, although there was nothing wrong with her, she was not taking his feelings into account. She works, is a mother, and stays in shape (what she described as "public perfectiveness," i.e., how the others perceived her and her life); therefore, she said, she felt as though she needed him to do things. It was her expectations. She was focused on the children, work, the gym, etc. "I'm perfect, but need you to be better," Jennifer said, not wondering whether he was happy. Expectations are hard to achieve. The thinking is that it is not me, i.e., her; it is everyone else, when it is really not. It comes at a price and we do not include that price in our expectations. Yet she also said that there was a breach of expectations because he did not say there was a problem. He did not speak with her about his issues as she expected that he would. He also did not ask how he could help. In short, there was a lack of communication (a word that she repeated) between them, which emerged as the primary negative pattern in the marriage. According to Jennifer, part of her mistake was not being sensitive to his needs. Jennifer viewed it as having self-responsibility. She said that she put herself in the situation, not that she was wrong, but that she made a personal choice. She cared only about her needs and did not give him attention, which he needed, that enabled his mind to wander. She was critical of him. She did not make him happy and she did not even know that he was not happy. Yet, she observed the lack of necessity of his personal accountability that led to the decision to do what he did.

Jennifer wants her children to be strong and to grow up not allowing the type of thing that their father did. But, before the decision to separate on the path to divorce, Jennifer determined that the children need a father, so she pretended the online communications did not happen primarily for the children's sake. Her objective was not to let the children see what was happening for it was not their business (or doing). But that only made it worse. She became bitter. It was a fake family. She was sad and in a horrible situation. She was trying to portray family harmony for the children; ironically, her desire to protect the children ended up "backfiring."

So how was the trust regained, despite the fact that he broke it, despite the fact that Jennifer was not going to be like her mom? Trust was regained through a determined process of working towards a greater understanding of the person and setting expectations. It is a truism, but the relationship was not "like [it was] when we first met." Reality sets in. What got lost is when they first realized that they would be good together—he made her happy, she made him happy, but not out of obligation. Which is why, Jennifer concluded that he sought fulfillment in another relationship. She did not ask him to change things that irritated her, but instead yelled at him. "Maybe he needs my attention," Jennifer suggested. He said to her that she was insensitive, and that he was hurting. There was an expectation that we just assume that we know the other person's expectations. He asked Jennifer what he needs to change to see if they can work on it. And there is forgiveness with the expectation that there will be no disloyalty if there is a future. Forgiving herself, her dad, and her mom; not just forgiving him. "To truly forgive someone you cannot assume that you are perfect," Jennifer said.

Their relationship is stronger at present. Knowing that problems can be worked through makes things stronger. "Accept and forgive or things will be worse," Jennifer stated.

Authors' Commentary

In Kreuter's view, the objective of a committed couple is for each party to be the willing custodian of the other person's dreams. This involves willing sacrifice of one's own preferences in order to help the other achieve his or her goals. Sacrifices (compromises) could involve major decisions about starting a family or having additional children, where to live, what kind of apartment to rent or house to buy. Even the concept of love evokes more than feelings, but a decision to be "in love" with someone. Kreuter adds that the problem with forgiveness is that the person who forgives usually does not let the other person forget that the forgiveness was given, which exacerbates the schema, creating, effectively, a rap-sheet against the other person. Marital discord is compounded when one or both spouses resurrect old hurts felt during the marriage when trying to resolve a current impasse. Karen (2001) wrote:

> If there can be no mercy, no leniency, no understanding, no forgiveness, or no simple tolerance for the magnificent complexity of being human—if we face every flaw or disliked quality as evidence that our blackened souls require rejection and banishment—we will not be captured by our own awareness motivated to change. (p. 111)

He adds:

> We feel our way toward new boundaries, toward using our anger and hurts in different ways, with the added ingredients of awareness and concern. 'I see what I do, I see how it can hurt myself and others, and I care about it. I don't like being that way.' Such awareness, such concern, creates its own mutation. It's central to the forgiving self. (p. 274)

While that could be the case, particularly depending on the depth of the breach of trust, Moltner does not necessarily agree with Kreuter. A person who truly offers forgiveness, especially someone such as Jennifer, who placed part of the responsibility for his transgressions on herself, will let the other person forget forgiveness was given. To remind him is contrary to the essence of forgiving. The act of forgiving, when it is sincere, does not mix well with the "Sword of Damocles" hanging over a person's head.

Case Studies Involving Thought Process

Samantha: The Concept of the Journey

Samantha is a woman in her 50s who, beginning in 2012, has undergone eye surgeries as a result of a detached retina. In February 2014, she had another surgery on her right eye to stabilize the retina, but will still be legally blind. Before that she never had any eye issues. She had great vision. One day, she saw black spots. She did not know what they were, but they went away. She had floaters, flashes of light, and felt tired. She lives on the east coast, but was on the west coast for the holidays when a relative saw her walking differently. She was tripping because of depth perception issues. She checked into it but a doctor said that she was fine. But after that, she was playing a board game but kept missing the board with the pieces. A relative was on the phone with a nurse and described what was happening. The nurse said that she had an issue with her eye and that Samantha should immediately go to a hospital. Samantha was about to leave on a flight back to the east coast and decided that she would go see a doctor when she returned back. She was getting off the plane when she saw people's heads not their shoulders and became scared. She was taken by ambulance to a hospital.

To understand Samantha's challenge and the way she has dealt with it, she discussed her background and her abiding faith. She has a survivor mentality that is derived from her "challenging" childhood, which was abusive. She "only knew survival" as a child. The fight for her sight was "more normal." Track and field was her ticket out of the house. She was a runner in college. She worked 90-hours weeks in corporate America and did well, but now believes that she "had limited vision" in the sense that she "only focused on work versus the blessings that work afforded my life and the blessing that God gave me each day of skill to work."

She had not been focused on marriage because, she stated, "I was married to work. I did not recognize the importance of being balanced." She wants that quality; she wants to share her life with someone. She wants to be a stepmother if, as the authors infer, she believes that she cannot have children of her own. She "did not align her goals to her personal dreams," she said.

She believes that life is in divine order and focuses on the positive. She has a "perfect" nephew and says, "I've been a mother to many as a mentor and friend." She has built strong and meaningful relationships. She knows that she will be "blessed with a beautiful family." As Samantha poignantly put it, "Although I yearn for love in my life I lived a blessed life with incredible opportunity. I truly trust in God's divine order, because of an abusive childhood, I'm a very kind and sensitive person who would wish no harm on anyone. Because of living a life of 'survival' I had very little social balance and I also did not understand how to value my 'worth.'" "The other blessing is that I learned and lived my life through core values related to the wisdom: 'do unto as you would want them to do unto you'…rewards don't come from man, they come from a higher power." With this background, we return to her continuing challenge and how she has dealt with it.

At the hospital, she was informed that she had a detached retina in her right eye which was going blind as the retina was detaching further. The retina is like wallpaper. It was peeling off. It cannot be replaced but can be repaired. Eight months later, she had a similar sensation in her left eye. She had eye surgeries. Dealing with the healing and reviewing medical records was emotionally draining. As a result of a last surgery, a cataract formed.

Her life changed suddenly. She could not do things that she used to do. She was trying to figure out why—did she have diabetes or something else internally, was she predisposed to it? Should a preventative measure have been taken for her left eye? She was depressed, feeling as though she was not in a position to fight, although she did not know it. But she realized that if she was negative "she would be dead." She could not "wrap her arms around this." What was going on made no sense. She had posttraumatic stress syndrome. But her attitude was not "why me?"

She was and is a person of deep faith and would deal with the challenge on the spiritual side. This was part of her journey, and no one said that it would be easy. She "walks by faith, not sight." And she relied on a higher authority to help get her through. Spirituality is very meaningful and real. It is bigger than her and, she said "I have to accept it." While preparing for the surgeries, she prays with the doctors, especially a week or two prior to the surgery. The day of the surgery, she prays by herself at the surgery room. She wants to feel peaceful before the surgery. She internalizes the Scriptures, and reads ones that are related to health. The Lord's Prayer brings her peace. She does not tell a lot of people before she has surgery because their anxiety is not good for her. The deity is using her, but she does not yet know for what—but there is a reason. Do what is right and the reward is greater than what people can give, she states.

We discussed the difference between faith and superstition. To Samantha, faith is a strong belief, the trust that something will happen. Faith is the divine order. Superstition is a hope that something will happen. It could be circumstantial or a fluke.

She also relied on the attitude that she adopted from her athletic background. She learned to jump over and lunge through to have stamina and train mentally. She was a former hurdler, and this was yet another hurdle. She is a positive thinker who "manifests energy." Samantha observed that the world is not set up for the vision-impaired. Rather, the perception is that people can see or are blind, not in between.

She has learned about herself. On different days of the interview, she stated that she sees life more clearly even though her vision is impaired because she sees what is important in life. She refuses now to live her life for others. As a result, she also learned a lot about medicine. Perhaps this was part of the legacy. She was uninsured, and learned a lot about foundations, the worth of networking skills, and the intellect it takes to navigate the process.

She has learned limitations as they happen, but she is adapting. She focuses on today. She has a daily devotion to health and fitness despite the sedentary life style that her vision issues impose and is sensitive to gaining weight. She no longer takes for granted the difference between grass and the sidewalk. She focuses on what she can do. Although not cleared to work, she works on projects and keeps active to stay mentally engaged.

She is intent that her vision will come back even better. She considers it a miracle the way her vision is, and that she might have better vision with glasses. She willed herself to have vision better than it was supposed to be after what she went through. She functions better than she sees.

"Although things have been challenging," Samantha said, "I say the scripture Proverbs 3 4–5 daily, 'Trust in the Lord with all thy might, lean not on your own understanding, and he will direct your path.'" "I don't evaluate life or fear it anymore. I'm grateful each day I wake up and I trust God to order my steps, I don't get caught up in my circumstances… the blessing is in the daily 'lesson'. I do my best. I trust the 'able' element of day versus the disability of my life."

It is a challenging medical time, yet "one of the most peaceful times" in her life because her "heart is at peace."

The following poem was written by Samantha's close friend Zonya Brewton (2014):

The Long Journey
with Will Rodgers Pioneer Foundation
From December 2010 to December 2013
I've traveled a road through my toughest 1100 days
From my life as I knew it I would have to learn to wean
Knowing that through it all I was to give Him Praise

From the beginning God assigned his angels to me
You are proof that Angels aren't always ones you cannot see
You walked with me down that long dark and often painful road
I could never repay the kindness and support that you showed
You supported me through five surgeries on my eyes
I went from 15/15 Vision to being legally blind
I was devastated by the news and my mind filled with whys
Even through my prayers there were no answers to find
I learned it is not up to me to ask the question why
But to literally learn to walk by faith and not by sight
I could no longer embrace my grief and sit around and cry
I had to take charge of my life and for my healing fight
In 2014 I will spend more time focusing on me
I lost myself in my work for others but it was hard for me to see
As important as it is to give to others it was more important to take care of me
My vision is impaired but thankfully it has helped me to see
It is said that when one sense is dulled another grows stronger
This journey has shown me that not all vision comes from your eyes
I have been able to see my life clearer and I'm a victim no longer
I am thankful for my family, friend and your foundation ties
I thank God for WILL RODGERS PIONEER FOUNDATION
And the support that you gave to a person losing her vision
But beginning to see; I thank God that he sent you to me.

Peter

Peter is a highly educated, gracious, and very eloquent man in his early 60s. He lives and works in New York City with his wife, two children, and two poodles, living a good life filled with all the things that would make most people envious of. Peter is also a very warm and kind man who notices the homeless and sufferers and does what he can to help them. He follows a model of behavior that he has passed down to his children: never to look down on another person regardless of his or her status in life. Peter helps his friends and will help those he comes in contact with. He shares his wisdom and takes people under his wing as a worthy mentor. However, Peter carries around inside him a troubled soul, one haunted by not what is outwardly threatening, but by internally created images and constructs that cannot be described in terms of actual existence. They are, in essence, fears.

When asked to write about his life, he readily agreed to do so and followed through with the following self-portrayal of his life described in his unique perspective. "Transformative writing is a way of completing those incomplete traumatic responses. It is, in fact, a way of creatively clearing one's way through the brushfire, and discovering a path forward, past the place we felt unable to go" (Reiter 2009, p. 1). His endearing and charming wife has explained to Peter that in order to understand him you have to consider his many levels. Peter's writing supports her impression. Peter's words:

> The sun is shining and there is a zero percent chance of rain, but I bring my umbrella because I know that this high pressure system will be the first to produce precipitation. I am in the top one percent of Americans in income and net worth, but I am always scouting

spots in New York City where I can live on the street when I am inevitably penniless. I strained my left shoulder playing squash, but the consequent discomfort is surely the early stages of heart disease. I am going to be sued by someone for something; no matter it has never happened in my sixty three years.

Pessimists are said to look at the glass half empty; to me there is nothing ever in the glass. I have walked out of my analyst's office for 33 years feeling good for anywhere from 5–30 minutes on average. He can't be right that I am blessed with a wonderful marriage, two great kids, and no serious problems. He doesn't know that disaster is lurking behind me 24/7 and will inevitably pounce, constantly taunting me for my inevitable fall.

Please don't feel sorry for me. Ninety-nine percent or more of what I worry about has no basis in reality and is completely self-manufactured. Growing up as an only child, my parents would make me look like an eternal optimist. They were abusive towards me on a regular basis both verbally and physically—not sexually—just a good smack or some saliva in my face. I was a great blessing to them, since they needed a battering-ram for all their multiple failures as people.

My life is a privileged one, by any reasonable standard. My wife and kids are the source of great love, support, and sustenance for me. I fight the demons every day, and as I get older and mellower, I am a more potent adversary for the demons. And I am determined to get even better. The darkness will never dissipate completely, but I am now lurking behind it 24/7 with a strong flashlight in my hand.

Peter's words, rewritten in the form of a poem (by Kreuter), using selected lines, we read as follows:

The sun is shining
But there is no rain.
I bring my umbrella
This high pressure system will produce precipitation.
I worry about that which is unlikely.
I am in the top one percent of Americans.
But I look for where I might live
On the streets
I will be penniless.
I am consumed with unsubstantiated worry.
I strained my shoulder
But the discomfort will lead to disease.
I am going to be sued by someone
But that has never happened.
Why am I so consumed with worry?
Pessimists look at the glass half empty.
To me there is nothing in the glass.
Disaster is lurking behind me 24/7.
I am taunted by the inevitable fall.
Why am I so worried about the future?
Ninety-nine percent of what I worry about has no basis in reality.
As a child I was brought up to be an optimist.
Yet, my parents abused me.
They took their frustrations out on me.
Why did they mistreat me?
My life is privileged.
I am loved and supported.
I fight the demons every day.
I grow in potency to fight them.
I will win the internal war one day.
The darkness will never dissipate.

But I am lurking in the shadows.
I have a flashlight.
I will illuminate the problems.
Then, and only then, will I defeat the demons.

Commentary by Eric Kreuter

Peter is a special person. He is thoughtful and sensitive and cares deeply about his family and friends. His internal struggle appears to be rooted in the young boy hurt by troubled parents who did not parent well. Yet, Peter survived and, for the most part, thrives. His internal river of fear flows rampant through the fabric of his life, soaking them in ever-present pain. It keeps him vigilant. He over-analyzes even the smallest issue, but, when he engages others, he does so with complete courtesy and fairness and avoids being overly demanding of others. Peter measures his words carefully and is never harsh. He raises his children much better than he was raised.

What his success in life testifies to is that he has successfully learned how to deal with the complexities of his existence in an admirable way. May (1975) wrote about the human capacity to handle struggles:

> We shall often be faced with despair, as indeed every sensitive person had been during the last several decades in this country. Hence Kierkegaard and Nietzsche and Camus and Sartre have proclaimed that courage is not the absence of despair; it is, rather, the capacity to move ahead in spite of despair. (p. 12)

While perhaps true that he will not ever shed the hurting skin that cloaks his persona with fear, he knows how to navigate life in such a way as to enjoy the fruits of a good life and, to a large extent, he does appreciate his relative affluence. It is how Peter works consistently towards resolving his thoughts that we can examine. "It is evident, then, that we have to consider the relationship between imaginations and reason if we wish to obtain an adequate account of the operation of the process of thought" (Bohm 2007, p. 62).

Peter does not flaunt his wealth. He may have been taught as a damaged child to feel guilty about whatever he has, but Peter knows better, at least intellectually. The war that occurs for Peter appears to be a psychically determined emotional war, albeit a very subtle one. Peter knows he cannot escape the influence of his internal paradigms. He makes himself unduly sad by the sight of a homeless man since this reminds him that he too could 1 day become that person.

Despite the seeming irrationality of this mindset, his perspective must be respected as presenting very real to him. Therefore, his fears compel Peter to believe that what he has could be taken away. He may, at some level, admire the already homeless man because not much remains to be taken from that person and the man has already, to some extent, acclimated to a life on the streets. Can Peter survive long in such an environment? That, ultimately, is probably the deepest driving fear boiling inside Peter that 1 day he will be put to the test of nothingness and he will be unable to cope and deal with that development.

While some would say that Peter's fears are nonrational, they are without doubt maladaptive. But, they are not very damaging in the sense of how he conducts himself in the world of reality. Daniels (2013) wrote:

> Modern man is even more sick in normality than in the asylum. He is a man in search of his soul. The last thing Jung wanted to do was to merely remove a person's sense of maladjustment. Mankind is in great danger, and the only solution is to become more conscious. (p. 2)

Peter continues to be eloquent, to render good decisions, to parent very aptly, and to love and be loved by family and friends. He copes and deals and thrives. His life activities can be described as one fully capable of high achievement. Therefore, Peter's negative schema is an internal one, but, still, quite potent. When he is in therapy, he uses this weekly opportunity to touch base with the objectively trained therapist to guide him back to center whenever his thoughts detour his mind to a place of extreme worry. Using this resource well, Peter stays grounded, connected, and well-centered, which helps him remain viable and mentally stable and towards his goal of emotional health. Peter's therapist read Peter's words as well as these commentaries and indicated to Peter that he thought they serve as a help to Peter along the path to progressing through his psychological issues towards greater relief from their relentless tormenting of him. His treatment acts as an antidote to the toxicity of his routinely delivered fear. For Peter, the inner world filled with fear, and largely imagined fear, conflicts, to a degree, with the outer world where there is a much smoother and controlled rhythm to his life. Peter feels as if the manifestations of his fear will always be there to haunt him, but he can keep them at bay as long as he does not let his guard down. For Peter, then, this is how he ultimately chooses to adapt and does so rather effectively. His story sends the message to others that having these kinds of fears does not have to debilitate or remove any part of the luster from his otherwise well-adapted existence. Erikson (1998) wrote about human adaptation:

> It is for psychosocial reasons, then, that it is not enough to speak of the ego's adjustment to an outer reality. For, conflictual as all human adaptation is, by the time the ego can be said to guide adaptation, it has already absorbed adaptive experiences and introjected intense identifications. (p. 89)

Commentary by Kenneth Moltner

Peter's challenges invoke a broader perspective (the following is thus not a commentary on Peter himself). The broader perspective is that of a person's internal, consuming unease, a discomfort that appears to constantly hover. The cloud is a constant, even if sometimes subliminal, shroud. It may not always be conscious but it is barely below the conscious surface. It is an underlying unease with oneself attempting to figure out his/her place in life, but unable to do so; an inability to find, or to live in, a comfort zone and maintain it. It is a gnawing sense of not being fulfilled in general, but not necessarily, if at all, attributable to a single cause, although it certainly can be exacerbated by a single cause.

This is not to suggest that life is a utopia in which one should or can always live in an emotional comfort zone. It is to suggest that the comfort zone, however broad or malleable that zone may be (which is a positive thing), should be the norm to which we emotionally strive. What is striking about Peter's poignant words is that he has not only financial stability but also emotional stability and happiness. For Peter, there is no apparent reason for his fear. To this author that is the point—there does not have to be a reason. Reason invokes logic; this type of a challenge invokes so much more. Peter is dead-on in his description of fear. Roosevelt famously intoned: "…the only thing we have to fear is fear itself."[7] But to an individual, fear is real, fear can be paralyzing. And it is a fear that cannot always or necessarily be identified. That Peter feels better for 5 or 30 minutes after therapy says so much about the nature of the temporary reprieve as starkly contrasted with a continuing comfort within oneself. This author would not be surprised if Peter's challenges apply to many. There are times that we do not know how we feel other than that we know that we too often do not feel as it might be expected we should because we know that we do not feel "good."

Descartes famously said, "I think therefore I am."[8] We say that we live because we feel. Perhaps, in one sense, we think too much and feel life too little. Do people become immune to life's beauties or get caught up in the vicious cycle of its challenges and worries? Instead of just living life as the precious gift that it is, do we allow ourselves live it? While we may well realize that we should, it is easier said than done no matter what emotional support or material possessions we possess. Why? Why is it so hard to enjoy? Why does the good seem to be temporary, but the pressures constant and never ending? Why cannot some let go of the angst and try though as hard as they may? Are we trying too hard? Are we creating a fight akin to Don Quixote's tilting at windmills?[9] On a general level, expectations play a role. We are not where we "should" be, we have challenges that we have not expected that seem, in a larger context, insurmountable.

Years ago, a friend gave me a mug that said, "Don't take life seriously, it isn't permanent." That is sound wisdom. But there is a reason that some cannot do so. The objective is to identify that reason, confront it, and overcome it.

Scott

Scott is a successful professional who is in his late 40s. He and his husband live in a metropolitan area, having been married shortly after the legalization of same sex marriage in New York. This is a long way from how his journey started back in the late 1980s when being gay was wrought with negative connotations and issues, particularly related to the AIDS crisis.

[7] This famous quote is taken from Franklin D. Roosevelt's first Inaugural Address on March 4, 1933.

[8] "Cogito ergo sum," which is Latin for Descartes's famous phrase. His philosophical meaning that the act of thinking guarantees the existence of the self is a fact that many philosophers take for granted.

[9] 'Tilting at windmills' derives from Cervantes's Don Quixote—first published in 1604, under the title The Ingenious Knight of La Mancha.

Scott grappled with his homosexuality during the late 1980s. Coming from a rather traditional, yet open minded family, he was not confident he would receive support for his lifestyle. Beyond that, the AIDS crisis was still being digested in America, and it was not uncommon to hear it referred to as the "gay disease," with untold thousands falling ill from this twentieth century plague. It was the toughest of times for a young man to come out and the risk both personally and professionally was great. Being gay had a clear stigma attached to it during this difficult time. Like other minorities before him (African–Americans and women, for example), trying to find a place of acceptance, Scott struggled with what the risks and rewards of coming out might mean. And in the midst of a health crisis as great as any in history, the time was not right for Scott to embrace his homosexuality, so he did not; instead he resigned himself to the fact that he must be bisexual.

Living a double life was never easy. Although there would be encounters with men, like many before (and after him) he chose to marry a woman when he was 28 years old, and they had two children. He was "outed" in 1997 when his ex- wife found that he had used a gay chat line. This was the impetus for self-realization, and ultimately following his divorce, he determined to no longer live a double life. He accepted that he was (and has always been) gay. He came out and his support from friends and eventually family was absolute. Now married to his partner of 11 years, Scott has found a place of peace within himself despite the difficulty of the journey.

How did he reconcile his emotions—his knowledge that his truth was that he was homosexual but the societal taboos of that time? He did so by facing them head on. He woke up 1 day and promised himself that there would be "no more bullshit." He was gay and was going to live his life judged for it or not, but unafraid of this truth. He was happy with who he is. Those who provided support were his real friends, he observed.

Times are different today and the challenges of nearly a generation ago exist at far less levels than they once did. Marriage is legal in almost half of the states in the union. The AIDS crisis has turned the corner and HIV, while still a huge problem, is managed far better than it has ever been. And the lesbian, gay, bisexual, and transgender (LGBT) community has been able to make so many aware of the normalcy of a lifestyle that not so long ago was considered anything but normal. Brave souls like Scott and others who emerged as proud and unafraid have made the journey for others better and the opportunities they have in life greater.

While there will always be those who struggle and there will always be hate, today, there is the highest level of acceptance on this front than ever before. Today, fear has been replaced by the reality that we are all equal and all deserve to be treated equally. What a remarkable journey indeed.

Madison

The "Developing" of The Message Within *FINGERPRINTS*—John Enger, Ph.D.

Fingerprints … does not sound like much of a story! Well it isn't a story really and the thought of "fingerprints" doesn't get one very excited unless you have a love of forensics and the science of "prints" themselves I suppose. I'm one of those "guys" who found a great fascination with fingerprints and their uniqueness to every person … past, present and future. That fascination along with the love of helping people were really the two things that drove me into the field of law enforcement besides my personal belief of accepting there is a God who placed in every one of us gifts and talents—your "purpose" or better stated, your "destiny." Ever feel like you are so unhappy in life and everything you are trying to do just plunges you deeper into frustration and depression? What's your destiny? When you come to the knowledge of what your true destiny/purpose is in life you will find the joy that you are looking for … and that is *every* part of your life by the way! And let me mention this … your destiny/purpose will have seasons and those seasons can be fruitful irrespective of the troubles and traumas encountered within each.

A good story contains a message…. I realize this. However, I have taken a different approach that the great majority of writers will disagree with. And you know what, that is fine with me. "Fingerprints" is an encapsulated cocoon that contains within it an *imprint* of a life and within that life is the key to understanding the incalculable importance you have on other people. Every person does so whether she/he realizes this or not! So, it's a *message,* and that message required me to relive the entire life and loss of my beautiful 3-year-old granddaughter, Madison. The journey in the development of that message was a most difficult one for me. Her death shook our family's belief in all ways. Not that I or any one of my family have not experienced losses of loved ones and friends. It is not that I had not experienced the traumas of seeing up close and personal what other human beings are capable of doing to each other because of hatred, anger and jealousy. These experiences have made me literally discouraged, disillusioned and very depressed at times over life and what its real purpose is. Madison's death however had a grip on me that I had never experienced. The darkest and deepest valley I had yet to encounter. One that also showed me some very troublesome things with many people I personally knew regarding her death that I had to overcome. Hundreds of "friends" of which only two called and prayed with me and encouraged me with their love and concern. I knew this much in my grieving … as the thought wanting some form of an elixir … alcohol or medication which may be a help, it was just a temporary "help" and a most deadly trap to a situation that must be somehow contained lest it destroyed me. I am no stronger emotionally than any other man or woman. I possess nothing more than any other human being does not possess. How did I, and how can countless others, come through things that I cannot imagine going through. How did they make it out of the deepest and darkest valleys in life? My darkest valley is not yours and vice versa. But I will assure everyone there are many deep valleys in life and we all will experience them to a lesser or greater degree.

So, what is the answer? How did I get through these deep and dark valleys? How did I maneuver through the darkest valley I have ever experienced? And how will I get through others I know will come in my life? And they will come … that is life!

ANSWER: CHOICE…it is YOUR CHOICE! You CHOOSE!

That seems pretty easy and quite logical. Yet, it is the truth! Once you are ready to choose if you will stay angry or not, hurt or not, devastated or not, disillusioned or not, convinced there is or is no hope, then your journey will be one of pain for a long time, for some decades or lifetimes and yet for a great many they choose another more devastating route by ending their own lives or taking others with them in the process. How tragic! It does all begin with choice.

I am a martial artist, defensive tactics instructor and have taught numerous law enforcement officers and the general public to stay alive. Sometimes it is much wiser to move to defend yourself than to do nothing and then in other situations it is much wiser *to do nothing* than to attempt a defensive tactic and die. The *CHOICE* not to move is nonetheless a tactic to stay alive. It is an *ACTION* based on purely *choices made*! Ah, you say you make a *choice* and may die anyway and that's not good! Very good observation! Now, that is the problem is it not? We convince ourselves that we may die or get seriously injured no matter what *CHOICE* is made and stay *paralyzed* by indecision based upon the circumstance(s) facing us. There are things in life that are beyond control no matter what we do! *Choosing* to understand this will free you from being paralyzed by all things that are beyond your control.

The horrific scene of watching my granddaughter die in the arms of my daughter and son-in-law is something that no one should ever have to endure…nonetheless it was my time, their time, our time to endure this. Why not me? Why us? Why my beautiful granddaughter Madison? WHY NOT? What made any us "special" or what "promise" was ever made that we would not have to endure such things in life. Certainly it was not a chosen and welcomed event. I am ordained Minister of the Gospel and was the person who presided over my granddaughter's dedication to God. I prayed earnestly that day that she would have His Hands of protection from sickness, illness and disease. I had faith that He would accomplish this "for me." Did not happen! God is God and He chooses to allow as He wills what will take place. Can He heal as He desires? Oh yes, I believe He can. He chose not to! I certainly could not have healed her nor restored her back to a healthy life…some of the best pediatricians in Florida could not do that! Even if I did not believe in God or a "higher power"…who do I blame? Who is there to get angry with? Who do I direct all negative feelings towards? I believe in God…do I get seriously miffed at Him. He's God…. I AM NOT! I may not understand the immediate reason for this but because in my trust in His omniscience I make a *choice* to believe there is a purpose.

Irrespective of whether anyone believes in a God, a higher power, statue or alien being…what is significant enough to break through the discouragement, the depression, the feelings of loss, anger and the many debilitating feelings that attach to the soul and steals hope? As I pondered these thoughts and what a 3-year old child had contributed to my life in such a short time, the thought of everyone's fingerprints crossed my mind over and over and how unique they are. If you have lost someone in your life, know this…their unique fingerprint ridge patterns will never be placed on anyone else in the world. Such is the case of life…their life's fingerprints have left a permanent mark on your life and many others. Just as yours have been left upon countless others…both in good and bad ways! You cannot escape this! There are also latent (hidden to the naked eye) prints left at times in your life by others and ones that you have left which are developed later in life. You cannot see them at the moment the words are spoken, or as the action unfolds—but those latent fingerprints will often be developed throughout life. You are leaving your fingerprints by your actions and words in life on someone else. Yes, even at the grocery store when you tell some to have a wonderful day and smile at them. Or when you gently touch the shoulder of a friend and tell him or her that you could not have done it without his or her help. And, you leave your prints on others by the negative, uncaring manner in which the issue was handled or how the person was spoken to. Can you imagine the prints that have left scars on those who have been abused or have watched horrific things take place in front of them. The good news is this…we can *choose* to deal with these bad prints in good ways which will leave wonderful prints on the lives of people now and in the future.

To overcome the stresses of life and at times the news or events that takes one deep in the darkest of valleys, you must *choose* to either leave there or stay there. *I have chosen to leave* and when I have been kicked back into a valley deeper and darker than the last *I have chosen to leave*. You must move or you will die in the valley. *Choosing* to stay in the valley is in fact leaving dark prints upon your own life and that of others.

I made a choice to take my granddaughter's life and share it with others so that her fingerprints will live on. My personal faith in a God who created me with a specific purpose and destiny in life is my resiliency. Knowing that I can leave innumerable fingerprints on others is an overwhelming thing to consider. I finally understood the importance of this by working through the loss of my granddaughter and writing the message of her life.

I think back on how decades ago now I left many fingerprints on others. I thought of them as just good deeds, being a decent and ethical human being. It was the right thing to do…yes it was. Then I thought of some of the negative fingerprints that I had left. I could change some and others were an impossibility…it all came with *my choice*. I asked God for forgiveness. Those who were no longer here I asked for forgiveness from them in prayer. And then *I chose* to forgive myself!

It matters not on who or what you are in life…. YOU LEAVE FINGERPRINTS IN THE LIFE OF EVERYONE YOU MEET.

Your life has value and it has meaning. No one enters or leaves this world without leaving your DNA behind. True…everywhere you go and every item you have touched has left your DNA fingerprint.

How important is a fingerprint… so important, so valuable, that I searched high and low for every little one I could find anywhere that were left by my granddaughter. Instead of yelling at them about leaving their prints on everything just think how valuable they may very well be to you. Instead we get far too busy cleaning them off of the objects touched.

We are created in God's image, Scripture says…that being the case and I believe it to be so, then we all have His fingerprints all over our lives!

Samuel (A Case of Positive Intervention)

Samuel is an articulate man, currently in his late 50s who had a professional career and was college educated. For many years, he has graciously taken on the role of competent surrogate parent of his nephew (Mark) in place of the nephew's living biological parents, who never married, have always lived apart, and are not capable of guiding Mark at this stage of his life due to their own financial, intellectual, and emotional limitations. Mark is currently midway through undergraduate college at a distant, top-rated state school, but has had great difficulties for the past 2 years, resulting in the risk of academic probation. These difficulties were unexpected due to Mark's superior high school academic performance.

Mark is a very bright young man, but was not honest with his uncle concerning the real reasons for his consistently poor grades. Mark's self-perception (including, ultimately, his self-deception) was that he was not using his time optimally or focused on his schoolwork, but, instead, became involved with risky behavior (alcohol use and smoking marijuana), leading to abuse and self-destructive patterns, thinking he could do this without jeopardizing school. Mark would routinely pacify Samuel's expressed concerns over his grades by stating how hard the courses are and how hard he was trying. Samuel asked Mark if he was partying too much, but Mark said that he was not doing this irresponsibly. Mark did, occasionally, express his concerns that the challenging academic environment may be too much for him, which made Samuel lessen the pressure of inquiry.

Samuel's overall concerns for his nephew's academic progress and future are admirable and clearly resulted in Mark's successful admission to this highly competitive college with the safety net of financial support from Samuel and other family members. Mark understood and welcomed Samuel's direct involvement in Mark's life, in general, and in Mark's academic performance, in particular, even though he was also concealing his negative behaviors.

With each report Samuel received on Mark's school performance, it became clearer that Mark was having much more than passing difficulty with his studies, resulting in a serious academic warning with the potential for dismissal. During a recent school break, Mark was staying with Samuel, which became the routine as there was no place else for Mark to stay during such breaks. It also provided Mark the opportunity to visit with his high school friends that he had not seen in months. One afternoon, Mark left Samuel's house stating that he was going to be with his friends. He left his laptop computer on and open sitting on a table in the family room. Though Mark typically left his computer open, after Mark had left the house, Samuel happened to bend down next to the computer to pick up a jacket and could not help but notice the open Facebook page, which was, at that moment, directly at Samuel's eye level.[10] Startled, Samuel realized for the first time that Mark's academic problems were due to more than bad study habits or the intense challenge of the curriculum. What Samuel learned through Mark's history of dialogue with his friends and his behavior, even before college and during college, involved Mark's joining the culture of problematic students who used substances, often to the level of abuse, even addiction. Samuel also was able to learn the identities of local drug dealers (at home and at school) and saw Mark's descriptions of various drug paraphernalia that he was using. It was how Samuel handled the crisis that speaks of a person's actions serving to catalyze a young person's maladaptive schema towards transformation into a good citizen, respectful of laws and focused on his academic performance and into respecting himself and his own physical and mental health, including being honest with his family as a result of his humiliation.

Samuel waited patiently for Mark to return home even though it was very late that night when Mark finally did come home. Samuel immediately confronted Mark about what was viewed on Mark's computer, but did so in a serious yet caring manner that opened the door to much needed dialogue. Samuel opened the dialogue about the discovery of Mark's excessive use/abuse of alcohol and marijuana. Though this instance of using alcohol and marijuana was supposedly an isolated event because Mark planned on going back to school the next day, Samuel challenged Mark that he learned the truth by reading not just the page that was opened on Mark's computer, but the entire history of entries as far back as he could, therefore, catching Mark in a massive lie, one in which he could not talk himself out of. At that point, Mark's affect changed. Samuel and Mark read every Facebook entry together and then Samuel asked Mark to explain terms and to describe in more detail what he was actually doing in the past. While this was uncomfortable to Mark, Samuel saw this as a condition of understanding the true meaning of Mark's Facebook communication. It also served to convince Mark that Samuel knew much of what Mark had been doing.

Through the ensuing discussion, Mark knew that returning to school was very much in jeopardy. Samuel was meanwhile quietly processing how to devise a plan for Mark to return to college. The break was ending soon, necessitating a decision. Samuel's stance was clear and convincing. Mark and Samuel established a new partnership of responsibility and accountability with each having dominant and submissive roles. Over the next few weeks, Samuel's actions led to very positive changes in Mark's attitude and in his life. Samuel contacted the college and spoke with the appropriate people who handle student problems such as Mark's. Together, they devised a plan for Mark, which included Mark's complete consent whereby Mark would be allowed to return to school, enter alcohol and substance abuse counseling, and submit himself to frequent drug screenings, all of which would be re-

---

[10] After inadvertently seeing the Facebook page and reading a few key words, which clearly indicated that Mark had planned to purchase marijuana and meet his friends, Samuel felt it prudent to continue probing the history of entries. He was shocked to learn that Mark had been involved with alcohol and marijuana since high school. The fact that Samuel looked through Mark's Facebook entries was never brought up by Mark as a deflection because Mark was obviously caught in his lies.

ported to Samuel. After very carefully chosen words about the severity of Mark's problems with substances and behavioral issues, Mark's mindset transformed with him first recognizing that he had made a mess of his life, then he started to do what was required of him to return to school and become more responsible for his new requirements and also led to a very positive turnaround of his grades. Mark has been fully compliant since this crisis. Samuel also explained to Mark that the ultimate goal was for Mark to learn how to become a responsible adult with respect to any future use of alcohol.

Through the management of the crisis, Samuel was able to emphasize to Mark the wonderful gift he had in the form of a college education and why drug use was counterintuitive, nearly resulting in termination of a valuable college education at a very good institution. Mark knew how valuable a college education was, but devalued the opportunity, thereby risking it to indulge his negative behavior. Samuel's efforts were to help Mark "fix what is obviously broken" in order to demonstrate a positive attitude towards his future. Mark acknowledged that it was time for him to start taking personal responsibility for his own life. By stating this to Samuel, Mark made it official that he understood and accepted his role in the management of his own life.

Mark likely would have failed out of school had it not been for Samuel's effective intervention. Thus, by capitalizing on the crisis to forge dramatic change, Mark's future became brighter. Had Samuel lashed out at Mark and simply punished him, taking away his college opportunity, Mark may have become bitter, which might have led to even larger problems for Mark and the family. It is, therefore, resolute management of a serious problem amidst chaos that can make a great difference in the outcome. Maladaptive patterns can be broken with a determined and level-headed approach, using a balance between toughness and leniency. In this case, the leniency was provided with a fool-proof system of verification. Since Mark realized that he either had to change his mindset or would have to leave school and then face a less than certain future, Samuel's approach proved quite effective.

Anna

Anna (pseudonym) is a vivacious, attractive person in her early 30s who exudes a zest for life. Anna was raised outside of the USA. Her parents were old fashioned and wanted her to stay close to home. Anna, however, wanted to follow her dreams. She not only went to school, commuting an hour away, but, when the opportunity presented itself, she also immigrated legally to the USA. This is a story of the challenges that are faced to pursue one's dreams.

After college, Anna started dancing and singing relatively later in life. Her hometown did not present the opportunity for her to pursue her dream of acting and singing. What she loved was what she felt in her heart. Initially, she commuted 1 hour a day and was able to work her way into TV and she did so successfully. She accepted a scholarship in the USA, which was more than 1000 miles from home, despite her parents' strenuous objections. She came to the USA alone with no family and no friends. She has managed to keep in touch with them through Skype. She had to learn English so she could speak and sing much better than she had. She had to adapt to a new culture, support herself, and fight the loneliness.

To obtain a visa, she was required to put together hundreds of pages of a book describing her work. She met with lawyers and had to endure the arduous process. She had to do extensive, time-consuming work to remain in the USA. There were, and are, no guarantees. She always had the option of going back "home," but her strong preference was to remain in this country legally to pursue her goals and follow her dreams. She was happy to pursue dancing, singing, and the theater, which requires hours of learning and practice.

Kenneth Moltner Commentary

We often hear the phrase "pursuing the American dream." For people such as Anna, being in this country constitutes the beginning of satisfying her personal goals. One can only imagine the internal fortitude that it took for Anna, as have many others, to come here, against her parent's will. She was, at least, able to taste success in her home country. She could have stayed in her home country, but apparently would have felt suffocated and would have regretted not taking the opportunity, requiring her to take a calculated risk. Anna found the confidence within herself to confront the many challenges of moving over a thousand miles away. "Most men lead lives of quiet desperation…" (Thoreau 2005/1849, p. 150). Anna has not. Anna should not have to look back and bemoan "what might have been" (Garret 1897, p. 4).

Deborah's Shift

Deborah's (a pseudonym) shift took a long time, and, of course, studied determination. Her determination to change began in the mid-1970s when she began a 12-step program to change her eating habits—she would eat at polar opposites, either not eating at all or bingeing. The Power greater than her was food. When she was eating in Italy, she "didn't know that Michelangelo painted the ceiling." Her focus was different.

She achieved "sobriety" in 1991, more than 15 years later. For 23 years now, she has measured three meals a day, and eaten nothing in between, wherever she may be. For Deborah, food was an addiction, and once she was able to control it, she "got her voice back"; she was able to free her mind from obsession. Prior to the shift, Deborah found false solace in not eating or in bingeing. It was her way of dealing with stress or uncomfortable situations. The shift saved her. It changed her victim mentality; it transformed how she saw things. She spoke up; she enforced her boundaries. Through the Program, she came to believe in a Higher Authority and practiced the distinctions of the Landmark Forum.

Deborah's shift and the program became a fundamental part of the foundation and motivation through which she took on another challenge. In 2011, she was run over by a cab. She had an outer-body experience, looking from above as she saw her body sprawled out. She thought that there were nurses and doctors on the street with her, but it turns out that was not so. There must have been angels, she concluded. Her sister, who does not live in the same state, was there that weekend which she considered to be a spiritual sign. Her friends, who never answer the phone if there is a number they do not recognize, picked up the witness's phone call. Her brother, who is often travelling, was home that evening. In Deborah's world, this all alluded to some kind of spiritual intervention.

Deborah went through multiple surgeries for fractures of her left leg, her knee, a broken femur bone, as well as pelvic and lumbar fractures. In addition, she had five painful procedures to relieve liquid that was building up on her lungs; the latter was life-threatening. Her body was wrapped in bandages; she had a cast around her chest and tubes coming out of her body. She faced the fear that she would not walk, but fortunately the doctors quickly assured her that she would but she had to do the painful work. She was in ICU for a month and then transferred to a rehabilitation center in a nursing home for 3 months, where she was surrounded by injured people and dementia patients. Rehabilitation was depressing. "These people were kids once," she thought to herself, and "look at their plight now." She had been independent, but now was lying with feces in her diaper. There was one aide for 12 patients, and she was too often given attitude when the aide came.

The doctors wanted her to gain weight and she was concerned whether, by doing so, she would regress from the progress that she had made. She could not weigh and measure food in the hospital or nursing home. She became obsessed whether the food was too much or too little.

Deborah's turning point came when she called a Leader of the Program. "What are you going to create?" he asked. "What am *I* going to create? What can I possibly create?" she thought. And then she realized what she could create, even [authors' note—or perhaps especially] in a rehabilitation facility. She could create the possibility of "fun," of "contribution," and of "aliveness." She went to the dementia unit, said hello, and engaged the patients. She founded a support group that ultimately had nine patients. Aides began attending as well. They named it "the Diaper Club!" It was a spiritual gathering, a place where patients could sing, talk, share, and focus on the question of what they could be grateful for. She found strengths that she thought that she never had. While she was in the hospital and during rehabilitation, the support that she received from family, friends, and the people in her life was also a source of strength and encouragement.

After rehabilitation, she was able to return to the paradigm shift that she had worked so hard to achieve. She made a commitment to herself and her close friends in the Landmark Education that by a certain date, against all odds, she would walk into the program's meeting. And she did.

The accident "cemented her beliefs." It was a stark reminder of the importance of being grateful. When you almost die, "when it happens to you," she said, you appreciate the little things. Deborah stated that she does not miss her younger years [authors' note—that many people seem to]. Her mind now clear once the food was controlled, gave her access to living a full and productive life. She is grateful every day. "Everyone can get through," she encourages.

Why then is it so hard for others? Deborah surmised that others may not have attempted to transform. Perhaps they, like her in the past, had a spiritual void. People become self-centered instead of "other-centered." "Challenges are part of life," Deborah maintains. "How we react to them is what matters." It is we who decide the kind of life we want. People have been brought up to think that "life is like a movie" all should be "fine and dandy." [The author inferred from Deborah's point that people may not be able to handle the challenges, sometimes extreme, with which they are faced]. The belief in a Higher Force reminds her that things happen for a reason.

It is not as though that Deborah never gets caught up in minor annoyances over things such as when a computer is not working properly. But she stops herself and has perspective.

Whatever the situation, Deborah can say to herself, "this is my gift." And she can act on it.

Commentary by Kenneth Moltner

Deborah's shift speaks to several themes that are discussed in this book. Most prominently are gradations of the shift, the fear of regression, and maintaining the shift. Deborah, as did and do so many others who have made or are striving to make a paradigm shift, worked long and hard. She was then confronted with an accident—an occurrence not of her making and not initially within her control—that could have led to a regression. Instead of the accident controlling her, she ultimately controlled it and its ramifications. For example, her way of being at the nursing home shifted from very understandable annoyance and upset to compassion and gratitude. Instead of regressing, not only did she overcome and regain that which she fought so hard to achieve, but that trying (to say the least) experience also cemented her shift.

Deborah's shift again raises the issue of the role that a Higher Authority and spirituality has played for so many in their shifts. Like Deborah, Samantha faced (she still faces) a severe physical problem which necessarily involved emotional and mental challenges. Both overcame with their faith as their foundation. See also discussion of faith earlier in the book.

Life of John Doe (Aaron Kreuter)[11]

John Doe was born to middle class family on February 29th, 1992. He grew up in a quiet neighborhood and attended a highly accredited public school. John and his friends all did well in school, played on sports teams, and rarely got into trouble. Sure, the neighborhood bully pushed him around a few times and called him a few names. So what? It did not matter, it happened to everyone. At least that is what the adults in his life always told him. All in all, John lived a pretty normal life. So what could possibly go wrong?

John awoke in the back of a police cruiser. He was pretty disoriented, but the wailing sirens were enough to tell him where he was. The officer turned around to speak with him. "Hey, looks like you're finally coming to. We picked you up down the street. You barely made it to the car before passing out." Through slurred speech, John told the officer "You guys won't tell my parents, will you? I really did nothing wrong." "The state you were in you're lucky to not be in the hospital. We're not going to bring you to jail, but we do have to bring you home to your parents and explain what happened." "Great," John thought." I'm going home in handcuffs again. What can they do to me anyway? I'm already grounded and my license is suspended. Probably just more talk of rehab." Next thing he knew, they were at John's house. The reality finally set in. This would be third time the police brought him home to his parents. When they finally got home, he received a stern lecture from the officer and went inside. He noticed that his parents seemed more concerned than angered this time. They asked how he had been drinking more and more and said that he should seriously consider getting help. John knew there was no way he could stop, since drinking was the only way to get along with his friends. His parents did not know what to do either. What had happened to the John they knew? The one that always did well in school and never got into trouble. Amazingly, they never even considered that all of John's problems could be traced to one person, Albert, the neighborhood bully.

It was a calm fall day when John and his friends were walking home from school. They had started the third grade only a few weeks ago and they really liked their teacher, Ms. Smith. She was kind to them and had a way of making even the most tedious division lessons interesting. As they were walking, they noticed Albert approaching them from down the street. He was in fifth grade, but, compared to them, he might as well have been a giant. "Hey nerds" he called to them. John knew they were in trouble. They had no hope of getting away from him and were convinced that his life's mission was to make them miserable. The only hope they had was that it seemed none of his friends were joining him today. "What do you want now?" John's friend Paul asked. Without answering, Albert shoved Paul on the ground. Seeing an opening to escape, John and his other three friends made a run for it. John almost made it out, but Albert caught him by the collar and yanked him down. He knelt on top of John and started punching him. No matter how much John squirmed

[11] Kreuter's 16-year-old son, Aaron, contributed this essay.

around, he knew there was no way he would escape without getting beaten. Albert was so much bigger than him that he knew his best hope was to lay there and try not to provoke Albert further. When he was done, Albert got up. He looked at John and laughed. “Maybe next time you won’t try to run. All I wanted was to say hello.” This infuriated John but he knew there was nothing he could do. This had happened before and he knew it would happen again. All of the adults he told said the same thing, to ignore Albert and he would go away. Well, that was not working and Albert was not letting up. John got up and brushed himself off. He had a few more blocks to walk and then he would finally be home. He wished he would never see Albert again. He wished he would never see anyone again.

“You should really turn that off,” John’s mom called. “It’s such a nice day, why don’t you go see if any of your friends are around? You’ve been such a recluse lately.” “I don’t care,” John called back. Lately, all he wanted to do was sit in front of the TV. It had been months since he saw any of his friends. His mother was worried, but she did not know what to do. It seemed John was always watching TV these days. She had discussed therapy with his father, but they never came to a decision. She decided she would bring it up at John’s physical in a couple of weeks.

“I’m fine mom, really. There’s never anything wrong me anyway.” John had always hated the doctor and today was no exception. As they pulled up to doctor’s office, his mom said “look, afterward we can go out for ice cream or something. Whatever you want. Just try to be on your best behavior today.” The exam went well, as usual. Dr. Schwartz asked them “so, any questions or concerns today?” “Well,” John’s mom started, “John’s been kind of lackadaisical lately. He doesn’t run around with his friends like he used to and he seems to be watching a lot of T.V.” “I see,” replied Dr. Schwartz. He turned to John. “Has anything been bothering you lately? Maybe your school work or perhaps the other kids?” “No, I’m fine” John replied. But he was not. And he knew it. Dr. Schwartz recommended finding a sport John likes. On the car ride home, John considered the proposal. “You know,” he said, “I have seen a lot of soccer on TV lately and it looks like fun. Maybe I can try that.” “Great idea!” his mom said. “There is a team forming in the local park. I can sign you up next week.”

At soccer tryouts, John was astonished by how quickly he picked up the sport. He found he could pass and shoot well, along with having a firm understanding of the rules. As a result, he made the team. He told his parents, and they were proud of him. Not so much for making the team, but for finding something he was interested in and enjoyed, while getting some exercise. John looked forward to middle school, which was approaching quickly. Next year, he could try out for the school team and play with his friends. “Middle school will be great,” John thought. “I can’t wait!”

The first day of middle school, John could not help but feel a little outcast from the other students. Everyone seemed to have their little group of friends, and none of these groups seemed to include him. This was not the exiting environment he had hoped for. He ran into Albert often, who at this point was entering his teen years. While Albert had changed physically (he was now approaching 6 ft tall), his hate for John did not. The frequent name calling and harassment from Albert were too much for John. He regressed from his friends and struggled in his schoolwork. He found solace in playing soccer, but that was about it. He felt anxious around other people, including those who were still kind to him. His mom suggested therapy several times, but John was adamantly against it. He was just so miserable, and did not know what to do.

This continued for many more years. John did not look forward to high school as he had to middle school. He rarely spoke to anyone. He did not speak unless spoken to, and never made an effort to make friends. Many members of the soccer team kindly approached him, but were discouraged by John's insistence to be left alone. Something was wrong. John's teachers, parents, and even John himself knew it. He always wanted to be alone and never reached out to other people. After a long conversation, John's parents decided they had to do something.

"Depression," Dr. Roberts said. After talking to his guidance counselors, John's parents finally decided to take him to therapy. At first, John was reluctant to go. However, a few minutes of talking with Dr. Roberts were enough to convince John that therapy was a good thing. He was diagnosed with mild depression, caused by his anxiety. "Is that treatable?" John asked. "Of course," said Dr. Roberts. "It takes some time but if you're willing to cooperate I can get you back to normal before you know it." "Sounds good," John said. "See you next week."

John actually started looking forward to therapy. Dr. Roberts was a great person to talk to, and he had answers to all of John's questions. They worked together, and John started improving. He was more talkative in school and even started to make a few friends. He even began to get along with his soccer team. As part of his therapy, John began going to the gym regularly. He found that his frequent workouts relieved stress as well as boosted his overall health. However, his new-found social life came with consequences. He was going out with his friends on weekends to parties that often included drinking. Unfortunately, these parties did not always end well. This all culminated with John being brought home in a police car for the third time.

As John spoke with his parents, they discussed the long journey John had been on. From being bullied back in elementary school to suffering from depression in high school, Albert was to blame for many of his problems. John recognized that his alcoholism was becoming an issue, but he did not know where to turn. His dad suggested an alcoholics anonymous (AA) meeting for young people at the nearby community college. One thing John had learned over the last few years was that seeking help was not always a bad thing. Thus, that Sunday night, he drove to the meeting and walked in.

"Hey, don't I know you from somewhere?" "Yeah," John said, "you look pretty familiar. You're Albert, aren't you?" "Yeah, who are you again? Wait, don't tell me. You look a little like a kid I used to pick on back in the day." "That is me. My name is John. Nice to see you again." John had to decide whether or not to tell him what he caused in John's life. Ultimately, he decided to let it pass and try to make amends. Clearly, Albert was having some issues too. They ended up getting along, and even became friends. Albert was a peer leader at the meetings and he was instrumental in curbing John's alcoholism.

With his alcoholism gone and his mental issues cured, John lived a pretty good life. He retained many of his friends and even got some of them into AA meetings too. That fall, he would go off to college to study education. He and Albert got along now and hung out regularly. As John looked back on his childhood, he was pleased with the progress he had made and the obstacles he overcame. Still, it amazed him how one neighborhood bully on his quiet street had such a profound impact on his life. It showed him how even someone in such an ideal environment could experience so many challenges at the hand of a single person. John vowed to not let anyone else go through what he did. He went on to begin his teaching career and establish an anti-bullying program in the school that he worked in. Under his watch, no one would suffer like he had to; that, he was sure of.

The Visit

Early in the new day, a beautiful woman lies in a near-wakeful coma, fatigued from the long evening of sleep, interrupted by the lights and sounds of the quiet of the still busy nursing home where so many rest similarly. Her eyes communicate terror and anguish though her words spill from her mouth like jumbled crumbs of the breakfast recently eaten. What is she trying to say? There is no means to decipher, as no code could be written. The listener can only smile, stroke her silky white hair, and whisper words of comfort, themselves probably not understood.

Outside the dreary room filled with items and shared with a nameless other, where there is no dialogue and seldom even baseline awareness of the presence of another human being, clatter of noise abounds—the constant delivery of dentist-office music combines with the unanswered calls for help from one of the more troubled residents. The engine noise of the work trucks outside mesh with the sounds of carts rolling up and down the corridors. Voices are overheard from passersby. Every now and then a nurse pops in to administer something in order to check a box on the never-ending list of procedures and protocols. The wheelchair is at the ready by the door when it is time for her to disembark from her lonely chamber of suffering—her rectangular home within a home for many, but earmarked for her exclusive use for as much more time there is allotted to her by God for the continuation of her progress towards the end—itself a new and happy beginning.

A tear forms in her eye, which is gently wiped away. Her arms tucked tightly by her sides under the cover of blankets despite the already rising temperature of the room. Sitting awkwardly, she is unable to move much, staring constantly out into the vastness of nowhere specific. Would it be better for a blind person who could then more easily rely on imagination or memories, but have these all gone astray as well?

Activities are announced over the loudspeaker, competing for attention, along with so many other sources of sound. Lunch at 12 noon, bingo at 4 p.m., but so what, there is nothing to do, nowhere to go. She does remember faces and some names, though these are mixed up. She can smile and that is the delight of the visit. Otherwise, there is nothing there. It is emptiness in the sharing of time with a person so loved in the normal rhythm of life. Now, the time passes slowly and horribly as the image of this poor shriveled woman, once beautiful to behold with a soothing voice and warmth, becomes chiseled in memory, replacing all happiness with severe depression and unspeakable grief. When will this end? Is it selfish to wish for it to be so?

A soft kiss, a vocalized affirmation of the love that can never be weakened and can never die is said to her followed by the end of touch on her still sweet face now so burdened; then, the visit is over, but the hopelessness commences, like a new episode of the same theme, just a week later. It is never good, but could always be worse. The fear is that this will continue to be the platform of existence, marking the final stages of the relationship—itself a cruel torture brought on by the vagaries of life. How delicate we are as creatures. Harris (2013) wrote: "My essence is not as an individual, autonomous human being living an isolated existence. My essence is a soul fashioned as a part of God's creative expression" (p. 11).

The sign-out sheet is ignored as usual—such a useless chore, a final trip to the restroom to wash and weep. They drive away always with the wonderment of the question whether it will be the last time or if this is merely just the beginning. Then, of course, the requisite feeling of selfishness robbing her of the sympathy and feeling stuck in an unwanted groove where there is no recording to enjoy. It is not the suffering of the visitor that should matter, but it is the one most able to be felt. Perhaps it boils down to the feeling that the death cycle is delayed in a state of frozen pain causing bittersweet thoughts, each one negating the happy times in the past, now so very distant. It is the muting of all positive feelings that destroy the will and fuel the anger, but there is no repository for such morsels of hurt. They just seep in deeper and deeper into the fabric of the soul so mourning this beloved person for having to live in such a state of near-death. Yes, the practice of faith soothes all the hurt and amplifies the love and trust, but it is the human equation that even God cannot remove as He created the mold. Perhaps we are meant to suffer so that we can know happiness when we stumble upon it. And, yes, we leave the pavement of the parking lot and go acquire coffee to drown our tears in, and we proceed to other things, working on our resilience. All true, but there is no masking of the silent penetration of the sadness felt so deeply inside the aching heart. There is no escape from this torment nor is one perceived as being deserved. It is the condition of living as a human, so must be accepted. And we do move past and find ways to engineer a smile and a laugh and renew the quest for our own purposefulness.

In the end, we may find ourselves in the bed, in the chair, in the state of emptiness with our loved ones peering down at us in pitiful sympathy or, worse, crying bitterly as we suffer. Perhaps the best hope is to experience a peaceful passing into the hands of God, while holding the reassuring hand of another. Even in the most hopeless environment, there is still hope.

Synopsis of Chapter

The specific cases we have explored show that some individuals are able to transform their paradigmatic thinking, allowing them to move from a maladaptive state to a progressive state. Others have been largely unable to transform, but show at least some signs of possible future resilience. For them, it remains open when they will shift their respective mindset in order to become more fully productive within society.

Chapter 10
Restarting Life at Any Age is Possible

Only those who do nothing at all make no mistakes… but that would be a mistake.

—Anonymous

Introduction

"Man being condemned to be free carries the weight of the whole world on his shoulders; he is responsible for the world and for himself as a way of being" (Sartre 1984/1943, p. 707). According to Sartre, absolute responsibility is not resignation; it is simply the logical requirement of the consequences of our freedom (p. 708).

What does it actually mean to hit the "restart" button? Perhaps, it equates to an inner resolve to make wholesale changes inside of one's life that, from an external viewpoint, appear dramatic and even startling. The earnest willingness to attempt such change may be brought about due to dissatisfaction with the present life circumstance, boredom, or some inner need to spice up life and develop some entirely new directions. It could also come about due to an internal feeling of urgency to make the best of the projected time left of active life and not "waste" any further time. Some people like to refer to a "Bucket List," a term made famous by the very successful 2007 American comedy-drama film in which two men with terminal lung cancer agree to fulfill a list of must-do activities before they die. The film importantly demonstrates the shared mission of two vastly different people, joined because of common and severe illness.

Some people begin a physical fitness regimen following a health scare, or stop smoking after being diagnosed with emphysema. They may stick with the new program or quit after a short while because they have not made a lasting change. Lasting change requires full determination, coaches, and, possibly, therapeutic intervention in order to be successful.

People can carry around grudges and even feelings of hate for others, perhaps for those who have caused harm. However, these negative feelings are, for the most part, self-destructive. While it is only natural to be angry with someone who has

E. A. Kreuter, K. M. Moltner, *Treatment and Management of Maladaptive Schemas*,
DOI 10.1007/978-3-319-06817-6_10,

caused harm, hate becomes toxic to the person who does the hating; rendering it, therefore, counterintuitive. Actions may suffice to deal with the energy and, assuming the actions fall under the legal domain, may be preferred to doing nothing. Kreuter and Moltner often run across clients who feel they have been harmed and who wish to bring on litigation, but, in many cases, they lack the fortitude (emotional and financial) to carry litigation through to the completion.

There are, however, problems associated with these types of "new leaf" turning. One problem is change that sounds good to the ear or looks fantastic on paper, but which soon dissipates because the person simply gives up. We can call this a false start or a truncated attempt to change. In addition, frustrating elements of changes in the patterns of a lifestyle can lead to giving up on the attempted changes. Setbacks can also interfere with progress towards the achievement of true and lasting change.

Interfering with true and lasting change are habits and general reluctance to stay in the course of a chosen new path because of one or more discernible obstacles. Setbacks often derail bold efforts to embark on new ways of life. One such obstacle or barrier is discomfort with the impact of the particular change. An example is a person deciding to quit a bad smoking habit. Often, the pangs of demand kick in, with the pleasure center of the brain demanding service in the form of re-inoculation with a fresh dose of smoke and the tar and nicotine to accompany the smoke. Essentially, the brain feels the impact of the behavioral change and is irritated at having now to put up with curtailment or, even more severe an adjustment, quitting cold-turnkey. A person who stops drinking alcohol may find it difficult to be around others who are drinking, thus, she/he may avoid certain social situations as a way to bypass this problem.

"The psychotherapist sees himself compelled, willy-nilly, to regard the individuality of a patient as an essential fact in the picture and to arrange his methods of treatment accordingly" (Jung 1983/1961, p. 354). "The human psyche is a thing of enormous ambiguity. In every single case we have to ask ourselves whether an attitude or a so-called *habit* is authentic, or whether it may not be just a compensation for its opposite" (p. 210). "But in psychotherapy it seems to me positively advisable for the doctor not to have too fixed an aim. He can hardly know better than the nature and will to live of the patient. The great decisions in human life usually have far more to do with the instincts and other mysterious unconscious factors than the conscious will and well-meaning reasonableness" (p. 210–211). "About a third of my cases are not suffering from any clinically definable neurosis, but from the senselessness and aimlessness of their lives" (p. 211).

Achievement of life change that appears more permanently ingrained in a person's life requires much hard work and a true and lasting change in attitude, plus the resilience to avoid the pitfalls of pressure to return to former ways of responding to common stimuli. Building upon one's initial success, making a change can lead to longer periods of sustainment. Having positive regard for oneself in the sense of internal satisfaction of a change made can also serve to keep the nagging pressures to resume negative behavior at bay.

A person can apply sheer will and determination to stay the course and avoid backsliding, but after awhile, the pressure to conform to the previous life pattern is so great that the person may cave under the pressure. Stress of just living out one's ordinary life can be so challenging that vices and negative or risky behavior patterns may seem attractive when opportunity presents, but, in fact, the potential for disaster looms ignored, which can lead to serious dilemma.

There is a dichotomy within a human existence that wants to both control a habit and continue status quo. Change requires effort. Effort consistently applied leads to change. They are very much related. A big change demands a larger and more consistent effort, which can become part of the primary means to overcome maladaptive schemas. Without material change, there can be little growth in a person; but do people really wish to grow or to become different? A person who lacks initiative to conquer a problem or to tackle a formidable goal may not be capable of success. It is even quite possible that succeeding is less a goal than it may seem.

"We cannot change habit directly; that notion is magic. But we can change it indirectly by modifying conditions, by an intelligent selecting and weighting of the objects which engage attention and which influence the fulfillment of desires" (Dewey 1922, p. 20). "Any impulse may become organized into almost any disposition according to the way it interfaces with surroundings" (p. 95). "In a definite sense, then, a human society is always starting afresh. It is always in a process of renewing, and it endures only because of renewal" (p. 95). "Ways of belief, of expectation, of judgment and attendant emotional dispositions of like and dislike, are not easily modified after they have once taken shape" (p. 108).

Success, itself, while on the surface, is something to be desired and strived for, but, once achieved, can be very stress-inducing. It is for this reason that some people fear success more than they do failure, because with success comes new and often loftier requirements, with the built-in natural assumption that the person who is seen as successful will have no problem performing any specific task. Thus, there is a hidden minefield of worry behind the curve on the road to a successful life. In order to be prepared for the impact of this minefield, a different type of preparation is needed. Development of a sense of humility and willingness to explore one's deep inner concerns can save a person from the impact of stress induced by a successful life and the lifestyle expected of the successful person. Others will apply their own unique brand of pressure on the successful person because they have no idea of any hidden limitation. Further, there is no real constancy between former and future abilities. Sometimes, people who are fully able to handle responsibility one day may become more tentative or even unable very soon after. When that happens, a crisis may occur. When such a crisis does occur, the person will do best exploring his or her life with a trusted other, such as a trained therapist, to resolve the causal impact of past issues that curtail furthering of success. Through voluntary effort, such a process of exploration can lead to new growth and an increase in dynamism within the individual. Thus, the problem is not having a problem, but the opportunity is dealing head-on with the problem, respecting its potency, but never giving in to the temptation of giving up.

Nietzsche found that we are strengthened by challenge, but it takes an optimist to accept this paradigm. A victim, who is languishing in his or her victimization, may see challenge as a weakening event. "Current research is clarifying the connections between stress, information processing, and the different forms of learning. It has long been known that stress can interfere with instrumental learning where as learning how to do something like solving 'puzzle boxes'" (Rossi 1993, p. 56).

The Need for Perfection

People want to strive for perfection. Failing the achievement of perfection, failure, then, becomes a possible notion. "It is my view, as it was Adler's that feelings of inferiority are *universal*, varying in degree and intensity, but not limited to 'neurotics.' It must be that we are unconsciously trying to prove to ourselves and the world that we are worthwhile, not inferior" (Sarno 2007, p. 101). The immense pressure placed on oneself can be, in itself, a debilitating force. In the workforce, there is a phenomenon of a fear of failure of success just as rich as the fear of failure, yet, not openly discussed either at the water cooler or in the performance review meeting. For example, once a person is promoted to the next level, more will naturally be required of the person. The promotion usually equates to the person being told she/he did an excellent job at the present level, and is ready to move up higher on the corporate ladder. Sometimes, the promotion requires substantial evidence of performance at the higher level and sometimes it is assumed that giving the person a higher level of responsibilities will undoubtedly result in continued stellar performance.

Managers of staff who are promoted often feel a sense of accomplishment themselves over the promotion of a subordinate. After all, they were probably instrumental in training and mentoring the person so, of course, there will be some potential for loss of objectivity. What this can lead to is the unmasking of a person's inner fears of moving ahead. The person may have grown quite accustomed to the present position and may not even desire the change in job content, increased responsibility, the new title, or even the associated increased compensation. Looking ahead at the new requirements, the person may feel that she/he is just not up for the new role. But, there may be a reluctance to speak openly about this fear, since it could lead to eventual demise of the relationship with the present employer. Fear of success may cause a person to avoid recognition for promotion—a subtle form of sabotage.

Those who can admit to this type of fear can avoid a negative pattern of career malaise through avoidance of exciting opportunities, through initiation of a therapeutic or coaching relationship. Trust is obviously of the utmost importance for this type of dialogue. For it to be of maximum benefit there needs to be complete disclosure and candor and a willingness to get into the weeds of personality and behavior. Examination of situational response to the stimuli of events at work, for example, can be introduced in the dyad and used to separate positive behavior from negative behavior. Once the negative patterns are uncovered, the work of reshaping can begin. This process may involve small steps of trial and error and may take a considerable amount of time to develop into an effective shift.

Equally important are the problems faced by people with problems in their relationships. They may experience difficulties in present relationships, leading to severance, or may find that starting new relationships has become quite difficult. In the case where there was formerly success in this area and now there is less than acceptable success, the mission is to explore what changed, why it changed, and how to re-energize the process. People give up, they fall back on succumbing to the aging process, they become disillusioned, even depressed, but much of this negative schematic thinking can, with assistance as necessary, be overcome.

The Importance of Momentum

In physics, specifically Newton's laws of motion, an object in motion tends to stay in motion. So too, in humans, our forward trajectory in our life endeavors portrays our desires for consistency and improvement in our lives. We want more good things and less bad things. Progress requires a fuel source. In a jet propulsion engine, we can use gas to create power. In a person, we use motivation, determination, ingenuity, a positive spirit, and, also, stubbornness. Some people just do not give up—they keep trying until they succeed, hence the cliché—"I will try until it kills me."

In the distance-running example, it is not the courage to finish the race, but the courage to start. The job hunt is as much in the preparation, planning, and process of going about the business of seeking employment as it is in the end result. Achieving an advanced degree begins with the notion to apply, then the application, then the commencement of classes, way before the commencement ceremony to receive the diploma. Even the term "commencement" used at graduations is not the end point, but the beginning point of reference.

It is for these reasons that most of us can wake up in a new day, be new in outlook, and start life over, in the sense that options are renewed to some extent and we can adopt a new attitude towards our own potentials. An overweight person can make a new decision to begin to diet and exercise and not look upon the past failed attempts as recipes for disaster going forward. Taking advantage of our ability to drive our engines through the propulsion of consistent effort only takes a decision; then it requires determination to succeed. Many times, we fail at projects because we give up or give in to some unseen force. This force is too often not external, but internal and can be itself fueled by abject laziness, naiveté, or because of a lack of guidance by a competent person or persons.

Reflecting on what worked in the past and what did not can help. "Reflection might start with culling your past experiences, looking at what worked and what didn't work in your old story. Then you see what you might want to pull forward into your new story in this new phase of life" (Leider and Webber 2013, p. 57).

Replacing bad habits with good ones provides an opportunity to shed a previous mindset and become transformed into a new person, one capable of more success. Hard workers can be labeled as workaholics, runners as obsessed, dieters as those destined to become anorexic. But, the first key to accomplish new great things is to become your own personal champion and learn to become unbothered by negative energy around you. Kreuter was given a lecture over a dozen years ago that marathon running is bad for you because of the toll it takes on the body. That is pure nonsense. Even peer groups can sometimes discourage a group member from breaking out into new endeavors because of the difference success would mean about that person as compared to the group. Even in the workplace, an extra achiever can be frowned upon because it sets the bar higher in terms of what work could be done if one were to try harder, work smarter, and accomplish more.

The standard for ourselves should be set by only one person—us. There can and should be allowances for considered influence by others, of course. But that does not mean to relinquish one's sovereignty to any other person. There are leaders and there are followers, and that makes perfect sense. But being a follower does not equate to becoming a "sheeple"—a person who cannot think for him or herself and needs constant direction and guidance to perform the simplest of tasks. Also, the herd mentality suggests going with the flow. Something that started out as being part of the flow becomes a legacy of a negative track record, one likely to be a haunting influence on the person long into the future. We are certainly capable of much better responsiveness to pressure and opportunities. Facing challenges and overcoming deficits makes us who we are. It is not having a problem that is the problem, but how we address the problem. By working into the equation definitive effort that we must do, we can become more active in the role we play as ourselves and start to break out of the pack. Otherwise, we could end up right back in the pack as sheeple.

Synopsis of Chapter

- Change requires inner resolve.
- Long-term successful change is hampered by short-term urges to give up.
- Enduring some pain is often necessary for a person to have lasting breakthroughs.
- Achievement requires hard work and dedication.
- Striving for perfection may hamper the will to achieve.
- Progress towards goals requires a sense of momentum.
- Retrospective thinking helps a person focus on what to do better next time.

Conclusions

> When you have gone so far that you can't manage one more step, then you've gone just half the distance that you're capable of—Greenland Proverbs

In the sequence of living a life, negative patterns can develop. These patterns can lead to maladaptive thinking, which can serve to temporarily or permanently derail the harmony formerly known to the person. If possible, the process of recovering from the aftermath of such negative schemas may take time and may require a professional coach or therapist to help the troubled person regain his or her foothold on life. It is the new perspective of resolving dilemma or problems with one's own thinking that elevates a person into a higher state of conscious awareness of their own ability to create turmoil in his or her life.

Various treatment regimens exist to help guide a person towards a more effective way of thinking. Treating symptoms can work for some; treating the whole person may work best for others. Treating the whole person requires gaining an understanding of the person's goals and objectives in life, as well as the currency of issues that the client feels are bothersome, requiring intervention. Because of the complexities of the human mind and spirit and the potential for some of the underlying negativity to be underneath the conscious level, therapeutic efforts may not be easy, may require significant effort and adequate time. Therapy is a gift (Yalom 2001). As such, clients who reach out to others for guidance avail themselves of the independent resources, which can serve as catalysts towards deeper exploration of the toxicity in everyday life. It is the road unblocked and the pathway newly cleared that enable someone to become truly new and awakened, ready to face the challenges, both chronic and new. By learning about one's own self, a person can then work on fine-tuning or adjusting his or her repertoire. In this process, new filters emerge and new abilities rise to the surface, enabling for noticeable and substantial change to take place.

The therapeutic aim is to create a working relationship with the client in order to achieve an effective strategy with the client for adoption into the client's repertoire. Effective therapy requires a cooperative and vocal client and an ethical and skilled professional to guide the process. Providing the client with assignments will enable the client to take greater responsibility for their therapy, providing them with a sense of ownership and empowerment. Tools can be given to clients who then can

E. A. Kreuter, K. M. Moltner, *Treatment and Management of Maladaptive Schemas*,
DOI 10.1007/978-3-319-06817-6, © Springer International Publishing Switzerland 2014

be encouraged to go out into the world and use the trial-and-error method to test the new ideas and see how they work in their own lives. The direct application of new concepts to ordinary and extraordinary life situations will serve to reinforce those that prove efficacious and may very well lead to lasting change once the new approaches are fully ingrained, which, then, equate to a shift in one's paradigms, leading to positive schema.

The causes of shifts in paradigmatic thinking, leading to negative schemas, can be explored to help the client determine his or her vulnerabilities. Doing so helps the client become more resilient against future encounters with similar issues and may fortify the person to withstand the onslaught of new issues that might turn the person towards negative thinking.

Treating the whole human being seems essential, which demands consideration of the person's life goals, fears, superstitions, spiritual essence, and raw abilities. Added to these is the benefit of assessing the person's level of creativity and his or her willingness to engage fully in the process of exploration towards an improved method of responding to stimuli.

Humans are most fortunate to have the gift of a cerebral cortex, allowing them to be both cunning and creative. The process of turning away from negativity, while entirely optional, somewhat uncomfortable, and perhaps risky, can help in the wonderfully exciting process of transformation.

The authors and the fine contributors of material for this book believe in the ability of the person to reconstruct his or her life through their voluntary efforts to look within the self for clues as to what works and what does not work so well.

Afterword

Cathleen M. Kreuter, MS-MFT

Being invited to write the afterword for this manuscript was such an honor. As the daughter one of the authors (Kreuter) and as a mental health clinician, I have had the pleasure of learning and growing as a person and a therapist/coach through my academic pursuit, as well as from the support and knowledge of this author. His dedication to the field of mental health has inspired me to meet and exceed my own expectations through self-discovery and positive reinforcement. Kreuter, as a publisher, has written several books that have inspired and motivated the lives of those he has had the pleasure of meeting, and I am no exception. Kreuter is a lifelong student and therefore he never stops learning; this being the mark of a true scholar and mental health/life coach.

With that said, it is not without great pride that I write about the context of this manuscript as it relates directly to the therapeutic modalities used among clients currently. The text describes transformation and how it comes from within, when coached from those with the knowledge to educate and support one's journey to heal and grow. As we look through the facets of this text, we find that Kreuter and Moltner use pertinent references and resources, as well as humor where appropriate to support their notion that "Coaching becomes essential to help the person overcome difficulties," or maladaptive schemas that are deeply rooted in their personality and life experiences.

While reading this manuscript, the reader will find that it covers many different elements including, but not limited to, paradigms and maladaptive thought, the involvement of spirituality (personal belief systems), therapeutic approaches to treatment of maladaptive schemas, and the dissection of how the problem presents itself. Kreuter and Moltner continue with how the problem becomes ingrained in personality, exploring the strength to overcome these ingrained behaviors, as well as case vignettes that demonstrate the use of coaching to shift these maladaptive schemas, and the lasting effects of the therapeutic relationship. By the end of the manuscript, it will be clear to see the pivotal purpose coaching plays on one's ability to overcome their maladaptive paradigms, but not without understanding that "Such help, while available, cannot begin without the person first admitting he/she has a problem and the desire to invest time, effort, and perhaps financial resources, to explore the problem and decide on new action steps."

E. A. Kreuter, K. M. Moltner, *Treatment and Management of Maladaptive Schemas*,
DOI 10.1007/978-3-319-06817-6,

As a therapist, the direction this manuscript takes inspires my coaching role because it reminds me of the reality of dynamics within a client's life, the ingrained life experiences we all have, and the support and knowledge that it can be very difficult to dissect and improve our maladaptive behaviors without the help and support of a neutral party. Working with different populations, all of whom come with different life experiences, childhood memories, and family dynamics, as well as from different socioeconomic statuses, therapists need to be mindful that not all therapeutic techniques are cookie-cutter models for treating such a wide array of problems. It should also be noted that not all problems are best treated by one sole modality. Therefore, this manuscript is the ideal text to help differentiate maladaptive schemas and the best practice for each individual, not each problem.

A perfect example of this would be treating two individuals who do not know each other and both suffer from depression. One of these individuals may be a young adult raising four young children whose father abandoned them after finding another woman. The mother of these children is now left as a single parent to raise the children in a one-bedroom apartment and is currently unemployed. The struggles and financial burden this woman now faces has left her feeling depressed. Whereas the other individual may be a 47-year-old man living with his wife and two teenage children in a modest three-bedroom house in an upscale part of town. The man maintains a job as a financial analyst and the family lives comfortably. The man, however, has been depressed for many years and is unsure why. Both of these individuals suffer from depression, but their causes remain individualized and, therefore, the treatment modalities and objectives must be accepted by each individual in order for their maladaptive schemas to be positively influenced.

Another concept discussed by Kreuter and Moltner in this book is their focus on maintaining a positive outlook on life for each individual we coach. Therefore, "…the best help we can give another human being is encouragement to develop them to become better, brighter, more aware and increasingly capable to withstand the mighty challenges ahead." Later in the text, the authors make another important point, fitting with the dialogue that focuses on maintaining a positive outlook, which is that one's "… validation of the achievements and efforts of others regardless of how small we may deem these to be by our own selfish definition." This concludes that if the coach does not maintain a positive outlook on their client's likely outcome and success, how might the client be able to do the same?

I believe that as an adult, not just a child, what we see effects how we behave. This does not in and of itself lead other people to behave the same way. However, a child may be more apt to see something he/she wants and takes it, leading to another child seeing him do it and getting away with it. This may then result in his or her desires to do the same thing. Although most adults understand that just because someone else does something does not mean they have to do it themselves, when behaviors are programmed into our brains (especially at a young age), we are more apt to subconsciously act and have less awareness of the choices we make. When this happens, I have heard people say "I can't help it" and truth be known that unless we are aware of our negative behaviors and have the support to change them, we will continue to repeat the same, unhealthy behaviors.

In conclusion, this manuscript will provide therapists and coaches alike with a broader sense of the meaning of maladaptive schemas and more insight into effective therapeutic techniques and coaching patterns. Sometimes, we must look inside ourselves and see our own maladaptive patterns to be able to understand the significance they have on our behaviors and actions. Once this has been accomplished, we can help others discover their own maladaptive behaviors, their causes, and possible solutions to improve their ability to control and/or change their maladaptive schemas. I do hope you enjoy reading this manuscript as much as I have, as it was a gift to do so.

Appendices

Appendix A

Template for a Shift in Thinking (Kreuter/Moltner Schema-Change Model)

As a way of providing readers, therapists, and coaches with a road map towards making a discernible shift in an aspect of their thought process, the following is a suggested model:

Name_______________

Date _______________

Statement of the problem

____

____

____

How long has the problem been a problem? _________________

In what ways does the problem impact of one or more aspects of life?

____

____

____

What have you tried in the past to control or eliminate the problem? What happened?____

____

____

____

Describe your ownership of the problem (your personal responsibility for it)

____

____

____

E. A. Kreuter, K. M. Moltner, *Treatment and Management of Maladaptive Schemas*,
DOI 10.1007/978-3-319-06817-6,

Who will your coach/therapist/mentor/ally in the process of improvement will be? ____

What is your goal for complete transformation of the problem? ________________

Write a personal statement of your commitment to begin the process of resolution
____
____
____
____
____

As part of the process of sharing your personal statement with another person or persons, write their advice or comments here
____
____
____

What do you see as the next five steps along the process, starting with the one most easily achieved?

1. ____________________
2. ____________________
3. ____________________
4. ____________________
5. ____________________

How will you measure the level of achieved success for each step?
____
____
____
____

If you stumble along the way how will you use your determination to renew your effort and resume the process of transformation?

____

____

____

____

Will you agree to maintain a log/diary describing your efforts and results? ____________

In what ways will you remind yourself of your goals?

____

____

____

Describe how your life will be once you attain your goal

____

____

____

How do you feel having made the commitment to change (or started the process)?

____

____

____

Date goal achieved ________________

After you achieved your goal, what will you do to maintain the changes thought-process?

____

____

____

Appendix B

Three Points in Time Essay

Purpose To help the person create a personal essay that explores the person he/she were, the person he/she are currently, and the person he/she would like to be in the future. This essay affords the individual with an opportunity to explore his or her inner thoughts pertaining to his or her honesty about him or herself reflective back and forward. The emphasis is on being in the moment, but using the historical reference to see where the person was and the evolution to the present moment to then propel the person towards projecting his or her future. In doing so, the burden of developing a road map to get from here there becomes clearer, enabling the person to set certain plans into action.

Essay:

Appendix C

Panic—Controlling the Beast Within the Domain of the Psyche

Before Onset

1. Realize situations that cause you to panic
2. Relax your physical body
3. Breathe rhythmically and slowly to lower heart rate
4. Settle your mind
5. Realize that stress is part of a normal life and can help your focus
6. Avoid disparate thoughts competing for attention
7. Prioritize your thinking to decrease flooding of immediate issues
8. Consider which aspects of the situation you can control
9. Remind yourself where you are, why your are there, and what is expected of you
10. Realize you have knowledge, skills, and abilities to handle all that is required and that you are really only responsible for doing, and can only do, your best—this includes breaking down the situation into manageable parts
11. Use a word or phrase to yourself that you have memorized as your calming mantra, such as: "I am fine and healthy and not having any problems" or "Nothing will happen today that I cannot handle"

If Feeling Onset

1. First, accept it and embrace the opportunity to practice control techniques
2. Inventory what is going on in the room and in your mind
3. Settle your mind to a less-complex place
4. Breathe deeply and slowly without racing your thoughts
5. Avoid catastrophic thoughts that the world is about to end
6. If the world actually is about to end, ignore 1–3 and run away

If you Feel Terrible

1. Sit quietly for a moment, close your eyes, and form a mental image of a happy place (beach, etc.)
2. Remind yourself this is temporary and you will get through it
3. See the feeling like a wave that ends

Meditative Exercise

Daily Sit on the floor in a comfortable position and focus your attention of a specific item in the room, such as a light. Narrow or limit your mind's attention to only that image. When your mind tries to wander, bring it back to the image. Stay in this posture until you feel completely relaxed and thinking of the one singular thought.

Appendix D

Inventory of the Positives

In all of our lives, there are some things that are positive and provide us with joy, provide us emotional sustenance, provide hope, or that just provide a moment or two to relax and take it all in. And, hopefully, the positives can be relied upon to help us begin to build a positive attitude. A friend of a close friend of Moltner suggested the following technique: Make a list of such things and every day look in the mirror and recite them out loud. In doing so, there can be a change in attitude. The following are some possibilities that may apply to you. Write up your own; it can be just a few. Write them in order if you prefer or in no particular order. All that is important is that they are meaningful to you. But write them up, and then look in the mirror:

1. Hugging, playing with, or just watching your children play or sleep
2. Your accomplishments (specifically, there are many more than you might first think)
3. Your spouse and the reasons you married or your girlfriend/boyfriend and the reasons you are with her/him
4. Your health
5. Your favorite exercise
6. Spending time with your friends
7. Spending time with your loved ones
8. A good night's sleep
9. Music, painting, dancing
10. Seeing a concert, a movie, a play
11. Reading
12. Writing
13. Traveling, experiencing different cultures
14. Eating different foods; trying different restaurants
15. Eating the same food at your favorite restaurants
16. Being at ease
17. Being passionate
18. Meeting new people
19. A sunny day
20. The sound of rain against the window
21. A funny joke

Appendix E

Poetry

The journey of a thousand miles begins with a single step.—Lao-tse

The Path Ahead
Nurturing from a distance,
yet so close at heart.
Rivers of solemn tears flow as silent whispers.
The only wish
is for you
to be well.
Whatever is necessary shall become the quest.
I gave you birth and you became my son.
This bond can never
be impeached
by struggle.
We are in this together, a family just the same.
Each lamenting over your trials and agony.
I feel immense pain
deep inside.
The hurt like daggers
stabbing at my soul.
Mothers are strong, but how will I make it through?
Questions and more questions.
Hope begets hope,
challenged by despair.
Then a moment of peace.
I see you smile.
Could happiness and resolve be just around the bend?
A little bit more struggle and just maybe.
Maybe?

Un homme élégant
Soft-spoken, but chose his words thoughtfully.
A gentle spirit, though he, like all, had his moments.
Caring for family was the constant.
He was a step above most and always accessible.
From France to Florida, with New Jersey in between.
Wherever he was he enjoyed all of life.
Working to sell and sell honestly, he never tired.
From plastics to residences, he knew his products.
Personable and debonair, he enjoyed people.
A card player and puzzler, he was clever indeed.
Dignified and respected, he found time to help in the community.
Rewarded with long life each moment was savored.
May the sea receive you and preserve your essence.
Reposer en paix.

Once then, but now
Once a little boy woke up and saw the sun
He smiled and rose to face the day

The boy grew up and became a man
He struggled with pain of childhood trauma
His life progressed and he had happy moments
But something was missing
He met a woman later in life
She was so beautiful
He was captivated by her charm and poise
His heart melted when she smiled
He remembered how he felt when he saw the sun
She became his new light and new warmth
He embraced her
Never ceasing, he embraces her
Always to love and cherish this special woman
To the end of days their hands must clasp
The love never setting
The passion not to be eclipsed
The pain of childhood would always be in his memory
But the love of his life will always be the cure
To hold, to hug, to kiss, to love
She is his everything; nothing remains undone
The sun in the world will set one day
But his love for her will endure through time

Never-Ending Beginnings
Newness arises like the tomorrow moon of yesterday.
Awakened to discover renewed resolve to become.
Destiny awaits the hungry soul seeking new horizons.
Toiling across the desert looking for the oasis.
Constancy of movement never stifled by self-doubt.
Where the direction is unclear the motivation remains strong.
Driven by the dim light of the setting sun.
Light shines from within like a beacon of hope.
There is strife, but the impact cannot endure.
Positive internal voice drowns out all negativity.
At junctions of assessment, always decision to continue.
Never ceasing; always creating; being, but thriving.

Magnum's Dream
The stars magically sparkle in the night air.
Warm summer winds cool my fur.
Cuddling with my Cathy was life to me.
I am part of the dream now, but a happy dream.
I am here and will always be here when you need me.
Just as you always loved me even I was naughty.
You understood me and I knew your heart.
We laughed and cried and walked and ran.
I became old, but had a wonderful life.
You cared for me in special way.
You are my best friend, my comfort, my delight.
My days were happy with you and ended with you by my side.
I wanted it just that way.
You are my every dream and will be forever.
My little body wore out, but I enjoyed my life with you.

Thank you for giving me my eternal rest and peace.
I love you, Cathy.
Your Magnum

My Favorite—You
I have many favorite foods,
But you are my favorite person.
One daughter is the favorite,
But I have only one daughter.
I do not have a favorite child,
But all my children think that they are.
When the moon glows, it is special,
But your eyes glow stronger and brighter.
The feel of the wind in my face when I run is glorious.
Yet, you provide the sustaining wind in my entire life.
Things of nature hold beauty and store value.
But, you are priceless and beyond measure.
When I have something important to say,
It is you who would be consulted.
In the small hours of the restless night,
It is your warm and sweet hand I reach for to hold.
No heartfelt longing ever could exceed
The passion's fire of missing you for a single moment.
Though age brings certain differences in ability,
There is only growth for us in the truest sense.
Within the love there is everlasting.
Within the lasting there is forevermore.
There can, then, never be more than forever.
I want to spend forever with you.
To live the favorite life,
The one I live happily with you.
So, for no other reasons,
You are my favorite.
But reasons are unnecessary
Because I can show you every day.
Sometimes a smile,
Then a hug; maybe a gift.
But in the warmth of the knowing,
Inside my soul, you see where you are,
Which is vested in that place,
That place known as the favorite,
Never to impeach, maybe to trial,
But always to triumph,
Always to remain strong.
The love burns longer than the candle's flicker.
My thirst for your essence never quenched.
Before my eyes close the last time, may they see you.

Endearing Granddaughter
Frequent vigil held in quiet sorrow.
Watching the life pass from his eyes.
Who he was, to her, was everything.
Now, he endures, in vibrant memory.

Nothing is lost, really, for the soul endures.
As the deer longs for running streams,
So, too, she longs for the sound of his voice.
But the rush of the wind still calls his name.
Even in agony, she knew he was there.
Testifying to the grandeur of her impressions of him,
She weeps and mourns and rightfully so.
The tears speak of love; the mourning of her deep pain.
He knew she was there even when he was asleep.
She will see him in her heart forevermore.
Nothing is lost, but only the presence of him in body.
What needs to remain vibrant will always be so.

A Relationship Between a Structure and a Tree

In the hills of Santa Rosa, CA, a very interesting relationship exists between a long-abandoned building, probably once used as a barn, and a very old tree whose main branch has grown at an angle up and over the roof of the building.

The tree is leaning severely on the roof, starting at the low end and bending again at the apex of the roof and down the opposite side. The tree is very much alive although the structure likely has not been used for many years. Yet the building stands and seems sturdy enough to perform its current function of providing support.

This scene, while perhaps too rustic for most photographers to bother turning their camera lens towards, does capture the imagination of the philosopher. One could wonder if the tree would have survived had it not been for the building. Perhaps the building is like an older person, wise from the years of experience. The tree, then, could resemble a younger individual, leaning on its mentor for support. This metaphor brings some sadness to one's heart, as surely the tree will never be able to break away from the building but will 1 day die either due to the natural physical deterioration of its components or as a consequence of catastrophe such as a fire. The tree may be sustaining the structure as a standing entity by providing shade to the roof, thereby lessening the impact of the sun on the materials.

Another element of this special relationship is one of a friend or relative placing a reassuring arm of support around the shoulder of a sufferer, perhaps someone who is dying. This idea brings a sense of calmness and beauty as the dying passes on while comforted by another who cares. It seems it would be sad to die alone. From the perspective of natural beauty, both the tree and the building would not have the same appeal as isolated entities. It is their close proximity and trust that creates such a striking picture of existence, purpose, and harmony.

Adapting the same story to distort the relationship to one of codependency:

It is possible that 1 day the side of the building closest to the trunk of the tree will be the first to deteriorate to the point of falling, only to be kept erect through the support of the tree. This now forms a reversal of roles and a change in the kaleidoscope of dependencies.

At such time that either the tree finally dies or the building finally falls down, one or both may continue to appear as representations or memories of their former selves. The tree will still look like a tree and the building will look like a pile of wood, once forming the structural support of a building. Thus, for at least awhile after the passing of both, their legacies will be observable. Even at the point of complete deterioration, their elements (both having origin in wood) will return to the earth together, providing new energy for future growth, even another tree. And 1 day, that tree could be harvested to make another building, or shade a new building next to the new tree.

Imagination begs one to think 200 years hence and form a mental picture of these two partners in their life-renewed state, like seeing the progeny of forefathers. To some, these are just two things in life. To others, they are a tribute to both the power and stark beauty of nature and the power of regeneration. They may even call to mind the power of God as creator (Kreuter 2003a, pp. 94–95).

Appendix F

Jewish Oncology: Okay, So We Got Cancer, Let us Eat!

Eric A. Kreuter, Ph.D.

Contents

Dedication

This appendix is dedicated to those who suffer or have suffered with cancer, both the survivors and the precious people who have died. Though the inspiration for this book was derived from the diagnosis and treatment of breast cancer in both Meryle and her sister, Lisa Hartman, and ovarian cancer in Linda Schumer (beautiful Jewish women), the intention is to inspire a sense of uplifting humor as part of the process of holistic healing. While some material may be viewed as overly stereotypical, no disparagement to anyone or any race or creed is intended. After all, as the typical cancer patient receiving chemotherapy, let his or her hair fall out; perhaps the reader can let their hair down and allow the writers to poke fun at people and the notions that comprise the pathology of everyday life.

Note from the Author

I am very proud of my beautiful wife Meryle for her brave handling of cancer and the aftermath of treatment. She maintains a wonderful balance between being sad and being happy. The outpouring of love and support from her family and friends shows how blessed she is. This book was born of her humorous idea amidst a moment of suffering and is an example of her deterministic spirit and her intrepid style of refusing to submit to adversary—in this case, disease. She is a noble example of the proud Jewish woman who steadfastly marches through surgeries and regimens of medical treatment just as the Jews marched triumphantly out of Egypt and across the Red Sea to escape the tyranny of Pharaoh.

Writing this for her is the highest honor for me. May it inspire other suffering or afflicted people of all walks of like endure by trusting God. Prayer and humor are good medicines to guide healing. From survival comes thriving again.

Eric A. Kreuter

Preface

Jews like to eat. Even during significant events like war and persecution, eating always maintains a prominent place in the thinking and strategizing of the Jew, whether orthodox, conservative, or reformed. Being observant of the need to eat, Jews strive to prepare meals suitable for any situation, in good times or times of strife. Even during the Passover, Jews sat and ate in their good travelling clothes while God was busy killing off all the first-born of the heathens. But, Jewish newbies were spared. And rightly so, we cannot afford to lose future cooks (or lawyers, doctors, and investment bankers for that matter). The food was even better though because our people were spared. We ate quickly and the bread was really flat, the herbs awfully bitter, but still it was food and food is, well, good. The fact is—Jews who have cancer still need to eat. And they need to eat well. They may puke-up whatever they eat, but this gives them a chance to taste the food going in and coming out. They may even need to eat more in order to heal. Even on a bad hair day, when strands or clumps are being lost from the civilized head of a Jewish person, meals continue to maintain their prominence in the daily planning and holiday ritual of the family. Eating a meal wearing a cap or wig or with a naked head is still an event of eating. So, this will reflect on the Jewish survivor of cancer and his or her unswerving appetite for good deli, fresh challah, tasty kugel, delicious marzipan, and good Manishewitz wine.

Chapter 1—Don't We Have Enough to Worry About?

Why cancer? Jews have already enough to worry about. Around the High-Holy days, you cannot find parking even close to Temple. Even sneaking out early backfires because some dumb-ass's BMW will be blocking your Mercedes from the extremely narrow exit path. "Selfish bastards!" And on Yom Kippur to do that to a fellow hungry Jew who cannot wait to get home and rifle through a meal or two to end the excruciating fast of what must have lasted for weeks of suffering. You find yourself hoping that the person gets warts and bedbugs. He/she probably is late paying his or her Temple dues and cheats on a golf score.

Is a diagnosis of cancer even fair? Is God still really mad at us? Was not 40 years of wandering around the desert like chickens without heads enough? Speaking of chicken—there are many great Jewish recipes for chicken dishes. Ask Grandma Etta for some of the old-world recipes.

So, once cancer is a definite, we have to deal with it, not put it off till after the holidays or when the kids return to school or when we are older and nothing better to do with our time. Do we have a choice? We start of course by complaining to anyone who will readily listen and we chase after a few soles who try to escape. "I've got cancer—oh boy, what am I gonna do now? This is terrible. My beautiful hair will fall out and I'll have to bend down and pick it up; my aching back—such pain, oy. I'll have to go to the hospital—the food there is awful. Nobody cares. Why me, why now, why not the Catholic down the block or the Lutheran across the street that always seems so damn healthy? I have to pee and I am hooked up to an IV. The tea sucks. What did I do wrong? Who did I offend?" And it goes on until the day the cancer is accepted. At that point, we parade our colorful headwear around hoping people will notice and ask: "How are you feeling? I heard you were sick." They really hope you will say: "I'm fine, gotta go." But, no, you take advantage of the opportunity and you talk and talk some more. You tell them the bitter details and drench their spirit in sympathy for you. The real angle is on scoring the promise of a delivery of food so you can avoid cooking a meal. Reheating is okay though.

> Hey Moshe—I had my last treatment today. I am a pro. I laugh at cancer. At my treatment I say to the shicksa nurse: 'Go ahead, give it to me. I can take it. I'm a Jew. Chemo is like liquid gefilte fish so pour it into my veins. I can take it.' Have you survived something like

> this? I didn't think so. You have no clue what it is like. I am strong. I am tough. Did I mention how much cancer hurts? Let me tell you. You think your stroke was a big deal? Nope, my cancer was much worse. I am lucky to be alive. Your brother's heart attack? That does not compare. This was much worse.

And so, the life of the Jew with illness is like a new form of plague. Sweet foods taste like they were dredged out of the Dead Sea. How can mealtime be enjoyed when chocolate bobka tastes like saltines? Such suffering we Jews with cancer go through. But, does anyone care? I think not.

Off to treatment means sitting in a room with other people who have probably not bathed this past week and will probably be otherwise completely annoying. The Jew will not be able to play tennis this weekend or go to services because he/she will be too tired, too sick, too grumpy, too whatever, but who cares anyway? Nobody calls. The Jew says: "I am left alone. I'll be all alone to suffer while everyone is having fun. Not fair? I give to the Temple. I pray most of the time. But still, I get this. Go figure. I won't be so nice after this is over; nope, not me. I survived cancer so I get to be free to shop, to do what I want, mostly to eat and eat and get fat. I earned the privilege, and justly so. Leave me alone, I say. I'll be fine. Don't you worry about me."

Chapter 2—The Hundreds of Phone Calls

Every day and late into the night people call to find out how I am doing. They usually inquire what I need, what can they do for me or if I need something from the store. Just as I am ready for a much needed nap there it goes again—that damn phone. And when I do not answer my cell phone they call the house and if I do not answer the house phone, they text me or send me an email or just brazenly drive over and ring the doorbell to see if I am okay. Suddenly, having cancer means accessibility. I bet hermits never get cancer.

It is like there is a sort of requirement for every person I ever met in the world to check in with me on a daily basis, sometimes twice. My mother's messages are special: "Hi, this is mom" (thank you for identifying yourself, after 49 years why would I recognize her voice?). "I don't want to disturb you if you are sleeping" (why worry about that, I had to get up in 2 hours anyway). "Just calling to see how you are feeling and to make sure you are getting enough sleep. I read that sleep is very important when you are undergoing chemotherapy. I could send you a few articles" (ironic, really). "You don't have to call me back" (of course not; then Jewish guilt kicks in, preventing further rest until I do call back and find out how the minute details of her life since the last call). "I'm fine" (the real purpose of the call to begin with was to report how she is doing and what ailments she is having this day and the one before and the one before that).

I love my friends and love to talk with them. Their calls are very much appreciated and they are a lifeline. It is just that telling the same story over and over and over again that can make me reach for the Advil bottle. How many times do I have to announce that my head makes Charlie Brown look like he needs a haircut? Maybe I will record a fresh message every day for the answering machine. For example, I could record: "This is Meryle. Today I feel like a Hummer ran me over and I was scrapped off the road and placed abruptly onto the couch where I plan to spend the entire day wishing for an out-of-body experience. I am nauseous, don't feel like eating, can't sleep, oh, and I am unusually cranky today. But thank you for calling. Please call again very soon."

Chapter 3—Food Deliveries—OMG! What to Do with all this Food?

It is Monday; at 9 a.m., food arrives in a large unmarked van. It takes two people three trips to lug in enough food-filled Tupperware for me to host a block party. Such food! Meats, fish, bread, pasta—what will I do with all this food? After 2 hours of sorting the fridge, I manage to shove everything in. I go back to my nap exhausted from rearranging. At 11:05 a.m., the doorbell rings; more food. This time I fill up the spare little refrigerator in the basement. At this rate, it will take 2 weeks to eat all this scrumptious food. People are so nice. I wonder if anyone considers the dilemma of multiple food deliveries within a span of a few days. Does anyone consider bringing extra toilet paper? Do they think people with cancer eat more? Food sent from Jews to Jews is especially important and always involves soup. Somehow, soup has become the healing mantra of the Zionistic crowd. Why does not some medical researcher synthesize soup and pour that into my veins.

The next day, guess what? Right, more food enters the house. It just keeps on coming; day after day, week after week. Well-meaning neighbors, friends, family, Temple members—the food multiplies. I start giving some away—sort of recycling. My house has become a distribution center and warehouse for prepared food.

Flowers arrive at an equally alarming rate. The local florists must be working overtime. My house is starting to resemble the NY Botanical Gardens. Pretty they are and beautiful are the people who sent or delivered them.

Cards are sent as well. And have I received so many. I am sure the postman has had to undergo surgery for a hernia. They are nice and express sympathy and hope. I cherish these cards because they show a true sense of caring from those who sent them.

Now, gifts—I think we are on to something very good and quite useful. That new scarf I wanted is now here. The blouse I had my eye on is now residing in my closet. Hey, this is, indeed, very good.

Chapter 4—Off to Chemo; then to the Diner

Another round of chemo scheduled for today. That means a poor night of sleep followed by getting up early; then a drive to the doctor's office only to wait. Who is in charge of scheduling that they do this to suffering people? First, I wait outside because nobody who works for the doctor is in the office (mind you it is past my appointment time). Like any other queue, cancer patients are anything but patient. “I was here first,” exclaims some old bitch with a weird hairpiece that makes her look like yesterday’s cleaning lady.

Finally, the office staff arrives and they try to be pleasant when all they really want is for the 5 p.m. buzzer to go off so they can go home. I sit in one of the extremely uncomfortable waiting room chairs and pick up a magazine that is several months old and get immediately bored. I notice the fake office plants have not been dusted in at least a century. Various notices are pasted on the walls asking for co-pays if you reasonably expect to be treated. Hum—no co-pay, no treatment. I believe I left my purse at home.

Once called, they proceed with boring small talk and poke a needle in my arm to draw some of my dwindling reserve of blood so they can check my white count. Since I am Caucasian you would think it should be 100 %, but I suppose it does not work that way; then, more waiting. Finally, a chair opens up and I am seated in one of the treatment chairs where they begin to install the dreaded port for the line of saline followed by a chemo chaser. “Excuse me, but may I have a vodka-tonic instead?” “No, now shut up and let me give you this wicked stuff. I am very busy and you are distracting me” says the chubby technician who probably failed out of nursing school. Geez—it is only 8 a.m. Such attitudes they have here.

I sit and sit and sit some more, staring out the window or reading something I do not care to read. My fellow chemo-recipients look morose, so I avoid eye contact. Surely, there will be no dialogue. Nobody here really gives a rat’s ass what kind of cancer you may have because everyone knows the common thread is cancer. The light bounces off the bald-headed guy across from me blinding me. “Next time I wear sunglasses,” I remind myself with a mental note that will be soon forgotten because I am also almost 50 so memory is fading faster that a desert sunset.

After several hours of chemo, they unhook me and I leave. I meet one of my girlfriends at the local diner and recant the awful things said and done to me these past few hours. I order some tea and a muffin to sooth my irritated nerves. We share small talk about our husbands’ respective bad habits and shortcomings and boast about our children as if we are the only ones with smart kids. After an hour of banter, we both pee and leave the diner.

Chapter 5—Bad Hair Day

Now that the new hairdo has been installed, going out in public is again possible. And, of course, the new hair “look” is much better than the old hair “look” as it transforms us to younger, prettier women. We deserve nothing less. So, we get ready, cut the labels off a few items of brand new clothes recently delivered by the nice people at Talbots Online, and pluck the hair off the Styrofoam dummy and plop it over our freshly shaved head. With a few (20 minutes worth) of primping and brushwork, we pronounce ourselves ready to meet the world. Hey, we still got it.

To make sure people notice, we gentle touch the curls when speaking to our girlfriends so they feel obligated to compliment us on how radiant we look. We feel better. First stop is the high-end retail store to select an even newer outfit to complement our new look. After all, recovery requires spoiling ourselves to the hilt. Such opportunities are far and few between.

Going outside on stormy days does present both a problem and a convenience. When there are very high winds there is concern that the hair will fly off and be carried away by some large bird for nest-making purposes. That would be a scene and we like to avoid scenes. Scenes are important fodder for gossip, especially among the female circuit, because they provide something to talk about other than our husbands, our children, and the lack of closet space in our house. In heavy rain, there is not such a problem because we can always toss the damn headpiece into the dryer for a few minutes. Try doing that with your own hair. Besides, in the time it takes for the hair to dry we can return five or ten phone messages or place one or two online orders.

If the new hair is not quite right, we can visit our favorite beautician who is more upset than we are about the loss of hair because it means the loss of a customer for a temporary period. Such is a chemo-disaster. So, the hair can be styled and trimmed if need be. Of course, we caution the stylist with 25 years experience not to cut too much because it will not grow back. This is not humorous for the poor beautician because she knows you probably will not be back for months.

Chapter 6—Bringing My Hair to the Beauty Parlor for an Overhaul

Now that it has been several months with my new wig, I feel it is time for some changes. A wig gives new meaning to the concept of a permanent. I bring the inanimate piece to my local beautician where he/she removes the built-up dust and wind-blown leaves that have accumulated and fix a few loose ends. While he/she renovates my temporary do, I am taking a few cell phone calls from my cadre of friends. They all suggest I might feel a bit better driving around in a new Lexus. I have very smart friends. I make yet another mental note to develop a plan of persuasion to use on my husband (aka—intense pressure) to achieve the newly formed goal of a new car. After all, he will do anything to make me happy, which is customarily interpreted as him doing just about anything to avoid me being unhappy. Leverage only gets better with cancer. The sympathy card can be played quite well, but should not be played too often. The real potency of this card is the uncertainty of when it might be deployed. It is sort of the secret weapon of the Jewish cancer survivor.

Equally effective is the application of guilt on the mother of a Jewish cancer survivor especially when she lives in the Promised Land (Florida). I can call her and complain of very uncomfortable side effects and deploy a few tears here and there to cause her to invariably say:

> Do you want me to fly to New York to help you? It would not be that much trouble. I can always reschedule my every Tuesday afternoon card game with my very dear friends that I hardly ever see and who probably will die soon and my dentist appointment to make much needed and long-deferred repairs that, if not made soon, will result in the loss of all my remaining teeth. They are hard to get appointments with as I am sure you know. And my teeth do need cleaning, even the false ones. But, it will be all right. And you know the air fares have gone up so much though my meager Social Security has stayed the same, but we can manage. Just let me know and I'll be there in a jiffy. You don't have to worry about me. I'll be fine.

The last thing you want or need on God's green earth is another visit from mom. Waiting on her hand and foot while you are undergoing treatment would be traumatic. So you simply pour on the charm and make her feel guilty for not being there by your side and let her off the hook so she does not travel to your house where there is no room anyway because your husband cannot provide a reasonably sized house for you and your child. But, you did not listen to mom when she said: "Oh, I guess he is nice, but you really ought to marry a real doctor." Mom is always right after all.

This way there is something in it for both of you: She gets to stay home in her comfort zone with zero maternal responsibilities and you achieved an important objective of transferring guilt from you for not visiting her on her birthday to her for not being there for you. Perfect! Jewish Oncology is the study of retro-transference of Jewish guilt. What a blessing. You will explain this technique while holding court next Tuesday at the diner with the "Chosen Ones"—your hand-picked girlfriends.

Chapter 7—Shopping and Cancer—the Best Medicine

What could be better therapy than a shopping excursion? Got to take my mind off cancer and continue to lead a productive life. So, off I go to that most wonderful oasis known to the Jewish woman—Bloomingdales. There I can cruise the floors, try on clothes, check out new makeup, try on new scarves, gloves, coats, hats, and enjoy an over-priced lunch in the store's restaurant where the point is to see and be seen. I can get lost inside Bloomies for two, maybe upwards of 3 hours without coming up for air.

There is a known therapeutic power attributed to shopping. It makes a Jewish woman feel complete, more so than being married (except being a Jewish spinster is to live a life of sheer misery, especially when Mom is around and a pure living Hell if you are unfortunate enough to have to actually live with mom). Unmarried 30-something, Jewish "girls" are pimped-out by their mothers in the form of establishment of numerous blind dates. Unfortunately, some of the very more than middle-aged men are either blind, bald, fat, smelly, or just plain unacceptable. They will, most assuredly have, though, several very acceptable qualities, all very endearing to the Jewish broad: being rich, owning a large house with plenty of vacant closet space, and, yes, they will be Jewish.

More than likely, most of them will be divorced, have thriving careers as physicians or attorneys, and love to display their girlfriends and wives (never simultaneously) decked-out in furs, diamonds, and *Manolo Blahnik* shoes.

Shopping provides a release more powerful than sex. It lasts far longer too and there are no messy sheets to change. Protection is not necessary unless you are shopping late at night and you parked in a dark corner of the parking lot. Even then, you can ask one of the hunky security guards to escort you to your car. That is a shopping bonus.

Jewish women have learned how to sneak packages into the house. Even if you happen to get caught, you can always whip out the sympathy card and let hubby know how generous he is and how good you will look in your new outfit(s) so he can be proud of you when you are in a crowd amid goyim trash.

Once safe at home, you begin the arduous task of finding room for those new shoes, new clothes, and other items. While moving other stuff around (much of which also have price tags still attached), you complain that you have inadequate closet space signaling the need for a larger home. You make yet another mental note to withhold sex until you have a chance to work on your husband's unreasonable resistance to moving. "Mortgage–shmortgage," you state emphatically as you roll over to that nirvana known as restful sleep after a trip to Bloomingdales. Your husband will have another restless night, but the mental pressure will soon bring him to his senses and he will be contacting the real estate agent very soon to arrange for suitable replacement headquarters for your expanded wardrobe as well as ample room for entertaining (showing off).

Chapter 8—Convenient Use of Cancer to Get Away with Things

While driving, we get distracted because we are also touching up our makeup and on the cell phone. A police officer finally gets our attention. How are we supposed to notice the flashing lights and siren when we are rushing to the store to check out the new line of boots at Macy's? "Ma'am, I will need to see your driver's license, insurance card, and vehicle registration card," barks the officer. "Is there a problem, officer?" we reply. "You were travelling 20 miles over the posted speed limit." "Oh, gee. I am very sorry officer. You see, I am a bit late for my chemotherapy treatment and then I have to get to the hospital to visit my poor old grandmother who is dying," we lie convincingly. Showing compassion, the officer leans down to the window and says: "You just drive careful and take care of yourself and say hi to your grandmother for me," the officer says with a smile, pat on the shoulder and a quiet, reassuring voice. Great, now we can race to the mall.

At the busy checkout counter in the grocery store, we notice very long lines. Making sure there is nobody in the store we recognize, we slip off our fake hair and start to look very upset. Everyone on line notices this "special needs shopper." People closer to the cashier take pity and offer to trade places, which we reluctantly, but graciously accept (take advantage of).

At a party, we overhear some chatty women discussing their medical problems. Some have bunions; others have knee problems. We mosey on over and chime in: "well, you think that is bad; I have cancer." The conversation quickly turns to us and we hold court for 20–30 minutes, garnering as much free sympathy as we can, but really just to monopolize the conversation. There is a way to embellish the agony of cancer treatment.

The next day more deliveries of food arrive, starting the cycle of excessive freebies all over again. But we enjoy the attention and the ability to turn small-talk into meaningful conversation because we are the main topic.

Chapter 9—Poking at my Veins; Where are the Veins?

A short poem:
Where are the veins?
Send in the veins.
My veins have collapsed.
I have no more veins.
Send in the veins.
Where are my veins?
Someone stole my veins, I'm sure.
No veins, no treatment today—okay.
Veins, schmeins; I need no veins.
I'll drink the stuff today, I will.
Why is today unlike any other today?
Because, today I have no veins.

Midway through my treatment plan, my poor veins have gone into double-secret hiding. Who could really blame them? The nurse tries and tries, but cannot locate anything even closely resembling a vein. So, instead of giving up, the bitch nurse keeps poking my arms, trying to be a hero by locating one of the last functioning veins I have left. "Um, nurse, dear, that f--ing hurts! Please stop," I beg in agony. "No way, lady," nurse Ratchet barks. "Doc says I have to give you this treatment or my fat ass is out on the street again, whoring and selling drugs just to feed my eight kids." "You have eight kids?" I had to ask; it helps take my mind off the extreme pain. "Or nine, I forget," the nurse says in a puzzling tone as she stabs me one last time like she was using a switchblade.

After 14 tries, the nurse finally locates a viable vein. It hurts so much. Some online shopping later will be necessary to recover. How much more can I take: no hair, no veins. All this suffering is putting a crimp on my scheduled house redecorating project. After 2 months of treatment, even my friends have pulled back from the initial flood of nonstop sympathy. Food deliveries have slowed to a crawl. The calls are fewer. Does anybody care? Why me? I know what it might be! I look so damn good in my new tight jeans and my replacement hair makes me look at least 10 years younger. My friends' husbands stare a lot at me. Cancer is the new high-maintenance burden. Go figure.

Chapter 10—Family Events—To Go or Not To Go?

Okay, so I am in the middle of my round of scheduled chemotherapy treatments and soon face the dreaded decision whether to attend a family function. After all, Jews love to gather because it is a convenient excuse to overeat. Further, someone else has to clean up. It also provides an above average opportunity for gossip. Paradoxically, where I used to look forward to these events in order to try to look better than the other females and be the center of attention, in my situation, I am more than likely already going to attract more than my fair share of attention, sympathy, questions, etc. "Do I really need this?" People will go out of their way to say the obligatory line: "You look great!" "Yes, having Drano pumped into my bloodstream makes one glow," I will reply. The will be dumfounded by my wit during crisis. "How does she stay so calm," they will say to themselves. I have achieved Jewish nirvana—both sympathy and envy from my girlfriends.

Yet, such events also provide the recovering person with unique opportunities to show the world how strong we are and how philosophical we have become. These revelations may take the form of doing the *Electric Slide* with more gusto than ever or the *Tango* in a very sensuous way. When talking with people, I can quote Nietzsche and Aristotle (as I will memorize several obscure sayings for use at convenient times). People will be amazed at how I am coping with disease and they will be amazed at how much smarter I have become. "Wow, isn't she amazing," some will mutter as they leave the crowd that will be surrounding me throughout the evening. I am a star.

When the family event becomes either extremely boring or the attention devoted to me starts to wane, I can revert to "Honey, I am feeling very tired and a little queasy. After I vomit, I think we should head home." My friends' husbands will trip over themselves trying to help me with my coat.

Shoes must be of the finest quality and the most current trendy style. The well-planned exit is as absolutely as important as the dramatic entrance done in style, aided by very new and expensive clothes. There can be no skimping on the amount of bling worn for the occasion. As I air-kiss every woman I see and press up against all the good-looking men, I will remember to instigate rounds of sympathy by telling a preselected group how appreciative I am of their thoughtfulness during my treatments. It is this group that will become unwitting catalysts to ensure the next food drive straight to my fridge. They will do so because they have been knighted to the legion of those having already done their share. Thus, the guilt card will be played around the room for the next several hours, reaching those who have procrastinated. Soon, freebies will be offered in my direction and life will be good again. After all, improvement of one's nails and stocking of one's pantry are part of the healing process.

The key sub-events will occur, of course, in the ladies restroom where all truth is always told and nothing is held back. "Meryle dear, you can tell me. How are you feeling dear? What can we do for you? Do you need food? Should I bring you some soup? Is Eric taking care of you?" To all I will cheerily reply: "Oh, I'm okay," but said with a worried voice and downcast eyes because we certainly never want to give up ground in the sympathy category. Tears form easily because, earlier, I made sure to stick myself in the eye with my eyeliner. “I’ll be fine. You don’t have to worry about me. I’ll manage,” said with a tiny quiver, which will, induce a hug. These well-timed responses will yield a new harvest of precooked meals delivered to my door, offers to go shopping, and free manicures and pedicures so my friends and relatives can really talk with me. Having cancer is real work. All this manipulation makes me hungry.

After the event, the requisite chain of telephone calls and email will commence. “Did you see how good Meryle looked?” Soon, chat rooms, Facebook pages, tweeting, etc. will be flooded with commentary about me. The leader of the subgroup will organize a food brigade so deliveries of my favorite foods will be well coordinated for the next several weeks. They will see this at doing a Mitzvah. I will see it as an escape from cooking—a win–win really.

Realistically, there are a lot of benefits to going through treatment for cancer; and why not? After all, I paid my dues; sat Shiva for families; donated surplus food and clothing at the Temple. Actually, the clothing drive for Jewish women equates to making room in the closets and dressers for upgrades to the wardrobe via online shopping and trips to Bloomies. After all, charity begins at home.

Chapter 11—Memory Has Been Forgotten

“What was I supposed to do today?” I cannot remember a single fact these days. I lose things often. Phone numbers, names, dates—all vacating my memory. Oh well, probably my memory will find its way back into my brain when I am done with the oncology people. “I was going to write more here, but just forgot.”

Chapter 12—Okay, I am Done with Treatment: I have Had Enough!

Five treatments of chemotherapy should be enough. I think I will call the doctor and announce that I am cured and will not be in need of either the sixth and final round of chemo or the planned 7 weeks of radiation. I am feeling physically okay, but mentally fatigued over all the poking and probing and would like to resume normal life. I also welcome the return of my hair. Wearing skullcaps and fake hair is just not the same and being as bald as a baby’s ass negates my spending quality time with the beautician on a regular basis. I am way behind on neighborhood gossip.

It takes more patience than I have to endure month after month of all this medical attention. Even though I know I will attend to the balance of the planned regimen, I will complain to all who will listen. After all, complaining is expected and I get lots of extra attention. At least from that perspective, being under the care of all these medical oncology people provides a convenient way for me to do what I want and not do what I do not want. It seems Jewish guilt goes out the window when one suffers from cancer. For example, I can now say: "Mom, I just could not return your twelve telephone messages because I was too busy puking up my guts. I am sure you will understand because I know you always do understand me." I say this bold-faced lie because I know (a) God will forgive a lying cancer patient and (b) the manipulation with Mom will be very effective and get her off my back for a few more weeks.

Besides, after the fifth treatment, I am starting to lose my eyebrows and eyelashes—the last vestiges of female beauty concerns. I look like a bowling ball with eyes, a mouth and a nose. I have started shopping online for falsies (not fake boobies mind you). I really do not want to look like I was struck by lightning at age five to explain why I am completely hairless.

Chapter 13—Posttreatment Attention Deficit Disorder (PTADD)

Perhaps the biggest fear (aka—horrific nightmare) faced by the mid-treatment survivor is: "OMG! What will I do once I am done with treatment and nobody pays any attention to me anymore?" This seems like it would be devastating, which, frankly, is unacceptable. For now, the calls continue to come in regularly, often jamming up my voice mailbox. When I feel so inclined, I can return the messages of my choosing; ignoring those from mother and other extremely annoying people. Food deliveries continue to trickle-in from the more guilt-ridden people in my circle and afternoons and dinners out with the girls have become a routine expectation. I garner extra sympathy with a flick of my little finger on a regular basis and my girlfriends constantly chatter how damn good I look now that I shed those few pounds of excess ballast. I have to admit, I do have a certain glow these days. Secretly, they refer to me as the "little bitch recovering from cancer." I love it! New boots will celebrate the attention-getting coup for this week.

But, once I announce that I am done with treatment, my friends and family will expect me to return to my normal life (read: slavery in the kitchen, cleaning the house, rough sex with my husband, etc.). Something must be done to avoid the dreaded toxic shock/posttreatment syndrome known as PTADD.

Perhaps I will float a few mysterious concerns to those in my girlfriend cadre that like to blab. I can tell a few: "Gee, I don't want to alarm my husband, but the doctor wants me to have more tests." Or, I can start a few rumors, which will increase my popularity with my more adventurous (slutty) friends, such as saying: "You know, I've always wanted to 'do' the UPS guy and show him my new and improved boobs." This way, my circle of doting friends will just continue to desire time with me to either provide the constant stream of sympathy I have become accustomed to or to probe me for information to add to the rumor mill. Either way I keep the attention right where it belongs—on me!

Chapter 14—My Husband Wants Another Child (Really?)

So, here is the current insanity. On the day of my last chemotherapy extravaganza my husband joins me for my examination before treatment. He watches me disrobe; admiring my delicious boobs that have been right-sized just as a corporation in a down economy. He knows that another man (a real Jewish doctor) is soon going to touch them. He considers this event to be a proxy for a three-way, though his preference has always been for the third person to be female. He is flexible so willing to settle for what he can get. The doctor comes in and immediately provides a reassuring hug and applies a kiss to my check. Hubby is sitting in a chair observing me get man-handled.

The doctor tore open my flimsy gown and starts to grab my boobies and feel my body all over. My husband observes his technique and extreme confidence and even takes a few notes. After all, the doctor is an expert in handling women. My husband is very excited and I know his adventurous mind is going places only possible in the land of his rather bizarre imagination. I knew he was damaged when I met him, but he can be overly mischievous. I am happy he is comfortable sharing his fantasies with me.

The doctor is explaining about how well I am doing and that I am very close to the dreaded land of mood swings known as menopause. Why menopause has the word “men” in it remains a mystery and is really unfair. My husband, being helpful (read: annoying) tells the doctor I already have serious mood swings. He responds that these will doubtlessly worsen. This converts my husband’s pallor to pale and pasty.

My husband, being relentless, asks the doctor how soon we can start working on another child.[1] He looks over and smiles, telling us to wait 2 years after the end of treatment. “No problem,” my husband exclaims. “She’ll only be 51,” he says to the doctor, who now realizes what I have been living with for the past 17 years. The poor kindly old doctor explains about fertility and viability of my dwindling supply of grade “A” ovary-fresh eggs and how there is only a 5 % chance of a pregnancy anyway. Of course, husband is thinking if we have sex 20 times in 1 week, the chances grow to 100 % (he is an idiot).[2] There is simply not enough jewelry on the planet to warrant such gratuitous sexual activity anyway. Sexual privileges must be earned and gaining access is not easy with Jewish women, regardless of cancer. Withholding is a right of the Jewish woman and abstinence is expected. This is why God invented the male art of begging and bribing. God is very wise.

Of course, my adoring husband agrees with the doctor that I look fantastic. He does, though, mention that I am starting to get a few grey hairs on my wig (did I mention he is an idiot?). At least he keeps me laughing. I will keep him around a few more years, at least until the new Lexus appears in my driveway and the kitchen

---

[1] Makes me wonder if he is being spontaneous or if he thought through this line of questioning.

[2] Meryle’s—Note to self: No sex for Eric for at least 6 months.

is completely remodeled to my satisfaction. After all, I deserve a major bonus for doing so well with my treatment. Some retail therapy is in order.

Men barely understand the functionality of a woman's body. Sure they know what to do with us, but internally they are usually dopey. When men think of eggs they think of scrambled or fried. The concept of being born with all the eggs a woman will ever have is beyond the grasp of the average male.[3]

On a positive note, love does abound between us; made stronger through the trials of treatment. With love, all suffering and worry can be overcome. Perhaps it is the comfort of the embrace at the end of each night that helps me drift off to sleep.

The problem with treatment for cancer is that the prescription for lifetime monitoring makes a person consider issues of mortality. This seems normal and can fit in with a thriving life. It takes some effort and having a husband who adores me and is willing to laugh at strife makes it easier. Maybe I will reward him later and let him play with my reconstructed bosom. He likes them and kisses them gently. Having a child with him, knowing he would want another provides warm feelings. While he may be quite delusional that it would be even remotely possible, the thought must be admired and cherished. Each stage of life has its own purpose, its specific limitations, and definite challenges. With a maturing relationship, a couple can go through these stages together with each helping the other with their personal struggle and efforts to actualize their individual destinies.

Chapter 15—Epilogue

Meryle's latest limerick:
I'm a little nauseous
Yes I am.
I just had my chemo,
Who knows which round?
In just about 5 days
I'll be fine.
Then back to chemo
I'm losing my mind.
Sung to the tune of I'm a little teapot.

[3] Though my husband is far from average, he does not really grasp this concept either. He feels why would God place all my eggs in one basket?

References

Adler, A. (1998). *Understanding human nature* (trans: B. Colin). Center City: Hazledon. (Originally published in 1927).

Agnew, R. (1992). Foundation for a general strain theory of crime and delinquency. *Criminology, 5,* 47–88.

Allport, G. (1955). *Becoming*. New Haven: Yale University Press.

Ambuel, D. (2007). *Image and paradigm in Plato's Sophist*. Las Vegas: Parmenides.

Andreason, N. C. (2005). *The creative brain: The science of genius*. New York: Penguin Books.

Anonymous. (2013). *Personal communication*. September 15, 2013.

Artemisia. (2011). *Paradigm shift*. http://www.taketheleap.com. Retrieved 21 Dec 2012.

Arntz, A. (2012). *Imagery re-scripting as a method to change emotional memories & schemata/representations* (pp. 1--10). The Netherlands: Maastricht University. http://www.kognitiv.no/filarkiv/File/Inspirasjonskonferansen%202013/ImageryRescript_works Shop_2013__Skrivebeskyttet___Kompatibilitetsmodus_.pdf. Retrieved 18 Dec 2013.

Bargh, J. (2014). Our unconscious mind. *Scientific American* (January), pp. 30–37.

Baresi, S. (2013). *Personal communication*. November 19, 2013.

Baresi, S. (2013). *Personal communication*. November 22, 2013.

Baumeister, R. F., Campbell, J. D., Krueger, J. I., & Vohs, K. D. (2003). Does high self-esteem cause better performance, interpersonal success, happiness, or healthier lifestyles? *Psychological Science in the Public Interest, 4*(1). American Psychological Society.

Becker, B. (1971). *The birth and death of meaning* (2nd ed.). New York: Free Press.

Beckley, K. (2013). Schema therapy, in contemporary psychotherapy (Winter 2013, pp. 1–6). http://contemporarypsychotherapy.org/vol-2-no-2/schema-therapy/. Retrieved 10 Dec 2013.

Berg, C. (1959). *Fear, punishment, anxiety and the Wolkfenden report*. London: Allen & Unwin.

Bishop, G. D. (2013). Understanding the human mind and behaviour: Psychological and related perspectives. *Innovation*. http://www.innovationmagazine.com/innovation/volumes/v5n3/coverstory1.shtml. Retrieved 5 Jan 2014.

Bloch, G. B. (1993). *How to train for and run your best marathon*. New York: Simon & Schuster.

Bohm, D. (2007). *On creativity*. London: Routledge.

Boysen, J., & Zarbock, G. (2012). Empirical evidence for schema therapy (May 3, pp. 1–11). Hamburg, Germany. http://www.isstonline.com/sites/default/files/empiricalevidenceST.pdf. Retrieved 27 Dec 2013.

Braden, G. (2008). *The spontaneous healing of belief: Shattering the paradigm of false limits*. Carlsbad: Hay House.

BrainyQuote.com. (2014). Donald Trump quotes. http://www.brainyquote.com/quotes/authors/d/donald_trump.html. Retrieved 9 Feb 2014.

Branden, N. (2013). Nurturing self esteem in young people. http://nathanielbranden.com/discussions. Retrieved 1 Feb 2014.

E. A. Kreuter, K. M. Moltner, *Treatment and Management of Maladaptive Schemas*, DOI 10.1007/978-3-319-06817-6,

Brehm, J. W. (1966). A theory of psychological reactance. In W. W. Burke, D. G. Lake, & J. W. Paine (Eds.). *Organizational change: A comprehensive reader (2009)* (pp. 377–392). San Francisco: Wiley.

Brewton, Z. (2014). *The long journey with Will Rodgers Pioneer Foundation*. Unpublished manuscript.

Broderick, P. (2009). To thine own self be true: A phenomenological investigation into the role of self in a moral dilemma (Abstract). http://digitalcommons.liberty.edu/doctoral/190/. Retrieved 6 Jan 2014.

Brown, S. L. (2012). Pathological relationships: Dealing with a problem partner. *Psychology Today*. http://www.psychologytoday.com/blog/pathological-relationships. Retrieved 27 Feb 2014.

Buber, M. (2000). *I and thou* (trans: R. G. Smith). New York: Scribner. (Originally published in 1958).

Caldwell, D. (2013). What's wrong with the Rangers? *The Wall Street Journal, October 15*(2013), A27.

Calliet, E. (1955). *The dawn of personality*. Indianapolis: The Dobbs-Merrill.

Capra, F. (1996). *The web of life: A new scientific understanding of living systems*. New York: Anchor Books.

Carter, S. B. (2011). Toxic relationships: A health hazard. *Psychology Today*. http://psychologytoday.com/blog/high-octane-women/201108/toxic-relationships- health-hazard. Retrieved 6 Jul 2013.

Casement, P. (2002). *Learning from our mistakes: Beyond dogma in psychoanalysis and psychotherapy*. New York: Guilford.

Caspi, A., & Moffitt, T. E. (1993). When do individual differences matter? A paradoxical theory of personality coherence. *Psychological Inquiry, 4,* 247–271.

Chappell, V. (2004). Locke on consciousness. http://philosophy.fas.nyu.edu/docs/IO/1650/chappell.pdf. Retrieved 7 Oct 2013.

Chesterton, G. K. (1994). *What's wrong with the world*? San Francisco: Ignatius. (Originally published in 1910).

Christian Research Institute. (2010). *The covering: God's plan to protect you from evil*. http://www.equip.org/bible_answers/what-is-the-biblical-definition-of-faith. Retrieved 28 Jan 2014.

Clarkson, P. (1989). In W. Dryden (Ed.), *Gestalt counseling in action* (3rd ed.). London: Sage.

Cockram, D. (2009). Role and treatment of early maladaptive schemas in Vietnam veterans with PTSD. Unpublished doctoral dissertation, Murdoch University. http://researchrepository.murdoch.edu.au/1309/2/02Whole.pdf. Retrieved 12 Dec 2013.

Corbett, R. (1980). The will to believe-William James: An outline. http://www2.webster.edu/~corbetre/philosophy/misc/james.html. Retrieved 10 Nov 2013.

Cummings, A. (2009). Greetings from cancerland. In S. Reiter (Ed.), *Writing away the demons: Stories of creative coping through transformative writing* (pp. 62–74). St. Cloud: North Star.

Cummins, D. (2013). Do you have "eyes on the prize" or "target fixation"? In Good thinking: Ideas that influence the way we think. http://www.psychologytoday.com/blog/good-thinking/201309/do-you-have-eyes-the -prize-or-target-fixation. Retrieved 3 Jan 2012.

Cyders, M. A., Flory, K., Rainer, S., & Smith, G. T. (2009). The role of personality dispositions to behavior in predicting first year college drinking. National Institute of Health. http://www.ncbi.nlm.nih.gov/pmc/articles/PMC2653206/. Retrieved 7 July 2013.

Daniels, V. (2013). Notes on Carl Gustav Jung. Sonoma State University. http://www.sonoma.edu/users/d/daniels/junglect.html. Retrieved 10 Jan 2014.

David, M. (2013). The correspondence theory of truth. In E. N. Zalta (Ed.) (Fall 2013 Edition). The Stanford encyclopedia of philosophy. http://plato.stanford.edu/archives/fall2013/entries/truth-correspondence/. Retrieved 3 Jan 2014.

Derr, W. J. (2001). *Righteousness or iniquity: Your choice and your just rewards*. Pittsburgh: Dorrence.

DeRubeis, R. J., & Beck, A. T. (1988). *Handbook of cognitive-behavioral therapies*. New York: Guilford.

Dewey, J. (1922). *Human nature and conduct: An introduction to social psychology*. New York: The Modern Library.

Divorce Statistics. (2014). Divorce statistics and divorce rate in the U.S.A. U.S. National Center for Health Statistics. http://www.divorcestatistics.info/divorce-statistics-and-divorce-rate-in-the-usa.html. Retrieved 11 Jan 2014.

Dowd, E., Clen, S., & Arnold, K. (2010). The specialty practice of cognitive and behavioral psychology. *Professional psychology research and practice, 41*(1), 89–95. American Psychological Association. http://www.psychologytoday.com/files/attachments/45869/pprp-article.pdf. Retrieved 23 Feb 2013.

Edwards, C. G. (2000). Creative writing as a spiritual practice: Two paths. In M. E. Miller & S. R. Cook-Greuter (Eds.), *Creativity, spirituality, and transcendence: Paths to integrity and wisdom in the mature self* (pp. 3–23). Stamford: Ablex.

Eligon, J., & Eckholm, E. (2014). For gay couples in Michigan, a day of joy ends in legal uncertainty (p. 1). http://www.nytimes.com/2014/03/23/us/gay-couples-in-michigan-seize-their-chance-to-be-married-after-ruling.html?rref=us&mobile=Ribbon&version=origin&region=Header&action=click&contentCollection=U.S.&pgtype=article. Retrieved 23 March 2014.

Eliot, G. (1878–1885). *The works of George Eliot* (Vol. 1–2). Edinburgh: W. Blackwood.

Elliott, F. A. (1984). The episodic dyscontrol syndrome and aggression. *Neurologic Clinics, 2,* 113–125.

Ellis, D. (1998). *Life coaching: A new career for helping professionals*. Rapid City: Breakthrough Enterprises.

Emerson, R. W. (1841). Essay II self reliance. http://www.emersoncentral.com/selfreliance.htm. Retrieved 4 Jan 2013.

Encyclopedia of Mental Disorders. (2014). Bibliotherapy. http://www.minddisorders.com. Retrieved 23 Feb 2014.

Enger, J. (2013a). Fingerprints. http://www.findmyfingerprint.com. Retrieved 26 Oct 2013.

Enger, J. (2013b). *Personal communication*. October 25, 2013.

Epstein, M. (2013). *The trauma of everyday life*. New York: Penguin.

Erikson, E. H. (1998). *The life cycle completed*. New York: W.W. Norton. (Originally published in 1982).

Florida State University. (2013). Robert Agnew's general strain theory. http://www.criminology.fsu.edu/crimtheory/agnew.htm. Retrieved 3 Jan 2014.

Fox, K. R. (1999). The influence of physical activity on mental well-being. *Public Health Nutrition, 2*(3a), 411–418.

Freud, S. (1955). *Psychopathology of everyday life*. New York: Mentor Books.

Frieswijk, N., Steverink, N., Buunk, B. P., & Slaets, J. P. J. (2006). The effectiveness of a bibliotherapy in increasing the self-management ability of slightly to moderately frail older people. *Positive Education and Counseling, 61,* 219–227.

Frost, R. (2014). Reluctance. In Great books online. Bartleby.com. http://www.bartleby.com/117/32.html. Retrieved 3 Jan 2014.

Furness, H. (2012). Key to career success is confidence, not talent. UK Telegraph. http://www.telegraph.co.uk/news/uknews/9474973/Key-to-career-success-is-confidence-not-talent.html. Retrieved 4 Jan 2014.

Gaisler-Salomon, I. (2014). Inheriting stress. The New York Times, March 7, 2014 (Sunday Review). http://www.nytimes.com/2014/03/09/opinion/sunday/can-children-inherit-stress.html?_r=0. Retrieved 8 Mar 2014.

Garret, P. (1897). *One hundred choice selections*. Philadelphia: Penn.

Gergen, K. J. (2000). The saturated self: Dilemmas of identity in contemporary life. New York: Basic Books.

Gerry, L. M. (2013). 10 signs you're burning out- and what to do about it. Forbes. http://www.forbes.com/sites/learnvest/2013/04/01/10-signs-youre- burning-out-and-what-to-do-about-it/. Retrieved 28 Nov 2013.

Ghougassian, J. P. (1972). *Gordon W. Allport's ontopsychology of the person*. New York: Philosophical Library.

Gibson, D. (2009). Is one man's faith another's superstition? *Wall Street Journal*. http://online.wsj.com/news/articles/SB123811509991753625. Retrieved 4 Jan 2014.

Goldsmith, B. (2013). Facebook study says envy is rampant on the social network. http://www.huffingtonpost.com/2013/01/22/Facebook-study envy_n_2526549.html. Retrieved 1 Jan 2014.

GoodTherapy.org. (2012). Past experiences influence therapeutic alliance. http://www.goodtherapy.org/blog/clients-past-experiences-influence-therapeutic-alliance-0626123. Retrieved 3 Jan 2014.

Graddy, D. B. (2001). Cognitive flexibility theory as a pedagogy for web-based course design. http://www.ipfw-edu/as/tohe/2001/Papers/graddy/graddy.htm. Retrieved 18 April 2007.

Graham, L. (2013). *Bouncing back: Rewiring your brain for maximum resilience and well-being*. Novato: New World Library.

Gregoire, C. (2013). How some of the world's most successful people discovered their spiritual side. http://www.huffingtonpost.com/2013/10/16/10-people-who-came-out-of_n_4086176.html?icid=maing-grid7%7Cmaing7%7Cdl23%7Csec1_lnk3%26pLid%3D393575. Retrieved 19 Oct 2013.

Grigsby, J., & Stevens, D. (2000). *Neurodynamics of personality*. New York: Guilford.

Grof, S., & Bennett, H. Z. (1992). *The holotropic mind*. San Francisco: Harper.

Grof, S. (2000). *Psychology of the future: Lessons from modern consciousness research*. New York: State University of New York Press.

Guarendi, R. (1971). *Fighting mad: Practical solutions for conquering anger*. Cincinnati: Servant Books. (Originally published 1946).

Guggenbuhl-Craig, A. (1980). *The emptied soul: On the nature of the psychopath*. Woodstock: Spring Publications.

Halbertal, M. (2014). *Maimonides: Life and thought* (trans: J. Linsider). Princeton: Princeton University Press.

Hall, C.S., & Nordby, V.J. (1973). *A primer of Jungian psychology*. Markham: New American Library.

Hagenaars, M., & Holmes, E. (2012). Mental imagery in psychopathology: Another step. *Journal of Experimental Psychopathology, 3*(2), 121–126. http://jep.textrum.com/index.php?art_id=69#.UsmyGfRDvmI. Reviewed 23 Dec 2013

Hanson, K. (2014). What is hope and how can we measure it? http://www.positivepsychology.org.uk/pp-theory/hope/100-what-is-hope-and-how-can-we-measure-it.html. Retrieved 20 Feb 2014.

Hanson, R., & Mendius, R. (2009). *Buddha's brain: The practical neuroscience of happiness, love, and wisdom*. Oakland: New Harbinger Publications.

Harris, S. J. (1953). *Columbia world of quotations*. New York: Columbia University Press 1996. http://quotes.dictionary.com/the_difference_between_faith_and_superstition_is_that. Retrieved 11 Jan 2014.

Harris, V. (2013). Abraham, great-great grandma Mary, & me. *Reform Judaism, winter,* 11–12.

Hegel, G. W. F. (1977). *Hegel's phenomenology of spirit* (trans: A. V. Miller). Oxford: Oxford University Press. (Originally published in 1807).

Heitz, D. (2013). *Self esteem* (medically reviewed on October 18, 2013 by George Krucik, MD, MBA). http://ask.healthline.com/health/self-esteem. Retrieved 1 Feb 2014.

Holmes, L. (2013). 8 ways to practice more positivity in 2014. http://www.huffingtonpost.com/2013/12/30/positive-new-year-resolut_n_4509532.html. Retrieved 1 Jan 2014.

Holmes, E., Arntz, A., & Smucker, M. (2007). Imagery rescripting in cognitive behavior therapy: Images, treatment techniques and outcomes. *Journal of Behavior Therapy and Experimental Psychiatry,* 297–305. http://www.mervin-smucker.de/fileadmin/user_upload/Dokumente/Holmes-EAImagery_rescripting-in-cognitive-behaviour-therapy-Images-Mervin-Smucker.pdf. Retrieved 28 Dec 2013.

Horney, K. (1957). *Our inner conflicts: A constructive theory of neurosis*. London: Routledge & Kegan Paul.

Hughes, M., Patterson, A. B., & Terrell, J. B. (2005). *Emotional intelligence in action: Training and coaching activities for leaders and managers* (p. 11). San Francisco: Pfeiffer.

Jacobs, J. (2013). *Personal communication*. July 11, 2013.

James, W. (1882). Rationality, activity and faith. *Princeton Review, 2,* 1–88.

James, W. (1907). Pragmatism: A new name for some old ways of thinking (Lecture VI, Pragmatism's Conception of Truth). New York: Longman Green and Co. http://www.authorama.com/pragmatism-7.html. Retrieved 1 Feb 2014.

James, W. (2004/1908). Letter to Helen Keller, December 17, 1908. In I. K. Skrupske & E. M. Berkeley (Eds.), *The correspondence of William James* (Vol. 12, April 1908–August 1910, p. 135). Charlottesville: University of Virginia Press.

John. (2013). *Personal communication*, December 21.

Johnston, A. (2013). Physics of the mundane: Kuhn's "Paradigm" & "Normal Science". http://physics.weber.edu/johnston/mundane/kuhn.htm. Retrieved 7 Oct 2013.

Jones, J. L. (2006). A closer look at bibliotherapy. *Young Adult Library Services, 5*(1), 24–27.

Joseph, S. (2013). What doesn't kill is. Psychology Today (April 11). http://www.psychologytoday.com/blog/what-doesnt-kill-us/201304/thine-own-self- be-true/comments. Retrieved 3 Nov 2013.

Jung, C. G. (1983). *The essential Jung: Selected writings*. (trans: R.F.C. Hull). Princeton: Princeton University Press. (Originally published in 1961).

Jung, C. G. (2010). *Synchronicity: An acausal connecting principle* (trans: R.C. Hull). Princeton: Princeton University Press. (Originally published in 1973).

Kaminker, A. (2013). *Personal communication*. September 17, 2013.

Kanter, R. M. (2004). *Confidence: How winning and losing streaks begin and end*. New York: Three Rivers Press.

Kaplan, A. G. (1991). Empathic communication in the psychotherapy relationship. In J. V. Jordan, A. G. Kaplan, J. B. Miller, I. P. Striver, & J. L. Surrey (Eds.). *Women's growth in connection: Writings from the Stone Center* (pp. 44–50). New York: Guilford.

Karen, R. (2001). *The forgiving self: The road from resentment to connection*. New York: Anchor Books.

Kawamoto, D. (2012). Billion dollar phobia? *Friday the 13th fears take a big economic toll*. http://www.dailyfinance.com. Retrieved 4 Jan 2014.

Kendall, B. (2014). High court halts Utah gay marriage. *Wall Street Journal,* A3. http://online.wsj.com/news/articles/SB10001424052702304887104593044116116601 06. Retrieved 26 Oct 2013.

Kernberg, O. (1985). *Borderline conditions and pathological narcissism*. Northvale: Jason Aronson.

King, C. H. (2014). *Personal communication*, January 24, 2014.

Kobasa, S. (1979). Stressful life events, personality, and health: An inquiry into hardiness. *Journal of Personality and Social Psychology, 37*(1), 1–11.

Knapp, P., & Beck, A. (2008). Cognitive therapy: Foundations, conceptual models, applications and research (pp. 54–64). http://www.scielo.br/pdf/rbp/v30s2/en_a02v30s2.pdf. Retrieved 9 Dec 2013.

Krasnova, H., Wenninger, H., Widjaja, T., & Buxmann, P. (2013). *Envy on facebook: A hidden threat to users' life satisfaction?* Institute of Information Systems at Berlin's Humboldt University. http://warhol.wiwi.hu berlin.de/~hkrasnova/Ongoing_Research_files/WI%202013%20Final%20Submission%20Krasnova.pdf. Retrieved 1 Jan 2014.

Kreuter, E. A. (2003a). *Love's journey: A book of reflections*. New York: 1st Books Library.

Kreuter, E. A. (2003b). The impact of identity theft through cyberspace. *The Forensic Examiner, 12*(5), 30–35.

Kreuter, E. A. (2004). Investigation of a psychopathic criminal's behavior as the wheels of justice slowly turn. *The Forensic Examiner, 13*(4), 28–35.

Kreuter, E. A. (2005). Transformation through poetic awareness of the inner pain of the prisoner. *Journal of Poetry Therapy, 18*(2), 97–101.

Kreuter, E. A. (2006a). *Victim vulnerability: An existential-humanistic interpretation of a single case study*. Hauppauge: Nova Science.

Kreuter, E. A. (2006b). Prose and cons: Use of poetry in existential-humanistic therapy for prisoners. *Journal of Poetry Therapy, 19*(1), 41–46.

Kreuter, E. A. (2006c). The psychopathic criminal mother: A case study of her two adult daughters' expression of basic mistrust. In A. Columbus (Ed), *Advances in psychology research* (Vol. 41, pp. 75–89). Hauppauge: Nova Science.

Kreuter, E. A. (2007a). Inside the psychopathic mind: A forensic interpretation based on dialogue with the victim cohort. *Advances in psychology research* (Vol. 48, pp. 279–292). Hauppauge: Nova Science.

Kreuter, E. A. (2007b). Creating an empathic and healing mantra for the soon-to-be-released prisoner. *Journal of Poetry Therapy, 20*(3), 159–162.

Kreuter, E. A. (2009). Catalyzing the inner spirit of the Type-A professional through poetic expression. *Journal of Poetry Therapy, 22*(3), 165–171.

Kreuter, E. A. (2010). Cyber psycho. In J. Wells (Ed.), *Internet fraud casebook* (pp. 349–358). New York: Wiley.

Kreuter, E. A. (2011a). *Victimization analyzed through the voices of a predator: Expansion of a single case study*. Hauppauge: Nova Science.

Kreuter, E. A. (2012a). *Victimization analyzed through the voices of a psychopathic predator: Expansion of a single case study*. Hauppauge: Nova Science.

Kreuter, E. A. (2012b). Research into the voices of the psychopathic predator: An analytical case study. *International Journal of Psychology Research, 7,* 2.

Kreuter, E. A. (2013a). *Fostering resilience for loss and irrelevance*. New York: Springer.

Kreuter, E. A. (2013b). *Propensity*. Unpublished manuscript.

Kreuter, E. A. (2013c). *Mother am I*. Unpublished manuscript.

Kreuter, E. A., & Reiter, S. (2013). Building resilience in the face of loss and irrelevance: Poetic methods for personal and professional. *Journal of Poetry Therapy* (in press).

Kreuter, M. (2013). *The starfish*. Unpublished manuscript.

Kreuter, M. (2014). *Personal communication*. February 12.

Kuhn, T. S. (1970/1962). *The structure of scientific revolutions* (2nd ed.). Chicago: The University of Chicago Press. (Originally published in 1962).

Kuhn, T. S. (1996). *The structure of scientific revolutions* (3rd ed.). Chicago: The University of Chicago Press.

Kuhn, T. S. (2002). *The structure of scientific revolutions*. Chicago: University of Chicago Press.

LaFave, S. (2005). Summary of theories of truth. http://instruct.westvalley.edu/lafave/Truth_theories.html. Retrieved 1 Feb 2014.

Lander, edu. (2013). Albert Camus, "Nobility of soul" Philosophy of life. http://philosophy.lander.edu/intro/camus.shtml#two. Retrieved 1 Sept 2013.

Lazarus, R. S. (1999). Hope: An emotion and a vital coping resource against despair. *Social Research, 66*(2), 653–678.

Leider, R. J., & Webber, A. M. (2013). *Life reimagined: Discovering your new life possibilities*. San Francisco: Berrett-Koehler.

Locke, J. (1975). In P. H. Nidditch (Ed.), *An essay concerning human understanding*. Book 11, Chapter xxii, Section 11, starting at page 294, line 1. Oxford: Clarenden. (Originally published London 1690).

Maddi, S. R., & Costa, P. T. (1972). *Humanism in personology: Allport, Maslow, and Murray*. Chicago: Aldine Atherton.

MarsOne. (2014). Astronaut requirements. http://www.mars-one.com/faq/selection-and-preparation-of-the-astronauts/what-are-the-qualifications-to-apply. Retrieved 3 Jan 2014.

Maslow, A. H. (1961). Existential psychology-What's in it for us? In R. May (Ed.), *Existential psychology* (pp. 52–60). New York: Random House.

Maturana, H. R., & Varela, F. J. (1987). *The tree of knowledge: The biological roots of human understanding*. Boston: Shambhala.

Matusiewicz, A., Hopwood, C., Banducci, A., & Lejuez, C. (2010). *The effectiveness of cognitive behavioral therapy for personality disorders*. NIH Public Access, Section. "Schema focused therapy" (unpublished manuscript), pp. 1–19. http://www.ncbi.nlm.nih.gov/pmc/articles/PMC3138327/. Retrieved 23 Dec 2013.

May, R. (1961). Existential bases of psychotherapy. In R. May (Ed.), *Existential psychology* (pp. 75–84). New York: Random House.

May, R. (1975). *The courage to create*. New York: W.W. Norton.
May, R. (1977). *The meaning of anxiety*. New York: W.W. Norton.
May, R. (1983). *The discovery of being*. New York: W.W. Norton.
McLeod, S. (2012). Jean Piaget. http:www.simplypsychology.org/piaget. Retrieved 11 Jan 2014.
Mlodinow, L. (2012). *Subliminal: How your unconscious mind rules your behavior*. New York: Vintage Books.
Moltner, K. M. (2013). Expectations vs. reality: A humanistic and practical perspective. In E. A. Kreuter (Ed.) *Fostering resilience for loss and irrelevance* (Chap. 10, pp. 215–280). New York: Springer.
Montgomery, D. (2013). Compass therapy: Christian psychology in action. http://compass-therapy.blogspot.com/2013/03/compass-therapy-interprets-personality.html. Retrieved 5 Jan 2014.
Morton, B. (2013). Fleshing out St. Augustine. http://www9.georgetown.edu/faculty/jod/texts/sundayheraldreview.html. Retrieved 29 Oct 2013.
Munro, A. (2013). Alice Munro wins nobel prize in literature. *New York Times, Oct 11*(2013), A1.
Murray, H. A. (1955). American Icarus. In A. Burton & R. E. Harris (Eds.), *Clinical studies of personality* (Vol. 2). New York: Harper.
Mutrie, N. (2001). The relationship between physical activity and clinically defined depression. In S. J. H. Biddle, K. R. Fox, & S. H. Boutcher (Eds.), *Physical activity and psychological well-being* (pp. 46–62). London: Routledge.
National Conference of State Legislatures. (2013). U.S. National Center for Health Statistics, National Vital Statistics Reports (NVSR), Births, marriages, divorces, and deaths: Provisional data for 2009, Vol. 58, No. 25, August 2010, and prior reports. http://www.ncsl.org/research/human-services/same-sex-marriage-overview. Retrieved 29 Dec 2013.
National Institute of Mental Health. (2013). What is obsessive-compulsive disorder. http://www.nimh.nih.gov/health/topics/obsessive-compulsive-disorder-ocd/index.shtml. OCD Retrieved 7 July 2013.
Naylor, G. (1998). Quote. In *A Helen Exley giftbook*. New York: Exley Publications.
New York Daily News. (2013). *Out of work and hope*. Editorial, 20, December 7.
Nisen, M. (2013). 5 reasons why people are getting married later and later in life. http://www.businessinsider.com/why-people-get-married-later-2013-10. Retrieved 9 Feb 2014.
Oliver, M. (1999). *Winter hours: Prose, prose poems, and poems*. Boston: Houghton Mifflin (Mariner).
Oxford Dictionary of Sports Science and Medicine. (2007). Consensus theory of truth (3rd ed.). http://www.oxfordreference.com/view/10.1093/oi/authority.20110803095633759. Retrieved 4 Jan 2014.
Padesky, C. (1994). Schema change processes in cognitive therapy (pp. 267–278). http://padesky.com/newpad/wp content/uploads/2012/11/schema_change_article_permissions.pdf. Retrieved 27 Dec 2013.
Parr, P. J. (1996). Further reflections on Late Second Millennium settlement in North West Arabia. In J. D. Seger (Ed.), *Retrieving the past: Essays on archaeological research and methodology in honor of Gus W. Van Beek*. Winona Lake: Eisenbrauns.
Pearl, M. (2013). What is schema therapy? http://www.schematherapy-nola.com/what-is-schema-therapy. Retrieved 1 Sept 2013.
Perry, J. (2008). *Personal identity*. Berkeley: University of California Press.
Peterson, L. (2013). It's healthy to work 'til you drop. http://jobs.aol.com/articles/2013/11/03/work-death-retirement/?icid=maing-grid7%7Cmain5%7Cdl1%7Csec1_lnk3%26pLid%3D400571. Retrieved 3 Nov 2013.
Peterson, C., Maier, S. F., & Seligman, M. E. P. (1993). *Learned helplessness: A theory for the age of personal control*. New York: Oxford University Press.
Pitchford, D. (2009). The existentialism of Rollo May: An influence on trauma treatment, *Journal of Humanistic Psychology,* 441–461. http://jhp.sagepub.com/cgi/content/abstract/49/4/441. Retrieved 4 Jan 2014.

Prasko, J., Grambal, A., Kamaradova, D., & Jelenova, D. (2012). Imagery re-scripting of traumatic or distressing stories from childhood. *Activitas Nervosa Superior Rediviva, 54*(3), 113–120. http://www.ncbi.nlm.nih.gov/pubmed/22504121. Retrieved 20 Dec 2013.

Provence, R. (2013). *Personal communication*. December 22, 2013.

Puff, R. (2012). Meditation for modern life. http://www.psychologytoday.com/blog/meditation-modern-life/201203/awareness-is -agent-change. Retrieved 3 Jan 2014.

Rappoport, J. (2013). The psychological crossroad of an unhappy life. Alex Jones' prison planet. http://www.prisonplanet.com/the-psychological-crossroad-of-an-unhappy-life.html. Retrieved 5 July 2013.

Ratzinger, J. (Card.). (1986). *Feast of faith*. San Francisco: Ignatius.

Reich, W. (1972). *Character analysis* (3rd ed.). New York: Farrar, Straus and Giroux. (Originally published in 1945).

Reiner, R., Brown, D., & Scheinman, A. (Producers), & Reiner, R. (Director). (1992). *A Few Good men* [Motion picture]. United States: Castle Rock Entertainment.

Reiter, S., & Contributors. (2009). *Writing away the demons: Stories of creative coping through transformative writing*. St. Cloud: North Star.

Rex. (2013). *Personal communication*. November 11, 2013.

Roach, J. (2004). Friday the 13th phobia rooted in ancient history. *National Geographic News*. http://news.nationalgeographic.com/news/2004/02/0212_040212_friday13_2.html. Retrieved 4 Jan 2014.

Roberts, E. (2012). The difference between self esteem and self-confidence. http://www.healthyplace.com/blogs/buildingselfesteem/2012/05/the-difference-between-self-esteem-and-self-confidence/. Retrieved 1 Feb 2014.

Rogers, C. R. (1988). *Client-centered therapy*. London: Constable & Robinson. (Originally published 1951).

Rogers, C. R. (1956). The necessary and sufficient conditions of therapeutic personality change. *Journal of Consulting Psychology, 21,* 95–103.

Rogers, C. R. (1995). *On becoming a person: A therapist's view of psychotherapy*. Boston: Houghton Mifflin. (Originally published 1961).

Rossi, E. L. (1993). *The psychobiology of mind-body healing: New concepts of therapeutic hypnosis, revised edition*. New York: W.W. Norton.

Ruback, R. B., & Thompson, M. P. (2001). *Social and psychological consequences of violent victimization*. Thousand Oaks: Sage.

Rykoff, A. (2011). Not so unlucky no. 13. http://espn.go.com/espn/print?id=6542266&type=story. Retrieved 29 Nov 2013.

Santanya, G. (1905). *Life of reason, reason in common Sense*. New York: Charles Scribner's Sons.

Sarno, J. E. (2007). *The divided mind: The epidemic of mindbody disorders*. New York: HarperCollins.

Sarte, J. P. (1984). *Being and nothingness: A phenomenological essay on ontology*. (Trans: H. E. Barnes). New York: Square Press. (Originally published in 1943).

Sartre, J. P. (1985). *Existentialism and human emotions*. New York: Kensington. (Originally published in 1957).

Savage, C., & Healy, J. (2014). U.S. to recognize 1,300 marriages disputed by Utah. http://www.nytimes.com/2014/01/11/us/politics/same-sex-marriage-utah.html?emc=edit_na_20140110&_r=0. Retrieved 10 Jan 2014.

Scaruffi, P. (undated). Essay truth. http://www.scaruffi.com/science/truth.html. Retrieved 11 Jan 2014.

Schneider, K. J. (2004). *Rediscovery of awe: Splendor, mystery, and the fluid center of life*. St. Paul: Paragon House.

Schutz, E., Sailer, U., Nima, A. A., et al. (2013). The affective profiles in the USA: happiness, depression, life satisfaction, and happiness-increasing strategies. https://peerj.com/articles/156/. Retrieved 15 Sept 2013.

Serban, G. (1982). *The tyranny of magical thinking: The child's world of belief and adult neurosis*. New York: E.P. Dutton.

Shakespeare, W. (between 1599 and 1601). *Hamlet*. http://shakespeare.mit.edu/hamlet/hamlet.1.3.html. Publication year ascertained from http://www.princeton.edu/~achaney/tmve/wiki100k/docs/Hamlet.html. Retrieved 1 Feb 2014.

Shanks, H. (2014). Where is Mt. Sinai? *Biblical Archaeology Review, 40*(2), 30–41.

Shubber, K. (2013). Mars One will take you to the red planet, if it can raise the cash. http://www.wired.co.uk/news/archive/2013-05/13/mars-one. Retrieved 18 Jan 2013.

Skinner, B. F. (1971). *Beyond freedom and dignity*. New York: Alfred A. Knopf.

Social Anxiety Institute. (2013). Social anxiety, chemical imbalances in the brain, and brain neural pathways and associations. http://socialanxietyinstitute.org/social-anxiety-chemical-imbalance-brain-neural-pathways. Retrieved 27 Nov 2013.

Solomon, A. (2014). *Personal communication*. February, 12, 2014.

Snyder, C. R. (2000). Hypothesis: There is hope. In C. R. Snyder (Eds.), *Handbook of hope theory, measures and applications* (pp. 3–21). San Diego: Academic.

Snyder, C. R. (2002). Hope theory: Rainbows in the mind. *Psychological Inquiry, 13,* 249–275.

Snyder, C. R., Irving, L., & Anderson, J. R. (1991). Hope and health: Measuring the will and the ways. In C. R. Snyder & D. R. Forsyth (Eds.), *Handbook of social and clinical psychology: The health perspective* (pp. 285–305). Elmsford: Pergamon. (Cited in Snyder, C. R. (2000). Hypothesis: There is hope. In C. R. Snyder (Ed.), *Handbook of hope theory, measures and applications* (pp. 3–21). San Diego: Academic Press).

Snyder, C. R., Sympson, S. C., Ybasco, F. C., Borders, T. F., Babyak, M. A., & Higgins, R. L. (1996). Development and validation of the State Hope Scale. *Journal of Personality and Social Psychology, 70*(2), 321–335.

Spinelli, E. (1989). *The interpreted world: An introduction to phenomenological psychology*. London: Sage.

Spiro, R. J., Feltovitch, P. J., Jacobson, M. J., & Coulson, R. L. (1995). Cognitive flexibility, constructivism and hypertext: Random access instruction for advanced knowledge acquisition in ill-structured domains. In T. Duffy & D. Jonassen (Eds.), *Constructivism and the technology of instruction*. Hillsdale: Erlbaum.

Stanford Encyclopedia of Psychology. (2003). http://plato.stanford.edu/entries/relativism/. Retrieved 11 Nov 2012.

Steckman, L. (2013). Afterword. In E. Kreuter (Ed.), *Fostering resilience for loss and irrelevance* (pp. 173–182). New York: Springer.

Stix, G. (2012). A Q & A with Ian Hacking on Thomas Kuhn's legacy as "The Paradigm Shift" turns 50. *Scientific American*. http://www.scientificamerican.com/article/kuhn/. Retrieved 29 Jan 2014.

Storr, A. (1983). Introduction. In C. G. Jung (Ed.), *The essential Jung: Selected writings* (pp. 13–27). Princeton: Princeton University Press.

Success.com. (2014). Online magazine. http://www.success.com/. Retrieved 4 Jan 2014.

Swedenborg, E. (2008). *Collected works of Emanuel Swedenborg*. Charleston: BiblioBazaar.

Szasz, T. S. (1974). *The myth of mental illness: Foundations of a theory of personal conduct*. (rev. ed.). New York: Harper & Row.

Taylor, E. (2009). R. W. Rieber (Series Ed. - Library of the History of Psychology Theories). *The mystery of personality: A history of psychodynamic theories*. New York: Springer Science+Business Media, LLC.

Thoreau, H. D. (2005/1849). *Civil disobedience and other essays*. Stilwell: Digireads.com. (Originally published in 1849).

Tillich, P. (2000). *The courage to be*. New Haven: Yale University Press.

Tolle, E. (2004). *The power of now*. Novato: New World Library.

Triskaidekaphobia.info. (2014). http://www.triskaidekaphobia.info. Retrieved 11 Jan 2014.

Twain, M. (1917). *What is man? And other essays*. New York: Harper. http://www.questia.com/read/149094/what-is-man-and-other-essays. Retrieved 1 Feb 2014.

Twain, M. (1992). *Pudd'nhead wilson those extraordinary twins the man that corrupted hadleyburg*. In R. D. Gooder (Ed.). Oxford University Press. http://www.questia.com/read/74335293/pudd-nhead-wilson-those-extraordinary-twins-the. Retrieved 1 Feb 2014.

United Artists. (1982). *Rocky II*. United States. R. Chartoff (Producer). S. Stallone (Director).

United States v. Windsor, __U.S. ___, 133S. Ct. 2675, 186L.Ed. 808 [June 26, 2013].
University of South Alabama. (2014). Cognitive flexibility theory. http://www.southalabama.edu/oll/mobile/theory_workbook/cognitive_flexibility_theory htm. Retrieved 20 Feb 2014.
Vaughan, F. (1979). Transpersonal psychotherapy: Context, content, and process. *Journal of Transpersonal Psychology, II*, 101–110.
Wall Street Journal. (2013). *Jobs and the Fed.* Editorial, December 7–8.
Wang, C. H., Lin, Y. J., Kuo, Y. C., & Hong, S. S. (2013). Reading to relieve emotional difficulties. *Journal of Poetry Therapy, 26*(4), 255–267.
Warrick, W. R. (undated). *Constructivism: Pre-historical to post-modern.* http://mason.gmu.edu/~wwarrick/Portfolio/Products/constructivism.html. Retrieved 1 Feb 2014.
Weegmann, M., & Cohen, R. (2002). *The psychodynamics of addiction.* London: Whurr.
White, R. E. (1966). *Lives in progress.* New York: Holt, Rinehart and Winston.
White, B. V. (1984). *Stanley Cobb: A builder of the modern neurosciences.* Boston: The Francis A. Countway Library of Medicine.
Williams, P., & Davis, D. C. (2002). *Therapist as life coach: Transforming your practice.* New York: W.W. Norton.
Withers, B. (1972). *Lean on Me.* Sussex Records.
Wooster, M. M. (2013). In education, positive reinforcement is important, but so are the basics. Philanthropy Daily. http://www.philanthropydaily.com/in-education-positive-reinforcement-is-important-but-so-are-the-basics/. Retrieved 4 Jan 2014.
Wonder, S. (1973). *Superstition.* Motown Records.
Wyatt, R. C., & Rogers, N. (2009). *Instructor's manual for person-centered expressive arts therapy.* Mill Valley: Psycotherapy.net.
Yalom, I. D. (1980). *Existential psychotherapy.* New York: Basic Books.
Yalom, I. D. (2001). The gift of therapy: *An open letter to a new generation of therapists and their patients.* New York: HarperCollins.
Yin, R. K. (1994). *Case study research: Design and methods series* (Vol. 5). Thousand Oaks: Sage.
Young, J. O. (2013). *The coherence theory of truth. The Stanford Encyclopedia of Philosophy.* In E. N. Zalta, (Ed.). http://plato.stanford.edu/archives/sum2013/entries/truth-coherence. Retrieved 3 Jan 2014.
Young, J., Klosko, J. S., & Weishaar, M. (2003). *Schema therapy: A practitioner's guide.* New York: Guilford.
Zebrowski, E. Jr. (2000). Scientist and artist within the mature self: The integration of two worlds. In M. E. Miller & S. R. Cook-Greuter (Eds.), *Creativity, spirituality, and transcendence: Paths to integrity and wisdom in the mature self* (pp. 151–166). Stamford: Ablex.

Index

E. A. Kreuter, K. M. Moltner, *Treatment and Management of Maladaptive Schemas,*
DOI 10.1007/978-3-319-06817-6, © Springer International Publishing Switzerland 2014

The manufacturer's authorised representative in the EU is Springer Nature Customer Service Centre GmbH, Europaplatz 3, 69115 Heidelberg, Germany. If you have any concerns regarding our products, please contact ProductSafety@springernature.com

Printed and bound by CPI Group (UK) Ltd, Croydon, CR0 4YY
01/10/2026
02225973-0004